Exiled Among Nations

How do groups of people fashion shared identities in the modern world? Following two communities of German-speaking Mennonites, one composed of voluntary migrants and the other of refugees, across four continents between 1870 and 1945, this transnational study explores how religious migrants engaged the phenomenon of nationalism. John P. R. Eicher demonstrates how migrant groups harnessed the global spread of nationalism to secure practical objectives and create local mythologies. In doing so, he also reveals how governments and aid organizations used diasporic groups for their own purposes, portraying such nomads as enemies or heroes in national and religious mythologies. By underscoring the importance of local and religious counter-stories that run in parallel to nationalist narratives, *Exiled Among Nations* helps us understand acts of resistance, flight, and diaspora in the modern world.

John P.R. Eicher is Assistant Professor of History at Pennsylvania State University-Altoona where his research focuses on Europe's global connections including colonialism, nationalism, migration, and religion. His research has been supported by numerous organizations including the German Historical Institute Washington, the Freie Universität Berlin, and the German Academic Exchange Service (DAAD), and his writing has won awards from the University of Iowa and the University of Winnipeg.

Publications of the German Historical Institute

Edited by

Simone Lässig

with the assistance of David Lazar

The German Historical Institute is a center for advanced study and research whose purpose is to provide a permanent basis for scholarly cooperation among historians from the Federal Republic of Germany and the United States. The Institute conducts, promotes, and supports research into both American and German political, social, economic, and cultural history; into transatlantic migration, especially during the nineteenth and twentieth centuries; and into the history of international relations, with special emphasis on the roles played by the United States and Germany.

A full list of titles in the series can be found at:
www.cambridge.org/pghi

Exiled Among Nations

German and Mennonite Mythologies in a Transnational Age

JOHN P. R. EICHER

Pennsylvania State University-Altoona

GERMAN HISTORICAL INSTITUTE

Washington, D.C.

and

CAMBRIDGE
UNIVERSITY PRESS

University Printing House, Cambridge CB2 8BS, United Kingdom

One Liberty Plaza, 20th Floor, New York, NY 10006, USA

477 Williamstown Road, Port Melbourne, VIC 3207, Australia

314-321, 3rd Floor, Plot 3, Splendor Forum, Jasola District Centre, New Delhi - 110025, India

103 Penang Road, #05-06/07, Visioncrest Commercial, Singapore 238467

Cambridge University Press is part of the University of Cambridge.

It furthers the University's mission by disseminating knowledge in the pursuit of education, learning and research at the highest international levels of excellence.

www.cambridge.org
Information on this title: www.cambridge.org/9781108731799
DOI: 10.1017/9781108626392

© John P. R. Eicher 2020

First published 2020
First paperback edition 2021

A catalogue record for this publication is available from the British Library

Library of Congress Cataloging in Publication data
NAMES: Eicher, John P. R., 1981– author.
TITLE: Exiled among nations : German and Mennonite mythologies in a transnational age / John P.R. Eicher.
OTHER TITLES: Now too much for us
DESCRIPTION: Washington, D.C. : German Historical Institute ; Cambridge, United Kingdom ; New York, NY : Cambridge University Press, 2020. | Series: Publications of the German Historical Institute | Revision of author's thesis (doctoral) – University of Iowa, 2015, titled Now too much for us : German and Mennonite transnationalisms, 1874–1944. | Includes bibliographical references and index.
IDENTIFIERS: LCCN 2019029280 (print) | LCCN 2019029281 (ebook) | ISBN 9781108486118 (hardback) | ISBN 9781108626392 (epub)
SUBJECTS: LCSH: Mennonites – Ethnic identity. | Mennonites – Cultural assimilation. | Mennonites – Paraguay – History. | Germans – Paraguay – History. | Emigration and immigration – History. | National characteristics, German. | Group identity. | Transnationalism.
CLASSIFICATION: LCC BX8115 .E33 2020 (print) | LCC BX8115 (ebook) | DDC 289.7/4309892–dc23
LC record available at https://lccn.loc.gov/2019029280
LC ebook record available at https://lccn.loc.gov/2019029281

ISBN 978-1-108-48611-8 Hardback
ISBN 978-1-108-73179-9 Paperback

For Julia, my love.

Contents

Figures

Maps

The maps are also available as an additional resource at www.cambridge.org/eicher

Acknowledgments

I have accrued an embarrassment of riches through an embarrassment of debts, far too many to be acknowledged in such a brief space. First, I am grateful to H. Glenn Penny and Elizabeth Heineman for their encouragement, advice, and the many letters written and sent on my behalf. Thank you. I also thank John D. Roth, for inspiring me to dedicate my future to the past, and Royden Loewen for his boundless enthusiasm for it.

Uwe S. Friesen, Christian Lopau, Colleen McFarland, Gundolf Niebuhr, Conrad Stoesz, John Thiesen, Frank Peachy, and Gary Waltner helped me navigate the archives they expertly administer. Peter Letkemann deserves special thanks for his spirited interest in my project and his vast archival knowledge. Victor Dönninghau, Benjamin Goossen, Jannis Panagiotidis, Hans-Christian Petersen, Richard Ratzlaff, Erwin Warkentin, the UT-Austin Religious Studies Colloquium, colleagues at the University of Iowa, colleagues at the German Historical Institute Washington (with special thanks to David Lazar), and the anonymous reviewers for Cambridge University Press, *Comparative Studies in Society and History*, and *German Historical Review* greatly improved portions of this manuscript. Though I arrived at Penn State Altoona when this project was nearly finished, my colleagues invited me into their intellectual community and I am thankful for their warmth and generosity.

I am deeply grateful to the institutions that made this work possible: The Berlin Program for Advanced German and European Studies (with special thanks to Karin Goihl), the German Academic Exchange Service, the German Historical Institute Washington, the Mennonite Historical Society, the Religious Research Association, and the University of Iowa.

Appreciation is also due to the Zerger family in Weierhof, Germany and Susie Fisher, Ryan Stoesz, and Caroline Fisher in Winnipeg, Canada for the generous use of their beautiful homes. Here, I should also like to note that I bear complete responsibility for the book's oversights and shortcomings. All translations are my own.

Jake Hall, Dennis Kuhnel, and Jason Moyer debated me on everything about anything when this book was still a dissertation and they have made me articulate myself in ways that I cannot articulate. I also thank various friends variously attached to 1605 9th St. and 625 E. Davenport St. for their many distractions. I thank my family for choosing the museum over the mall and National Parks over theme parks. Finally, I thank Julia for being a partner with me in this project, for her intelligence, creativity, imagination, and for most everything that is good in my life, especially our two brilliant daughters, Colette and Daphne.

Abbreviations

AO	Auslandsorganisation (Foreign Organization)
BDMP	Bund Deutscher Mennoniten in Paraguay (League of German Mennonites in Paraguay)
BiN	Brüder in Not (Brethren in Need)
CMBC	Canadian Mennonite Board of Colonization
CPS	Civilian Public Service
DAI	Deutsches-Ausland Institut (German Foreign Institute)
DDP	Deutsche Demokratische Partei (German Democratic Party)
DVP	Deutsche Volkspartei (German People's Party)
DVfP	Deutscher Volksbund für Paraguay (German League for Paraguay)
JDC	Jewish Joint Distribution Committee
KfK	Kommission für kirchliche Angelegenheiten (Commission for Church Affairs)
KPD	Kommunistische Partei Deutschlands (Communist Party of Germany)
MC	(old) Mennonite Church
MCC	Mennonite Central Committee
VDA	Verein für das Deutschtum im Ausland (1908–1933) Volksbund für das Deutschtum im Ausland (1933–1945) (Association for Germandom Abroad)
VoMi	Hauptamt Volksdeutsche Mittelstelle (Central Welfare Office for Ethnic Germans)
VRD	Verband der Russlanddeutschen (Association of Russian Germans)

WP   Reichspartei des deutschen Mittelstandes (Reich Party of the German Middle Class)

Z   Deutsche Zentrumspartei (Center Party)

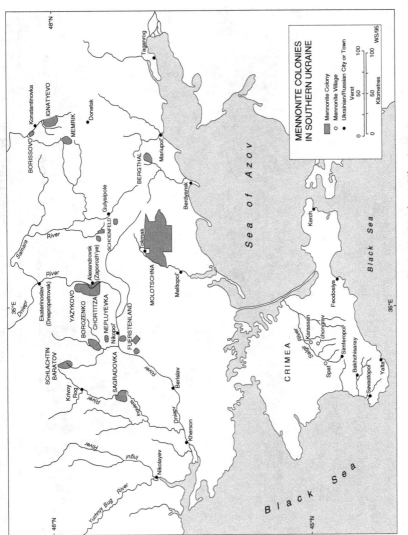

MAP 0.1 Mennonite colonies in Southern Ukraine

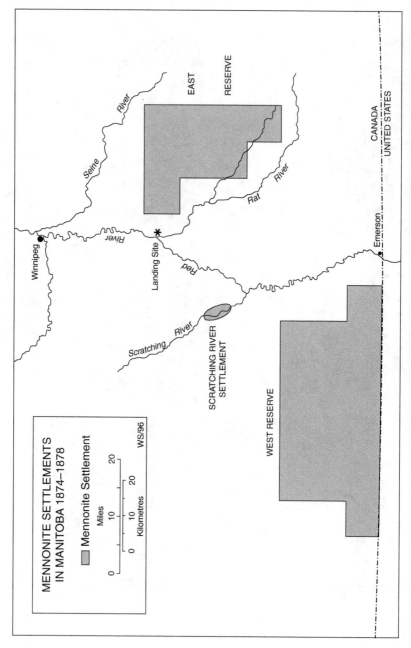

MAP O.2 Mennonite settlements in Manitoba 1874–1878

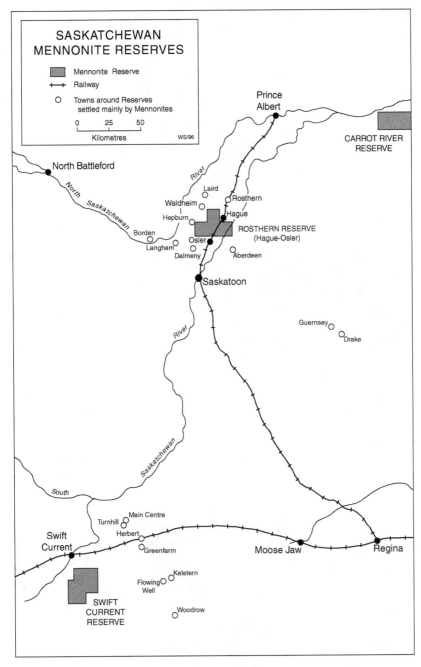

MAP 0.3 Saskatchewan Mennonite reserves

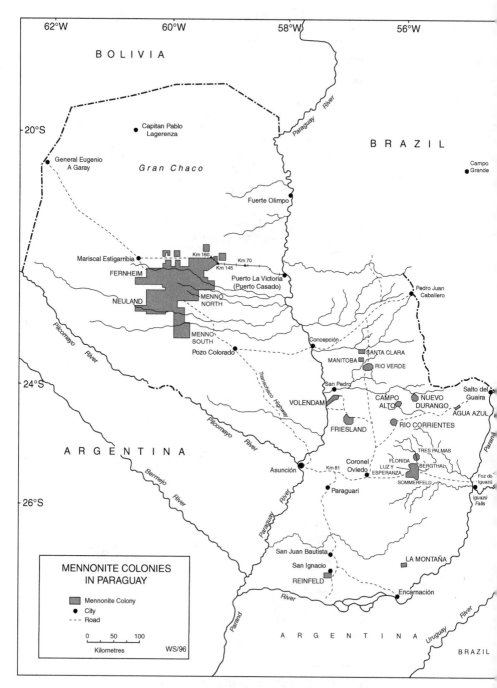

MAP 0.4 Mennonite colonies in Paraguay

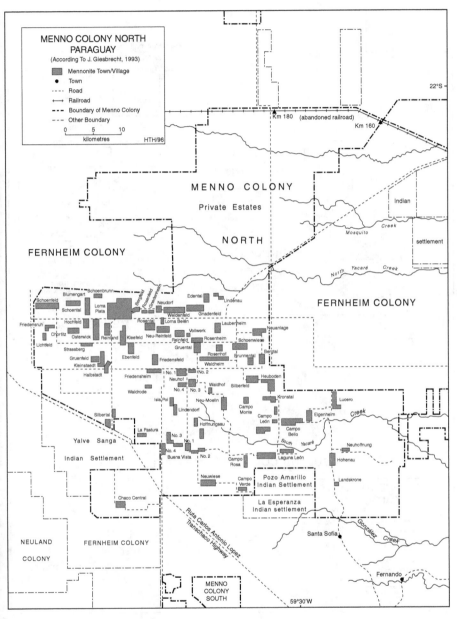

MAP 0.5 Menno Colony North Paraguay

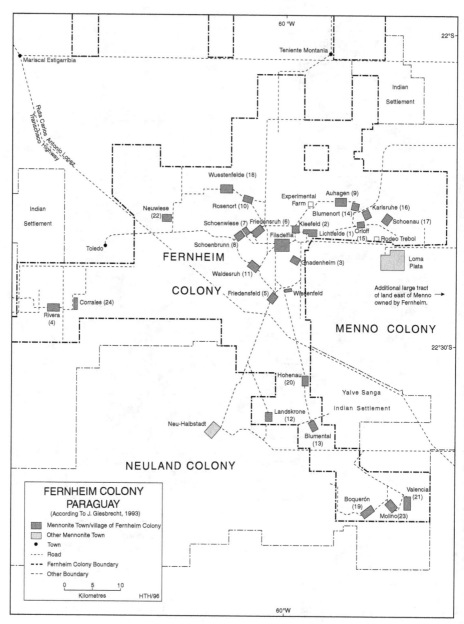

60 °W

22°S

Mariscal Estigarribia

Teniente Montania

Indian
Settlement

Ruta Carlos Antonio Lopez
Transchaco Highway

Indian
Settlement

Wuestenfelde (18)

Experimental
Farm

Auhagen (9)

Neuwiese
(22)

Rosenort (10)

Blumenort (14)

Karlsruhe (16)

Schoenau (17)

Schoenwiese (7) Friedensruh (6)

Kleefeld (2)

Toledo

Schoenbrunn (8)

Filadelfia

Lichtfelde (1)

Orloff
(15)

Rodeo Trebol

FERNHEIM

Loma
Plata

Gnadenheim (3)

COLONY

Waldesruh (11)

Friedensfeld (5)

Wiesenfeld

Additional large tract
of land east of Menno
owned by Fernheim.

Corrales (24)

Rivera
(4)

MENNO COLONY

22°30'S

Hohenau
(20)

Yalve Sanga

Landskrone
(12)

Indian Settlement

Neu-Halbstadt

Blumental
(13)

NEULAND COLONY

Valencia
(21)

FERNHEIM COLONY
PARAGUAY
(According To J. Giesbrecht, 1993)

Boquerón
(19)

Molino(23)

Mennonite Town/village of Fernheim Colony

Other Mennonite Town

Town

Road

Fernheim Colony Boundary

Other Boundary

0   5   10

Kilometres   HTH/96

60°W

MAP 0.6 Fernheim Colony Paraguay

Introduction

Man ... is the story-telling animal. Wherever he goes he wants to leave behind not a chaotic wake, not an empty space, but the comforting marker-buoys and trail-signs of stories. He has to go on telling stories. He has to keep on making them up. As long as there's a story, it's all right.
Graham Swift, *Waterland*

This book poses two questions: How do mobile populations fashion collective narratives as nations, religions, and diasporas? Specifically, how did German-speaking Mennonites – a part of the larger German-speaking diaspora – conceive of themselves as Germans and Christians during the era of high nationalism? I answer these questions by tracing the movements of two groups of Mennonites between 1874 and 1945. One was composed of 1,800 voluntary migrants, the other of 2,000 refugees. Both groups originated in nineteenth-century Russia, took separate paths through Canada and Germany, and settled near each other in Paraguay's Gran Chaco between 1926 and 1931. The settlement of voluntary migrants was named the Menno Colony. The settlement of refugees was named the Fernheim Colony. Through an analysis of both groups and the eight governments and four aid agencies that they encountered along the way, this book advances two overarching theses: First, it argues that diasporic groups harnessed the global spread of nationalism and ecumenicism to create local mythologies and secure evolving local objectives. Second, it argues that governments and aid organizations in Europe and the Americas used diasporic groups for their own purposes by portraying them as enemies or heroes in their evolving national and religious mythologies. This comparative study positions the groups at the center of how we understand mobile populations who were forced to reckon with the twin developments of nationalism and Christian ecumenicism in the modern era.

The theses advanced in this book help us understand the global forces of nationalism, citizenship, ethnicity, and displacement. As the twentieth century unfolded, there were millions of individuals who were voluntarily or coercively relocated because they did not fit a particular government's prescribed national, racial, or class demographics. Many resisted participating in assimilative or corporate bodies and many more were indifferent to them. Though this work traces the lines of two small movements of people across the globe, it engages universal challenges experienced by mobile groups such as how they negotiate hybrid identities and perpetuate local cultures under a variety of circumstances. It also engages the ways that mobile groups confounded institutions – both state and religious – that attempt to impose singular, comprehensive identities on them. It does so by mapping the shifting contours of the Mennonites' local narratives and of the national and religious narratives promoted by governments and aid agencies that wished to exclude them from or absorb them into their ranks.

The groups' troubled relationships with national and religious assimilation are therefore not unique to Mennonites, or even the millions of German speakers who poured out of Europe during the late nineteenth and early twentieth centuries. Indeed, many other national and religious groups in Europe and around the world struggled to come to terms with what homogenized nations and religions meant for their larger cosmologies – from Polish-speaking Catholics living in Germany, to German-speaking Jews living in the Dominican Republic, to Chinese nationalists living in Singapore.[1] Myriad groups existed outside the paradigm of national and religious uniformity and some were required to take to the road. The Mennonites in this book traveled farther and longer than most.

MENNONITES' *LONGUE DURÉE*

Mennonites have a long history of contrarianism and mobility, extending back to the confession's inception in Central Europe's sixteenth-century

---

[1] James Bjork, *Neither German nor Pole: Catholicism and National Indifference in a Central European Borderland* (Ann Arbor, MI: University of Michigan Press, 2008); David Kenley, *New Culture in a New World: The May Fourth Movement and the Chinese Diaspora in Singapore, 1919–1932* (New York: Routledge, 2003); Allen Wells, *Tropical Zion: General Trujillo, FDR, and the Jews of Sosua* (Durham: Duke University Press, 2009).

Anabaptist movement.[2] Anabaptists wished to establish a pure and literal understanding of the Bible and purge all ecclesial traditions from Christianity that did not conform to their interpretation. Under the loose direction of an apostate Dutch priest named Menno Simons, the Mennonites emerged from the skein of the Anabaptist movement, and believed that Christians should follow the example of the early, persecuted church in Rome. Most importantly, Mennonites believed that the church should be composed of voluntary members who confessed their faith and were baptized as adults. On a social level, Mennonites accentuated precepts of nonviolence, closed communities, and the separation of church and state. Nevertheless, individual communities perpetuated additional doctrines within their local contexts regarding such things as occupation and dress, which they believed were essential to the faith.

Mennonites maintained the Anabaptist focus on purging and purity by emphasizing the spiritual integrity of local communities, issuing bans against errant members, and engaging in numerous schisms. Central European magistrates likewise aspired to purge religiously errant groups under the stipulations of the Peace of Augsburg (1555), which promulgated the idea "Cuius regio, eius religio" ("Whose realm, his religion"), in their pursuit of ecclesial and social purity. Branded as heretics by Europe's Catholic and Lutheran authorities and scattered to the wind, the Mennonites never solidified around a geographic center, agreed upon a specific theology, or forged a set of shared practices.

One of the most effective strategies that Mennonites discovered for maintaining their communities was fleeing to marginal lands on imperial borders. The fact that Mennonites quarreled often and divided frequently certainly did not hinder their physical dispersal. During the seventeenth and eighteenth centuries, hundreds of Mennonites living in a broad swath between Switzerland and the Low Countries immigrated to North America, where they settled in Pennsylvania and Virginia and then traversed the Appalachian Mountains to the Midwest and Ontario.

---

[2] I use the word "confession," rather than "denomination" or "church," to describe the Mennonites, since the latter terms imply centralized or ecclesiastical authority, often with government oversight. According to Thomas Finger, "Mennonites are neither a creedal church nor a confessional one in the sense of adhering to a single authoritative confession. They are confessional, however, in the sense of having authored numerous confessions that at times have played important roles in church life." See "Confessions of Faith in the Anabaptist/ Mennonite Tradition," *Mennonite Quarterly Review* 76, no. 3 (2002): 277–97.

At about the same time, the free cities of Gdańsk and Elbląg invited Mennonites living in the Low Countries to cultivate the swamplands of the Vistula delta. In exchange, authorities granted them legal, economic, religious, and social guarantees, which was a common practice in the early modern European legal system. After the first and second partitions of Poland (respectively, 1772 and 1793), Frederick II ("the Great") of Prussia affirmed Mennonites' religious freedoms but he limited their land holdings and required annual compensation for military exemption.[3] The stipulations eventually became too onerous for some Mennonites and they looked east for new land in the Russian Empire.

The eighteenth century witnessed the rise of large, multiethnic empires that replaced ecclesial law with civil law and were governed by monarchs who sought capable pioneers to settle their expanding territories. Instead of emphasizing religious purity, they asserted their "enlightened" benevolence, tolerated religious minorities, and legitimated their imperial plurality with a religious and royal metaphor: "so we, though many, are one body."[4] When successful, this type of government practiced what Jane Burbank and Frederick Cooper call the "contingent accommodation" of heterogeneous interests.[5] Specific groups – merchants, craft guilds, intellectuals, religious minorities, and the like – pledged loyalty to the Crown in exchange for specific concessions or a degree of autonomy. This balancing act resulted in neither "consistent loyalty nor consistent resistance," but worked for its intended purposes.[6] In a worldview described by Northrop Frye as, "imperial monotheism," the monarch represented God on earth and was "tolerant of local cults, which it tend[ed] increasingly to regard as manifestations of a single god."[7] In 1763, Catherine II ("the Great") of Russia issued a Manifesto directed at German-speaking farmers living in Central Europe that gave prospective settlers a charter of privileges in exchange for making her southern and eastern territories economically productive. Western farmers' economic standing as free settlers from Europe – rather than Russian

[3] Adolf Ens, *Subjects or Citizens? The Mennonite Experience in Canada, 1870–1925* (Ottawa: University of Ottawa Press, 1994), 4–5; James Urry, *Mennonites, Politics, and Peoplehood: Europe-Russia-Canada 1525–1980* (Winnipeg: University of Manitoba Press, 2006), 44–51.

[4] Romans 12:5 (ESV). See Northrop Frye, *The Great Code: The Bible and Literature*, ed. Alvin A. Lee (Buffalo: University of Toronto Press, Scholarly Publishing Division, 2006), 118.

[5] Jane Burbank and Frederick Cooper, *Empires in World History: Power and the Politics of Difference* (Princeton, NJ: Princeton University Press, 2010), 14.

[6] Ibid.   [7] Frye, *Great Code*, 112; Urry, *Mennonites, Politics, and Peoplehood*, 44.

serfs, whom the regime counted as less productive – mattered more to Catherine II than their religious, cultural, or linguistic preferences.[8]

From 1787 to 1789, Mennonites living in Prussia took up Catherine II's invitation to settle the Empire's vast steppes. Twelve years later, Tsar Paul I confirmed a Mennonite *Privilegium*, or list of Mennonite-specific privileges that included clauses that ensured their exemption from military service and swearing oaths in court. Mennonites viewed the agreement as a personal covenant between their colonies and the monarch and believed that his descendants would respect their privileges in perpetuity.[9] The guarantees prompted other Mennonites from Prussia to emigrate to southern Russia and especially the regions of Ukraine and Crimea. Here, they created Mennonite spaces in Russian places by retaining their *Plautdietsch* (Low German) dialect, cultural and religious customs, village structures, and even their village names, though their constituent churches remained at odds with each other over religious practice and doctrine.

Russia's Mennonites fit into a broad milieu of German-speaking minorities. Stefan Manz identifies three primary groups: The first two included German speakers from the burgher class who began filtering into the Empire's cities in the fifteenth century, and social elites living in the Baltic region who were absorbed by the Empire in the eighteenth century. Both groups maintained separate ethnic communities and retained a German nationality. By 1871, there were about 250,000 of them living in the Russian Empire. The third group was composed of Catherine II's invitees who accepted Russian nationality with important caveats enshrined in the Manifesto. This group included farmers, tradesmen, and professionals. Most were Catholic and Lutheran but smaller pietistic confessions dotted their ranks. They established hundreds of colonies in the Black Sea and Volga regions and soon represented the plurality of German speakers in the Empire, which by the late nineteenth century numbered about 1,800,000 individuals.[10]

Between 1789 and 1870, the Empire's Mennonite population grew to more than 50,000 members spread across several settlements from Odessa

---

[8] E. K. Francis, *In Search of Utopia: The Mennonites in Manitoba* (Glencoe, IL: Free Press, 1955), 18; Dirk Hoerder, "The German-Language Diasporas: A Survey, Critique, and Interpretation," *Diaspora* 11, no. 1 (2002): 18–19.

[9] Urry, *Mennonites, Politics, and Peoplehood*, 85–88.

[10] Stefan Manz, *Constructing a German Diaspora: The "Greater German Empire,"* 1871–1914 (New York: Routledge, 2014), 145–46; Frank H. Epp, *Mennonite Exodus: The Rescue and Resettlement of the Russian Mennonites Since the Communist Revolution* (Altona, MB: Canadian Mennonite Relief and Immigration Council, 1962), 14.

to the Volga River.[11] Mennonites established villages of about twenty to fifty families, with their homes laid out in a *Strassendorf* (street-village) structure of single-family houses arranged in two rows down the sides of a broad street. Fields extended from behind each property, except for those of landless individuals who worked as hired laborers or in non-farming occupations. Villages maintained their own churches, windmills, primary schools, and cemeteries. In addition, there were usually one or two larger villages within a colony that contained factories, granaries, hospitals, post offices, secondary schools, administrative buildings, and retail stores.

During the 1860s, Tsar Alexander II introduced a series of modernizing initiatives that threatened the Mennonites' standing as autonomous colonies. Russia's military loss during the Crimean War (1853–1856) led the Tsar to conclude that his heterogonous and agrarian population was a determent to the Empire's status as a world power. His initiatives – broadly referred to as "Russification" – included freeing serfs, tightening bureaucratic control over the provinces, implementing educational programs, and introducing universal military conscription.[12] Naturally, the country's Mennonites were disturbed by the new policies, especially the military service requirement, which they feared would cause their young men to imbibe Russian militarism. Mennonites had adapted to Russian legislation in the past – provided they were allowed to do so on their own terms – but the slate of new reforms, introduced quickly and impartially, led Mennonites to wonder whether they were the privileged minority that they had assumed themselves to be. It is this moment of crisis that sets the stage for this book.

MENNONITES' *BREF DURÉE*

During the 1870s, approximately 17,000 Mennonites relocated from the Russian Empire to North America's western prairies because they preferred to live on a new frontier rather than under the Tsar's new laws. Yet it was not long before this frontier was integrated into the national fabrics of Canada and the United States as part of their own homogenizing

---

[11] F. H. Epp, *Mennonite Exodus*, 17–20.

[12] James Urry, "The Russian State, the Mennonite World and the Migration from Russia to North America in the 1870s," *Mennonite Life* 46, no. 1 (1991): 14. On Russia's nineteenth-century reforms see Ben Eklof, John Bushnell, and Larissa Zakharova, eds., *Russia's Great Reforms, 1855–1881* (Bloomington, IN: Indiana University Press, 1994).

schemes. By the 1920s, governments around the world had begun censuring individuals who did not accept national identifications. Resembling the purifying fervor of sixteenth-century European reformers, early-twentieth-century communists and nationalists persecuted dissidents by harshly enforcing existing assimilation policies and formulating new understandings of purity based on race, religion, class, or nationality.[13] Mennonites met the challenge by making peace with the initiatives – either through compromise or emigration – which again raised questions of religious purity within the confession. In the mid-1920s, 1,800 individuals voluntarily left Canada for Paraguay's remote Gran Chaco on account of the nationalizing policies embedded in Canadian public education, and fears that their coreligionists had become too "worldly." Here, they created the Menno Colony. The Menno colonists emphasized their adherence to biblical examples of itinerancy and resistance to political power by rejecting all outside attachments. In contrast, those who stayed in Canada reinterpreted questions of separation and religious purity into questions of confessional unity and personal morality.

In 1929, approximately 3,800 of the Soviet Union's Mennonites fled to Moscow after the Soviet government labeled them as kulaks and purged them from their villages. Now refugees, they sojourned in Weimar Germany for several months. With the aid of the German government and a US relief agency named the Mennonite Central Committee (MCC), 1,500 of these individuals relocated to Paraguay and created the Fernheim Colony, adjacent to the Menno Colony. More refugees arrived from Poland and China, swelling the Fernheim Colony's ranks to 2,000. Once the refugees were settled, they engaged in fierce battles over what it meant to be Mennonite, German, or Paraguayan. Some argued that God had called them to the Chaco to proselytize to their indigenous neighbors on behalf of the global Mennonite Church. Others believed that God wanted them to be good Paraguayan citizens and help the Paraguayan Army fight Bolivia during the Chaco War (1932–1935). Still others believed that God would restore them to their Russian homeland if they collaborated with the ascendant Nazi Party.

---

[13] Incidentally, communists and nationalists articulated their claims of authenticity in a Judeo-Christian religious framework, which accepts that authority is singular, is transmitted textually, and develops chronologically. Consequently, communists and nationalists unified populations around the singular purity of class or nationality, claimed authority using Marxist writings and primordial national mythologies, and established chronologies through dialectical materialism and the "awakening" of national consciousness. Frye gets at this similarity in *The Great Code*, 105.

Simultaneously, a growing number of Mennonites in North America embraced higher education and absorbed liberal humanist attitudes about church–state relations. These Mennonite intellectuals reinterpreted the confession's traditional tenets of voluntary membership in the church and the separation of church and state as analogous to the democratic tenets of individual freedom and religious pluralism.[14] They worked to create conferences, institutions, and aid agencies, including the MCC, that supplanted the confession's local expressions of "Mennoniteness" with a few key principles that were easily articulated to an external audience of politicians and journalists. Despite the reality that most of the world's Mennonites were indifferent or opposed to their idealistic goals, Mennonite intellectuals reasoned that a new era of Mennonite history had arrived that legitimated the confession's transnational solidarity and permanent settlement in democratic and liberally oriented countries.

During the interwar years, the MCC attempted to incorporate both colonies into an imagined global Mennonite body: a Mennonite nation, so to speak. Nazi representatives – some of whom were Mennonites – also tried to incorporate the colonies into a transnational German nation. The Paraguayan government likewise assumed that the Mennonites were part of the national fabric, particularly during the Chaco War. Each external entity agreed that the modern world required clearly defined populations, with clearly defined loyalties, who lived within clearly defined boundaries. They conflated settlement with stability and believed that identities were (or should be) circumscribed and singular. Mobility and fluid identifications were "problems" requiring "solutions." Thus, the Menno Colony's local group identification was too narrowly focused and the Fernheim Colony's divergent group identifications were too widely scattered to merge with larger national or religious narratives. In separate ways both the Menno and Fernheim Colonies crystalize the problems faced by individuals who did not fit into prescribed national and religious molds during the era of high nationalism.

---

[14] In the US context, James C. Juhnke refers to these individuals as "Mennonite progressives." See *Vision, Doctrine, War* (Scottdale, PA: Herald Press, 1989), 164–65; In the German context, Benjamin W. Goossen considers them "Mennonite activists." See *Chosen Nation: Mennonites and Germany in a Global Era* (Princeton, NJ: Princeton University Press, 2017).

GERMANNESS AND MENNONITENESS

Each colony possessed national and religious identifications that were self-contradictory in many important respects. On one hand, both colonies claimed to be Christians and Mennonites, but they held different ideas about scripture and Mennonite principles. On the other, both colonies were composed of German speakers living outside of the German nation state, but they possessed contrasting ideas of what it meant to be German. Generally speaking, outsiders such as the MCC and the German government regarded both groups as members of a distinct ethno-religious minority (*the* Mennonites) who were culturally, ethnically, or racially German. This book therefore makes a point of examining outsiders' shifting notions of Germanness – the constellation of qualities regarded as essential for being German – and Mennoniteness – the constellation of qualities regarded as essential for being Mennonite. The payoff is that we can see how national and religious identifications unite or divide populations depending on time, location, and circumstances.

Germanness, or *Deutschtum*, is a nebulous concept used to define a nebulous category of people, and one which was highly susceptible to revision. It first came into use during the nineteenth century as Europe's German-speaking liberals struggled to create a German civic and cultural taxonomy.[15] During this century, the idea of Germanness and the geographic space of Germany referred to German-speaking locales concentrated in Central Europe, regardless of the political realm in which they happened to be situated. Germanness also existed in tandem with the concept of *Heimat*, a word peculiar to the German language that connotes an individual's sentimental attachment to a specific location.[16] In short, Germanness was a trans-state identification while *Heimat* was a substate identification, and both concepts existed prior to the formation of the German nation state in 1871.[17]

During the early twentieth century, both identifications – Mennoniteness and Germanness – generated problems for German nationalists who wished to gather the world's German speakers under

---

[15] David Brodbeck, *Defining Deutschtum: Political Ideology, German Identity, and Music-Critical Discourse in Liberal Vienna* (New York: Oxford University Press, 2014), 6–10.

[16] See Peter Blickle, *Heimat: A Critical Theory of the German Idea of Homeland* (New York: Camden House, 2004). On the early-twentieth-century *Heimat* Movement see Celia Applegate, *A Nation of Provincials: The German Idea of Heimat* (Berkeley, CA: University of California Press, 1990).

[17] Richard Ned Lebow, "The Future of Memory," *Annals of the American Academy of Political and Social Science* 617 (2008): 30.

the leadership of a single regime or within a single geographic location. By the first decades of the century, the concept of *Heimat* in Germany existed alongside, and eventually buttressed, German nationalist propaganda that promoted loyalty to the German nation state.[18] Meanwhile, many German speakers who occupied their own "Heimats Abroad" – in Asia, Africa, and the Americas – responded tepidly to German nationalism.[19] According to Manz, "*The* German abroad did not exist. What did exist were extremely heterogeneous groups or individuals of different geographical regions, political convictions, religious beliefs and social backgrounds, all moving into, and within, very different contact zones [emphasis added]."[20]

After the First World War, Germanness became politically charged as new citizenship laws in Central European countries required individuals to choose a nationality, which sometimes entailed relocating to a new state. Abroad, the Weimar government harnessed the concept of Germanness to promote economic and cultural ties between Germany and communities of *Auslandsdeutsche* (German speakers living abroad), while the Nazi government reformulated the idea as a scientific category to promote the racial allegiance of *Auslandsdeutsche* to Germany.[21] As Germanness transformed from a vague and voluntary category to an academic and ascriptive one, German speakers living outside of the German nation state found themselves in the crosshairs of heated debates in Germany and their host states concerning their national bona fides. During the late nineteenth and early twentieth centuries Mennonites' Germanness helped convince a range of governments that they were desirable pioneers. Nonetheless, after the creation of the German nation state and especially after the Nazis' rise to power, their Germanness raised

---

[18] Applegate, *A Nation of Provincials*, 107, 198.

[19] See Krista O'Donnell, Renate Bridenthal, and Nancy Reagin, eds., *The Heimat Abroad: The Boundaries of Germanness* (Ann Arbor, MI: University of Michigan Press, 2005); Manz, *Constructing a German Diaspora*, 3.

[20] Manz, *Constructing a German Diaspora*, 4.

[21] Christopher Hutton, *Race and the Third Reich: Linguistics, Racial Anthropology and Genetics in the Dialectic of Volk* (Cambridge, UK: Polity, 2005), 58–59. Like *Deutschtum*, *Auslandsdeutsche* is a nebulous concept. The Nazis considered *Auslandsdeutsche* to be German citizens abroad, while *Volksdeutsche* were ethnic Germans abroad, and both constituted the *Deutschtum im Ausland*. Other definitions merge *Reichsdeutsche* (German citizens) with *Volksdeutsche* (persons of German descent) to form the *Auslandsdeutsche*. See Max Paul Friedman, *Nazis and Good Neighbors: The United States Campaign Against the Germans of Latin America in World War II* (Cambridge, UK: Cambridge University Press, 2003), 15.

troubling questions in host countries about whether they were loyal citizens, loyal to Germany, or even a dormant Nazi fifth column.

Less precise still is the concept of Mennoniteness. Indeed, it is a word that lacks historical provenance. Generally speaking, it is a catchall term indicating a set of attributes that twentieth-century Mennonite intellectuals bundled together to articulate the confession's essential religious, cultural, and sometimes even racial, character. Yet owing to Mennonites' history of biblical literalism and ecclesial disunity, their communities held durable, yet imprecise, understandings of how their religious culture affected their daily lives. They lacked scholarship, High-Church practices, and the refined sacramental theology of other Christian denominations, all of which kept them from parsing religion from other aspects of daily life or establishing a systematic connection between culture and faith. Indeed, their cultural attributes were not handed down by church authorities but manifested from the bottom up.

Thus, the *Gemeinde* (local community) was the arbiter of culture and every other aspect of life. In Russia's Mennonite communities, the cultural and religious life of the *Gemeinde* was supervised by an *Ältester* – sometimes translated as "bishop" or "elder" – who was elected from the colony's ministers. The geographic area in which the *Ältester* could reasonably traverse in a day or two limited the size of the colony and encouraged compact settlements. The *Ältester* looked after baptisms, ordinations, weddings, and funerals and possessed a great deal of influence in the community beyond the religious sphere. He was aided by an elected team of *Prediger* (lay ministers) who supervised the moral life of each village.[22] Together they comprised the *Lehrdienst*.[23] Likewise, an elected official named the *Oberschulze* represented a colony's social organization and governed its internal and external affairs. The *Oberschulze* and his assistants, called *Besitzer*, combined to form the *Gebietsamt*, a governing body that looked after a colony's civic functions: healthcare, schools, insurance, and economic development.[24] Village administration was composed of a *Schulze* (mayor) and his assistants who maintained the village's infrastructure, fire

---

[22] Royden Loewen, *Family, Church, and Market: A Mennonite Community in the Old and the New Worlds, 1850–1930* (Toronto: University of Toronto Press, 1993), 50; Uwe S. Friesen, "Ältester," in *Lexikon der Mennoniten in Paraguay*, ed. Gerhard Ratzlaff et al. (Asunción: Verein für Geschichte und Kultur der Mennoniten in Paraguay, 2009), 20.

[23] Andreas F. Sawatzky, "Lehrdienst," *Lexikon der Mennoniten in Paraguay*, 262–63.

[24] Ens, *Subjects or Citizens?* 6; Heinrich N. Dyck, "Oberschulze," *Lexikon der Mennoniten in Paraguay*, 318–19.

safety, local justice, and church attendance.[25] Civic and religious leaders were always men, though lay members – also men, but often in consultation with their spouses – collectively held a broad range of powers including taxation, hiring teachers, and assigning crop rotations.[26]

Divisions between Mennonites' civic, economic, and religious spheres were never completely clear, which meant that every aspect of life was a part of ones' Mennoniteness. In the small, closely knit village setting there were frequent instances where civic and religious leaders clashed over the boundaries of their particular jurisdiction.[27] Family connections, historic precedent, and strong personalities often had as much sway as official rules. Altogether, the *Gemeinde* was

more than an organization. It was the all-encompassing community and articulator of culture: it interpreted the historical stories that gave members a common identity; it pronounced the mercies and judgments of God that gave meaning to daily disasters and fortunes; it legitimized social arrangements that structured community and defined boundaries; it built social networks that tied together distant places; and it set the agenda for discourse, debate, and conflict. It extolled the virtues of an envisaged yesterday, and it confronted ideas and trends that threatened that vision in the present.[28]

As *Gemeinden* moved from one environment to another, they incorporated and perpetuated cultural characteristics that they absorbed along the way: in the Low Countries, Prussia, Russia, Canada, and Paraguay. This in turn led to an ongoing discussion within and between *Gemeinden* over which aspects of culture were important to their articulation of Mennoniteness and which were not.

One debate that is particularly germane to this observation was waged in 1921 between Abram A. Friesen and Benjamin H. Unruh. Both individuals left the Soviet Union in 1920 as part of a Russian Mennonite study commission, which had been tasked with finding immigration possibilities in the wake of Soviet persecution. A. Friesen eventually settled in Saskatchewan, Canada while Unruh settled near Karlsruhe, Germany.

[25] Ens, *Subjects or Citizens?* 5–6; Gerhard Ratzlaff, "Schulze," *Lexikon der Mennoniten in Paraguay*, 378–79.

[26] Ens, *Subjects or Citizens?* 5–6. Mennonite households were embedded in thick intergenerational kinship ties, which often gave women power in communal decision-making beyond their ability to vote. See R. Loewen, "The Children, the Cows, My Dear Man and My Sister': The Transplanted Lives of Mennonite Farm Women, 1874–1900," *Canadian Historical Review* 73, no. 3 (1992): 348.

[27] Various instances are noted in James Urry, *None but Saints: The Transformation of Mennonite Life in Russia 1789–1889* (Winnipeg: Hyperion Press, 1989).

[28] R. Loewen, *Family, Church, and Market*, 50.

Throughout the 1930s and 1940s, Unruh was the main point of contact between the Fernheim Colony, the MCC, and the Weimar and Nazi governments.[29] He viewed German culture as intimately tied to Mennonites' religious practice and part of their fundamental Mennonite "nature" (i.e. their Mennoniteness), while A. Friesen believed that cultural features were malleable and tangential to religious fidelity. Unruh argued that it was a "right of all peoples" to "speak one's mother tongue, to pray in one's mother tongue, to know and love what our forefathers . . . have known and loved." He conflated Germanness with Mennoniteness. Alternately, A. Friesen argued that Mennonites should be willing to adapt to the cultural norms of their host societies, wherever they may be, while remaining on guard for threats to their religious convictions. He argued, "The [Soviet] government's attacks were not directed against the Mennonites as a confessional body, but against the Mennonites as a national construct," because they maintained a separate language, culture, and social organization.[30] Similar disagreements arose in the United States as Mennonites debated higher education, dress, and other aspects of culture and conduct that set them apart from or aligned with broader society.

Geoff Eley and Ronald Suny assert, "Culture is more often not what people share, but what they choose to fight over."[31] Between the 1870s and the 1940s, Mennonite communities and conferences across the Americas and Europe battled each other over a broad spectrum of issues, from personal appearance, to occupation, to attending public schools, to participating in government. Similar to other minority groups during this era, the Mennonites' internal conflicts led to a remarkable degree of

---

[29] Harold S. Bender, "Unruh, Benjamin Heinrich (1881–1959)," *Global Anabaptist Mennonite Encyclopedia Online*, last modified November 24, 2013, http://gameo.org/index .php?title=Unruh,_Benjamin_Heinrich_(1881–1959)&oldid=103975, last accessed June 7, 2018; Jakob Warkentin, "Brüder in Not," *Lexikon der Mennoniten in Paraguay*, 56–57. For a longer, hagiographic account of Unruh's life, see Heinrich B. Unruh, *Fügungen und Führungen: Benjamin Heinrich Unruh, 1881–1959: Ein Leben im Geiste christlicher Humanität und im Dienste der Nächstenliebe* (Detmold, Germany: Verein zur Erforschung und Pflege des Russlanddeutschen Mennonitentums, 2009).

[30] Both are quoted in Abraham Friesen, *In Defense of Privilege: Russian Mennonites and the State Before and During World War I* (Winnipeg: Kindred Productions, 2006), 260, 264. For Unruh's position, see Benjamin H. Unruh, *Bote* "Praktische Fragen," #757 (23 March 1938). For A. A. Friesen's position, see A. A. Friesen papers, Mennonite Library and Archives (hereafter, MLA), Bethel College, North Newton, Kansas.

[31] Geoff Eley and Ronald Grigor Suny, "Introduction: From the Moment of Social History to the Work of Cultural Representation," in *Becoming National: A Reader*, ed. Geoff Eley and Ronald Grigor Suny (New York: Oxford University Press, 1996), 9.

polarization that caused them to move centripetally inward toward a manifest sense of local unity or centrifugally outward toward an imagined sense of confessional or national unity. In doing so, they redefined the meanings of Mennoniteness and Germanness to align with their collective narratives about the past, present, and future.

INTERVENTIONS AND FRAMEWORK

The Menno and Fernheim Colonies help us understand a range of migrants and refugees who interpreted nationalism and ecumenicism through local lenses. My framework traces each group's narrative warp through time and space while teasing out the weft of national and religious identifications that entangled the groups during their travels. I therefore begin from the premise that national and religious identifications are not objective and immutable but are tied to subjective mythologies that unfurl through time as collective narratives.

Mennonites' primary allegiances were generally not directed at the nations to which they ostensibly belonged. Consequently, building an analytical framework based on national labels is as misleading as it is dangerous. For example, Russia's Mennonites often understood themselves to be less a part of the German nation – or any nation for that matter – and more a part of their local communities. Their Germanness was likewise created and sustained at the local level.[32] They did not perpetuate German cultural characteristics – such as using Luther's translation of the Bible, German village names, and farming practices – in order to maintain a connection to the German state, but rather to maintain a historical link to their ancestors. In short, they held to German cultural characteristics because they were Mennonites, not because they were Germans. Not surprisingly, historians writing about the Mennonites are mostly uninterested in exploring the confession's Germanness since they are aware that Mennonites emphasize the separation of church and state and know that most Mennonites never lived within the political borders of Germany. Though Russia's Mennonites may not have actively cultivated a sense of German *political* nationalism, they nonetheless shared features

---

[32] Pieter Judson argues that the term "German" has for too long "privileged the German state founded in 1871 as the social, cultural, and political embodiment of a German nation." See "When Is a Diaspora Not a Diaspora? Rethinking Nation-Centered Narratives About Germans in Habsburg East Central Europe," in *The Heimat Abroad*, 219.

in common with other German-speaking locales in the Russian Empire and the Americas. In addition to a shared written culture, German speakers of all faith backgrounds negotiated special privileges, were more loyal to their colonies than to national or international attachments, and entwined culture and religion in unique and enduring ways.[33] In this way, Mennonites were "real" Germans, even if they did not always articulate this identification in the public sphere.

It is common practice for scholars of migration and diaspora to use state borders to describe mobile groups, but this jeopardizes our understanding of how mobile populations understood themselves. For example, historians writing about Germans living abroad frequently merge a wide variety of German-speaking groups under the label of their host countries (e.g. German Canadians, Russian Germans, and Paraguayan Germans).[34] These histories promote a uniform and essentialist understanding of "the Germans," which neglects local variations and obscures individuals' self-identifications.[35] Mennonite historians likewise tend to rely on national paradigms for framing their histories by writing about "Russian Mennonites," "Canadian Mennonites," and "Paraguayan Mennonites," instead of "Russia's Mennonites," "Canada's Mennonites," or "Paraguay's Mennonites."[36] The former designations assume that Mennonites' most relevant descriptor is the geographic area in which they originated or resided. The latter designations place Mennonites within state territories but they do not assume their loyalty to the state.[37] The distinction matters because it opens up an avenue for

---

[33] Manz, *Constructing a German Diaspora*, 3.

[34] See for instance Jonathan Wagner, *A History of Migration from Germany to Canada, 1850–1939* (Vancouver: University of British Columbia Press, 2006); Grant Grams, *German Emigration to Canada and the Support of Its Deutschtum During the Weimar Republic* (New York: Peter Lang, 2001).

[35] Hoerder draws attention to this disparity. See "German-Language Diasporas." So does H. Glenn Penny's historiography of German enclaves in Latin America. See "Latin American Connections: Recent Work on German Interactions with Latin America," *Central European History* 46, no. 2 (2013): 362–94. For examples of writing German history without privileging the nation state or essentializing "Germanness," see O'Donnell et al., *The Heimat Abroad.*

[36] R. Loewen makes a similar observation in *Village Among Nations: "Canadian" Mennonites in a Transnational World, 1916–2006* (Toronto: University of Toronto Press, 2013), 5.

[37] In a similar vein, Tobias Brinkmann demonstrates that scholars of Jewish immigration retroactively assign national identifications to their subjects. See "'German Jews'? Reassessing the History of Nineteenth-Century Jewish Immigrants," in *Transnational Traditions: New Perspectives on American Jewish History*, ed. Ava F. Kahn and Adam Mendelsohn (Detroit, MI: Wayne State University Press, 2014), 145.

examining the fluid nature of Mennonites' external attachments. Historians' reasons for using national frameworks are seldom engaged directly, but they likely have as much to do with ease and convention as they do with the persistent belief that there is something essential about defining a group of people by geographic territory.[38] I accept that state-centered paradigms tell us valuable things about some Mennonites' relationship with specific states, but other Mennonites thrived under a variety of governments even as they remained indifferent to national loyalties and state borders. In such instances, they shared a great deal in common with other German-speaking communities who were tepid about their host states and German nationalism. My framework is sensitive to national cultures and political borders, but it does not conflate them with state or national allegiances. Doing so would risk telling us more about the state's narrative than the Mennonites'.

At various times, Mennonites – and the historians who write about them – have cast those of that confession as victims of government efforts to nationalize new territories; however, I show that Mennonites were not victims of these processes and actually provoked them. Hence, building a framework out of Mennonites' persecution at the hands of a generic "State" is misleading. Mennonites routinely sought out states with weak or amorphous borders where they could establish agrarian communities that were relatively free from state control. Yet due to their proclivity for transforming marginal terrain into productive farmland, they invited the attention of authorities and made it possible for governments to consolidate authority over them. Then, when states demanded that Mennonites abandon their local cultures and integrate into the host nation, they relocated to new frontiers in other lands. Some Mennonites rode a wave of nationalism from borderland to borderland, thereby preserving their communities and their cultures even as they literally sowed the seeds of their own dispersal. In this way, groups like the Menno Colony Mennonites used transnational means to attain transchronological ends.

---

[38] Oddly, national labels are even found in the self-generated histories of Mennonites who patently chose to avoid national citizenship. See for example John D. Thiesen, *Mennonite and Nazi? Attitudes Among Mennonite Colonists in Latin America, 1933–1945* (Kitchener, ON: Pandora Press, 1999). An important exception is R. Loewen, *Village Among Nations*. Oddly, national labels are even found in the self-generated histories of Mennonites who patently chose to avoid national citizenship. See for example Martin W. Friesen, *Canadian Mennonites Conquer a Wilderness: The Beginning and Development of the Menno Colony First Mennonite Settlement in South America*, trans. Christel Wiebe (Loma Plata, Paraguay: Historical Committee of the Menno Colony, 2009).

They successfully replicated their early modern privileges in the modern era by relocating to new, unnationalized spaces.

It is unwise to assume that Mennonites were always "victims" of nationalism. However, I also contend that it is unwise to assume that their integration into host societies or an international fraternity of Mennonites was a given, even if "official" narratives make it appear so. By the end of the First World War, the promises of modern citizenship had led a majority of the world's 516,300 Mennonites to make peace with national identifications and state borders.[39] For example, Mennonite intellectuals in Germany aimed to unite the world's Mennonites under a shared ethnicity, while Mennonite intellectuals in North America – organized under the MCC – tried to unite the world's Mennonites under a shared set of religious principles. Yet owing to Mennonites' local cultures and religious peculiarities, early-twentieth-century Mennoniteness was marked more by disunity than by collaboration. Large numbers of Mennonites remained as recalcitrant to their intellectuals' high-minded entreaties for solidarity as they were to the alleged virtues of nationalism. This observation is important, because it demonstrates that Mennonite intellectuals were as prone to corporatist thinking as nationalist politicians, and the two groups experienced similar problems in uniting diverse constituencies.

Now that I have described what my framework is not, I will now describe what it is. At the broadest level, this book's structure demonstrates how nations and religions exist as mythologies that are arranged as narratives across time. In doing so, it intervenes in the literatures of European-style nationalism, religious ecumenicism, and modern diasporas.

In the 1980s, scholars of nationalism advanced structural explanations of the phenomenon by focusing on nationalism's political and social dimensions. Yet they did not generally engage its mythical qualities.[40]

---

[39] An 1850 estimate places the number of Mennonites at 67,500, which represents a sevenfold increase between 1850 and 1925. For population estimates, see Bender, Sam Steiner, and Richard D. Thiessen, "World Mennonite Membership Distribution," *Global Anabaptist Mennonite Encyclopedia Online*, last modified November 17, 2013, http://gameo.org/index.php?title=World_Mennonite_Membership_Distribution&oldid=103542, last accessed June 7, 2018.

[40] Benedict Anderson, *Imagined Communities: Reflections on the Origins and Spread of Nationalism* (London: Verso, 1983), 11–12; Eric J. Hobsbawm, *Nations and Nationalism Since 1780: Programme, Myth, Reality* (Cambridge, UK: Cambridge University Press, 1990); Ernest Gellner, *Nations and Nationalism* (Ithaca, NY: Cornell University Press, 1983).

Although Benedict Anderson's concept of "imagined communities" gets at nationalism's transcendent nature, he does not account for its affective and moral qualities, which breathe life into the phenomenon.[41]

I argue that nations – and by extension, denominations – exist as mythologies in the space where imagination merges with sentiment.[42] Nations and denominations embody a corpus of myths, which Ernst Renan regards as "common glories" and "regrets."[43] These myths are welded and wielded by political or religious "entrepreneurs" who compete among themselves to fashion them into mythologies.[44] This definition resonates with Anthony Smith's concept of "mythomoteurs" since it focuses on how mythologies succeed or fail based on how closely their constitutive myths resonate with a population's lived reality.[45] Thus, myth and mythology should not be confused with the oft-used concept of "memory" as a means of social agency, since any number of memories may or may not be enshrined in a particular population's corpus of myths.[46]

---

[41] Anderson's concept of "imagined communities" describes nations as groups of people who share a sense of affinity and equality with each other without having ever met. See Anderson, *Imagined Communities*, 6–7; Anthony D. Smith, *Nationalism* (London: Verso, 2006), 89.

[42] Along similar lines, nationalism can be understood as ideology, though the latter differs from mythology in a few important aspects. On one hand, ideologies tend to be future-oriented and project a vision of how the world *should* be. Politics and economics are the principle tools of change. On the other, mythologies hold either a linear or cyclical view of time that may or may not privilege the past, present, or future. Mythologies present a vision of the world as it *appears* to be, and the principle agent of change is either God or an indeterminate "spirit" of history. In general, ideologies are positions that people hold; mythologies are worlds in which people live. Though I agree that nationalism is also ideology, I engage it as mythology to better account for the religious disposition and political ambivalence of my subjects. See Etienne Balibar, "The Nation Form: History and Ideology," in *Race, Nation, Class: Ambiguous Identities*, ed. Etienne Balibar and Immanuel Wallerstein (London: Verso, 1991), 86–106.

[43] Ernest Renan, "What Is a Nation?" in *Becoming National*, 52–53.

[44] Rogers Brubaker, *Ethnicity Without Groups* (Cambridge, MA: Harvard University Press, 2004), 12.

[45] According to Smith, "mythomoteurs" provide an ethnic group with an "overall framework of meaning." Without one, "a group cannot define itself to itself or to others, and cannot inspire or guide collective action." See *The Ethnic Origins of Nationalism* (Oxford: Basil Blackwell, 1986), 24–25.

[46] Duncan S. A. Bell argues that even if "we accept the more rigorous social agency definition of memory – in both its individual and collective senses – then there are at least two major problems with the manner in which it is more commonly employed. Firstly, 'memory' is not transferable (as memory) to those who have not experienced the events that an individual recalls, which means that it cannot be passed down from generation to generation." For another, "it is often a question of perspective, that different sets of people 'remember' different things." Alternately, myths are transferable

Understanding national "mythscapes," where battles over collective memories are won and lost, is not simply an intellectual exercise.[47] It has significant consequences for how we understand acts of resistance, insurrection, flight, and dispersion. One need only consult the headlines to witness stories of émigrés and refugees who for one reason or another defy dominant national narratives with their own interpretations of history and "the nation." The same goes for so-called "cults" that challenge dominant religious narratives with alternative interpretations of church doctrine and scripture. If the nation is an "idea," then it is for good reason that theorist Anthony Smith reminds us of Émile Durkheim's dictum that "ideas, once born, have a life of their own."[48] Unorthodox ideas about nations and denominations are dynamic engines that reveal the essential malleability of a given "mythscape."

Yet how do we understand nationalism's mythical characteristics without ourselves becoming entrapped by them? In the words of Timothy Snyder, "Refuting a myth is dancing with a skeleton: one finds it hard to disengage from the deceptively lithe embrace once the music has begun, and one soon realizes that one's own steps are what is keeping the old bones in motion."[49] I propose that we do not attempt to refute mythologies (after all, one cannot kill a skeleton) but rather treat them as objects of historical inquiry. A way forward is to focus attention on group narratives that challenge the logic and structure of dominant narratives. By tracing the fluctuations of subaltern narratives (the Menno Colony migrants) and the formation of new ones (the Fernheim Colony refugees), historians can denaturalize governing mythologies about a particular group: national, religious, or otherwise. The center is illuminated from the periphery.

By the early 2000s, historians of Central Europe had begun reevaluating nationalism as an artifact of modernity by taking up Hobsbawm's call to analyze it from below.[50] They did so by focusing on expressions of "national indifference" – instances when modern individuals identified themselves outside of national strictures, usually on a local or regional

---

and necessarily require a "believer" to accept a specific perspective. See "Mythscapes: Memory, Mythology, and National Identity," *British Journal of Sociology* 54, no. 1 (2003): 73, 76–77. On memory as social agency see Emmanuel Sivan and Jay Winter, eds., *War and Remembrance in the Twentieth Century* (Cambridge, UK: Cambridge University Press, 1999).

[47] On the concept of "mythscapes" see Bell, 66.   [48] A. Smith, *Nationalism*, 72.

[49] Timothy Snyder, *Reconstruction of Nations: Poland, Ukraine, Lithuania, Belarus, 1569–1999* (New Haven, CT: Yale University Press, 2003), 10.

[50] Hobsbawm, *Nations and Nationalism*, 10–11.

level.[51] These scholars were aided by Rogers Brubaker's concept of "groupness," which he defines as highly contingent "moments of intensely felt collective solidarity" that may or may not crystalize into group mobilization.[52] Their work confirmed that the formation of ethnic or linguistic national blocs (composed of individuals who supposedly shared a perennial solidarity) was not inevitable or even particularly desirable for large numbers of Europeans well into the twentieth century.[53]

Yet it is not enough to focus on the (mostly) political aspects of nationalist-minded and nationally indifferent individuals. Nor is it sufficient to restrict our field of view to nationalism's vicissitudes and victims within a specific locale or region. We must also cultivate an understanding of the counter-stories, religious and otherwise, that run parallel to nationalist narratives – cosmologies that apparently explain nationalism better than it explains itself. In the early twentieth century, Catholic Silesians, Budweiser activists, and Bohemian parents contested their German, Czech, or Polish nationalities in editorials, referendums, and parent–teacher conferences, but they had little doubt that membership in a state (of their choosing or not) was a given. If their local identifications were threatened, few conceived of voluntarily abandoning their homes and property, though mobility is no less of a natural human condition than settlement.

Scholars of nationalism and its discontents succeed at describing the presence or absence of a population's collective identifications, and how these identifications change, but they do not do an especially good job of pegging their observations to broader mythologies. *Moments* of "groupness" happen and individuals recall *specific* memories, but questions

[51] See Tara Zahra, "Imagined Noncommunities: National Indifference as a Category of Analysis," *Slavic Review* 69, no. 1 (2010): 93–119.

[52] Brubaker, *Ethnicity Without Groups*, 12. Brubaker likewise argues that ethnicity, community, identity, and diaspora are not "things" so much as "perspectives" or "stances" that are manifested in specific instances. See Brubaker, "The 'Diaspora' Diaspora," *Ethnic and Racial Studies* 28, no. 1 (2005): 1–19; Brubaker et al., *Nationalist Politics and Everyday Ethnicity in a Transylvanian Town* (Princeton, NJ: Princeton University Press, 2006), 15.

[53] Kate L. Brown, *A Biography of No Place: From Ethnic Borderland to Soviet Heartland* (Cambridge, MA: Harvard University Press, 2004); Bjork, *Neither German nor Pole*; Pieter M. Judson, *Guardians of the Nation: Activists on the Language Frontiers of Imperial Austria* (Cambridge, MA: Harvard University Press, 2006); Jeremy King, *Budweisers into Czechs and Germans: A Local History of Bohemian Politics, 1848–1948* (Princeton, NJ: Princeton University Press, 2002); Zahra, *Kidnapped Souls: National Indifference and the Battle for Children in the Bohemian Lands, 1900–1948* (Ithaca, NY: Cornell University Press, 2008).

persist about how they are woven into longer narratives. Like Hobsbawm's "traditions," mythologies may be "invented" and ahistorical, but naming them as such does not diminish their power.[54] I argue that historians of nationalism should not leave questions of narrative and myth to the pernicious pushers of primordialism and their "just-so" ethnic and nationalist stories. This book examines the shifting terrain of collective mythologies, for they too are the stuff of history.

Obviously, Mennonites' local organization, movements across state borders, and use of multiple identifications challenge the notion that we can discover or create a Mennonite identity.[55] Instead, I demonstrate that diasporic groups such as the Mennonites do not have identities so much as narratives.[56] Therefore, the central goal of this book is to account for the ways that diasporic groups maintain alternative narratives against nationalist ones or incorporate fragments of nationalist narratives into their communal stories. As Alexander Freund reminds us, "Europeans migrated to 'America' rather than Canada [or any specific country], to a 'story' rather than a reality."[57] Yet migrants brought their own stories with them, so my approach pays special attention to how Mennonites' group narratives – often rooted in specific understandings of the Bible – affected their actions and allegiances in new lands. In doing so, I demonstrate how ethno-religious diasporas connect their earthly communities to transcendent national and religious mythologies.

Mennonites interpreted the world through the Bible. This book is not simply a collection of laws and prophecy, but in the words of Don Cupitt, is a "story to live by."[58] Yet owing to the open-ended nature of biblical exegesis, a more apt description of the Bible is that it provides "stories to live by." The Bible animated Mennonites' ambivalence to nation-building schemes, mediated their relationship to the environment, helped them make sense of their migrations, and gave existential meaning to their

---

[54] Hobsbawm and Terence Ranger, *The Invention of Tradition* (Cambridge, UK: Cambridge University Press, 1983).

[55] In other words, identity is constantly being modified as its bearers move through time and space. See James Clifford, "Diasporas," *Cultural Anthropology* 9, no. 3 (1994): 302–38; Linda Basch, Cristina Blanc-Szanton, and Nina Glick Schiller, *Towards a Transnational Perspective on Migration: Race, Class, Ethnicity, and Nationalism Reconsidered* (New York: New York Academy of Sciences, 1992).

[56] Historically, Mennonites did not use the term "diaspora" to describe themselves, but the term is nevertheless useful to describe Mennonites' dispersion throughout the world.

[57] Alexander Freund, "Introduction," in *Beyond the Nation? Immigrants' Local Lives in Transnational Cultures* (Toronto: University of Toronto Press, 2012), 3–17, 5.

[58] Don Cupitt, *What Is a Story?* (London: SCM Press, 1991), xi.

lives. According to Royden Loewen, "When crops failed, children died, cattle fell to rinderpest, storms threatened lives, farmsteads burned, wives became ill, and governments abolished special privileges," Mennonites "conceded and uttered, 'what God does He does well' or 'He takes all and gives all.'"[59] The church congregation was the arbiter of Mennonites' communal narratives, binding the living to the dead, the past to the present, the world to heaven, and connecting everything to the Bible. Believing that the Mennonites were, in a sense, God's chosen people, Mennonites' interpretations of their history are often as mythical as they are historical: the faithful heretic who evades capture by God's hand, the martyr who meets death with a prayer, a safe passage through the wilderness, or the "worldly" ruler stirred to Christian compassion. Thus, "The literal basis of faith in Christianity is a mythical and metaphorical basis, not one founded on historical facts of logical propositions."[60]

Frye's Theory of Modes, which is discussed in his seminal *Anatomy of Criticism*, is useful for interpreting how Mennonites applied biblical concepts such as "wandering" and "exile" to their collective narratives and how they articulated their migrations as "tragic" or "comic" plot progressions. In chronological order, Frye's modes, or literary epochs, are "mythic," "romantic," "high mimetic," "low mimetic" and "ironic."[61] The point of using Frye's modes is not to suggest a collective "progress" of Mennonite theology or a Hegelian culmination of history, but rather to arrive at a better understanding of how theology is expressed in narrative form and changes across time and space. When Mennonite migration is viewed from this perspective, a new layer of interpretation arises in the Mennonites' *longue durée*.

Two of Frye's modes, romantic and high mimetic, are useful for mapping the trajectory of the Mennonites' wanderings. Mennonites emerged from the Anabaptist movement with a narrative corresponding to Frye's romantic mode. They understood themselves as perpetual wanderers, trying to follow the spiritual precedent of the early persecuted church.[62] Protagonists in romantic narratives are killed when there is a tragic plot structure (for example the stories recorded in the Anabaptist/Mennonite *Martyrs Mirror* martyrology), or survive in a comic plot structure where

[59] R. Loewen, *Family, Church, and Market*, 52.

[60] Frye, *The Double Vision: Language and Meaning in Religion* (Toronto: University of Toronto Press, 1991), 17.

[61] Frye, *Anatomy of Criticism: Four Essays*, ed. Robert D. Denham (Toronto: University of Toronto Press, 2006).

[62] Ibid., 40, 54.

the hero is absorbed into a pastoral life (for example the cliché of Mennonites as "the quiet in the land").[63] Either way, Mennonites took the path of diaspora. They remained separated from society and lived (or died) in opposition to the world.[64]

With the increasing affluence and physical expansion of nineteenth-century Russia's Mennonite colonies – what some historians have dubbed the "Mennonite Commonwealth" – some Mennonites began interpreting their story in a high mimetic mode, which is thematically associated with a city or nation.[65] The "Commonwealth" represented a happy resolution to the Mennonites' wanderings. Their Russian "homeland" was the gathering place of God's people on earth, autonomous of "earthly" influences and secure under the protection of a benevolent monarch's "eternal" privileges. Nevertheless, in the 1870s, a third of Russia's Mennonites again followed a "romantic" path by migrating to North America and fifty years later a smaller number sustained this path by moving to South America. Alternately, those who remained in the Russian Empire reached their material and organizational zenith in the first decade of the twentieth century, which reinforced a mimetic connection to Russia and lingered on even after the Bolsheviks' seizure of power.

The Mennonites who fled to Canada and thence to Paraguay interpreted their collective story as a comic plot progression: They experienced a falling-out with government authorities and their coreligionists who disagreed with them, underwent the physical and moral tests of migration, and were spiritually renewed in subsequent locations.[66] By way of example, in 1900 Gerhard Wiebe, an *Ältester* in Manitoba's (West Reserve) Chortitzer *Gemeinde*, recorded a meandering chronicle of the Christian Church defined by moments of rupture and restoration:

---

[63] The full title of Thieleman J. van Braght's *Martyrs Mirror Is The Bloody Theater or Martyrs Mirror of the Defenseless Christians Who Baptized Only upon Confession of Faith, and Who Suffered and Died for the Testimony of Jesus, Their Savior, from the Time of Christ to the Year A.D. 1660* (Scottdale, PA: Mennonite Publishing House, 1950). On folk literature as a social behavior in exiled groups see Daniel L. Smith, *The Religion of the Landless: The Social Context of the Babylonian Exile* (Bloomington, IN: Meyer-Stone Books, 1989), 11.

[64] On diaspora as a rule rather than an exception in the Bible see John Howard Yoder, "Exodus and Exile: The Two Faces of Liberation," *Cross Currents* 23 (Fall 1973): 304.

[65] Frye, *Anatomy of Criticism*, 54. For an appraisal of the term "Mennonite Commonwealth" as a description of Russia's Mennonites, see James Urry, "The Mennonite Commonwealth in Imperial Russia Revisited," *Mennonite Quarterly Review* 84, no. 2 (2010): 229–47.

[66] Frye, *Great Code*, 190.

For approximately three hundred years God had upheld the teaching of humility, but then through arrogance it sank to an animal level. The Jews foundered due to false prophets and amorous alliances with the Assyrians. Four hundred years after Christ the Christians denigrated to an animal level through worldly wisdom and false priests, yet the Lord always safely hid his own. We have seen that God's Word first came from southern France to Bohemia, and a hundred years later to Switzerland, Germany, Holland, Poland and Austria. In 1789 the Mennonites began to move to Russia, and by 1862 or 1863 the rest of the Mennonites had left Germany. Now they were all gathered together in the vast Russian empire, and nowhere else have they been able to live out their faith and principles of freedom as undisturbed as in Russia. Yet, through arrogance, quarreling and contentiousness they departed more and more from the simple life until the beast could dare to enter into battle with them.[67]

When Mennonites such as Wiebe confronted "the beast," they moved to a new location where they were spiritually renewed.

By contrast, the Mennonites who fled from the Soviet Union to Paraguay in 1929 collectively experienced what scholar Robert Zacharias describes as a "break event." Each family interpreted their story of expulsion from the Soviet Union as a tragic plot progression, which rose to a point of peripety when they fled their homes, and plunged downward to catastrophe when they were "exiled" to Paraguay.[68] Fernheimers therefore remained divided over the meaning of the colony's heterogeneous and tragic beginnings, and were skeptical that they could redeem their individual tragedies with a greater collective purpose and somehow recast tragedy into comedy. Both the Fernheim and Menno Colonies believed that they were acting as Mennonites, but their separate pasts and different interpretations of scripture led them to articulate contrasting interpretations of their present situation and of an

---

[67] Gerhard Wiebe, *Causes and History of the Emigration of the Mennonites from Russia to America*, trans. Helen Janzen (Winnipeg: Manitoba Mennonite Historical Society, 1981), 15.

[68] Frye, *Great Code*, 197. Robert Zacharias argues that retelling the story of Russia's Mennonite Commonwealth and its swift dismemberment after the Bolshevik Revolution "has taken on the status of a supplementary scripture." See Robert Zacharias, *Rewriting the Break Event: Memories and Migration in Canadian Literature* (Winnipeg: University of Manitoba Press, 2013), 2. Novelist Robert Kroetsch notes that Mennonites who fled the Soviet Union wrote their history as "a story of the fall from a golden age (the departure from an ideal world somewhere in the past which was apparently in Russia, somewhere, in the late 19th century)." See "Closing Panel," in *Acts of Concealment: Mennonite/s Writing in Canada*, ed. Hildi Froese Tiessen and Peter Hinchcliffe (Waterloo: University of Waterloo, 1992), 225. On understanding exile from the subjective point of view of the exiled see D. L. Smith, *The Religion of the Landless*.

overarching Mennonite narrative, which kept them divided in Paraguay and led them to make very different choices.[69]

IDENTIFICATIONS AND NARRATIVES

Before proceeding, it is important to establish the difference between group identifications and group narratives, as the concepts are easily conflated. Group identifications are a shorthand way of making a particular group legible to outsiders at a particular moment. Identifications such as nationality and religion are singled out from a range of possibilities for the sake of simplicity or to convey a desired sentiment. For example, Canadian officials identified incoming Mennonite settlers as "Germans" in order to lump them together with a well-known and well-respected ethnic group.[70] Then again, some Mennonites referred to themselves as "Germans" when their audience knew who the Mennonites were and may have found the confession distasteful.[71] In short, identifications are used for a specific purpose, within a specific context, to indicate cohesion. Of course, given the complexity of human nature it may be tempting to simply claim that every individual is a unique kaleidoscope of identifications, each with his or her

---

[69] On like groups' construction of different narratives for a shared event see Liisa Malkki's discussion of "mythico-histories" in *Purity and Exile: Violence, Memory, and National Cosmology Among Hutu Refugees in Tanzania* (Chicago: University of Chicago Press, 1995). On the challenges of reconciling competing historical narratives see William Cronon, "A Place for Stories: Nature, History, and Narrative," *Journal of American History* 78, no. 4 (1992): 1347–76. On the relationship between historical narratives and communities see David Carr, "Narrative and the Real World: An Argument for Continuity," *History and Theory*, 25, no. 2 (1986), 117–31. In a similar vein, Susan Schultz Huxman and Gerald Biesecker-Mast point out that when speaking to governments, "Mennonites typically adopt paradoxical rhetorical strategies: *separatist* arguments derived from their faith's tragic orientation; *assimilative* arguments derived from the comic orientation of their yearning to be good citizens." See "In the World but Not of It: Mennonite Traditions as Resources for Rhetorical Invention," *Rhetoric and Public Affairs* 7, no. 4 (2004): 539–54.

[70] See for example F. H. Epp's two volume, *Mennonites in Canada, 1786–1920: The History of a Separate People* (Toronto: Macmillan of Canada, 1974), 185–86; Wagner, *A History of Migration from Germany to Canada*, 76.

[71] See for example "Statement to Hon. Robert F. Forke," March 6, 1929, Canadian Mennonite Board of Colonization (hereafter, CMBC), Immigration Movement I, c. Organizations, Individuals and Transactions related to Immigration and Relief, 1923–1946, vol. 1270, 605, Mennonite Heritage Centre (hereafter, MHC), Winnipeg, MB; Fritz Kliewer, "Letter to Landesleiter des VDA Landesverbandes Weser-Ems," November 18, 1937," R127972d, 52, Politisches Archiv des Auswärtigen Amtes (hereafter, PA AA), Berlin, Germany.

own private agendas, and leave all notions of collectivism by the wayside. But that is to deny both reality and humanity. Humans are collectivist, but oftentimes they are more attached to – and unified through – shared narratives than to shared identifications.

Like shared identifications, shared narratives describe groups of people but they include the element of time, which is a uniquely human conception. Paul Ricœur theorizes that narratives constitute the very center of humans' ability to identify and be identified as anything in the first place. They necessarily presuppose all attempts to incorporate the past into the present and consequently "individual and community are constituted in their identity by taking up narratives that become for them their actual history."[72] Under such a theory, one can never be quite certain if a corporate memory is the literal truth or simply the best, fleeting attempt to reconcile a fractured past with present contingencies. Importantly, Ricœur argues that the "selective function" of narrative is the process through which memory is most susceptible to ideology – religious, political, or otherwise.[73]

A collective narrative is therefore a curated assembly of myths, events, and identifications that offer a tidy and meaningful alternative to the clutter and chaos of history. It may be substantiated in part by scholarship but finds its most robust articulation as the story of a distinct culture, from the smallest *Gemeinde* to the largest nation. Since collective narratives are embedded in time, they are susceptible to transformations as groups experience new events and incorporate and dismiss various identifications. Yet the story remains. For example, the Menno colonists emphasized the continuity of their narrative as nomadic Mennonites despite numerous relocations and being identified variously as "Russians," "Canadians," and "Paraguayans." By contrast, the Fernheim Colony was composed of sundry individuals and families, each of whom had been torn from preexisting narratives as members of specific communities across the Soviet Union and now had to create a new narrative in Paraguay. To do so, they first had to discover or invent a set of shared attributes – the untested flotsam and jetsam of identifications they carried with them (or that others gave them) – that they could fashion into a collective story.

Ultimately, collective narratives err more toward mythology than history. Zacharias observes that "narrative itself always 'strains' to project

---

[72] Paul Ricœur, *Time and Narrative*, vol. 3, trans. Kathleen Blamey and David Pellauer (Chicago: University of Chicago Press, 1988), 247.
[73] Ricœur, *Memory, History, Forgetting* (Chicago: University of Chicago Press, 2004), 85.

an artificial coherency and completeness onto its subject," even as it wields a remarkable power to shape past, present, and future.[74] Mennonite migrants' "break events," "plot points," or moments of rupture are often historical events burnished with mythological meaning. For instance, it is a historical fact that none of the ships carrying the 1874 Mennonite migrants to Canada sank in the Atlantic Ocean, but in the Mennonites' collective narrative this fact is only relevant because God protected them. Likewise, histories go to great pains to clarify causality (did Mennonites leave Canada due to new public education laws or did they have other reasons?), while group narratives are remarkably clear on the point: The Menno Colony Mennonites left Canada because it was "Babylon."[75] Histories plunge into detail, while group narratives float above historical nuance, such as G. Wiebe's tidy summary of his *Gemeinde*'s past. Finally, histories move outward, seeking to incorporate more factors into their analysis, while group narratives remain tightly focused on a specific and highly meaningful storyline.

As we move from Russia, through Canada, Germany, China, Paraguay, Bolivia, and up to the United States over the span of seventy-five years, the chapters in this book accentuate the ways that Mennonite migrants and refugees situated their religious and national identifications within their collective narratives and how outsiders influenced these developments. Here, at the nexus of myth and migration, narrative, and nationalism, lies this book's center of gravity.

CHAPTER OVERVIEW

This book comprises six chapters. The first chapter follows the movement of voluntary migrants from the Russian Empire to Canada to Paraguay between 1870 and 1926. It shows that members of this cohort underwent a contentious process of integrating state citizenship and Mennonite unity into their collective narratives or rejecting it in favor of local narratives that prized religious separation. Chapter 2 examines the discourse between governments, aid agencies, and the press concerning the Mennonite refugees who fled from the Soviet Union to Paraguay via Germany and China between 1929 and 1931. This chapter contends that the refugees were both aided and inhibited by their national,

---

[74] Zacharias, *Rewriting the Break Event*, 5.
[75] Guenther, "*Ältester* Martin C. Friesen (1889–1968): A Man of Vision for Paraguay's Mennogemeinde," *Journal of Mennonite Studies* 23 (2005): 189.

religious, and economic identifications, which left them with an ambiguous collective narrative. The first two chapters also demonstrate how governments used each group to define their own constituencies along the lines of class, nationality, citizenship, and religion.

The third chapter grounds us in the local context of the Chaco and examines each colony through three lenses. The first concerns the colonies' interpretations of the natural environment. The second focuses on their actions during the Chaco War. The third is about their interactions with indigenous peoples after the war. This chapter shows that each colony's collective narrative – as faithful nomads and as displaced victims – led them to make profoundly different choices vis-à-vis the Paraguayan government, and kept the groups divided during the 1930s.

Chapter 4 looks to the United States to explain why the colonies found themselves in the crosshairs of the MCC's emerging mission as the arbiter of a narrative of global Mennonite unity, while Chapter 5 looks to Germany to explain why the colonies found themselves in the crosshairs of the Nazi State's bid for transnational German unity. Each of these chapters demonstrates that the colonies frustrated outsiders' initiatives for unity due to their local conceptions of Mennoniteness and Germanness.

The sixth and final chapter shows how the Fernheim Colony's collective narrative reached a point of crisis (and violence) between 1937 and 1944 as colonists became divided between those who continued to believe that they should remain in Paraguay, as per the wishes of the MCC, and those who thought they should relocate to Europe under Nazi jurisdiction. Meanwhile, the Menno Colony remained indifferent to Germany's oscillating fortunes, as they preferred to maintain their local expressions of Mennoniteness and Germanness. This chapter highlights the ambiguity caused by a quick reversal of a group's collective narrative – from an anticipated comic outcome to a tragic one. Combined with Chapter 5, it also indicates that Latin America's German-speaking communities exhibited a wide range of attitudes toward the Nazi state, from political indifference to overwrought anticipation.

This work is neither a micro history that comprehensively describes the groups' social, religious, and political dimensions nor a macro history that uses multiple categories of analysis to analyze a large diaspora.[76] Rather, it focuses on two group narratives, often crafted by the community's

---

[76] R. Loewen has made significant contributions to our understanding of mobile Mennonites on each of these counts. For a local, comparative study, see *Family, Church, and Market*. For a broader survey of transnational Mennonite networks, see *Village Among Nations*.

leaders as their groups moved in and out of several national contexts. As a result, it necessarily contains several analytical limitations. For one, the thousands of other Mennonites, Jews, and other migrants who moved across borders in Europe, Asia, and the Americas during this tumultuous era are acknowledged but remain unexamined. For another, the material and economic aspects of the colonies are not discussed in detail. Likewise, I refer to the colonies' organizational structures – such as economic cooperatives and municipal governments – insofar as they relate to the argument at hand, but I do not elaborate on their internal mechanics. Class and gender are important lenses for understanding the effects of power and inheritance within agrarian communities and they provide us with reasons why individual families elected to stay or leave a given country.[77] Yet I am primarily concerned with the community-level narratives that illuminate how Mennonites' national and religious identifications mediated their wanderings. These narratives generally emerged from the groups' internal hierarchies, which placed landowning, male leaders from recognized families at the fore.[78] Thus, many of the primary sources I use concerning the colonies – such as the work of Martin W. Friesen – were written by colony elites. Beyond using these works to relate basic chronologies and statistics, I do not uncritically accept their interpretations of events. Rather, I use their interpretations to exhibit and analyze the truth claims and justifications made by elites as they crafted unifying narratives. These individuals were generally men, their Bible-based theology was patriarchal, and their decisions to migrate were grounded in masculine issues: Boys received a longer formal education, and young men were targets of the draft. Adult men were allowed the franchise in Canada and were most at risk of incarceration in the Soviet Union. Older

---

[77] In keeping with 1 Peter 3:7, which states that men and women are co-heirs of the grace of life, Russia's Mennonites practiced bilateral partible inheritance, which gave women a degree of influence over financial decisions. See Marlene Epp, *Mennonite Women in Canada: A History* (Winnipeg: University of Manitoba Press, 2008), 36; R. Loewen, "The Children, the Cows, My Dear Man and My Sister,'" 360–63.

[78] Naturally, individuals create personal narratives of migration – both for and against – but understanding them is best achieved through oral interviews or an analysis of diaries and letters. On gender and personal narratives see Brigitte Bönisch-Brednich, "Migration, Gender, and Storytelling: How Gender Shapes the Experiences and the Narrative Patterns in Biographical Interviews," in *German Diasporic Experiences*, ed. Mathias Schulze, James M. Skidmore, David G. John et al. (Waterloo: Wilfrid Laurier University Press, 2008): 331–44; Sandra K. D. Stahl, *Literary Folkloristics and the Personal Narrative* (Bloomington, IN: Indiana University Press, 1987). For an example of using this approach in the Mennonite context see R. Loewen, *Hidden Worlds: Revisiting the Mennonite Migrants of the 1870s* (Winnipeg: University of Manitoba Press, 2001).

men preached sermons, administered the colonies, and organized migrations. As Marlene Epp notes, Mennonite theology and leadership "had nothing to say specifically to women, who had no military service obligations to their country, [or] about how they might live out nonresistant beliefs within their sphere of activity."[79] Of course, this is not to say that Mennonite women lacked theological convictions, agency, and feelings of excitement or apprehension over the possibility of migration, but they were generally articulated at the interpersonal or family levels.[80] Insofar as one or both family heads found Mennonite leaders' arguments for migration persuasive or unpersuasive, this book speaks to those decisions. Finally, wherever Mennonites went, they demanded indigenous displacement as a condition of settlement. There is much to be said about this conspicuous irony – given Mennonites' presumed interest in nonviolence – but my line of argument necessarily foregrounds the relationships between colonists and state governments that accepted Mennonites into and/or rejected Mennonites from their national communities.

As a history, this book is organized as a *Weltgeschichte*, an attempt to answer the question "What should I have seen if I had been there?"[81] Yet I am writing the history of a people who interpreted their story as a *Heilsgeschichte* and who would have answered, "This may not be what you would have seen if you had been there, but what you would have seen would have missed the whole point of what was really going on."[82] This project operates in the space where these views collide: It considers the evidential causes and effects of migration and nationalism while remaining attuned to how those processes were interpreted by Mennonites. Henry Glassie notes that scholars are often "tempted to dismiss religious people as marginal (which they are to histories painstakingly arranged around secular centers) and to probe beneath religious motives for worldlier goals deemed to be more real."[83] Brown likewise argues the "myth" of using rational approaches is that "even when [humans] act irrationally, their actions when examined reveal an underlying political, social, psychological, or economic motivation."[84] This "hermeneutic of suspicion" may be more insidious to our understanding

---

[79] M. Epp, *Mennonite Women in Canada*, 13.

[80] According to M. Epp, the female partner may "indeed have been the one who pushed her family to go, perhaps because she feared for the future security of her children, or perhaps because she had an adventurous spirit." See M. Epp, *Mennonite Women in Canada*, 28.

[81] Frye, *Great Code*, 66.   [82] Ibid., 66.

[83] Henry Glassie, *Material Culture* (Bloomington, IN: Indiana University Press, 1999), 21.

[84] K. L. Brown, *A Biography of No Place*, 69.

of historical individuals than simply misunderstanding their motives, since it "destroys the very possibility of understanding historical difference" between past and present, "us" and "them," and "imposes on past events modern, a priori assumptions intent on separating the 'ideological' from the 'authentic.'"[85] As Frye reminds us, "mythical and typological thinking is not rational thinking and we have to get used to conceptions that do not follow ordinary distinctions of categories and are, so to speak, liquid rather than solid."[86] Human identifications, both past and present, are likewise more liquid than solid. They are active, dormant, aspirational, disposable, and frequently irrational. In the same way that the quark – a fundamental constituent of all matter – is too ephemeral to be studied in isolation, human identifications are elusive things that are best observed during moments of collision. These interactions are in turn part of larger mythologies that are best captured in narrative form.

I am neither a theologian nor a literary critic and so my work is primarily focused on the applied dimensions of Mennonites' *Heilsgeschichte*: how, why, and where they migrated and the interpretations they recorded along the way. Yet on a broader level, this book turns a mirror on the secular *Heilsgeschichten* advanced by nationalists to understand the position that mobile and nationally resistant individuals occupied within national mythologies. In doing so, I aim to uncover the insecurities and ambiguities that accompanied the formation of modern nation states, which was the largest and most destructive experiment in the history of social engineering.

---

[85] Brad Gregory, *Salvation at Stake: Christian Martyrdom in Early Modern Europe* (Cambridge, MA: Harvard University Press, 1999), 14, 15; John D. Roth, "The Complex Legacy of the Martyrs Mirror Among the Mennonites in North America," *Mennonite Quarterly Review* 87, no. 3 (2013): 283.

[86] Frye, *Great Code*, 195.

I

No Lasting City (1870–1930)

The morning of August 21, 1927, was unseasonably cool and rainy in the small Manitoba village of Osterwick.[1] Here, Martin C. Friesen, the young and handsome *Ältester* of the Chortitza Mennonite *Gemeinde*, delivered his farewell address to several hundred spectators, including the faithful and the merely curious. According to one reporter's account, 200 cars and 100 buggies crowded the property and lined the muddy road.[2] M. C. Friesen's sermon – based on the apocalyptic passage of Jeremiah 51 – conjured up imagery of punishment and escape. There is no record of the exact section M. C. Friesen focused on, but the verse is a relentless condemnation of corrupt regimes:

Flee from the midst of Babylon; let every one save his life! Be not cut off in her punishment, for this is the time of the Lord's vengeance, the repayment he is rendering her. Babylon was a golden cup in the Lord's hand, making all the earth drunken; the nations drank of her wine; therefore the nations went mad ... Forsake her, and let us go each to his own country, for her judgment has reached up to heaven and has been lifted up even to the skies.[3]

M. C. Friesen's message was accompanied by the hymn "When Lot and Abraham Separated," based on the biblical passage Genesis 13:5–13. This section describes a scene in which the Jewish patriarch Abraham senses conflict with his nephew Lot and tells him "separate yourself from me. If you take the left hand, then I will go to the right, or if you take the right

---

[1] Osterwick was later renamed New Bothwell.
[2] Titus F. Guenther, "Ältester Martin C. Friesen (1889–1968): A Man of Vision for Paraguay's Mennogemeinde," *Journal of Mennonite Studies* 23 (2005): 189, n. 29.
[3] Jeremiah 51:6–9, ESV.

hand, then I will go to the left."[4] The pragmatic and opportunistic Lot chose the land before him – the fertile Jordan Valley, located ominously near the cities of Sodom and Gomorrah. Ever faithful to the Lord's inscrutable will, Abraham chose the unknown land of Canaan.

Surely the significance of this verse and song was not lost on the audience. Before M. C. Friesen led nearly 1,800 Mennonites from the Bergthal (Saskatchewan), Chortitza (East Manitoba), and Sommerfeld (West Manitoba) communities out of Canada and into the wilds of Paraguay's Gran Chaco, he wanted to explain to everyone present why his flock had made this decision. The Canadian government likely represented the all-encompassing state, drunk on power, and indifferent to a righteous minority. The Mennonites who remained in Canada presumably represented Lot. They were not evil, but they did not completely trust God. M. C. Friesen wanted to be clear that his group was taking the path of Abraham and that it was God, and not himself, who was their leader. Two days later, his family accompanied the second-to-last group of Mennonites bound for Paraguay.[5] They believed that the journey, and the primitive conditions that greeted them, represented a sacred renewal of God's unfolding promise.

M. C. Friesen's group left Canada because of their belief that Mennonites should remain autonomous from nationalist activities and institutions. A focal point of their concern was compulsory, public, English-language schooling. Beginning in the last decades of the nineteenth century and culminating after the First World War, western Canada's provincial authorities made education the focal point of Canadization and national citizenship. However, many Mennonites believed that Canada's Dominion government, under the headship of the Crown, guaranteed them indefinite and exclusive control of their schools. Yet the latitude given to Mennonites when they arrived in the 1870s was more a symptom of the frontier's fluid society than an expression of the government's permanent intentions. As Canada shifted from an imperial frontier to an independent country, Mennonites faced the question of whether they would participate in Canadian education, politics, and society. In Manitoba and Saskatchewan, the decision accompanied a rupture among the Mennonites wherein locally oriented *Ältester*-led communities were eclipsed by new leaders who advocated the founding of teacher-training institutes, holding national church conferences, and conciliation with government authorities.

---

[4] ESV.   [5] Guenther, "*Ältester* Martin C. Friesen," 189.

This chapter contrasts Western Canada's Mennonites using two broad categories that emerged between 1890 and 1914 and solidified during the First World War: (1) Associative Mennonites were willing to participate in Canada's democratic system. They engaged the government as individual, enfranchised citizens who agreed to a set of evolving rights and responsibilities. Associative Mennonites viewed Canada as their homeland and established educational institutions and national conferences. (2) Separatist Mennonites rejected Canada's democratic system. Most were naturalized British subjects – a requirement for claiming land – but they did not avail themselves of the tools of Canadian citizenship such as joining political parties, voting, and public education. Instead, they engaged the government as a community of subjects who did not recognize any country as their homeland. Instead, they lived in Canada as autonomous units wishing to retain their local identifications.[6] The separatist Mennonites who moved from Russia to Canada to Paraguay, therefore, were voluntary migrants since they exited Canada on their own terms and after much debate. The Menno Colony was not a collection of disparate individuals, but a group that possessed a strong, self-generated understanding about its relationship to states and its members' identification as religious nomads.

Despite Mennonites' communal orientation, Russian, Canadian, and Paraguayan authorities shared the belief that they belonged to the German nation. Western governments valued German-speaking settlers for their presumed heartiness and attracted Mennonites to their frontiers by offering them concessions that assured their separation from society. Yet once Mennonites helped nationalize new territories, authorities reevaluated their concessions and demanded that they shed their Mennoniteness and Germanness, and nationalize themselves. When Mennonites refused to comply, they departed for new states where authorities and local circumstances favored them once more. Though Mennonites may have rejected

---

[6] There are several ways of grouping Canada's Mennonites, each of which is insufficient for neatly describing their differences. For instance, one could divide their communities and congregations by their schisms in Europe and North America, their adaptation of certain technologies or participation in government, their organizational structure (whether *Ältester*-oriented or conference-oriented), or the timing of their migration to North America, including their subsequent migrations across the continent. For the argument at hand, Adolf Ens's *Subjects or Citizens? The Mennonite Experience in Canada, 1870–1925* (Ottawa: University of Ottawa Press, 1994) nonetheless provides a particularly germane categorization. On page 46 Ens notes that Mennonites "were quite prepared to be subjects of the realm, but reluctant to accept the privileges and obligations of full citizenship in the nation."

the social and political aspects of "Germanness," they did not deny the identification's usefulness when it aided their migrations.

This chapter makes three contentions: First, I show that Canadian officials transitioned from identifying Mennonites as enterprising and valuable German-speaking settlers in the 1870s – when they promoted a narrative of Canadian national expansion, to viewing them as insular and subversive German-speaking dissidents in the 1920s – when they promoted a narrative of Canadian national cohesion. Second, I demonstrate how Canada's Mennonites developed contrasting narratives about Canadian citizenship. Associative Mennonites believed that God willed them to carve out a place within Canada's national narrative. Separatists believed that God willed Mennonites to accept perpetual migration as a necessary burden of faith. Third, I contend that separatist Mennonites harnessed modern transnational technologies – such as transportation, communication, and financial systems – to secure the transchronological goal of living as early-modern subjects. In other words, separatist Mennonites used the tools of nationalism and modernity in an attempt to flee from them.

CONSCRIPTION AND CRISIS IN IMPERIAL RUSSIA

The 1860s was a watershed decade for Russia's Mennonites and their relationship to the imperial state. During this time, a large schism among the Mennonites coincided with a government plan to modernize the empire's bureaucratic, educational, financial, judicial, military, and social systems. The changes prompted a third of Russia's Mennonites (roughly 17,000 of 50,000 members) to depart for North America. In keeping with the confession's tradition of disunity, migrants accused those who stayed of compromising with worldly authorities, while those who stayed accused the migrants of zealotry. The migrants' justification for leaving and the remainders' justification for staying foreshadow the separatist/associative split that occurred fifty years later when Canada's provincial governments passed its own modernizing initiatives. In both instances, what was at stake for authorities was the ability to guide their populations toward a more nationally integrated future. What was at stake for the Mennonites was whether religious fidelity was best preserved by rejecting these schemes or adapting to them.

During the first half of the nineteenth century, Russia's Mennonites were small, freeholding farmers primarily clustered in two large settlements: the older and demographically stable Chortitza Colony, which was settled between 1789 and 1811, and the younger, socially dynamic Molotschna Colony, which was settled between 1803 and the 1840s.[7] In due course, industrialization and the expansion of the international grain market prompted Russia's 50,000 Mennonites to shift from subsistence farming to commercial grain production. The move entailed the creation of capital-intensive industries, increased contact with non-Mennonites, and led to greater economic disparities between landowners and non-landowners.[8] These developments, in turn, provoked migration to new settlements in the Black Sea and Volga regions.[9] The 1860s witnessed a painful division that split colonies along religious lines, most notably the emergence of the revivalist Brüdergemeinde (Mennonite Brethren Church) and Krimmer Mennoniten Brüdergemeinde (Krimmer Mennonite Brethren Church) from the old, established Mennonitengemeinde (Mennonite Church, also called Kirchengemeinde).[10] Both Brüdergemeinde groups adhered to Mennonite principles of nonviolence, simple living, and abstaining from oaths, but stressed a more spiritually earnest lifestyle. The Mennonitengemeinde, for its part, feared the new groups would jeopardize their status as a distinct and privileged minority.

In the midst of these changes, Tsar Alexander II introduced his Great Reforms, which were intended to modernize the empire after its defeat in

---

[7] James Urry, "The Russian Mennonites, Nationalism and the State 1789–1917," in *Canadian Mennonites and the Challenge of Nationalism*, ed. Abe J. Dueck (Winnipeg: Manitoba Mennonite Historical Society, 1994), 27.

[8] R. Loewen, *Family, Church, and Market: A Mennonite Community in the Old and the New Worlds, 1850–1930* (Toronto: University of Toronto Press, 1993), 15; James Urry, "The Russian State, the Mennonite World and the Migration from Russia to North America in the 1870s," *Mennonite Life* 46, no. 1 (1991): 14–15.

[9] For instance, in 1865, 700 Kleine Gemeinde Mennonites who had been living in the Molotschna Colony migrated to Borosenko, 160 km to the northwest. See R. Loewen, *Family, Church, and Market*, 19–20.

[10] The biggest rupture occurred on January 6, 1860, when a group of Molotschna Colony Mennonites formed the Brüdergemeinde. Mennonitengemeinde leaders were alarmed by this development because the Brüdergemeinde tried to maintain their Mennonite privileges while openly proselytizing to Russian peasants, which angered the Orthodox Church. See Abraham Friesen, *In Defense of Privilege: Russian Mennonites and the State Before and During World War I* (Winnipeg: Kindred Productions, 2006), 109–12; Urry, "The Russian State," 14–15; Sergei I. Zhuk, *Russia's Lost Reformation: Peasants, Millennialism, and Radical Sects in Southern Russia and Ukraine, 1830–1917* (Baltimore, MD: Johns Hopkins University Press, 2004), 159–63. John B. Toews wryly notes, "In one sense the [Brüdergemeinde] dispute of 1860 reaffirms continuity in the history of a rather contentious people." See "Brethren and Old Church Relations in Pre-World War I Russia: Setting the Stage for Canada, *Journal of Mennonite Studies* 2 (1984): 42.

the Crimean War (1853–1856). Until the middle of the century, the Imperial government's "Rossification" agenda allowed national minorities to remain culturally autonomous from Russian society and conduct business with the state in their chosen vernacular. For the Mennonites, this was High German, which was the closest officially recognized language to *Plautdietsch*. Ironically, both Russian and German governments would eventually regard Russia's Mennonites as "Germans" based on their bureaucratic use of High German. Nevertheless, Alexander II's new "Russification" policies included a cultural dimension that made Russian the official language of government and promoted the integration of minority subjects.[11] Accompanying this plan, in 1866 the government's Fürsorge-Komitee für die Kolonisten der südlichen Gebiete Rußlands (Guardians' Committee of the Foreign Colonists in the Southern Regions of Russia) required Mennonites to begin teaching Russian in their schools.[12]

The Great Reforms indicated a new direction for Russia's government, one that took a more active interest in the lives of its subjects. Many of the reforms – including taxation and land use – permitted the state to engage subjects directly rather than through communes or estates.[13] The reforms align with James C. Scott's concept of state "legibility," which describes state attempts to standardize, and thus control, local practices – from weights and measurements to systems of communication and education.[14] For the most part, Mennonites did not mind making their commerce and industry more legible to the state – after all, Jesus instructed his followers to "Render to Caesar the things that are Caesar's" – yet some were concerned that changing the cultural aspects of their communities would interfere with their faith.[15] They implicitly knew, as Scott explicitly states,

[11] For a detailed discussion of "Rossification," and "Russification," see Urry, "Mennonites, Nationalism and the State."

[12] Cornelius Krahn, "Fürsorge-Komitee (Guardians' Committee)," *Global Anabaptist Mennonite Encyclopedia Online*, last modified June 15, 2014, http://gameo.org/index.php?title=F%C3%BCrsorge-Komitee_(Guardians%27_Committee)&oldid=123221, last accessed June 7, 2018.

[13] On the reforms' ambiguities and inconsistencies see Don K. Rowney, "Imperial Russian Officialdom During Modernization," in *Russian Bureaucracy and the State: Officialdom from Alexander III to Putin*, ed. Don K. Rowney and Eugene Huskey (Basingstoke: Palgrave Macmillan, 2009), 26–45; Yanni Kotsonis, "'Face-to-Face': The State, the Individual, and the Citizen in Russian Taxation, 1863–1917," *Slavic Review* 63, no. 2 (Summer, 2004): 221–46.

[14] James Scott, *Seeing Like a State: How Certain Schemes to Improve the Human Condition Have Failed* (New Haven, CT: Yale University Press, 1998), 2–3; 183–84.

[15] Mark 12:17, ESV.

that preserving one's "illegibility ... has been and remains a reliable resource for political [or in this case, religious] autonomy."[16] The Tsar did not call on Mennonites to participate in Russian politics, but he did ask them to adjust their social order to the state's new political direction.

One of the most important goals of a modernizing state is the creation of a professional military. To this end, the Tsar introduced universal mandatory military conscription, which directly threatened Mennonites' convictions.[17] Harry Loewen argues that even though some *Ältesten* were outspoken in their support of biblical nonresistance, the government believed that the Mennonite laity "did not take their principle of non-resistance all that seriously" since many had vocally and materially supported Russia's efforts during the Crimean War. Ultimately, "at stake was not only exemption from military service, but also their rights and policies with regard to education, the German language and control of their colonial affairs" generally.[18] Military conscription thus set off a battle for local control. Language and education reforms would affect individuals within the colony, but military service would literally remove individuals from it.

When the Mennonites caught word of the Imperial Court's decision to implement mandatory conscription, the Chortitza and Molotschna colonies dispatched an ad hoc delegation led by elders Gerhard Dyck and Leonhard Sudermann to St. Petersburg. They intended to remind the government of the concessions enshrined in their *Privilegium*.[19] At the meeting, officials spoke wryly of the confession's contradictions as a people of peace. They had "shelves full of records ... which told the stories of quarrels among Mennonites concerning religious and educational matters."[20] If Mennonites fought each other, why should they not fight on behalf of the state? Naturally, it did not help that the delegates could not

---

[16] Scott, *Seeing Like a State*, 54.

[17] The nobility also feared conscription since they were wary of their children fraternizing with peasants. See Urry, "The Russian State," 185.

[18] Harry Loewen, "A House Divided: Russian Mennonite Nonresistance and Emigration in the 1870s," in *Mennonites in Russia 1788–1988: Essays in Honour of Gerhard Lohrenz*, ed. John Friesen (Winnipeg: CMBC Publications, 1989), 127.

[19] Frank H. Epp, *Mennonites in Canada 1786–1920* (Toronto: University of Toronto Press, 1974), 184; James Urry, *Mennonites, Politics, and Peoplehood: Europe-Russia-Canada 1525–1980* (Winnipeg: University of Manitoba Press, 2006), 99. For more on the origins of the Russian *Privilegium*, see John Staples, "Religion, Politics, and the Mennonite *Privilegium* in Early Nineteenth Century Russia: Reconsidering the Warkentin Affair," *Journal of Mennonite Studies* 21 (2003): 71–88.

[20] H. Loewen, "A House Divided," 127.

speak Russian. On a deeper level, the Mennonites' request was terribly out of step with the emerging government position that minority populations should conform to Russian society.[21] After being chastised by the president of the Imperial Court for their temerity, the delegates returned home with an ultimatum: Comply with the new laws or emigrate within ten years. Mistrustful of the big colonies, the smaller and less prosperous Bergthal Colony (which was formed by landless Chortitza Mennonites between the 1830s and 1850s) dispatched representatives to conduct separate negotiations.[22] They received the same reply. In an act of conciliation, however, the government granted Mennonites an exemption from military service through working in state forestry units, hospitals, fire brigades, railways and factories.[23]

Rejecting the Tsar's "olive branch" of alternative service, a third of the country's Mennonites sought land in North America. They were aided by the Prussian-born Mennonite Cornelius Janzen, who was a grain broker and former representative of the Prussian consulate in Berdyansk, Russia. Janzen had business contacts in the colonies, diplomatic contacts in England and the United States, and Mennonite and Quaker friends in both countries. Upon hearing of the Mennonites' proposed exodus, he worked to bring these disparate groups into contact.[24] In 1873, the Borozenko (Kleine Gemeinde), Bergthal, and Molotschna colonies dispatched representatives to survey land in the western United States and Canada.[25] In the United States, there were already about 20,000 Mennonites living in a band from the Mid-Atlantic States to eastern Iowa.[26] In Canada, there were about 10,000 Mennonites, who mostly resided in southern Ontario, a

---

[21] F. H. Epp, *Mennonites in Canada 1786–1920*, 184; Urry, *Mennonites, Politics, and Peoplehood*, 99.

[22] Martin W. Friesen, *New Homeland in the Chaco Wilderness*, 2nd ed., trans. Jake Balzer (Loma Plata, Paraguay: Cooperativa Chortitzer Limited, 1997), 19.

[23] H. Loewen, "A House Divided," 132.

[24] Gustav R. Gaeddert, "Jansen, Cornelius (1822–1894)," *Global Anabaptist Mennonite Encyclopedia Online*, last modified January 15, 2017, http://gameo.org/index.php?title=Jansen,_Cornelius_(1822–1894)&oldid=143620, last accessed June 7, 2018; Mark Jantzen, "'Whoever Will Not Defend His Homeland Should Leave It!' German Conscription and Prussian Mennonite Emigration to the Great Plains, 1860–1890," *Mennonite Life* 58, no. 3 (2003): n. pag.

[25] Mennonites also considered Turkestan and Australia. See Frances Swyripa, *Storied Landscapes: Ethno-Religious Identity and the Canadian Prairies* (Winnipeg: University of Manitoba Press, 2010), 36.

[26] This estimate is based on Henry King Carroll, "Statistics of Churches," *Census Bulletin*, no. 131 (Washington, D.C.: United States Census Office, October 25, 1891).

world away from the prairies.[27] Now there would be a third large grouping of Mennonites in North America. Between 1874 and 1880 Russia lost over a third of its Mennonite population.[28] About 10,000 members of the Mennonitengemeinde and Brüdergemeinde hailing from the Borozenko (Kleine Gemeinde), Molotschna, and Volhynia colonies settled in the United States while another 6,931 Mennonitengemeinde individuals from the Bergthal, Kleine Gemeinde, Chortitza, and Fürstenland colonies settled in the newly formed province of Manitoba.[29]

United States–bound migrants were enticed by the promises of better weather, lower tariffs, less contact with American Indian populations, and better transportation links. Military conscription was not a federal issue in the United States, but state officials convinced settlers that they would be granted military exemption if the country went to war. Less affluent and more culturally conservative Mennonites pursued the Canadian option due to the prospect of free land, granted as a contiguous block, and the Dominion's guarantee of complete exemption from military service. They also chose Canada because of their familiarity with monarchical governance.[30] Yet a settler's choice between Canada and the United States was not necessarily final. One pragmatic Mennonite farmer happily quipped that "one can always still move to [Canada]" in the event of US military conscription.[31] Though government authorities in Ottawa and Washington, D.C. aspired to clear and permanent national borders, the indigenous and settler populations who actually lived there imagined the space according to their local or transnational loyalties.

Russia's Mennonites conceived of their relationship to governments using the analogy of a family wherein they were the children of a paternalistic state. Mennonites did not feel obliged to adopt the manners and morals of the government's other "children" – be they Russian peasants or members of a fleeting democratic majority. This suited the Russian regime, but the situation was different in the United States, since

[27] This estimate is based on the 1841 and 1901 census data found in F. H. Epp, *Mennonites in Canada, 1786–1920*, 74–75, 304.

[28] Ibid., 185.

[29] Ibid., 194–200, especially Table 3, listing number of immigrants by year of departure. See also R. Loewen, *Family, Church, and Market*, 74.

[30] F. H. Epp, *Mennonites in Canada 1786–1920*, 195; R. Loewen, *Family, Church, and Market*, 108–11.

[31] See Jacob Klassen to Heinrich Ratzlaff, October 4, 1874, John K. Loewen papers, C. J. Loewen Family, Giroux, Manitoba. Quoted in R. Loewen, *Family, Church, and Market*, 109.

Mennonites were required to consult a wide cast of characters including railroad agents, land speculators, and democratically elected politicians. On the other hand, Canada was less bewildering since their Canadian broker, the German-born agent Wilhelm Hespeler, spoke directly with the Crown's Dominion representatives. In general, the closer Mennonites came to dealing with the highest levels of government, the more secure they felt as privileged "children."

Mennonites initially had good reason to feel special in the eyes of Canadian authorities since the government granted them a direct assistance loan in the amount of $100,000 CAD – an advantage that it had not previously given to non-British settlers.[32] Furthermore, Secretary of Agriculture John Lowe's 1873 letter to the Mennonite delegation cast the Dominion's guarantees in the language of a *Privilegium*, even though most of the terms were part of its standard immigration policy.[33] Importantly, one of the document's main guarantees – the exclusive management of schools – actually remained outside the Dominion's jurisdiction since education matters were handed over to the provinces under the British North American Act of 1867. Its inclusion in Lowe's letter to the Mennonites eventually caused serious misunderstandings when Manitoba indiscriminately forced public education on its population.[34]

The division of Russia's Mennonites was not amicable. Migrants disparaged those who stayed as being more political than pious since they conceded to state demands. From an economic perspective it was a buyer's market when departing Mennonites sold their assets. Migrants told stories

---

[32] Gerald E. Dirks, *Canada's Refugee Policy: Indifference or Opportunism?* (Montreal and London: McGill-Queen's University Press, 1977), 30. See also Ernst Correll, "The Mennonite Loan in the Canadian Parliament, 1875," *Mennonite Quarterly Review* 20, no. 4 (1946): 255–75.

[33] See F. H. Epp, *Mennonites in Canada 1786–1920*, 192. E. K. Francis writes "The Mennonites have always referred to Lowe's letter as the 'privileges' and regarded it as their Magna Carta." See *In Search of Utopia: The Mennonites in Manitoba* (Glencoe, IL: Free Press, 1955), 47.

[34] The letter's tenth point states, "The fullest privilege of exercising their religious principles *is by law* afforded the Mennonites, without any kind of molestation or restriction whatever, and *the same* privilege extends to the education of their children in schools [emphasis added]." Yet prior to the document's ratification by Order-in-Council it was amended to read "The Mennonites will have the fullest privileges of exercising their religious principles and educating their children in schools, *as provided by law*, without any kind of molestation or restriction whatever [emphasis added]." The former enshrines Mennonite autonomy within law while the latter makes it subject to the law. Quoted in F. H. Epp, *Mennonites in Canada 1786–1920*, 338–39. The discrepancy between Loewe's letter and the Order-in-Council has provoked much debate in the historiography. See Ens, *Subjects or Citizens?* 141–42.

of their calculating coreligionists who had waited until their day of embarkation to make a final offer on their land.[35] Echos of these hard feelings were recorded in Peter M. Friesen's influential *Die Alt-Evangelische Mennonitische Brüderschaft in Russland (1789–1910), im Rahmen der Mennonitischen Gesamtgeschichte*. Published in Russia in 1911, the book argues that the emigrants were "incapable of God-willed and God-permitted closer association with Russian society … it was good for Russia which is now free of these unmanageable, pious foster children whom it was impossible to satisfy," even as it includes a section on Russian-Mennonite patriotism.[36]

The Mennonites who stayed in Russia maintained that acquiescing to "Russification" was acceptable, since Christian submission to the state was justified in scripture. They derisively referred to those who left as "Kanadier" and stereotyped them as inflexible zealots.[37] In their high mimetic, "Whig" interpretation of the Mennonite narrative – of which P. Friesen's book is an excellent example – Russia's Mennonites viewed the departure of this group as the beginning of a "golden age" of Mennonite history that lasted until the First World War. By 1914, Mennonite farmers held a total of 728,008 hectares of property, while Mennonite industrialists commanded 6 percent of the Russian market in agricultural machinery and owned 38 brick and tile factories. Mennonites supported a large educational apparatus and their General Conference of Mennonite Churches in Russia (Allgemeine Bundeskonferenz der Mennonitengemeinden in Rußland) presented a united front to outsiders (Fig. 1.1).[38] Nevertheless, individuals who left remembered "Russification" as an insidious first step toward Mennonites' abandoning their communities for the wider world. Later in life, one migrant believed that:

It was the angel of the Lord who also led Israel through the desert till they reached Canaan; indeed, Jehovah's angel was also our escort and protector on this long burdensome journey, by water and by land. Even a captain said to me in 1875: "It

---

[35] Delbert F. Plett, "'Poor and Simple?' The Economic Background of the Mennonite Immigrants to Manitoba, 1874–1879," *Journal of Mennonite Studies* 18 (2000): 120.

[36] Peter M. Friesen, *The Mennonite Brotherhood in Russia (1879–1910)*, trans. J. B. Toews (Fresno, CA: Mennonite Brethren Board of Christian Literature, 1978), 592–94.

[37] Plett, "Poor and Simple?" 114. See also Urry, "Of Borders and Boundaries: Reflections on Mennonite Unity and Separation in the Modern World," *Mennonite Quarterly Review* 73, no. 3 (1999): 503–24.

[38] Frank H. Epp, *Mennonite Exodus: The Rescue and Resettlement of the Russian Mennonites Since the Communist Revolution* (Altona, MB: Canadian Mennonite Relief and Immigration Council, 1962), 17, 21.

FIGURE I.I Built in 1912, the central school in Orloff, Molotschna Colony showcases the wealth and modernity of Russia's Mennonites at the height of the so-called Mennonite Commonwealth in Russia. Standing in front are young men in official uniform, either Russian servicemen or members of the Mennonites' Forestry Service. n.d. Source: Archivo Colonia Fernheim

is remarkable that since 1874 twenty-five ships have stranded and wrecked, but not a single one with emigrants or your Mennonites."[39]

Both groups of Mennonites were concerned with the "correct" answers to essential questions about scriptural interpretation, separation from state and society, and the trajectory of history. These questions were not laid to rest with the Russian schism but followed the Mennonites to Canada and beyond.

CANADA'S "GERMAN" MENNONITE "CHILDREN"

German-speaking Mennonites did not come to North America to become US or Canadian citizens, much less to preserve their Germanness. Like most German-speaking migrants, Mennonites wished to recreate their

[39] Gerhard Wiebe, *Causes and History of the Emigration of the Mennonites from Russia to America*, trans. Helen Janzen (Winnipeg: Manitoba Mennonite Historical Society, 1981), 40.

local cultures in new locations, but unlike most German-speaking migrants they wished to preserve an early-modern relationship with host states.[40] As a result, Canada's granting of "privileges" and its short-lived experiment with immigrant block settlements led Mennonites to believe their goals could be realized in perpetuity.

The Dominion government did not intend for immigrant reserves to be permanent. They were simply a way to organize the land, attract pioneers and private capital, and prepare settlers for integration into Canadian society.[41] Ryan Eyford states the reserve system that morphed from the 1872 Dominion Lands Act was formed through a "process of negotiation and contestation as Indigenous peoples pushed for the recognition of their claims to their traditional territories, and as European migrants, who could choose to relocate to any one of several settlement frontiers, negotiated the conditions under which they would settle in Canadian territory."[42] The gambit would simultaneously attract group-minded settlers, help Canada avoid the pitfalls of waging US-style Indian wars on behalf of individual homesteaders, and allow Canadian officials to colonize land from a position of weakness rather than strength, which foreshadowed the Paraguayan government's use of Mennonite colonies in the Chaco. Ironically, the block settlements that Mennonites thought would ensure their local autonomy were actually conceived of as laboratories for Canadian citizenship.

Once in Manitoba, Mennonites created the East Reserve, the West Reserve, and the smaller Scratching River Reserve. They had little interest in using the reserves to experiment with Anglo-Canadian politics and culture, but instead used them to sustain their continuity with the past. Mennonites even restructured their sectional homesteads to recreate a communal *Strassendorf* arrangement.[43] They also gave their villages the same names that they used in Russia – Hoffnungsfeld, Osterwick,

---

[40] Gerhard P. Bassler argues that "national origin has rarely been a rallying cause" among Canada's German speakers. See "German-Canadian Identity in Historical Perspective," in *A Chorus of Different Voices: German-Canadian Identities*, ed. Angelika E. Sauer and Matthias Zimmer (New York: Peter Lang, 1998), 92.

[41] Ryan Eyford, *White Settler Reserve: New Iceland and the Colonization of the Canadian West* (Vancouver: UBC Press, 2006), 10, 52–54. For an overview of the Dominion's view of the prairielands, see John C. Lehr, John Everitt, and Simon Evans, "The Making of the Prairie Landscape," in *Immigration and Settlement, 1870–1939*, ed. Gregory P. Marchildon (Regina: Canadian Plains Research Center, 2009), 13–56.

[42] Eyford, *White Settler Reserve*, 5. For more on the reserve system's origins, see 55–57.

[43] Mennonite rezoning was recognized by an amendment to the 1872 Dominion Lands Act. See *An Act to Amend the Dominion Lands Act*, S.C. 1876, 39 Vic., c. 19, s. 9.

Schoenthal. The names were not meant to honor the new German nation state, but rather to sustain the memory of previous settlements.[44] Initially, Bergthaler and Kleine Gemeinde families settled the East Reserve and Scratching River locations, while families from Chortitz and Fürstenland (collectively, the Reinländer or Old Colony) settled the West Reserve. Within a few years about 300 Bergthaler families had become unsatisfied with their land and moved to the more promising West Reserve.[45]

Canadian authorities regarded German speakers as expert farmers and model pioneers, and lauded their perceived sobriety and industriousness.[46] Underlying such assumptions were contemporary theories about the superiority of so-called "northern races" – variously labeled Aryan, Caucasian, Nordic, and Teutonic.[47] Despite the fact that the Mennonites were born in the Russian Empire, James Zohrab, the British counsel stationed in Berdyansk, claimed that Mennonites and other German speakers from Russia were a "valuable acquisition" for the realm since "they are very hard working and, therefore, in proportion to each man, they bring a much larger quantity of land under cultivation" than Russians.[48] In a conversation with the 1873 Mennonite delegation, Manitoba's lieutenant governor Alexander Morris stressed a special affinity between the British Crown and German speakers due to Queen Victoria's Germanness.[49] Once settled, officials continued to view the Mennonites as Germans. The Governor General of Canada, Lord Frederick Hamilton-Temple-Blackwood and his wife Lady Hariot Hamilton-Temple-Blackwood lauded the group's Germanness. While touring the Mennonite colonies in 1877, Lady Hamilton-Temple-Blackwood recorded: "The Mennonites are most desirable emigrants:

---

[44] Mennonite place names differed from those of other ethnic groups on the frontier. For instance, Ukrainian immigrants embraced *fin-de-siècle* Ukrainian nationalism and gave their villages explicitly nationalist names such as Bohdan (the name of a Cossack leader known for his 1648 revolt against Polish rule), Szewczenko (a nineteenth-century poet), and Myroslaw (a student who assassinated the Polish governor of Galicia in 1908). See Swyripa, *Storied Landscapes*, 50; Peter P. Klassen, "Die Namen der Dörfer wanderten mit," *Jahrbuch für Geschichte und Kultur der Mennoniten in Paraguay* 13 (2012): 7–30.

[45] Krahn, "West Reserve (Manitoba, Canada)," *Global Anabaptist Mennonite Encyclopedia Online*, last modified February 20, 2014, http://gameo.org/index.php?title=West_Reserve_(Manitoba,_Canada)&oldid=106431, last accessed June 7, 2018.

[46] Swyripa, *Storied Landscapes*, 19.   [47] Eyford, *White Settler Reserve*, 24.

[48] Public Archives of Canada (PAC), Shortt papers, M.G. 30, D45, vol. 57, J. Zohrab to E. Granville, 3 February 1872. Quoted in F. H. Epp, *Mennonites in Canada 1786–1920*, 185–86.

[49] F. H. Epp, *Mennonites in Canada, 1786–1920*, 191.

they retain their best German characteristics, are hardworking, honest, sober, simple, hardy people."[50] Along similar lines, Lowe argued that "German immigrants have been found to be specially adapted for settlement on the Prairies of the North West of the Dominion."[51] Each commentator believed that despite the Mennonites' religion and origin, their Germanness gave them a special connection with Canada and the British Empire.

The positive stereotypes associated with German-speaking immigrants and the notion that there was an affinity between German and Anglo cultures were buttressed by German liberals in central Europe. After the failed 1848 revolutions, they reimagined Germandom as a transnational community, unbounded by central European borders, and trumpeted the accomplishments of overseas Germans in publications such as *Die Gartenlaube, Globus, Die Grenzboten* and *Die Deutsche Erde*. Writers lustily proclaimed that overseas Germans had contributed to the development of Russia and the United States and were essential to the industry of the British Empire.[52] Especially in Anglo-dominated locations, Germans were believed to "improve the moral and cultural fiber" of British stock and "militate against the 'feminizing' impact of the French emigrants and stultifying influence of the Irish."[53] In the years before 1871, British authorities had little to fear from German nationalism because German-speaking immigrants lacked a nation state that could claim their loyalty.[54] In general, Mennonites profited from nationalist

---

[50] Hariot Georgina Hamilton-Temple-Blackwood, Marchioness of Dufferin and Ava, *My Canadian Journal 1872–8: Extracts from My Letters Home Written While Lord Dufferin Was Governor-General* (London: John Murray, 1891), 332.

[51] John Lowe, Secretary of Agriculture, to Dr. Hahn, May 30, 1879, Library and Archives of Canada, Ottawa, Canada, RG 25, accession A-1, vol. 3, 11. Quoted in Jonathan Wagner, *A History of Migration from Germany to Canada, 1850–1939* (Vancouver: University of British Columbia Press, 2006), 76.

[52] "Deutsche Wissenschaft in England," *Gartenlaube* 9 (1865): 141; see also "Verdienstvolle Deutsche in Amerika," *Gartenlaube* 10 (1866): 159–60.

[53] Bradley Naranch, "Inventing the Auslandsdeutsche: Emigration, Colonial Fantasy, and German National Identity, 1848–71," in *Germany's Colonial Pasts,* ed. Eric Ames, Marcia Klotz, and Lora Wildenthal (Lincoln, NE: University of Nebraska Press, 2005), 28.

[54] Sebastian Conrad notes that toward the end of the nineteenth century, host governments grew increasingly worried about the political influence of their German minorities and even the "colonial ambitions of the emigrants' 'mother countries.'" See *Globalisation and the Nation in Imperial Germany* (Cambridge, UK: Cambridge University Press, 2010), 320–21.

assumptions about the value of German pioneers without needing to demonstrate their German bona fides.

In the 1870s, Manitoba was at the very margins of Anglo-Canadian geography and society. Wittingly or not, Mennonites changed this situation by cutting trails, draining fields, removing rocks, and experimenting with wheat cultivation. Ironically, their work sparked further immigration, which increased provincial scrutiny. Eventually a diverse cast of characters arrived on the prairie to battle nature, displace indigenous people, and participate in the reserve system.[55] A group of Icelanders inaugurated a block settlement on the shore of Lake Winnipeg in 1875, while the French-speaking, Roman Catholic Society for the Colonization of Manitoba partially succeeded in creating a reserve for French Canadians from the United States. Other reserve ventures failed or never materialized, including German, English, Scottish, Swedish, and Swiss settlements. Nine reserves were established on the prairie before the Mackenzie government deemed the system a failure in 1877 and promoted individualized freeholding.[56] In the ensuing decades, tens of thousands of speakers of English, German, Hungarian, Polish, Romanian, Russian, and Ukrainian, from Eastern Europe, Russia, and the United States arrived in western Canada and established their own rural and urban networks.[57] Despite a shared language and presumed national identification, the Mennonites had very little to do with new German-speaking arrivals. The reason, of course, is that German speakers practiced their ethnicity in different ways, which sent them along different trajectories as they engaged the Canadian state.[58] Their Germanness was an "ethnocultural and not national-political identity."[59]

[55] Eyford, *White Settler Reserve*, 15.
[56] Ibid., 58–59; James M. Richtik, "The Policy Framework for Settling the Canadian West 1870–1880," *Agricultural History* 49, no. 4 (1975): 613–28, 626; Kenneth Michael Sylvester, *The Limits of Rural Capitalism: Family, Culture, and Markets in Montcalm, Manitoba 1870–1940* (Toronto: University of Toronto Press, 2001), 14.
[57] See Gregory P. Marchildon's edited collection *Immigration and Settlement, 1870–1939* (Regina: Canadian Plains Research Center, 2009) and Swyripa, *Storied Landscapes*.
[58] See Bassler, *German-Canadian Identity*, 90. R. Loewen likewise speaks to the diversity of nineteenth-century German-speaking women's "lifeworlds" on the prairies in "'As I Experienced Them Myself': The Autobiographical German-Language Immigrant Woman in Prairie Canada, 1874–1910," in *A Chorus of Different Voices: German-Canadian Identities*, ed. Angelika E. Sauer and Matthias Zimmer (New York: Peter Lang, 1998), 119–42.
[59] Bassler, *German-Canadian Identity*, 92.

THE FLUID FRONTIER MEETS THE SOLIDIFYING STATE

During the 1870s, Manitoba's small bureaucracy did not have the ability to implement legislation across its great territory, so Mennonites' self-perception as "subjects" or "citizens" was of little consequence. Yet the Mennonites' industry worked to undermine the reserves' insularity from within, while government-funded cadastral surveys, integrated transportation networks, and especially public education undermined it from without. Compulsory public schooling was not a new idea (it had already been inaugurated in Ontario) but questions about the language in which Manitoba's public schools would be taught and the entity administering them were firmly entwined with ethnicity and religion.[60] As far back as the mid-nineteenth century, Canada's foremost public-school promoter, Egerton Ryerson, argued that "The State, therefore, so far from having nothing to do with the children, constitutes their collective parent, and is bound to ... secure them all that will qualify them to become useful citizens to the state."[61] Provincial governments were jealous parents of "Canada's children," and foresaw a time when all would be enrolled in public, monolingual schools. It proved to be a long custody battle.

In 1890, Manitoba's ruling Liberal Party passed its Public School Act, which repealed provincial funding for parochial schools, established a tax-based public-school system, and insinuated that its curriculum would be taught in English.[62] The Act was primarily aimed at checking the spread of francophone, Roman Catholic culture outside of Quebec, but not all Roman Catholics spoke French (for example Irish Canadians) and francophone Catholics considered themselves to be just as Canadian as their anglophone, Protestant neighbors. The legislation opened up a Pandora's box of disputes, which lasted for six years until the Laurier–Greenway Compromise permitted a loophole for bilingual instruction. The controversy's political machinations mostly roiled above the Mennonites' heads, but it sharpened their attitudes about education and

---

[60] Alison Prentice, *The School Promoters: Education and Social Class in Mid-Nineteenth Century Upper Canada* (Toronto: McClelland and Stewart, 1977), 17–18.

[61] Canada (Province). Dept. of Public Instruction for Upper Canada and Egerton Ryerson, *Special Report on the Separate School Provisions of the School Law* (Toronto, 1858), 14–15.

[62] The Public School Act did not explicitly name English as the official language of instruction in provincial schools, but a second act passed by the government in 1890 stipulated the use of English in all government, legislative, and judicial matters. It was therefore widely assumed that English would also be the primary language of instruction in government-supported schools. See Ens, *Subjects or Citizens?* 106–7.

paved the way for a schism between associative Mennonites who accepted government-directed schooling and their separatist brethren who did not.

Like the Tsar, Manitoba's government pursued standardized education to increase the legibility of its population and thereby control it. While it is true that Manitoba's Public School Act promoted a state-directed, English-language curriculum for some bureaucratically practical reasons, it was also intended to advance Anglo-Canadian civilization.[63] At the time, Canadian school promoters were inclined to see "the community as a dangerous or unsuitable environment for the child."[64] Through the supposedly politically neutral school system, educators could anchor "the conditions of political governance in the selves of the governed."[65] In other words, violence and coercion may control recalcitrant individuals for a time, but education controls them from within, forever. The Public School Act would at once standardize the province's education system, teach children to be loyal citizens, and make them "better" than their elders.

Mennonites were not opposed to education or even learning English.[66] They were simply opposed to the British and Canadian nationalisms that were embedded in a public-school curriculum. Mennonites feared that school marches resembled military drills, sports would draw children away from home, and advanced skills might encourage youths to leave the community.[67] They valued education as a path to running a family farm and to participating in religious life. For these specific purposes, girls aged six to twelve and boys aged six to fourteen were instructed in reading, writing, arithmetic, and the Bible.[68] Even the schoolhouse was endowed with religions meaning, since it doubled as a church.[69] The Mennonites' fears were justified. In the Ontario context, Benjamin Bryce states, "From the moment German was no longer used as a language of

---

[63] Benjamin Bryce, "Linguistic Ideology and State Power: German and English Education in Ontario, 1880–1912," *The Canadian Historical Review* 94, no. 2 (2013): 208–9.

[64] Prentice, *School Promoters*, 20.

[65] Bruce Curtis, *Building the Educational State: Canada, West, 1836–1871* (London, ON: Falmer, 1988), 15.

[66] It is important to remember that Mennonites' first language was *Plautdietsch*. In addition to German – which was important for religious reasons – English would effectively be their third language. Francis, *In Search of Utopia*, 167–68; Guenther, "*Ältester* Martin C. Friesen," 189.

[67] F. H. Epp, *Mennonites in Canada, 1920–1940: A People's Struggle for Survival* (Toronto: Macmillan of Canada, 1982), 105.

[68] Harold J. Foght, *A Survey of Education in the Province of Saskatchewan* (Regina: King's Printer, 1918), 174.

[69] Guenther, "*Ältester* Martin C. Friesen," 192.

instruction, there were no German schools in Ontario."[70] When there were no German schools, Mennonites were anxious that there would be no Mennonite schools and when there were no Mennonite schools, parents feared their children would be lost to Anglo-Canadian society.

The school question reveals the challenge of determining which aspects of faith and culture were essential for maintaining the Mennonite confession. It also reveals common problems shared by other diasporic religious groups. Was education a cultural or religious matter? What of dress, food, and occupation? What of nonresistance? Generally speaking, was Mennoniteness a seamless cultural-religious way of life or a set of so-called "essentials," carved out of an essentially secular lifestyle? Werner Schiffaur records a similar quandary in his study of Turkish Muslim peasants who relocated to Germany, noting that "during sacred times, society no longer changes into a religious community but, rather, one leaves the society and enters the religious community ... since the opposition between secular and sacred times is now determined by the more fundamental notions of the working day and leisure."[71] Mennonites wrestled with the question of whether the working day – or in this case the school day – was a discrete, areligious interval in daily life or simply one facet of a unified cultural-religious whole.

Already by the mid-1880s, some of Manitoba's Mennonites were carving a middle path between private and public education by establishing a teacher-training institute to prepare Mennonite teachers for work in public schools. One such individual was the Bergthal (West Reserve) *Ältester* Johann Funk. His progressive position was often informed as much by his theology as his enthusiasm for conflict. Despite strong opposition, he pushed the Bergthaler Mennonites to create a teacher-training institute in Gretna, Manitoba named the Gretna Normal School.[72] Another individual who promoted the teacher-training institute was school inspector Heinrich (Henry) H. Ewert. Born in West Prussia and educated in Kansas, Iowa, and Missouri, he was a cosmopolitan educator who wanted Mennonite children to become Canadian citizens. When he moved to Manitoba in 1891, he served as a principal of the Gretna teacher-training institute and as Manitoba school inspector, a dual position that let him

[70] Bryce, "Linguistic Ideology and State Power," 232.

[71] Werner Schiffauer, "Migration and Religiousness," in *The New Islamic Presence in Western Europe*, ed. Thomas Gerholm and Yngve Georg Lithman (London: Mansell, 1988), 150.

[72] It was later renamed the Mennonite Educational Institute, and then the Mennonite Collegiate Institute.

assess Mennonite schools from both a church and state perspective. Although he received a degree of support among J. Funk's Bergthaler community, he remained a controversial figure due to his Prussian background, identification with the United States, level of education, and government salary, which meant that his loyalties were compromised.[73] Mennonites who advocated the teacher-training institute and public schooling also looked beyond the reserves for support by consulting Mennonites in the United States and reaching out to the Provincial Board of Education's George Bryce, who encouraged the initiative. Both moves foreshadowed the growth of Mennonite conferences and government cooperation across North America.

With the passage of the Public School Act, separatist detractors were faced with having to pay for both private and public schools, even if they did not use the latter. When these groups complained to the Dominion's Deputy Minister of Justice, he replied that the government's hands were tied since municipal issues fell under provincial sovereignty.[74] Angered by their modernizing coreligionists, stymied by the Dominion's lack of jurisdiction, and unwilling to vote in provincial elections, Mennonites who were skeptical of the new legislation directed their displeasure toward other Mennonites. Manitoba's Mennonite reserves were ripe for discord.

Between 1890 and 1893, the Bergthal (West Reserve) church splintered over the teacher-training institute, accepting government money for schools, Manitoba's new municipal government system, and new railheads and trading centers on the reserves.[75] These disputes sharpened the line between the province's *Ältesten*. J. Funk occupied the minority position. His group kept the Bergthal name, though they retained only 61 of 476 families. The majority took the name "Sommerfelder," since their new *Ältester*, Abram Doerksen was from the village of Sommerfeld. The original East Reserve Bergthaler group also changed their name – in protest against the West Reserve Bergthalers – to "Chortitzer" since their *Ältester*, G. Wiebe (grandfather-in-law of M. C. Friesen) came from the village of Chortitz (Canada). Thus, the Sommerfelder (East Reserve) and Chortitzer (West Reserve) bodies were opposed to the

---

[73] F. H. Epp, *Mennonites in Canada, 1786–1920*, 341–42.

[74] William Janzen, *Limits on Liberty: The Experience of Mennonite, Hutterite, and Doukhobor Communities in Canada* (Toronto: University of Toronto Press, 1990), 90.

[75] Lawrence Klippenstein, "FUNK, JOHANN," *Dictionary of Canadian Biography* 14, www.biographi.ca/en/bio/funk_johann_14E.html, last accessed June 7, 2018; Richard J. Friesen, "Saskatchewan Mennonite Settlements: The Modification of an Old World Settlement Pattern," *Canadian Ethnic Studies* 9, no. 2 (1977): 72–90, 74.

modernizing initiatives but remained organizationally and geographically divided. Meanwhile, the original West Reserve Reinländer Mennonites led by *Ältester* Johann Wiebe sided with the conservative Sommerfelders, but remained ecclesiastically separate from them. Now there existed three Mennonite factions in Manitoba that were opposed to the reforms: the Sommerfelders (who moved from the East Reserve to the West Reserve), the Chortitzers (East Reserve), and the Reinländers (West Reserve). Despite their alliance over the school issue, the groups remained separate from each other because unifying would mean forming an organization that transcended the authority of the *Gemeinde*.

In 1896, Canadian Prime Minister Wilfrid Laurier and Manitoba Premier Thomas Greenway came to an agreement over the 1890 Act and implemented the Laurier–Greenway Compromise, which permitted religious instruction in public schools between 3:30 and 4 p.m., and bilingual instruction in rural schools where more than ten non-English-peaking pupils were present.[76] Though French-speaking Catholics had done much of the legwork for battling the Public School Act's Anglo-Protestant agenda – and had even secured the support of Pope Leo XIII – they were chagrined that the compromise reduced the status of French from parity with English to a minority language.[77] In contrast, the country's German speakers lacked a shared understanding of what the German language meant to their Germanness or their varied religious sensibilities – atheist, Anabaptist, Catholic, Protestant, Jewish – and did not politically organize around ethnolinguistic lines.

Many of Canada's German speakers actually believed that the maintenance of their German ethnicity did not require German-language schooling. In the country's most populous province of Ontario, "by the 1890s, state regulation along with local trustees and parents' lack of protest ensured that English was the language of instruction at all 'German schools.'"[78] Manfred Prokop offers an explanation by suggesting that Canada's German speakers made a distinction between their linguistic and cultural heritages, with the applied behavior required by

---

[76] In urban schools, the requirement was twenty-five non-English-speaking pupils. "Terms of Agreement Between the Government of Canada and the Government of Manitoba for the Settlement of the School Question, November 16, 1896," https://slmc.uottawa.ca/?q=leg_laurier-greenway_compromise, last accessed June 7, 2018.

[77] Leo XIII, "Affari Vos: Encyclical of Pope Leo XIII on the Manitoba School Question," http://w2.vatican.va/content/leo-xiii/en/encyclicals/documents/hf_l-xiii_enc_08121897_affari-vos.html, last accessed June 7, 2018.

[78] Bryce, "Linguistic Ideology and State Power," 210, 228.

the former displaced by the abstract symbolism of the latter.[79] Along similar lines, Gerhard P. Bassler's research suggests that German speakers were mostly ambivalent about the school issue owning to a "weakness or absence of political nationalism," which would have given language retention a more programmatic edge.[80] In the Prairie Provinces specifically, Heinz Lehmann argues that the "low level of education and weak ethnic consciousness of German-speaking immigrants" (85 percent of whom did not come from Germany), combined with a political influence that was "virtually nil" led to a general ambivalence over German ethnicity.[81] Associative Mennonites, for their part, could not conceive of spurring other German speakers to action because they viewed the German tongue as their ethno-religious language and not as a building block for an ethno-national alliance.

Altogether the Laurier–Greenway Compromise benefited the increasingly associative Bergthaler and Kleine Gemeinde communities, who were assured that they could use German in their public schools. However, it was of much less importance to the emergent separatist Mennonites, who remained suspicious of all government initiatives and maintained their private school system.

SPREADING SECTARIANISM TO SASKATCHEWAN

Mennonites' growing religious stratification fueled the sense that the authority of *Ältesten*-led *Gemeinden* was being eclipsed. Individuals involved with business and education, families that settled outside the reserves, and individuals who moved to urban areas formed churches with fluid relationships to Canadian society. Moreover, the late nineteenth century saw the arrival of Mennonite families from the United States and Germany who came to the prairie unaffiliated with established Mennonite *Gemeinden*. Less bounded by geography and communal leaders, such Mennonites nevertheless developed a leadership elite who

---

[79] Manfred Prokop, *The German Language in Alberta: Maintenance and Teaching* (Edmonton: University of Alberta Press, 1990), viii. See also Rudolf Kalin and J. M. Berry, "Ethnic, National and Provincial Self-Identity in Canada: Analyses of 1974 and 1991," *Canadian Ethnic Studies* 27, no. 2 (1995): 1–15.

[80] Bassler, *German-Canadian Identity*, 92.

[81] Heinz Lehmann, *The German Canadians: Immigration, Settlement, and Culture*, ed. and trans. Gerhard P. Bassler (St. John's, NL: Jesperson Press, 1986), 282, 339. Taken from Lehmann's *Zur Geschichte des Deutschtums in Kanada* (1931) and *Das Deutschtum in Westkanada* (1939).

established Mennonite conferences, promoted Mennonite institutions, and advised churches on social and political matters. According to Frank H. Epp, "At one and the same time, [Mennonite organizations] represented an adjustment to a society which was obsessed with organizations and institution-building, and a protection from that society through institutions uniquely Mennonite."[82] Thus, the division of associative and separatist Mennonites solidified in the first decade of the twentieth century. The former viewed Canada as their homeland and merged their Mennonite narrative with Canada's nationalist one, while the latter maintained a communal narrative that was unbeholden to a nation.

A new wave of Mennonite migrations between 1890 and 1905 brought the public-school debate to the District of Saskatchewan (Saskatchewan became a province in 1905). In the 1890s, Manitoba's burgeoning Mennonite population spawned migrations of conservative Reinländer and Sommerfelder families to points further west, where they created the Rosthern Reserve, about 70 km north of Saskatoon, and the Swift Current Reserve, about 40 km south of Swift Current.[83] After the move, 1,000 Sommerfelders resurrected the Bergthaler name, so now there were two Bergthaler groups in Canada: the progressive Manitoba group and the conservative Saskatchewan group.[84] In 1932 Gerhard Ens, Rosthern Colony leader and future district representative to the province, described the Saskatchewan migration in biblical language with an ethnic twist:

Our first impression reminded us strongly of the story of the creation in the Bible ... A prairie fire had destroyed everything ... Immediately the cars were cleared and converted to living quarters ... . Soon smoke was rising happily from each car. The fragrance of fried German bacon filled the air.[85]

Associative Mennonite also filtered into Saskatchewan. In 1891, a group of families from West Prussia migrated to the territory on account of Germany's new military conscription laws. They settled near Rosthern and were amenable to forming broad-based organizations similar to the

---

[82] Epp, *Mennonites in Canada, 1920–1940*, 49.

[83] Francis, *In Search of Utopia*, 147; R. Loewen, *Family, Church, and Market*, 146–47; Bender, Ens, and Jake Peters, "Sommerfeld Mennonites," *Global Anabaptist Mennonite Encyclopedia Online*, last modified January 31, 2014, http://gameo.org/index.php?titl e=Sommerfeld_Mennonites&oldid=112425, last accessed June 7, 2018; Ens, *Subjects or Citizens?* 109.

[84] Bender et al., "Sommerfeld Mennonites," *Global Anabaptist Mennonite Encyclopedia Online*.

[85] Quoted in Lehmann, *German Canadians*, 199.

ones they had belonged to in Germany.[86] Families from the United States also made the district their home, particularly after the outbreak of the Spanish–American War in 1898.[87] They too accepted public schooling with little debate.[88]

In 1905, Saskatchewan Mennonites who were inclined toward public education established a teacher-training institute in the town of Rosthern, named the German-English Academy. Like the Gretna Normal School, the Academy was tasked with educating bilingual teachers for implementing a public-school curriculum in Mennonite communities.[89] In 1906, the stocky, kind-faced David Toews became the school's principle. He served in the position until 1917.[90] Perhaps more than any other individual during the twentieth century, D. Toews promoted a vision of Canadian Mennonite unity and state cooperation. In 1884, he migrated from Russia to Kansas, where he studied under Ewert. He then moved to Manitoba in 1893, where he taught under Ewert's inspectorship for four years.[91] Like Ewert, he was an interloper among Western Canada's Mennonites, but by 1914 he was elected *Ältester* of the associative-minded Rosenort, Saskatchewan Mennonite community and was made the moderator of the Conference of Mennonites in Central Canada.[92] After the First World War, he organized the Canadian Mennonite Board of Colonization (CMBC), which helped 20,000 of the Soviet Union's war-stricken Mennonites relocate to Canada.

Mennonite public schooling therefore went hand in hand with the creation of Mennonite church conferences and the creation of a leadership elite, which, in turn, brought associative Mennonites into

---

[86] Krahn and R. D. Thiessen, "Regier, Peter (1851–1925)," *Global Anabaptist Mennonite Encyclopedia Online*, last modified September 8, 2013, http://gameo.org/index.php?title=Regier,_Peter_(1851–1925)&oldid=101381, last accessed June 7, 2018.

[87] Helmut Harder, *David Toews Was Here, 1870–1947* (Winnipeg: Canadian Mennonite University Press, 2006), 55. On the opening of the Saskatchewan prairie to settlers see P. L. McCormick, "Transportation and Settlement: Problems in the Expansion of the Frontier of Saskatchewan and Assiniboia in 1904," in *Immigration and Settlement, 1870–1939*, ed. Gregory P. Marchildon (Regina: Canadian Plains Research Center, 2009), 81–102.

[88] Ens, *Subjects or Citizens?* 114. W. Janzen, *Limits on Liberty*, 27.

[89] H. Harder, *David Toews Was Here*, 73.

[90] Ibid., 68; John G. Rempel and R. D. Thiessen, "Toews, David (1870–1947)," *Global Anabaptist Mennonite Encyclopedia Online*, last modified February 13, 2014, http://gameo.org/index.php?title=Toews,_David_(1870–1947)&oldid=112895, last accessed June 7, 2018.

[91] Ens, *Subjects or Citizens?* 114.

[92] F. H. Epp, *Mennonites in Canada, 1786–1920*, 351.

closer contact with each other and the government. In the 1890s, Ewert and D. Toews organized a series of Mennonite teaching conferences where educators could meet and exchange information.[93] By 1900, the conferences gave rise to the German-English Teachers' Association of Southern Manitoba, which invited Mennonite teachers to benefit from innovations in pedagogy introduced by the Department of Education. A corollary goal of the Association was to influence provincial legislation, which neatly combined education, democratic participation, and supralocal Mennonite organization.[94] Significantly, the two Mennonite communities that possessed a teacher-training institute, the Manitoba Bergthaler and Saskatchewan Rosenort Mennonites, organized the Conference of Mennonites in Central Canada in 1903. This organization aimed to "promote the fellowship of the Spirit among the various Mennonite congregations and to encourage and strengthen one another."[95] Its annual meetings welcomed "fraternal visitors" from Mennonites across Canada and the United States.[96] By 1913, the Manitoba Bergthaler, Brüdergemeinde, and some Sommerfelder Mennonites had formed a school commission that petitioned the Manitoba government to recognize it as the official Mennonite representative for education issues.[97] Thus, the teacher-training institutes not only prepared teachers for public schools but

---

[93] The organization called itself the Western Local Conference of Public School Teachers of the Mennonite Settlement in Manitoba. See Lawrence Klippenstein, "Western Local Mennonite Teachers' Conference – An Early Minute Book," *Manitoba Pageant* 22, no. 2 (1977), www.mhs.mb.ca/docs/pageant/22/mennoniteteachers.shtml, last accessed June 7, 2018.

[94] Ens, *Subjects or Citizens?* 113.

[95] Johann G. Rempel (ed.), *Fuenfzig Jahre Konferenzbestrebungen, 1902–1952* (Erster Teil 1902–1927), Zweiter Teil (1928–1952) (Rosthern, SK: Konferenz der Mennoniten in Canada 1952,) 27. Quoted in H. Harder, *David Toews Was Here,* 67. The Conference of Mennonites in Central Canada was later renamed the General Conference of Mennonites in Canada and the Conference of Mennonites in Canada.

[96] H. Harder, *David Toews Was Here,* 68. South of the forty-ninth parallel, Mennonite leaders including Goshen College president Noah E. Byers and *Mennonite* editor I. A. Sommer organized a series of meetings between 1913 and 1936 titled the "All-Mennonite Convention" for US Mennonites from any congregation or conference interested in mending historic differences and addressing common problems. As with the Conference of Mennonites in Central Canada, the meetings appealed to a limited audience, which resulted in a closed loop of affirming US associative Mennonites' preexisting aspirations. See C. Henry Smith, "All-Mennonite Convention," *Global Anabaptist Mennonite Encyclopedia Online,* last modified January 17, 2017, http://gameo.org/index.php?title=All-Mennonite_Convention&oldid=90797, last accessed June 7, 2018.

[97] Ens, *Subjects or Citizens?* 113.

also prepared Mennonites to cooperate with provincial authorities and organize on a trans-local, and even transnational, basis.

Ewert and D. Toews resembled the growing number of Mennonites in Germany, Russia, and the United States who viewed the liberal, late-nineteenth-century zeitgeist as providential for the confession.[98] By compromising with governments over specific issues, such as education or military conscription, they could sustain the faith and share the fruits of modernity. Ironically, some Mennonites who had left Russia in the 1870s over such issues began resembling their Russian counterparts who had accepted alternative military service and Russian-language education.[99] In the United States, Mennonite intellectuals, such as C. Henry Smith, disparaged the confession's isolationism and argued that Mennonite values, including the separation of church and state and freedom of conscience, were *democratic* values. Mennonites should not fear acculturation but accept it as the confession's destiny.[100]

Yet separatist Mennonites impeded the move toward modernity by retaining their own organizational structures. At the Rosthern Academy's annual meeting in 1909, D. Toews stated, "Every good endeavor has its opponents ... We are not surprised by the fact that our school project in Saskatchewan is not recognized by all in our community."[101] In contrast, the reactive Chortitzer (East Reserve) leader G. Wiebe – who by this point was firmly against public schooling and Mennonite institution-building – argued that the "heavy battle against the princes of the world" was increasingly strenuous since "the wicked enemy knows how to throw such clever slings," such as public education. He speculated that its proponents are "from Babylon, that is, they produce confusion ... the

---

[98] For accounts of this phenomenon in the German, Russian, and US contexts, see respectively, Benjamin W. Goossen, *Chosen Nation: Mennonites and Germany in a Global Era* (Princeton, NJ: Princeton University Press, 2017); Urry, "Constitutionalism and Solidarity (1905–1908)," in *Mennonites, Politics, and Peoplehood*, 111–36; James Juhnke, *Vision, Doctrine, War* (Scottdale, PA: Herald Press, 1989).

[99] J. B. Toews, "The Russian Mennonites: Some Introductory Comments." *Mennonite Quarterly Review* 48, no. 3 (1974): 403–8, 405; Peter Braun, "Education Among the Mennonites in Russia," *Global Anabaptist Mennonite Encyclopedia Online*, last modified August 23, 2013, http://gameo.org/index.php?title=Education_Among_the_Mennonites_in_Russia&oldid=91640, last accessed June 7, 2018.

[100] See Perry Bush, "'United Progressive Mennonites:' Bluffton College and Anabaptist Higher Education, 1913–1945," *Mennonite Quarterly Review* 74, no. 3 (2000): 357–80.

[101] H. Harder, *David Toews Was Here*, 74.

fruit of worldly knowledge and arrogance."[102] Theologically, separatist Mennonites believed that God worked exclusively through their local communities, while associative Mennonites held that God was at work in the whole world.

In 1908, the division of Saskatchewan's Mennonites over public schooling drew provincial authorities into the fray and completed the divisions between separatist and associative Mennonites. It also confirmed provincial authorities' suspicions that the Mennonites were a contentious group of people. Under the leadership of *Ältester* Jacob Wiens, the Reinländer Mennonite Gemeinde – which numbered 950 members, spread across three churches – began excommunicating families who sent their children to public schools.[103] The stakes were high, since excommunicated members were banned from the church and perhaps heaven too.[104] D. Toews' Rosenort church received the excommunicated families, which no doubt displeased the Reinländers.[105] The dispute soon came to the attention of Premier Thomas Walter Scott, who threatened not only to remove Reinländer leaders' ability to solemnize marriages, but also to force public-school attendance on their community.[106] The threat was met with silence, so the government set up a Royal Commission of Inquiry at Warman in December 1908.

D. Toews and J. Wiens were both present at the meeting and took different positions on compliance with authorities and an overarching Mennonite narrative. Through an interpreter, a provincial delegate asked J. Wiens whether the Bible commands Mennonites to refuse to send their children to public schools. He responded with a passage from Deuteronomy 11:19 that instructs God's people (the Israelites in this instance) to teach the word of the Lord to their children.[107] By contrast,

---

[102] G. Wiebe, *Causes and History*, 63. In G. Wiebe's view, there were only three *Ältesten* who were "standing up to the beast [presumably, the beast of Revelation]": Chortitzer (East Reserve) [David?] Stoesz, Sommerfelder (West Reserve) [Abraham?] Dörksen, and Reinländer (West Reserve) Johann Wiebe.

[103] Alan M. Guenther, "'Barred from Heaven and Cursed Forever': Old Colony Mennonites and the 1908 Commission of Inquiry Regarding Public Education," *Historical Papers 2007, Canadian Society of Church History: Annual Conference, University of Saskatchewan*, 27–29 May 2007 (2008): 129–48.

[104] Guenther, "Barred from Heaven," 136.

[105] H. Harder, *David Toews Was Here*, 55.

[106] [Walter Scott], Memorandum for Mr. Calder, marked "Confidential," 2 Sept. 1908, File Ed. 12 d., SAB. Cited in Guenther, "Barred from Heaven," 133.

[107] To the annoyance of government representatives, Wiens deferred questions about his authority to the Reinländer members in attendance because he did not consider himself to be a "leader" so much as the first among equals. See Guenther, "Barred from

D. Toews stated, "Our Church believes in public schools and progress all along" and that it favored "public schools, progressive schools, and they [Reinländer] don't believe in them."[108] The Reinländer elders subsequently assembled their congregations and declared they could not accept the claims of their "rebelling" brethren, come what may.[109] The face-off settled into a stalemate. The government did not press the issue and Mennonite leaders eased off of excommunicating parents who sent their children to public schools.[110]

The confrontation testifies to a clear separation of Canada's Mennonites. Associative Mennonites were comfortable with rights rather than privileges. In contrast, separatist Mennonites believed the rules of citizenship did not apply to them – all the more so, since they appealed to scripture and their presumed special privileges.[111] On an existential level, separatist Mennonites viewed the world through a mythical, biblical lens that evaporated nuance and rendered history and chronology irrelevant. For example, among the (East Reserve) Chortitzer Mennonites, G. Wiebe had no problem comparing Israel's departure from Egypt, King David's battle with the Amalekites, and stories about Jesus' disciples to the situation of the Mennonites in Canada.[112] In their view, the "correct" interpretation of the Bible was obvious to anyone who studied it with enough humility. Individuals could obey it and remain in the *Gemeinde* or reject it and (literally) go to hell. Separatist Mennonites' comprehension of reality was therefore quite similar to an early-modern European worldview, which reversed the places of Christianity and science. According to Jacques Barzun, "in earlier times people rarely thought of themselves as 'having' or 'belonging to' a religion ... just as today

---

Heaven," 133. Other scriptures used by Reinländer Mennonites to justify the excommunications include Matthew 18:15–18; Mark 7:21–24; Romans 16:17–18; Thessalonians 3:6, 14; 2 John 9, 10; 2 Timothy 3:1–6; 2 Timothy 3:15. See "Inquiry re Practices of Old Colonier Mennonite Church: Minutes of Evidence," Proceedings of Commission of Inquiry at Warman, Dec. 28 & 29, 1908, File Ed. 12 d., Saskatchewan Archives Board, Saskatoon, SK. Quoted in W. Janzen, *Limits on Liberty*, 102.

[108] "Inquiry re Practices of Old Colonier Mennonite Church," 43. Quoted in Guenther, "'Barred from Heaven,'" 131.

[109] "Rev. Jacob Wiens, bishop to the Government of Saskatchewan, Regina," January 21, 1909, Scott Papers, Saskatchewan Archives Board, 12d, 118G. Cited in W. Janzen, *Limits on Liberty*, 103.

[110] W. Janzen, *Limits on Liberty*, 103.

[111] Guenther observes during the Reinländer testimony: "The language of 'privilege' rather than 'right' pervades the ministers' discourse." See "'Barred from Heaven,'" 142.

[112] G. Wiebe *Causes and History*, 4–5.

nobody has 'a physics'; there is only one and it is automatically taken to be the transcript of reality."[113] Accepting a modern, "scientific" narrative of progress implicitly acknowledges that humans control time and space, which in turn denies God's authority. To be sure, Separatist Mennonites were a literate people with a nuanced understanding of the past, but it was not an historical one that accorded humans unlimited agency. This type of mythological thinking was an existential threat to associative Mennonites and government authorities since notions of human progress – including the "beginning" of Mennonite institutions and the "expansion" of Anglo-Canadian culture – *require* historical, chronological thinking. Associative Mennonites and Canadian officials were irritated that the Reinländer Mennonites did not acknowledge their progressive narrative, which they believed was manifestly obvious. For the nation to function and for the modern zeitgeist to be realized, separatist *Gemeinden* would have to deny God's ahistorical authority and accept Canada's national history as transcendent – a fantastic and perverse proposition.

Ironically, the separatist Mennonites' stance against Canadian integration provoked admiration from confused German nationalists who viewed language preservation as an expression of patriotism. According to one 1908 article in the *Berliner Zeitschrift*, most German-speaking individuals lost their language and culture upon landing on North America's shores, but the Mennonites retained their Germanness despite having not lived in Central Europe for generations. Separatist Mennonites were, however, as uninterested in preserving a link to Germany as they were in establishing one with Canada. They confounded German ethnolinguistic nationalists and Canadian provincial authorities in equal measure.

As the British system of governance transformed from empire to Commonwealth, and as the Crown's "contingent accommodations" for minority groups gave way to the rights and duties expected of Canadian citizens, government officials no longer tolerated local diversity and, in fact, often feared it. This happened gradually at first but transformed decisively during the first two decades of the twentieth century, and especially after the First World War. Blessed and sustained by nationalist movements around the world, the war placed separatist Mennonites' German-speaking, pacifist culture squarely at the center of the nation's Canadizing aims.

---

[113] Jacques Barzun, *From Dawn to Decadence: 500 Years of Western Cultural Life: 1500 to the Present* (New York: HarperCollins, 2000), 24.

A FIGHT FOR FREEDOM DURING THE "WAR FOR DEMOCRACY"

The seeds sewn by western provinces wishing to make their populations legible in the 1880s and 1890s bore the fruits of dedicated educational bureaucracies in the early twentieth century. They were aided by precise population statistics, reliable transportation networks, armies of school inspectors, and legal systems amenable to government activism. In the words of one prominent Manitoba journalist, schools were "blast furnaces" for the Canadian melting pot, which would create a "fusion of races" and "the new Canadian."[114] However, provincial efforts to consolidate schools around Anglo-Canadian culture were met with new resolve by separatist Mennonites and a flood of immigrants that poured into western Canada. Owing to their prolific reproduction, Manitoba's and Saskatchewan's Mennonite population jumped from 18,997 to 41,839 between 1901 and 1921.[115] The provinces' German speakers likewise grew from about 39,000 in 1901 to 103,000 in 1911, out of a combined population that ballooned from 316,490 to 953,826 during this same period.[116] Both increases coincided with the arrival of about 2.5 million immigrants entering Canada between 1896 and 1914, a significant number considering that the country's population stood at 4,833,239 in 1891.[117] About half of the new arrivals settled in the Prairie Provinces of Manitoba, Saskatchewan, and Alberta, so that on the eve of the First World War the number of immigrants living in each province ranged from 41 to 57 percent of the population.[118] The immigration boom provoked fears that immigrants could live in western Canada without being educated as Canadians. Manitoban schools were especially singled out for their low attendance and high illiteracy rates. One "well informed authority" speculated that on any given day more than 30,000 children skipped school, while a British observer condescendingly described the province's education system as "almost a generation behind the rest of the civilized world." Manitoba's Conservative premier Rodmond Roblin – who relied on the support of ethnic minorities – retorted by calling the

[114] George Fisher Chipman, "Winnipeg: The Melting Pot," *Canadian Magazine*, September 1909, 410.
[115] F. H. Epp, *Mennonites in Canada, 1920–1940*, 7.
[116] Lehmann, *German Canadians*, 145, 298.   [117] Wagner, *History of Migration*, 118.
[118] Monica Boyd and Michael Vickers, "100 Years of Immigration in Canada," in *The Changing Face of Canada: Essential Readings in Population*, ed. Roderic P. Beaujot and Don Kerr (Toronto: Canadian Scholars Press, 2007), 146.

pundit "a jelly-bag of an Englishman," but the fact remained that Manitoba (and Saskatchewan) would need to deploy bureaucratic tools with double force if they wished to forge their polyglot populations into unified citizenries.[119] The Mennonites were no exception. The situation was untenable for a nation at war, especially a nation at war with the progenitor of the Mennonites' German culture. Yet the First World War was not the catalyst of the provinces' struggle against non-English-language schools generally, nor Mennonite schools specifically, but the culmination of a quarter-century of policies that advanced Anglo-Canadian culture as the only legitimate culture in the land.

Government officials and the Anglo-Canadian press believed that the process of turning immigrant communities into Canadians began when minorities rejected Old World traditions. Conservatives took an imperialistic position by demanding that minorities become thoroughly "infused with British patriotism." Though Liberals relied more on immigrant support (including that of the Mennonites), they still wanted minorities to embrace a Canadian identity. Neither party was willing to argue for the advantages of heterogeneity since it portended the "Balkanization" (i.e. regression) of the country's population.[120] In a unique twist on a biblical story that was favored by Mennonites, Anglo-Canadians voiced concerns that the country was building a "Tower of Babel" by allowing ethnic enclaves to retain their languages. Whereas Mennonites used the story to emphasize the hubris of a monolingual society, Canada's Anglo commentators emphasized the story's abominable polyglot consequences. Aside from biblical analogies and blurry platitudes, educationalist Neil Sutherland summarizes that Anglo-Canadians "projected their fear for the future much more clearly than they did the vision of it."[121]

At no time was foreign integration a more acutely controversial topic in the Canadian context than after the First World War. Canada's sacrifices in the conflict, its independent signing of the Versailles Peace Treaty, and its membership of the League of Nations created an opportunity for provincial leaders to frame their postwar narratives as the full flowering of Canadian independence. Though the war provoked a strong sense of national identity in its Protestant, English-speaking, middle class, the general population remained fractured along lines of ethnicity, class,

---

[119] C. B. Sissons, *Bi-lingual Schools in Canada* (London: J. M. Dent, 1917), 119–20.

[120] Neil Sutherland, *Children in English-Canadian Society* (Toronto: University of Toronto Press, 1976), 211.

[121] Ibid., 211.

region, and religion.[122] The war also cultivated the notion that Canada stood on the side of democracy, and officials soon conflated this objective with monolingualism. John Herd Thompson summarizes,

"Democracy" was a word into which the people of the West could sink their teeth, teeth cut on direct legislation, the initiative, referendum and recall ... It was a concept used to explain the need to assimilate the immigrant, and to justify the need for unilingual education. What better reason to fight a war?[123]

Democracy was such a broad and righteous justification that the Dominion did not require a sophisticated wartime propaganda machine. Patriots emerged spontaneously at the municipal level to denounce Germany and promote displays of citizenship, such as English-language public schooling. Once democracy, the war, and public education were conflated, University of Saskatchewan president Walter Murray felt confident proclaiming to a group of graduating schoolteachers that prior to the war "the problem of racial assimilation quickened our interest in the schools as agencies for ... the adoption of a common language. Today the war has intensified our interest in education as a factor in nationalization."[124] Fighting the German language in Saskatchewan schoolhouses was as good as fighting German soldiers at Vimy Ridge.

Canadian patriotic activity may have been promoted metaphorically, but the Dominion's aggressive policies were anything but figures of speech. Donald Avery states that "During the years 1914–19 individuals and groups were deemed loyal or disloyal, law-abiding or revolutionary, according to how their behaviour conformed to the values and norms of the middle-class Anglo-Canadian community."[125] Owing to the upsurge of non-British immigrants prior to the war and the continued existence of urban and rural immigrant enclaves, there was a bewildering array of such individuals. Concerning enemy aliens specifically, Canada's 1911 census shows that there were 393,320 from the German Empire, 129,103 from the Austro-Hungarian Empire, 3,880 from the Ottoman Empire, and a

---

[122] Tom Mitchell, "The Manufacture of Souls of Good Quality: Winnipeg's 1919 National Conference on Canadian Citizenship, English-Canadian Nationalism, and the New Order After the Great War," *Journal of Canadian Studies* 31, no. 4 (1996–1997): 21.

[123] John Herd Thompson, *The Harvests of War: The Prairie West, 1914–1918* (Toronto: McClelland and Stewart Limited, 1978), 30.

[124] Walter Murray, *Western School Journal*, May 1917, 193–98. Quoted in ibid., 43.

[125] Donald Avery, "Ethnic and Class Relations in Western Canada During the First World War: A Case Study of European Immigrants and Anglo-Canadian Nativism," in *Canada and the First World War: Essays in Honour of Robert Craig Brown*, ed. David MacKenzie (Toronto: University of Toronto Press, 2005), 272.

few thousand Bulgarians.[126] The biggest concern facing enemy aliens was the government's view that they were a "problem" that had to be "solved." On August 22, 1914, Ottawa passed its War Measures Act that allowed for the arrest, detention, exclusion, and deportation of enemy aliens. The act, which "created the category of enemy alien, made synonymous in the public mind the idea of foreigner and enemy."[127] Two months later Ottawa passed the draconian Order-in-Council 2721 which "established a system of enemy alien registration, declared destitute enemy aliens could be interned as prisoners of war, and resolved that, as prisoners of war, they could be put to work."[128] It essentially conflated unemployment with crime during a time of general recession, seasonal unemployment, and rising xenophobia.[129] Only 8,579 enemy aliens wound up in internment camps, yet "the very threat of internment – and the sense of rejection by Canadian society as a whole – was felt by all who were at risk."[130] In time, the Dominion passed even more discriminatory measures in the form of the Wartime Elections Act of 1917. The Act disenfranchised not only enemy aliens, but all conscientious objectors and individuals of enemy origin who had arrived in Canada after 1902. Incidentally, Mennonites welcomed the Act since, in a roundabout way, it reaffirmed their status as conscientious objectors.[131]

The country's German-speaking population was an especially hot topic in Canadian social and political discourse. What began as tolerance in the early months of the conflict had transformed to harassment and persecution by the war's end. If nationality was something that was primordial and permanent – as many contemporaries assumed – then there was every reason to oppress German speakers as a matter of national security. Everywhere, the stereotype of the hardworking German was recast into the militaristic Hun, and speaking German or possessing even a tenuous connection to the geographic region between the Rhine and the Dnieper Rivers provoked suspicion or abuse. Bizarrely, much of the country's initial paranoia was directed south of the border, where the presence of an estimated 7 million German Americans stoked Canadian fears of a

[126] Ibid., 276. Bohdan S. Kordan, *No Free Man: Canada, the Great War, and the Enemy Alien Experience* (Montreal and Kingston: McGill-Queen's University Press, 2016), 19.

[127] Kordan, *No Free Man*, 76.   [128] Ibid., 124.   [129] Ibid., 69–76.

[130] Avery, *Ethnic and Class Relations*, 276. The demographic breakdown of internees included 2,009 Germans, 5,954 Austro-Hungarians, 205 Turks, 99 Bulgarians, and 312 classified as "miscellaneous."

[131] Rutherdale, *Hometown Horizons: Local Responses to Canada's Great War* (Vancouver: University of British Columbia Press, 2004), 80–81.

covert attack on the Empire.[132] From remote districts like Happyland, Saskatchewan to the metropolis of Toronto, government officials received countless reports of alleged subversive activities.[133] In Calgary, vigilantism was encouraged against German sympathizers, Winnipeg witnessed the stoning of its German club, and Vancouver businesses assumed to be foreign-owned were smashed by a mob.[134] In a particularly violent episode, a group of about 500 soldiers and veterans marched up Toronto's Yonge Street, attacked "enemy" businesses, and forcefully rounded up alleged enemy aliens, regardless of whether they were from Central, Entente, or neutral powers.[135]

In general, Mennonites escaped the worst abuses of Canada's patriotic zeal owing to their status as British subjects, high levels of employment, rurality, and the fact that they had little contact with secular German organizations. Yet the heady wartime atmosphere gave provincial educationalists ammunition against separatist Mennonites' private schools and associative Mennonites' bilingual public schools.[136] According to one journalist writing for *The New Outlook* on Mennonite education, "When the war spirit got hold of the West, and to poor equipment were added the dual sins of pacifism and German speech, the patience of ... officials could no longer stand the strain. Recourse was had to compulsion."[137] In 1915, the Liberal candidate Tobias Norris replaced Roblin as Premier of Manitoba. Following in his predecessor's footsteps, Norris called for compulsory, English-language, public-school attendance for the province's children. In the same year, Liberal candidate William Martin became the Premier of Saskatchewan and heightened his

---

[132] J. L. Granatstein, "Conscription in the Great War," in *Canada and the First World War: Essays in Honour of Robert Craig Brown*, ed. David MacKenzie, 62–75 (Toronto: University of Toronto Press, 2005), 66; Robert Rutherdale, *Hometown Horizons*, 136.

[133] Kordan, *No Free Man*, 18, 30; Adam Crerar, "Ontario and the Great War," in *Canada and the First World War: Essays in Honour of Robert Craig Brown*, ed. David MacKenzie (Toronto: University of Toronto Press, 2005), 254.

[134] Kordan, *No Free Man*, 30.

[135] Crerar, "Ontario and the Great War," 259. Moreover, the country's German publications were censored, suspended, or forced to be published in English. Lehmann, *German Canadians*, 275, 288–89.

[136] Aside from a great deal of red tape and a few scandals over unbaptized Mennonite men avoiding the draft, Dominion authorities largely accommodated Mennonites' refusal to serve in the military – though press antagonism of their German and nonviolent culture remained strong. See "The War and Military Exemption," in Epp, *Mennonites in Canada 1786–1920*, 381.

[137] *The New Outlook* (New York), March 7, 1928. Quoted in Francis, *In Search of Utopia*, 180, n. 19.

predecessor's threats against Mennonites by fining parents who did not send their children to public schools.[138] Despite the government's hardened stance, Mennonites and other minority-language populations remained assured of the 1890 proviso and by the end of 1915, nearly 2,600 Mennonite children mostly from the Bergthaler (West Reserve) and Kleine Gemeinde (East Reserve) groups had been enrolled in Manitoban public schools.[139] Another 1,000 students – from the Chortitzer (East Reserve) and Reinländer (West Reserve) groups – attended private schools.[140] A similar division existed in Saskatchewan.

All of this changed in January 1916 when Manitoba's Superintendent of Education, C. K. Newcombe, released a highly influential report that was critical of the province's bilingual schools. In response to a combination of factors including the report, Canada's patriotic atmosphere, French Canadians' tepid support for the war, and increased public criticism for allowing two "enemy" languages (German and Ukrainian) to be used in taxpayer-funded schools, Manitoba passed the School Attendance Act on March 10, 1916, which made schooling compulsory and overturned the bilingual proviso.[141] Saskatchewan followed suit in 1917 with the passage of its Attendance Act, which dictated compulsory public-school attendance for all provincial children within range of a public school and modified existing legislation to make all public schools monolingual. It then set about building public schools within range of Mennonite communities.[142]

Mennonites were aware of the proposed change before it went into effect and its associative wing – including Bergthaler, Kleine Gemeinde, and some Sommerfelder Mennonites – appealed to the government on political grounds by threatening to not support Norris's Liberal Party.[143] Other ethnic minorities made similar appeals via government

---

[138] Ens, *Subjects or Citizens?* 116.

[139] Epp reports this was an all-time high, with over sixty schools receiving public money. See *Mennonites in Canada 1920–1940*, 97; Ens, *Subjects or Citizens?* 113.

[140] Ens, *Subjects or Citizens?* 113, 153; Epp, *Mennonites in Canada 1786–1920*, 352.

[141] Rose Bruno-Jofre, "Citizenship and Schooling in Manitoba, 1918–1945," *Manitoba History* 36 (Autumn/Winter 1998–1999), last modified October 23, 2011, www.mhs.mb.ca/docs/mb_history/36/citizenship.shtml, last accessed June 7, 2018.

[142] Ens, *Subjects or Citizens?* 134. See School Attendance Act, *The Revised Statutes of Saskatchewan, 1920*, Chapter 111 (Assented to November 10, 1920), www.publications.gov.sk.ca/redirect.cfm?p=66948&i=74287, last accessed June 7, 2018.

[143] Ens, *Subjects or Citizens?* 156. Other groups were likewise affected by the laws. In Manitoba, for instance, French bilingual schools enrolled 7,393 pupils (with 3,465 students attending) while Ukrainian and Polish schools enrolled 6,513 students (with 3,885 attending). See Sissons, *Bi-lingual Schools*, 141.

representatives and protest meetings, but accepted the basic premise that the government was the ultimate authority in education matters. In Saskatchewan, one observer noted that "Among the French and Ruthenians [Ukrainians] ... any defects in their schools are not due to their being outside State control so much as to the difficulty of making acknowledged State control effective."[144] Thus, like other ethnic minorities, associative Mennonites pursued dissent within the political system, not outside of it.[145]

Separatist Mennonites also petitioned to withhold passage of the Act, but they did not avail themselves of a political threat because they did not vote. They continued to treat the government as a monarchy that could grant special concessions to its minorities at will. While the associative Bergthaler petition stated that they "put their confidence in the Liberal Party," the Reinländer petition started from the premise that the Canadian government was "ordained of God."[146] In another letter, separatist Chortitzer Johann Schroeder wrote that "with prayer to God, we ask you, as high officials, also to hold this alliance sacred; for it is not the custom of the English government to consider such [the *Privilegium*] as a scrap of paper. It is our desire that Canada may be a loving and benevolent mother to us for a long time."[147]

The petitions drafted by associative and separatist Mennonites testify to a different understanding of Mennonites' relationship to the state. The former acted like enfranchised citizens who were invested in the democratic process. Alternately, separatist Mennonites from the Chortitz (East Reserve) and Reinländer (West Reserve) groups acted as subjects whose only options were to beg the government to rescind the law or threaten to migrate.[148] Their reasoning did not originate in liberal philosophy since they neither wrote nor spoke of "inalienable rights," nor did they threaten to overthrow the unjust rule of authorities for violating them. Rather, they articulated their position in the language of collective privileges – attendant to their *Privilegium* but also grounded in a particular understanding

---

[144] Sissons, *Bi-lingual Schools*, 165.

[145] Some groups were entirely unconcerned. For example, the Icelandic colony had used English for school instruction since the 1870s. See ibid., 165; Epp, *Mennonites in Canada, 1920–1940*, 110; Eyford, *White Settler Reserve*, 11.

[146] *Manitoba Free Press*, May 18, 1920, 15; vol. 544, no. 47, Mennonite Heritage Centre. The latter is quoted in Ens, *Subjects or Citizens?* 156.

[147] This quote is from a letter accompanying the "Petition on behalf of the Chortitza church council directed to the Department of Naval Service in Ottawa," October 2, 1919. Quoted in M. W. Friesen, *New Homeland*, 41.

[148] Ens, *Subjects or Citizens?* 234.

of Romans 13:1, which holds that Christians are subject to authorities unless it causes them to violate their allegiance to Christ.[149] Adolf Ens insists that separatist Mennonites actually trusted governments *more* than associative Mennonites since the former had an "intrinsic obligation to ... keep its promises" while the latter "had already developed a sense that the ruling party had a political obligation to them," which was merely predicated on the last election.[150]

Before the passage of Manitoba's legislation, Premier Norris and his ministers assured Mennonites that private schools would remain unaffected by monolingual legislation.[151] As a result, *Gemeinden* who had accepted public schools in the past but disliked the monolingual initiative privatized their schools so that by November 1918 only thirty remained public.[152] Yet the dramatic rise in private schools led the government to impose public schooling on private schools that failed to submit an annual census, which many did not.[153] Combined with separatist Mennonites' multiple failed attempts to secure legal sanction at provincial, dominion, and imperial levels, this made it increasingly clear that Mennonite private schools were both pedagogically and legally unacceptable to the state. In the face of this hardened stance, and with mounting public scrutiny, most of Manitoba's Bergthal and Kleine Gemeinde communities agreed to monolingual public schooling by 1920.[154]

The war years' emphasis on patriotism and the introduction of increasingly strict education legislation eliminated all leeway for independent Mennonite education and any doubt that Canada's separatist Mennonites shared the same trajectory as their associative brethren. As the Mennonites diverged philosophically, some chose to diverge physically and leave their brethren to the "clever snares" of the world.

---

[149] A 1920 letter from the Reinländer churches to the Saskatchewan Premier Johann F. Peters speaks directly to the Romans passage by stating, "We want to be subject to the authorities. But you must also allow us our rights. If you force us to violate our teaching, who will then bear the punishment?" Translated by and quoted in Ens, *Subjects or Citizens?* 147.

[150] Ens, "Becoming British Citizens in Pre-WW I Canada," in *Canadian Mennonites and the Challenge of Nationalism*, ed. Abe J. Dueck (Winnipeg: Manitoba Mennonite Historical Society, 1994), 85.

[151] Ens, *Subjects or Citizens?* 120–21.   [152] Epp, *Mennonites in Canada 1920–1940*, 97.

[153] Ens, *Subjects or Citizens?* 124.

[154] The Sommerfelder case defending the legality of Lowe's *Privilegium* letter made it to the Judicial Committee of the Privy Council in London, which was the highest court of appeals in the British Empire. Epp, *Mennonites in Canada 1920–1940*, 107–9.

AMBIGUOUS CONCLUSIONS AND CLEAR SOLUTIONS

With the war in Europe sputtering to an armistice, the battle over public education in the western provinces became even sharper. The winter of 1918–1919 was a turbulent time on the prairie. Returning soldiers introduced a public health crisis in the form of "Spanish" influenza, which killed 50,000 Canadians in a matter of months.[155] The postwar depression sent grain prices falling and unemployment soaring, and instigated a general strike in Winnipeg. The chaos seemed to justify officials' reasoning that dissident groups were a threat to national security. Lehmann succinctly states that after the war, "The cultural offensive against the non-British population was thus in no way abandoned, but rather intensified."[156] Separatist Mennonites viewed the developments less as a political turning point and more as a sign of divine retribution against a pugnacious and prideful nation.[157]

After the passage of the Manitoba and Saskatchewan Attendance Acts and with no recourse at dominion or imperial levels, the roughly 14,000 Mennonites living in the provinces had three alternatives:[158] (1) They could accept public schools and hope that private instruction would make up for it (2); they could supply qualified Mennonite teachers from their teacher-training schools to public-school districts with Mennonite populations, thereby teaching a state curriculum while retaining a semblance of Mennoniteness; or (3) they could emigrate. The majority of Manitoba and Saskatchewan Mennonites explicitly or implicitly favored the first two options. Yet members of the Reinländer (West Reserve), Bergthal (Saskatchewan), Chortitz (East Reserve), and Sommerfeld (West Reserve) communities pursued the third option, while organizing a rearguard defense against the legislation.

By 1919, the Manitoba government was commandeering private Mennonite schools that refused to comply with the new laws.[159] They also built schools in areas that lacked them and hired discharged soldiers as teachers.[160] When Mennonites refused to sell land and materials for the

---

[155] Mark Osborne Humphries, *The Last Plague: Spanish Influenza and the Politics of Public Health in Canada* (Toronto: University of Toronto Press, 2013), 3.

[156] Lehmann, *German Canadians*, 324.

[157] Royden Loewen, *Village Among Nations: "Canadian" Mennonites in a Transnational World, 1916–2006* (Toronto: University of Toronto Press, 2013), 20.

[158] This number is compiled from Table 9, "Mennonite Congregational Families in Canada," in F. H. Epp, *Mennonites in Canada 1920–1940*, 20–21. Epp places the population of Canada's Mennonites in 1920 at 58,800.

[159] Ens, *Subjects or Citizens?* 125–27.   [160] Lehmann, *German Canadians*, 322.

new schools, the government simply expropriated the land and imported materials from Winnipeg.[161] Parents in contempt of the legislation risked heavy fines or jail sentences. Instead of prosecuting every case – a move that threatened to clog the courts – authorities took a scattershot approach by imprisoning and fining random individuals.[162] This was too much for the remaining Bergthaler (East Reserve) communities, who caved under the pressure.[163]

Saskatchewan's tactics were even more punitive. In 1920 and 1921 the province opened 2,935 cases against Mennonites who did not avail themselves of public schools. Of these, 2,346 individuals were fined a total of $20,984 CAD ($296,372 in 2019 CAD).[164] Sometimes police resorted to seizing property – from cows to cured hams – and sold it at auction. Unluckier still were twelve Mennonites who were jailed. Like the Russian government in the 1870s, Canadian provincial authorities assured themselves that separatist Mennonites' would eventually bend to the new laws. According to Saskatchewan's Premier Martin, "These people ... have been here a long time and while they are deluded in thinking they have special privileges in Saskatchewan over other citizens, at the same time we have got to use reasonable toleration in our treatment of them."[165] Separatist Mennonites offered to settle the wilds of northern Manitoba – even to the shores of the Hudson Bay – if they were allowed their privileges, but the proposition was as creative as it was unfeasible.[166] Nation, state, and territory were increasingly indivisible. In the same spirit, though in a different time and place, one eighteenth-century French politician bluntly stated, "To the Jews as a Nation, nothing; to the Jews as individuals, everything."[167]

---

[161] After the schools were built, state-appointed teachers sat alone for weeks in empty schoolhouses or fought with private-school teachers to occupy the same building. Ens, *Subjects or Citizens?* 127; 144; W. Janzen, *Limits on Liberty*, 96.

[162] Ens, *Subjects or Citizens?* 144.   [163] Ibid., 124.

[164] Ibid., 147–48. The inflation adjustment was made with the Bank of Canada inflation calculator, www.bankofcanada.ca/rates/related/inflation-calculator/, last accessed August 8, 2019. W. Janzen places the amount in fines for these years at over $26,000, but his estimate is taken from an earlier publication by Ens. See n. 82 in W. Janzen, *Limits on Liberty*, 328.

[165] Quoted in J. Castell Hopkins, *The Canadian Annual Review of Public Affairs* (Toronto: The Canadian Annual Review, Ltd., 1920), 552; even once the exodus was underway, the premier remained confident that they would return to Canada.

[166] Epp, *Mennonite Exodus*, 96.

[167] "Opinion de M. le Comte Stanislas de Clermont-Tonnerre, dèputè de Paris, le 23 decembre, 1789," reprinted in *La Rèvolution française et l'émancipation des Juifs*, vol.

Amid the postwar turbulence, associative Mennonites endeavored to clarify their differences from separatist Mennonites. This objective was particularly acute for members of the CMBC, including D. Toews and Ewert, who wished to resettle impoverished Mennonites from the Soviet Union. Following the First World War and its many privations, the Russian Revolution and Civil War (1917–1922) all but obliterated Russia's Mennonite settlements. Especially in Ukraine and southern Russia, where the bulk of Russia's Mennonites lived, the Bolshevik Red Army, the anti-Bolshevik White Army, and the Anarchist Black Army demolished everything in their path. Faced with complete desolation, Mennonite communities collaborated with other German speakers to create ad hoc *Selbstschutz* (self-defense) militias in 1918 and 1919, using weapons donated by the German and White armies. Despite such measures – which entirely violated Mennonites' nonviolent beliefs – hundreds of Mennonite men, women, and children were killed and raped, mostly by Nestor Makhno's anarchist army (Fig. 1.2).[168] The chaos of the Civil War subsequently provoked a devastating famine. Under the auspices of the newly formed MCC, associative Mennonites in the United States organized a relief program to help Mennonites in Russia, while Canada's associative Mennonites directed their energies toward helping them relocate to Canada.

In 1919 the Dominion issued an Order-in-Council barring further Mennonite immigration due to their "peculiar habits, modes of life and methods of holding property."[169] As a result, in 1921 D. Toews, Ewert, and a visiting delegation of Russian Mennonites – the study commission mentioned in the Introduction, which included A. A. Friesen and Unruh – approached Canada's acting premier, D. M. Reesor to clarify *their* version of Mennoniteness.[170] The group claimed that the "Dutch" Mennonites of Russia were, like most of Canada's Mennonites, "a most progressive people and would give the government no trouble in school matters."[171] A. A. Friesen followed up the meeting with a letter to the Canadian

---

7, 13. Quoted in Paula E. Hyman, *The Jews of Modern France* (Berkeley and Los Angeles, CA: University of California Press, 1998), 27.

[168] For more on the Selbstschutz, see John B. Toews, "The Origins and Activities of the Mennonite *Selbstschutz* in the Ukraine (1918–1919)," *Mennonite Quarterly Review* 46, no. 146, no. 1 1972): 5–39.

[169] "A Hundred Years of Immigration to Canada 1900–1999," *Canadian Council for Refugees*, last modified May 2000, http://ccrweb.ca/en/hundred-years-immigration-canada-1900–1999, last accessed June 7, 2018.

[170] F. H. Epp, *Mennonite Exodus*, 102.

[171] Report on interview by delegation dated July 20, 1921. Quoted in ibid., 102.

FIGURE 1.2 Mennonite mass burial in Blumenort, Molotschna, Russia during the
Russian Civil War, 1920. Gerhard Lohrenz photo collection 44–312, Mennonite
Heritage Archives

Minister of Immigration, James A. Calder. In an act of normalizing the
associative Mennonites' worldview against the separatists, A. A. Friesen
argued,

> I am aware that there is a certain branch of the Mennonite church in western
> Canada which endeavors to keep aloof from the Canadian people and perpetuate
> some foreign customs and practices, but this branch can not stand as
> representatives of Mennonites in general. In my travels among the brethren of
> my faith in the US I have found that everywhere they have unquestionably adopted
> the public schools … The same attitude is taken also by the Mennonites of
> Ontario, as well as by a large part of the Mennonites in the west …[172]

Incoming Premier W. L. M. King was favorably disposed to the immi-
gration scheme since he had grown up among the acculturated
Mennonites of Waterloo County, Ontario. He repealed the Order-in-
Council and between 1923 and 1927, the Dominion government allowed
about 20,000 Mennonites to emigrate from the Soviet Union to Canada.
The immigration was supervised by the CMBC, facilitated by the

---

[172] Letter from A. A. Friesen to J. A. Calder, July 25, 1921. Quoted in Epp, *Mennonite
Exodus*, 102–3.

Canadian Pacific Railroad, and had the ostensible financial backing of "The Mennonite Church of Canada," whom D. Toews claimed to speak on behalf of.[173] Nevertheless, the CMBC's ledger was always in the red, it lacked broad-based participation, and it encountered outright hostility from many separatist and associative Mennonites who felt they owed nothing to Russia's Mennonites, whom they pejoratively dubbed "Russländer."[174]

History, nevertheless, would favor the CMBC and Canada's associative Mennonites. Within the official (i.e. academic) twentieth-century historiography, the associative Mennonites' greatest champion was Frank H. Epp, the prolific writer, history professor, and president of Conrad Grebel College in Waterloo, Ontario. His account of the resettlement, *Mennonite Exodus*, and his influential two-volume magnum opus, *Mennonites in Canada*, took for granted a world organized into nation states while tirelessly promoting Mennonite unity.[175] F. H. Epp regarded early-twentieth-century Mennonite disunity as an "internal weakness" that "significantly impaired their ability to deal effectively with the problems of the day."[176] Separatist Mennonites were "stubborn" while those who pursued a "middle-of-the-road position" by emphasizing a select set of religious "essentials," "kept the best that tradition had to offer and allow[ed] adjustments which were believed to be necessary and useful."[177] Similar in many respects to the Russian Mennonites who damned the 1870s migrants as "poor" and "backward," F. H. Epp's view of Mennonite history assumes that associative Mennonites' "problems of the day" were objectively more relevant than those of their separatist brethren. Private German-language schools were not "essential" for *Canadian* Mennonites.

Over the course of fifty years, associative Mennonites came to believe that God had brought them to Canada to maintain their religious "essentials" while allowing them to carve out a place in modern civil society. This was a mythological process that combined Mennonites' distinct sense of peoplehood with national governance that was amenable to its existence. Like other mythologies, nationalism is not imparted wholly and immediately. Individuals first experience it to be true and only then believe it to be real. This is what gives a conversion story its power, since it really *is* miraculous to

---

[173] Epp, *Mennonite Exodus*, 103; 121.
[174] For a complete description of the scheme, see Epp, "Part V. Debts and Developments in the Immigrant Community," *Mennonite Exodus*.
[175] On F. H. Epp's national vision, see Swyripa, *Storied Landscapes*, 127–28.
[176] F. H. Epp, *Mennonites in Canada 1920–1940*, 1.   [177] Ibid., 18.

change one's reality. For associative Mennonites, this conversion happened gradually as they transitioned from demanding collective *privileges* as autonomous communities to accepting individual *rights* as Canadian citizens. Especially after the Second World War, and especially in contrast to the United States, Canadian Mennonites took pride in Canada's modest presence on the world stage and its reluctance to engage in warfare. Writing in the 1990s, Rodney J. Sawatsky notes that "Mennonites in Canada seem comparatively comfortable as Canadian citizens and are actively involved in politics ... In turn, Canadian Mennonites tend to consider the political order as a means to pursue common ends rather than as the Mennonite enemy."[178] By marrying their sense of peoplehood to a Canadian national narrative of anti-militarism and mild socialism, Canadian Mennonites could reasonably argue that their government shared their nonbelligerent and humanitarian ethos.

Separatist Mennonites also felt the Lord's guidance – sometimes quite literally. With the education storm gathering wind, the intractable Reinländer J. Wiens was standing in his wheat field on a warm summer day in 1913 when he heard a voice say "you will not be able to stay here forever; the church will once again have to take up the walking staff." Reinländer diarist, Isaac M. Dyck, located the reasons why God willed the Mennonite faithful to be perpetual wanderers. In R. Loewen's analysis, I. M. Dyck articulated that "religious rebirth and commitment could occur only in exile" for it was during these times that God truly revealed himself. According to I. M. Dyck, the *Privilegium* had given the confession a false sense of security. Though it exempted Mennonites from military service, their prosperity and acquiescence to public school made them accomplices in building a new "Sodom" and a "Canadian tower of Babel." The only option was to follow Christ in the "footsteps of grief," by seeking out earthly Zions until they finally reached the "upper Zion" of heaven.[179]

NO REST FOR THE RIGHTEOUS

Between 1919 and 1922, separatist Mennonites sent a total of seventeen delegations to Argentina, Brazil, Mexico, Paraguay, Uruguay,

---

[178] Rodney J. Sawatsky, *History and Ideology: American Mennonite Identity Definition Through History* (Kitchener, ON: Pandora Press, 2005), 104.

[179] Isaak M. Dyck, "Emigration from Canada to Mexico, Year 1922," trans. Robyn Dyck Sneath, 2005 (unpublished manuscript in possession of R. Loewen). Quoted in R. Loewen, *Village Among Nations*, 4, 14–15, 19–20.

Mississippi, and Quebec, to scout for land and privileges.[180] On February 20, 1921, a Reinländer delegation was granted an audience with President Obregon in Mexico City. Eight days later, the President and his Minister of Agriculture put their names on a Mennonite *Privilegium*. The Reinländers' only reservation – and the reason why other Mennonites did not choose Mexico – was that the agreement was not embedded in the Mexican Constitution. Nevertheless, between 1922 and 1926, 5,350 Reinländers and 600 Sommerfelders immigrated to Mexico where they purchased more than 100,000 hectares in Chihuahua and Durango.[181] According to E. K. Francis, many individuals pragmatically retained their Canadian citizenship and bank accounts in the event that they might have to return (Fig. 1.3).[182]

During their search, the Reinländer delegates initiated contact with New York banker Samuel McRoberts, president of the Metropolitan Trust Company. In 1919, they visited him to inquire about financing an immigration scheme, but he turned them away.[183] According to Mennonite sources, his fundamentalist Christian wife, Harriet Skinner, subsequently intervened on the Mennonites' behalf owing to her fascination with their faith.[184] McRoberts then solicited the aid of the Norwegian-born ex-millionaire and freelance explorer Fred Engen to look into settlement possibilities. After reviewing options in Africa and Asia, the two agreed that South America held the best possibility of success. Engen departed for South America in 1919.[185] Concluding his trip, Engen wrote to McRoberts that he had "found the promised land."[186]

McRoberts visited South America in July 1920 intending to settle the Mennonites in Argentina. Yet on the steamer from New York to Buenos Aires, he met the newly elected Paraguayan president, Manuel

---

[180] F. H. Epp, *Mennonites in Canada, 1920–1940*, 110, 120.

[181] On the Old Colony immigration to Mexico, see F. H. Epp, *Mennonites in Canada, 1920–1940*, 109–28; R. Loewen, *Village Among Nations*, 14–65. For a transcript of Mexico's charter of freedoms, see J. H. Doerksen, *Geschichte und Wichtige Dokumente der Mennoniten von Russland, Canada [sic], Paraguay und Mexico* (n.p., 1923), 125–26.

[182] Francis, *In Search of Utopia*, 192.   [183] M. W. Friesen, *New Homeland*, 58.

[184] Bender, "McRoberts, Samuel (1868–1947)," *Global Anabaptist Mennonite Encyclopedia Online*, last modified April 12, 2014, http://gameo.org/index.php?title=McRoberts,_Samuel_(1868–1947)&oldid=118554, last accessed June 7, 2018; Bernhard Toews, *Reise-Tagebuch des Bernhard Töws 1921: Chacoexpedition mit Fred Engen* (Kolonie Menno, Paraguay: Abteilung Geschichtsarchiv, Schulverwaltung der Kolonie Menno, 1997), 13.

[185] M. W. Friesen, *New Homeland*, 59.   [186] Ibid., 64.

FIGURE 1.3 A boy plowing with horses on the Mennonites' West Reserve in Manitoba, Canada. The house and barn are representative of the typical farms that the Menno Colony Mennonites sold when they left for Paraguay; n.d., Lawrence Klippenstein photo collection 53–61, Mennonite Heritage Archive

Gondra Pereira, and his traveling companion, Minister of Foreign Affairs and future president, Eusebio Ayala. McRoberts relayed the Mennonites' story to the pair and praised them as pioneers and efficient farmers. Listening attentively, Gondra and Ayala viewed a settlement in the Chaco as an excellent means of consolidating Paraguayan power over the region. Once in Buenos Aires, McRoberts' negotiations with the Argentines stalled over the Mennonites' *Privilegium*, so he traveled up the Paraná River for Asunción to resume negotiations with the more pliant Gondra. The president immediately approved the Mennonites' terms and organized a publicity campaign to convince Paraguay's press and citizenry that settling German-speaking Mennonites was a national opportunity. Gondra also threw a banquet for McRoberts to which he invited key representatives in the government, and organized a two-day cruise up the Paraguay River with Asunción's business elite, government ministers, and members of the Catholic clergy.[187]

Like the Canadian government in the 1870s, Gondra was acutely aware that his country was low on the list of destinations for prospective immigrants, especially white, self-sufficient, German-speaking agriculturalists. Before the First World War, German-speaking immigrants to South America typically favored costal countries owing to their better land opportunities, transportation, and infrastructure. Yet by the 1920s, speculators were reevaluating Paraguay as a good location for German settlement.[188] Anticipating a transfer of continental Germans, Paraguay's Congress proposed creating a propaganda and immigration office strategically located in Hamburg. The Deutsche Volksbund für Paraguay (German League for Paraguay, DVfP), also printed a pamphlet titled *Paraguay: Winke für Einwanderer* (*Paraguay: Hints for Immigrants*) that aimed to steer Germans to Paraguay.[189]

It was within this context that Mennonites from Canada were easily conflated with German speakers from Europe and were promoted as excellent agriculturalists and entrepreneurs. Ayala had worked for the Liberal Party newspapers *El Liberal* and *El Diario*, and these publications swung behind the cause. The former gushed, "It is said these people are very industrious ... They are rich. Some 40,000 of them propose to come to Paraguay. They are bringing with them everything needed for developing a flourishing settlement."[190] Like Canada fifty years earlier, Paraguay's liberal government overlooked the Mennonites' religious peculiarities, emphasized their culture of industry, and assured skeptics that they would be good citizens.[191]

Throughout 1921, Paraguayan newspapers waged a battle over whether the Mennonites should be allowed to settle in Paraguay. *El Liberal* steadfastly maintained that Mennonites would "civilize" the Chaco.[192] Advocates argued that the Mennonites did not wish to create

---

[187] Ibid., 64–66.

[188] Stefan Rinke, "German Migration to Latin America," in *Germany and the Americas: Culture, Politics, and History, a Multidisciplinary Encyclopedia*, vol. 1, ed. Thomas Adam (Santa Barbara, Denver, Oxford: ABC CLIO, 2005), 27–31, 29–30.

[189] Joseph Winfield Fretz, *Immigrant Group Settlement in Paraguay: A Study in the Sociology of Colonization* (North Newton, KS: Bethel College, 1962), 38.

[190] *El Liberal* (Asunción), August 30, 1920. Quoted in M. W. Friesen, *New Homeland*, 67.

[191] The debate in the Paraguayan legislature preceding the passage of Law 514 is found in Cámara de Senadores, Paraguay. "Franquicias a los Menonitas," *Diario de Sesiones Del Congreso – Cámara de Senadores, 32 Sesion Ordinaria*, July 12, 1921. Asunción: Imprenta Nacional, 1921.

[192] *El Liberal* (Asunción), July 20, 1921.

a state within a state but merely to reestablish their farming communities in a familiar style. Other Paraguayans were less enthusiastic about the prospect of thousands of foreigners living in the country's hinterland. They thought that the Mennonites offered Paraguay little incentive other than a vague promise that they would eventually develop the Chaco.[193] Striking an alarmist note, the Conservative *La Tribuna* argued that Mennonites would turn Paraguay into a German-speaking state and threaten the Paraguayan race.[194] Others maintained that by agreeing to the Mennonite privileges, the state was actually creating two classes of citizens: Paraguayans who shared a set of duties and rights, and Mennonites who would be an aloof minority.[195]

The Paraguayan situation also reflected Canada's territorial anxieties from the 1870s, namely the existence of an undefined border with a larger and more powerful neighbor. Since Paraguay's defeat in the War of the Triple Alliance (1864–1870), the country had remained embroiled in a dispute with Bolivia over the Chaco.[196] A massive and immediate transfer of settler-farmers to the area promised to check Bolivian ambitions. With Paraguay's dissenting Conservatives in a minority position and geopolitical concerns outweighing civic equality, the Paraguayan government approved Mennonite immigration.

When McRoberts returned to the United States, he informed the Reinländer Mennonites of Paraguay's terms, but the group had already decided on Mexico.[197] In their place, the Saskatchewan Bergthaler Mennonites registered interest in the Chaco and organized a delegation in 1921.[198] Their mission was to consult with McRoberts in New York, rendezvous with Engen in Buenos Aires, meet with Paraguayan authorities

---

[193] M. W. Friesen also provides a detailed overview of press attitudes toward Mennonite settlement in *New Homeland*, 111–18.

[194] *La Tribuna* (Asunción), 8, July 23 and 25, 1921.

[195] Bridget María Chesterton, *The Grandchildren of Solano López: Frontier and Nation in Paraguay, 1904–1936* (Albuquerque, NM: University of New Mexico Press, 2013), 97–101.

[196] Bruce W. Farcau, *The Chaco War: Bolivia and Paraguay, 1932–1935* (London: Praeger, 1996), 7.

[197] M. W. Friesen, *New Homeland*, 68.

[198] The delegation was composed of Johann Friesen, Jakob Neufeld, and Aaron Zacharias (Bergthal, Saskatchewan); Isaak Funk and Bernhard Toews (Sommerfeld, West Reserve); and Jakob Doerksen (Chortitz, East Reserve). Two were ministers and three were farmers, including one who was also a private-school teacher. Johann Priesz of Altona, Manitoba, accompanied the group and was responsible for its legal matters. Ibid., 71, 74.

in Asunción, and explore the Chaco.[199] At the time, the Paraguayan state had legal title to no more than about 375,000 hectares in the Chaco. The vast majority was divided between 821 private owners.[200] During the delegates' layover in Buenos Aires, they met with one of the largest Chaco landowners, José Casado.[201] His company, Carlos Casado S. A., was a major wheat grower and livestock producer that also specialized in extracting tannin from the quebracho tree. At 1.2 million hectares, Casado's Chaco real estate constituted the largest single private landholding in the world.[202]

In Asunción, Ayala and Gondra received the delegates and endorsed their list of privileges pending the Mennonites' approval of the Chaco.[203] Continuing up the Paraguay River, the delegates stopped at Puerto Casado before venturing inland. Everywhere they went, the delegates were intensely interested in the weather, farming, industry, and transportation. They were correspondingly less interested in the country's culture, history, and politics. Once the delegates were back in Asunción, they again met with the president, who put in motion the passage of Law 514, which ensured the Mennonites' privileges. Though the state expected that Mennonites would eventually be naturalized as Paraguayan citizens, the law guaranteed that their communities would receive special treatment. It would reproduce in function, if not in form, their desire to remain autonomous subjects of a benevolent government.

The years 1921 and 1922 were economically difficult in Canada and Paraguay, so McRoberts placed the immigration plans on hold until the price of land stabilized. Moving forward in 1925, McRoberts established three corporations, in conjunction with Philadelphia investment banker Edward Robinette, to manage the finances: (1) the Intercontinental Company Limited, which handled the purchase and resale of the Mennonites' Canadian acreage; (2) the Corporación Paraguaya, which handled the purchase of land from Carlos Casado S. A.; and (3) the American Continental Company, which was based in Philadelphia but

---

[199] For a complete itinerary, see B. Toews, *Reise-Tagebuch*.

[200] Jan M. Kleinpenning, *Integration and Colonisation of the Paraguayan Chaco* (Nijmegen: Katholieke Universiteit Nijmegen, 1986), 20.

[201] B. Toews, *Reise-Tagebuch*, 28.

[202] M. W. Friesen, *New Homeland*, 87. The land figure is taken from Willard H. Smith, "Corporación Paraguaya," *Global Anabaptist Mennonite Encyclopedia Online*, last modified August 20, 2013, http://gameo.org/index.php?title=Corporaci%C3%B3n_Paraguaya&oldid=79930, last accessed June 7, 2018.

[203] The full list of privileges is found in M. W. Friesen, *New Homeland*, 81–82.

organized in the Dominican Republic, to hold the Corporación Paraguaya stock. In total, the Mennonites exchanged 17,805 hectares of land in Canada for 55,814 hectares in Paraguay. The sale price for the Canadian land was valued at $902,900 in American gold (about $13,137,038 USD in 2019) while the Corporación Paraguaya was capitalized at $750,000 (about $10,912,370 USD in 2019).[204]

Before leaving Canada, Paraguay-bound Mennonites attempted to unite as a single church and economic unit. They succeeded on the second count by organizing a commission to handle land transactions. It was named the Fürsorge-Komitee in memory of the name the Russian government had given to its colonial administrative apparatus. Yet religious unity remained impossible after Aaron Zacharias of the small Bergthaler (Saskatchewan) group approached the larger Manitoba groups with a list of demands. The Sommerfeld (West Reserve) and Chortitz (East Reserve) churches rejected these, however, stating that they were not willing to impose an outside system of laws on their people, particularly the rejection of cars and telephones.[205]

Between 1926 and 1930, about 1,800 Mennonites from Bergthal (Saskatchewan), led by Aaron Zacharias; Sommerfeld (West Reserve), led by Heinrich Unruh; and Chortitz (East Reserve), led by M. C. Friesen (whose wife, Elisabeth Wiebe, was the granddaughter of the group's former leader G. Wiebe), sold their land, packed their bags, and moved to the Chaco, where they established the Menno Colony.[206] Groups were subdivided into *Strassendorf* villages of about 10–16 families each, located about 5–10 km apart. Like the Reinländer

---

[204] Peter G. Sawatzky, "The Paraguayan Corporation: The Agency Which Facilitated the Mennonite Settlement in the Chaco" (History Senior Seminar paper, Goshen College, 1965), 15–18; Bender, "Intercontinental Company, Limited," *Global Anabaptist Mennonite Encyclopedia Online*, last modified December 8, 2013, http://gameo.org/index.php?title=Intercontinental_Company,_Limited&oldid=104872, last accessed June 7, 2018; Walter Quiring, "The Canadian Mennonite Immigration into the Paraguayan Chaco," *Mennonite Quarterly Review* 8, no. 1 (1934): 36. The inflation adjustment was made with the Bureau of Labor Statistics (CPI) Inflation Calculator, www.bls.gov/data/inflation_calculator.htm, last accessed August 8, 2018.

[205] M. W. Friesen, *New Homeland*, 141–42.

[206] The exact number is uncertain. Estimates range from 1,742 to 1,876. For a list of sources and figures, see F. H. Epp, *Mennonites in Canada, 1920–1940*, 136, n. 123. See also Guenther, "*Ältester* Martin C. Friesen," 188; Cornelius J. Dyck, M. W. Friesen, and U. S. Friesen, "Menno Colony (Boquerón Department, Paraguay)," *Global Anabaptist Mennonite Encyclopedia Online*, last modified November 18, 2013, http://gameo.org/index.php?title=Menno_Colony_(Boquer%C3%B3n_Department,_Paraguay)&oldid=103606, last accessed June 7, 2018.

FIGURE 1.4 Schoolhouse in the Menno Colony village of Schoental, n.d. Samuel McRoberts photo collection 713-BK6-174, Mennonite Heritage Archives

Mennonites, some families pragmatically retained their Canadian citizenship on the chance that Paraguay did not work out.[207] Out of a total Manitoba and Saskatchewan population of approximately 45,000 Mennonites, 7,735 left for Mexico and Paraguay, and repeated once again the measures that their ancestors had taken in the 1870s (Fig. 1.4).

Under the constellation of power, money, and politics that made the immigration possible, separatist Mennonites continued to view themselves as humble subjects rather than assertive citizens. In lieu of a tsar or queen, the separatist Mennonites now looked to McRoberts, Casado, and the Paraguayan government as adopted monarchs to whom they would obsequiously communicate their wishes. A 1930 letter from Menno Colony member Peter A. Falk to McRoberts testifies to this observation. The letter concerned a financial discrepancy that Falk had

---

[207] Acquiring a Canadian passport was expensive, so most migrants traveled under the colony's group passport. Into the 1930s, enough Menno Colony residents retained their status as British subjects for the German legation in Paraguay to make note of it. See Dr. Hans Karl Paul Eduard Büsing, "Nr. 371, 2 Durchdrucke," R127972e, PA AA.

encountered when working with employees of the Corporación Paraguaya. As a salutation Falk stated,

Now my dear sir, you will probably, after looking through this imperfect writing, think or say to yourself, how presumptuous and daring it is for one so insignificant to be so bold as to write a letter to me personally, and you certainly have a right to think so for I am in fact as compared with you in worldly reputation and standing a nobody, but in spite of this I make this imperfect appeal to your Christian character ...[208]

Separatist Mennonites were not afraid to speak to the highest authorities but they did so in the language of subjects and not citizens.

In the late nineteenth century, Mennonites became British subjects to claim their land, yet by the 1920s Canadian citizenship entailed more than simply plowing the prairie. It required adopting rights and responsibilities inimical to separatist Mennonites' insularity. By contrast, Mennonites such as the (West Reserve) Bergthalers and the (East Reserve) Kleine Gemeinde moved in and out of the associative category for decades, sometimes adopting public schools, sometimes reverting to private status, but slowly adapting to representative democracy. Leaders such as Ewert and D. Toews provided a vision for associative Mennonites, but it remained just that – a hazy picture of confessional solidarity and state citizenship that may be achieved with the next conference or annual report. Public schooling was inevitable under this mindset. As in Russia, Mennonites' tendency toward division and mobility in the face of growing state power prompted a new round of Mennonite migrations to the margins of weaker states.

In 1920, the *Manitoba Free Press* summarized the popular view that the separatist Mennonites' case rested on the "assumption that it is a fundamental natural right of any sect, group or nationality to set up a state within the state and arrogate to itself one of the state's prime functions, that of seeing that children are suitably educated to discharge the duties of citizenship."[209] Yet separatist Mennonites did not demand more rights, their own state, or even citizenship. Rather they desired a set of privileges in exchange for their communal autonomy as subjects. Unlike other minorities who balked at Anglo Canadization (such as the French Canadians), separatist Mennonites rejected the liberal language of natural

---

[208] Peter A. Falk, May 3, 1930 letter to McRoberts, Corporación Paraguay: Letters from Mennonites, January 1927–January 1931, IX-3-3 Paraguayan Immigration 6/32, Mennonite Central Committee Archives (hereafter, MCCA), Akron, PA.

[209] "The Plea of the Mennonites," *Manitoba Free Press*, May 18, 1920, 15.

rights, legal equality, and personal freedom. As a result, they could not articulate their worldview in terminology that provincial governments or associative Mennonites were willing to acknowledge.

And so, the separatist Mennonites who created the Menno Colony voluntarily moved to a new state that admired their industry and ethnicity and where they again separated themselves from society. Though they continued to correspond with family members in Canada, they remained detached from the conferences that they felt had deceived their brethren. Before their departure, the emigrants wrote a polite letter to the Ottawa government thanking them for decades of peace and prosperity. This quaint and deferential gesture placed separatist Mennonites in a different time, and so they were required to live in a different place, where they would once again be labeled as citizens but would be allowed to live as privileged subjects.

2

A Sort of Homecoming (1929–1931)

At 11:00 p.m. on November 9, 1929, the Neufeld family packed thirteen bags and a featherbed into their horse-drawn wagon and set off across the frozen Siberian landscape. Their destination was Moscow. Kornelius A. Neufeld had already sold everything of value at a fraction of its cost and the family left at night to avoid being noticed. Given the immense distance and the regime's growing harassment of Mennonites, the Neufelds feared they might not even make it past the regional capital of Omsk. The Neufelds were successful farmers who spoke Plautdietsch, read High German, and were members of a small Mennonite community near the Trans-Siberian Railway line. In the preceding weeks, news had filtered through Siberia's Mennonite villages that families were being granted exit visas by the presidium of the All-Russian Central Executive Committee. Without a backup plan, the Neufelds hoped to migrate to Canada.[1]

Across the Soviet Union, and especially in Siberia, thousands of Mennonite families made a similar decision to abandon their homes in the face of Stalin's burgeoning war against the so-called kulak class of farmers.[2] As early as February – but especially from September to

---

[1] Kornelius K. Neufeld, *Flucht aus dem Paradies: Damals vor Moskau* (Weisenheim am Berg, Germany: Agape, 2005), 25–28.

[2] The flight to Moscow was highly disorganized and those involved included German-speaking Lutherans, Catholics, Baptists, and Adventist families who lived near Mennonite settlements. Some families had had their properties confiscated in the preceding months while others, like the Neufeld family, had abandoned their properties because they feared that confiscation was imminent. Fritz Adalbert Ernst von Twardowski, "Memorandum by Twardowski," November 5, 1929, Russland Politik. Mennoniten – Deutschstämmige. Deutsche in Russland, GFM 33/4538: L192441, National Archives (hereafter, NA), Kew, England.

December – thousands descended on the capital to request exit visas from the government. Those with money rented dachas in the suburbs and those without money slept wherever they could find shelter.[3] By the end of November, the total number of these individuals had reached 13,000[4] (10,000 of whom were Mennonites[5]).

The Soviet Union's Politburo was aware of the influx by mid-October but did not know what to do with the supposed kulaks.[6] The German government also received news of the situation and identified the group as *Auslandsdeutsche*. Concerned German citizens, led by the relief organization Brüder in Not (Brethren in Need, BiN) – which was initially founded by the German Red Cross in 1922 to help German-speaking victims of the Russian famine – was quickly reorganized to raise public awareness in Germany. Though most individuals hoped to settle in Canada, tensions between Ottawa and the country's provincial governments discouraged the plan. Instead, the United States–based MCC stepped in to find them a new home in Latin America. Within a few weeks, the ragged collective became a critical topic of Soviet, German, and Canadian diplomacy, a symbol of transnational religious and national solidarity, and an important item in the international press.

During the interwar years, mobility rose to new heights and threatened to destabilize the world order.[7] The category of "refugee" was especially vexing for the world's governments because individuals designated as such existed outside the nation-state paradigm. The number of individuals who fell through the cracks is staggering. By one estimate, in 1922 there

---

[3] Ibid., L192460.

[4] Oskar Trautmann, "Memorandum by Trautmann," November 25, 1929, R29275, E160405–E160410, PA AA. Most sources place the number of refugees at 13,000, but some estimates range as high as 18,000. See also Harvey Dyck, *Weimar Germany and Soviet Russia 1926–1933: A Study in Diplomatic Instability* (London: Chatto and Windus, 1966), 163.

[5] "Memorandum," November 15, 1929, GFM 33/4538: L192381, NA; Trautmann, "Memorandum by Trautmann," November 1929, GFM 33/4538: L192405, NA; Dyck, *Weimar Germany*, 163.

[6] Andrey I. Savin, "The 1929 Emigration of Mennonites from the USSR: An Examination of Documents from the Archive of Foreign Policy of the Russian Federation," *Journal of Mennonite Studies* 30 (2012): 47.

[7] On the growth of early-twentieth-century nationalist and philanthropic movements that aimed to address the phenomenon see Sebastian Conrad and Dominic Sachsenmaier, "Introduction," *Competing Visions of World Order: Global Moments and Movements, 1880s–1930s*, ed. Sebastian Conrad and Dominic Sachsenmaier (New York: Palgrave Macmillan, 2007), 1–25. The broad scope of early-twentieth century long-distance migration is covered in Adam McKeown, "Global Migration, 1846–1940," *Journal of World History* 15, no. 2 (2004): 155–89.

were nearly 850,000 Armenian and Russian refugees in Europe, with countless other individuals "trapped" as citizens within hostile states.[8] By 1926 the League of Nations had granted disenfranchised individuals within the Soviet Union the status of "refugee" but it did not provide a normative definition of the term.[9] Clearly much had changed since the 1870s, when 7,000 German-speaking Mennonites relocated without passports from the Russian Empire to the British Empire and transplanted their *Privilegium*, village structures, and religious culture with them *in toto*. Now, governments curated their populations in an attempt to mold them into ideal citizens. They enforced immigration quotas and demanded that their populations conform to a growing list of social, cultural, political, economic, and racial characteristics. Groups that held a wide range of identifications were particularly confounding to authorities. Though Mennonites in the Soviet Union possessed Dutch surnames, they were not Dutch nationals and though they spoke German, they were not German nationals. Technically, they remained Soviet citizens until they left the country. Yet their property was confiscated when they left their villages and their citizenship was a hollow artifact once they were labeled as kulaks. They were first homeless, then rightless, then stateless.

We often assume that governments regard refugees as "a problem" or "a crisis" since they threaten the solidarity of national populations and the integrity of national borders.[10] Yet a tacit feature of a refugee crisis is that it provides domestic interest groups with an opportunity to articulate refugees' similarities or differences to their constituencies. In other words, state and nonstate actors use refugees as a rhetorical tool to

---

[8] See John Hope Simpson, *The Refugee Problem: Report of a Survey* (London: Oxford University Press, 1939), 558–59.

[9] League of Nations, "Arrangement with Respect to the Issue of Certificates of Identity to Russian Refugees," July 5, 1922, *League of Nations Treaty Series* 13, no. 355, www .refworld.org/docid/3dd8b4864.html, last accessed June 7, 2018; League of Nations, "Conference on Russian and Armenian Refugee Questions, Report by the High Commissioner, June 5, 1926," 3, https://biblio-archive.unog.ch/Dateien/CouncilDocs/C -327-1926_EN.pdf, last accessed June 7, 2018. For the term's interwar uses and limitations. see Peter Gatrell, *The Making of the Modern Refugee* (Oxford: Oxford University Press, 2013); Michael Marrus, *The Unwanted: European Refugees from the First World War Through the Cold War* (Philadelphia, PA: Temple University Press, 1985); Claudena M. Skran, *Refugees in Inter-War Europe: The Emergence of a Regime* (New York: Oxford University Press, 1995).

[10] Gatrell, *Making of the Modern Refugee*, 5; Liisa Malkki, *Purity and Exile: Violence, Memory, and National Cosmology Among Hutu Refugees in Tanzania* (Chicago: University of Chicago Press, 1995), 7.

advance normative national and religious identities, collective national and religious narratives, and their visions of an ideal world.

This chapter shows how a range of state and nonstate actors used the Mennonites' varied identifications as farmers, Germans, and Mennonites to advance their own interests and define their constituencies around issues of class, nationality, race, or religion. As a result, this chapter focuses on the conversations surrounding the refugees – the efforts to assign them significance – rather than details about the group itself.[11] The Soviet government labeled the refugees as kulaks and wanted to banish them from the country or exile them internally. The Weimar government considered the group to be German farmers and wished to resettle them in Brazil, where they could establish economic ties to Germany and preserve their Germanness. The rising Nazi Party viewed them as "race comrades" while the Kommunistische Partei Deutschlands (Communist Party of Germany, KPD) argued that helping the refugees was a betrayal of Germany's proletariat. Meanwhile, the faith-based charity BiN viewed the group as national and religious brothers, whose story could be used to raise awareness of Soviet atrocities. Across the Atlantic, Canada's provincial leaders worried that the refugees were sectarians who would thwart their "Canadization" efforts, while the Paraguayan government perceived them as sturdy German pioneers who could solidify solidify the country's nebulous northern border. Meanwhile, the MCC was unconcerned with the refugees' nationality. It wished to settle the group in the Chaco, where they could sustain their "Mennoniteness" and advertise the concept of transnational Mennonite unity in the United States. External groups therefore imbued the 1929 refugee movement with symbolic meanings that far outweighed the refugees' actual strength or numbers.

As the debate over the refugees played out in the press and ricocheted between Moscow, Berlin, Ottawa, Asunción, and La Paz, it also swirled around the refugees and gave them a formative understanding of their shared economic, national, and religious similarities. Consequently, this chapter demonstrates how outsiders' interpretations provided the Fernheim Colony refugees with new ways to collectively understand

---

[11] Several Mennonite memoirs detail the refugees' personal stories. See for example Neufeld, *Flucht aus dem Paradies*; Helmut Isaak, *Your Faith Will Sustain You, and You Will Prevail: The Life Story of Jacob and Elisabeth Isaak* (Norderstedt, Germany: Books on Demand, 2014); H. J. Willms, *At the Gates of Moscow: God's Gracious Aid Through a Most Difficult and Trying Period*, trans. George G. Thielman (Yarrow, BC: Columbia, 1964).

themselves as heroes, victims, Mennonites, Germans, and Paraguayans. The refugees that formed the Fernheim Colony held a few general similarities and many specific differences. They were all German-speaking Mennonites from communities that had witnessed growing prosperity, increased education, and greater cooperation with the Russian state during the so-called Mennonite "golden age" from 1870 to 1914. They had also experienced abuses and setbacks during the First World War and its revolutionary aftermath. Aside from these generalities, they hailed from different local circumstances. By 1932, the Fernheim Colony was composed of three separate groups: the 1,572 refugees who had assembled in Moscow in 1929, 57 voluntary migrants[12] from Poland, and another 370 refugees from Siberia via Harbin, China.[13] A majority of the collective came from Siberia but most had only moved to that region from older settlements in southern Russia in the previous twenty years. They also belonged to different religious branches (of which the Brüdergemeinde and Mennonitengemeinde were the largest) and were members of different economic organizations – the Verband der Bürger Holländischer Herkunft (Association of Citizens of Dutch Descent) in Ukraine and the Allrussischer Mennonitischer Landwirtschaftlicher Verband (All-Russian Mennonite Agricultural Association) in Russia, which maintained different relationships with the Soviet state.[14]

On a personal level, the refugees had different occupations, levels of education, family histories, and migration experiences that inhibited their unity. Some individuals, such as Nikolai Siemens – who founded the Fernheim Colony newspaper *Menno-Blatt* – were cosmopolitan. N. Siemens was born in Crimea in 1895, visited the United States with his family, and settled in Siberia in 1910. After marrying a Polish–German Baptist named Anna Wosnjak Fessner, he attended a Bible school in

---

[12] For the sake of simplicity, I collectively refer to the Fernheim Colony Mennonites as refugees, since less than 1 percent of its population were voluntary migrants.

[13] John D. Thiesen, *Mennonite and Nazi? Attitudes Among Mennonite Colonists in Latin America, 1933–1945* (Kitchener, ON: Pandora Press, 1999), 76–77; P. Klassen, *The Mennonites in Paraguay Volume 1: Kingdom of God and Kingdom of This World*, trans. Gunther H. Schmitt (Filadelfia, Paraguay: Peter P. Klassen, 2003), 81–82.

[14] Peter F. Froese, "Allrussischer Mennonitischer Landwirtschaftlicher Verein," *Global Anabaptist Mennonite Encyclopedia Online*, last modified August 23, 2013, http://gam eo.org/encyclopedia/contents/A446.html, last accessed June 7, 2018; Benjamin B. Janz, "Verband der Bürger holländischer Herkunft," *Global Anabaptist Mennonite Encyclopedia Online*, last modified August 23, 2013, https://gameo.org/index.php?titl e=Verband_der_B%C3%BCrger_holl%C3%A4ndischer_Herkunft, last accessed June 7, 2018.

Tchongrav, Crimea for pastoral training and then returned to Siberia, where he became a Brüdergemeinde preacher in the village of Smolyanovka.[15] Others were less educated and more sedentary, such as the farmer and eventual Fernheim *Oberschulze* Jakob Siemens. He was born in the Chortitza Colony in 1885, where he received a primary-school education. After moving to Siberia, he participated in the Forest Service, married his wife, Sara, and farmed until 1927, when his family was forced to join a collective. On the night of December 17, 1930, they led 217 Mennonites across the frozen Amur River into China on 63 sleds.[16]

Once in Paraguay, the refugees shared with their Menno Colony neighbors the advantage of finding a country that was keen to attract "German" immigrants, but the similarities in their migration stories end there. Menno Colony residents firmly believed that God had ordained their movement to the Chaco, while the Fernheim colonists were more ambivalent about their purpose. Moreover, the Menno colonists had the luxury of researching destinations and purchasing land and supplies prior to the move. The refugees were at the mercy of others. The tenuous circumstances under which the Fernheim Colony was formed began when individuals and families placed their lives in the hands of governments and nongovernmental organizations who saw within them the fears and possibilities of a new world defined by nation states and transnational connections.

CREATING KULAKS

In 1928, the Soviet Union's Stalinist bloc made the destruction of kulaks the focal point of progress in the countryside, through forced grain requisitions, mass exile, and collectivization. Stalin rejected the conventional wisdom of Lenin's New Economic Policy (NEP), which held that if the peasantry were better educated, this would lead to their rationality and atheism. Instead, he argued that the battle for

---

[15] On N. Siemens' life see Alfred Neufeld, "Siemens, Nikolai," in Gerhard Ratzlaff et al., *Lexikon der Mennoniten in Paraguay* (Asunción: Verein für Geschichte und Kultur der Mennoniten in Paraguay, 2009), 387–88; Frieda Siemens Kaethler and Alfred Neufeld (eds.), *Nikolai Siemens der Chacooptimist* (Weisenheim am Berg, Germany: Agape, 2005).

[16] Sara Siemens and children, "Ein Nachruf," *Menno-Blatt* (Fernheim, Paraguay), January 1941, 2–3. See also Helmut T. Huebert, *Events and People: Events in Russian Mennonite History and the People That Made Them Happen* (Winnipeg: Springfield Publishers, 1999), 201–7.

communism was a fundamental struggle between good and evil. Dark forces lurked in the countryside that could rise up and destroy the Bolsheviks' bright future.[17] As with other entities that are based more on myth than reality, the figure of the kulak had myriad local interpretations. Unsurprisingly, most resembled the opposite of the average Russian peasant: wealthy, "foreign," and not members of the Russian Orthodox faith.[18] Due to their socially and economically privileged status before the First World War, the country's large and diffuse German-speaking population made easy targets for local officials who wanted to fulfill their kulak incarceration quotas.[19] In 1929, the German embassy in Moscow estimated the number of German speakers living in the Soviet Union at about 1.2 million individuals.[20] This included 91,134 Mennonites, but even more Catholics and Lutherans, who had accepted Catherine the Great's eighteenth-century manifesto.[21] In general, there was more separating these groups of German speakers – religiously, culturally, politically, and historically – than there was uniting them as a class or nationality.

Poor harvests in Ukraine, Crimea, and the North Caucasus between 1927 and 1930 shifted the center of gravity for essential government grain procurements squarely on Siberia and specifically on the heads of its prosperous farmers.[22] Siberia was consequently the epicenter of Stalin's war against kulaks. Mennonites especially embodied the kulak threat due to their insularity, agricultural unions, relative wealth, and foreign contacts with

---

[17] James Hughes, *Stalinism in a Russian Province: Collectivization and Dekulakization in Siberia* (Basingstoke, UK: Macmillan, 1996), 132.

[18] Golfo Alexopoulos, *Stalin's Outcasts: Aliens, Citizens, and the Soviet State, 1926–1936* (Ithaca, NY: Cornell University Press, 2003), 46; Sheila Fitzpatrick, *Everyday Stalinism: Ordinary Life in Extraordinary Times* (Oxford, UK: Oxford University Press, 1999), 122; Hughes, *Stalinism*, 8.

[19] Some of the Soviet government's highest officials believed that all German-speaking villages were composed of kulaks. See Terry Martin, *The Affirmative Action Empire: Nations and Nationalism in the Soviet Union, 1923–1939* (Ithaca, NY: Cornell University Press, 2001), 320.

[20] Otto Auhagen, "Memorandum by Auhagen," October 11, 1929, GFM 33/4538: L192467, NA.

[21] This number is tallied from Adolf Ehrt's population statistics. His count relies on the Mennonite's Kommission für Kirchenangelegenheiten (Committee for Church Affairs, KfK) 1926 census, which stated that there were 46,830 Mennonites in Ukraine and 44,304 in the Soviet Union (excluding Ukraine). See Ehrt, *Das Mennonitentum in Russland von seiner Einwanderung bis zur Gegenwart* (Berlin: Verlag von Julius Beltz, 1932), 152.

[22] Hughes, *Stalinism*, 22.

coreligionists abroad.[23] Before 1914, they had established about 59 colonies in Siberia and their numbers had reached 21,000.[24] The majority of their settlements were located in the vicinity of Omsk, Slavgorod, and Pavlodar. Whether in Siberia or Ukraine, Mennonites' insularity bothered local and regional authorities. One official noted, "The class differences of the Mennonite population are not outwardly apparent, they are so good [at hiding them] as to be unnoticeable. The poor and laborers are themselves Mennonites, that is to say sectarians, therefore, it is very difficult to use them as a weapon against the sect."[25] A second bluntly stated, "The Mennonite communities are run by wealthy preachers."[26] Linguistic ties did not ensure solidarity among alleged German-speaking kulaks. Some German Lutherans labeled Mennonites "Dutch bandits"[27] and Mennonites likewise held their German-speaking neighbors in contempt.[28] In a few instances, non-landowning Mennonites joined the Bolsheviks and helped liquidate their erstwhile brethren.[29] In the final analysis, the Bolshevik quest to discover a class of individuals that embodied the kulak typology failed – but labeling disparate individuals as kulaks and blaming them for any number of crimes was expedient for welding together a diverse and indifferent peasantry.

Despite Mennonites' self-perception as "the Quiet in the Land," they possessed a leadership elite that had been attuned to events in Moscow since the 1870s.[30] Even after the Revolution, Mennonites retained

[23] Martin, "The Russian Mennonite Encounter with the Soviet State, 1917–1955," *The Conrad Grebel Review* 20, no. 1 (Winter 2002): 31; Colin Neufeldt, "The Flight to Moscow, 1929," *Preservings* 19 (2001): 35.

[24] Petr P. Wiebe, "The Mennonite Colonies of Siberia: From the Late Nineteenth to the Early Twentieth Century," *Journal of Mennonite Studies* 30 (2012): 26. Wiebe bases his figures on Horst Gerlach, *Die Russlandmennoniten: Ein Volk unterwegs* (Kirchheimbolanden, Germany: Horst Gerlach, 1992), 49.

[25] Hildebrandt, *Die Mennoniten in der Ukraine und im Gebiet Orenburg: Dokumente aus Archiven in Kiev und Orenburg* (Göttingen, Germany: Der Göttinger Arbeitskreis, 2006), 101.

[26] Ibid., 99.   [27] Ibid., 45.

[28] See Neufeldt, "Liquidating" Mennonite Kulaks (1929–1930)," *Mennonite Quarterly Review* 83, no. 2 (2009): 221–91.

[29] H. Loewen, "Anti-Menno: Introduction to Early Soviet-Mennonite Literature (1920–1940)," *Journal of Mennonite Studies* 11 (1993): 23–42; Neufeldt, "Re-forging Mennonite *Spetspereselentsy*: The Experience of Mennonite Exiles at Siberian Special Settlements in the Omsk, Tomsk, Novosibirsk and Narym Regions, 1930–1933," *Journal of Mennonite Studies* 30 (2012): 275.

[30] Mennonites elected representatives to the third and fourth Dumas (1907–1917). See Abe J. Dueck, "Mennonite Churches and Religious Developments in Russia 1850–1914," in *Mennonites in Russia 1788–1988: Essays in Honour of Gerhard Lohrenz*, ed. John Friesen (Winnipeg: CMBC Publications, 1989), 174.

FIGURE 2.1 Mennonite dairy in Slavgorod, Siberia. When connected to a horse, the wooden frame in the foreground supplied power to the enterprise. The operation is broadly representative of the comfortable but modest lifestyle of Siberia's Mennonites before the flight to Moscow and Harbin, China, 1927. Source: Archivo Colonia Fernheim

influence in the Ministry of Agriculture and Food where they counted People's Commissar for Agriculture, A. P. Smirnov, as a friend.[31] Moreover, their agricultural skills were badly needed by the nascent government, since agriculture was the engine of the Soviet economy.[32] For this reason, Communist officials allowed the Mennonites to establish economic unions in Ukraine and Russia (Fig. 2.1).[33] Ostensibly, the unions' prerogatives were confined to agriculture but they were also the vanguard protecting Mennonites' social and religious autonomy. As they

[31] Urry, "After the Rooster Crowed: Some Issues Concerning the Interpretation of Mennonite/Bolshevik Relations During the Early Soviet Period," *Journal of Mennonite Studies* 13 (1995); 26–50, 48, n. 39.

[32] James W. Heinzen, *Inventing a Soviet Countryside: State Power and the Transformation of Rural Russia, 1917–1929* (Pittsburgh, PA: University of Pittsburgh Press, 2004), 4.

[33] A filed report to the Executive Committee of the All-Ukrainian Central Executive Committee on July 16, 1924, stated "The existence of the Association of Mennonites as an economic institution is rated very positive because it has set a goal to increase agricultural production." See Hildebrandt, *Mennoniten in der Ukraine*, 28, my translation.

had under the Tsars, Mennonites played to their economic strengths, cultivated powerful friends, and guarded their religious privileges.

Nevertheless, the political changes that accompanied the rise of Stalinism destroyed the fragile truce built on the strengths of Mennonite organization and the weaknesses of the NEP. By the middle of 1929, Mennonites' economic and religious organizations had been terminated, their leaders imprisoned, and their sympathetic contacts in the People's Commissariat of Agriculture dismissed or relocated.[34] Dekulakization represented a new type of homogenizing initiative that was altogether more thorough and more threatening than what they had experienced in the 1870s, and what their coreligionists had experienced in Canada in the early 1920s. Mennonites were not offered a chance to leave, or fined for their presumed transgressions. Instead, the Soviet government demanded their complete and immediate removal from society. With nowhere else to turn, Mennonites looked abroad for salvation. As unlikely as it may have seemed to them, both the German government and the Mennonites in North America were highly interested in their fate.

THE DIPLOMATIC DILEMMA

In keeping with their history of mobilization and migration, thousands of Siberian Mennonites fled to Moscow at the end of 1929. More would have followed if not for government agents that scrambled to staunch the movement. Prospective emigrants often traveled to multiple towns and cities hoping to find a station where they could buy tickets unnoticed. Refugees' long train rides were usually followed by difficulties obtaining food and shelter in the capital. Families disembarked at stations several kilometers outside Moscow – Djangarovka, Perlovka, Kljasma, and Pushkino – where rents were cheaper and where they would not attract attention. Early arrivals had a modest amount of money because they had had more time to sell their possessions, but the majority of refugees were poor.[35] Bread and fuel were especially difficult to find, since disenfranchised individuals could not procure ration cards. In spite of this reality, the *Moscow Review* held that most refugees were of the landed classes (i.e. kulaks) (Fig. 2.2).[36]

---

[34] Urry, "After the Rooster Crowed," 48, n. 39.

[35] Ibid., L192460, L192472-L192473; Hans Kasdorf, *Design of My Journey: An Autobiography* (Fresno: Center for Mennonite Brethren Studies; Nürnberg, Germany: VTR Publications, 2004), 21.

[36] Carl Dienstmann [?], "Aufzeichnung," October 29, 1929, Russland Politik, Mennoniten – Deutschstämmige, Deutsche in Russland, GFM 33/4538: L192456, NA.

FIGURE 2.2 Refugee Peter Kasper with his wife and his cousin in Moscow, Russia. In the background is a dacha rented by the refugees while they awaited their exit to Germany, 1929. Source: Archivo Colonia Fernheim

By this point, it did not matter how wealthy the refugees actually were. They were kulaks and they were attempting to evade justice.

Mennonites contacted every powerful group that they could think of who might grant them exit visas and passports. Women and children took the lead since they were less likely to be arrested. Most wished to go to Canada, under the auspices of D. Toews' CMBC. Mennonites therefore visited or wrote letters to the Soviet Central Committee, the Politburo, and Lenin's wife, Nadezhda Krupskaya. Some wrote to Maxim Gorky, who was exiled in Italy.[37] A number of Mennonite women and children staged a protest in the waiting room of President Mikhail Kalinin's office.[38] The group even mailed petitions to six government offices, closing with the threat that if they were not allowed to emigrate, they would commit suicide on the Kremlin's steps.[39]

Like other German-speaking communities in Eastern Europe before the First World War, Russia's Mennonites did not necessarily understand

---

[37] Auhagen, "Aufzeichnung," October 29, 1929, L192473-74, NA.
[38] Neufeldt, "Flight to Moscow," 39.   [39] Ibid.; Willms, *At the Gates of Moscow*, 62.

themselves to be part of a "German diaspora," or view Germany as their homeland. Their Germanness was defined locally or regionally and involved no clear attachment to the German nation state.[40] Despite Mennonites' indifference to Germany, they did view its embassy and its agricultural attaché, Dr. Otto Auhagen, as potential allies, since Auhagen and the German Foreign Office were already interested in them.[41] The German Foreign Office possessed a highly developed analytical paradigm for interpreting the refugees as *Auslandsdeutsche*. After the First World War, German fears about the country's loss of colonies and territory merged with fears about *Auslandsdeutsche* losing their Germanness, to create the perception that the German nation was weak and in need of support.[42] The Foreign Office therefore monitored and aided *Auslandsdeutsche* around the world by directing money and resources through embassies and back-door channels to fund German business and farm loans and support German newspapers, charities, and schools.[43]

One of the most pressing concerns facing the Weimar government was whether *Auslandsdeutsche* from eastern countries deserved citizenship in the German state. One German-speaking writer in the Soviet Union argued in *Deutsche Post aus dem Osten* that Russian Germans were real Germans, though "when you read the writings about us, you sometimes get the impression that we are a newly discovered people."[44] Annemarie Sammartino summarizes the view from Germany thus: "Germans from

---

[40] Pieter M. Judson, "When Is a Diaspora Not a Diaspora? Rethinking Nation-Centered Narratives About Germans in Habsburg East Central Europe," in *The Heimat Abroad: The Boundaries of Germanness,* ed. Krista O'Donnell, Renate Bridenthal, and Nancy Reagin, 219–47 (Ann Arbor, MI: University of Michigan Press, 2005), 221.

[41] Auhagen, "Aufzeichnung," October 29, 1929, L192473, NA.

[42] On Germany's concern for Russia's German-speakers see James E. Casteel, "The Russian Germans in the Interwar German National Imaginary," *Central European History*, 40, no. 3 (2007): 429–66; James Casteel, "The Politics of Diaspora: Russian German Émigré Activists in Interwar Germany," in *German Diasporic Experiences: Identity, Migration, and Loss,* ed. Mathias Schulze, James M. Skidmore, David G. John, Grit Liebscher, and Sebastian Siebel-Achenbach (Waterloo: Wilfrid Laurier University Press, 2008), 117–29.

[43] Brubaker, *Nationalism Reframed: Nationhood and the National Question in the New Europe* (Cambridge, UK: Cambridge University Press, 1996), 123–24; Thomas Lekan, "German Landscape: Local Promotion of the *Heimat* Abroad," in *The Heimat Abroad: The Boundaries of Germanness,* ed. Krista O'Donnell et al. (Ann Arbor, MI: University of Michigan Press, 2005), 153; Nancy R. Reagin, "German Brigadoon? Domesticity and Metropolitan Perceptions of *Auslandsdeutschen* in Southwest Africa and Eastern Europe," in *The Heimat Abroad: The Boundaries of Germanness,* ed. Krista O'Donnell et al. (Ann Arbor, MI: University of Michigan Press, 2005), 254.

[44] *Deutsche Post aus dem Osten* (Berlin), March 28, 1920, 1.

across the political spectrum – save the extreme left – shared a belief that citizenship should only be available to those who had proven their German identity."[45] Yet there was a lack of agreement among federal and state authorities and between government and private organizations as to what denoted German identity. The German citizenship law of 1913 remained in effect during the Weimar era, but it often yielded to prevailing political winds. The law stated that descendants of a "former German" could be granted citizenship but it did not enumerate the specific attributes of "former Germans" or reveal how far back one could claim German ancestry.[46] During the Weimar years, citizenship was not simply an issue of legal membership in Germany but a battleground for defining the German nation, state, and individual.

Throughout the 1920s, the German government was willing to grant permission for *Auslandsdeutsche* from eastern countries to stay in Germany until they could find new homes elsewhere. The German Red Cross headed up the effort by creating a network of camps. About 100,000 German speakers from Russia alone fled during the First World War, the Bolshevik Revolution, and the ensuing Civil War. As of 1925, about 58,000 remained in Germany.[47] Mennonite refugees from the Soviet Union were a small part of the flood. By the mid-1920s, Camp Lechfeld, a former German army barracks in Bavaria, was a way station for about 20,000 Mennonites who were headed to Canada.[48] For those who attempted to remain in Germany, federal and state governments granted citizenship on an arbitrary basis or left the decision up to local officials. In one instance, an official at the Prussian Welfare Ministry encouraged the *Oberpräsident* (governor) of Kassel to adopt a more cultural understanding of Germanness rather than a legal or technical

---

[45] Annemarie Sammartino, "Culture, Belonging and the Law: Naturalization in the Weimar Republic," in *Citizenship and National Identity in Twentieth-Century Germany*, ed. Eley and Jan Palmowski (Stanford, CA: Stanford University Press, 2008), 59.

[46] "German Imperial and State Citizenship Law. July 22, 1913," *The American Journal of International Law* 8, no. 3, Supplement: Official Documents (1914): 217–27. Germany's citizenship laws generally excluded newcomers and privileged Germans abroad. See Howard Sargent, "Diasporic Citizens: Germans Abroad in the Framing of German Citizenship Law," in *The Heimat Abroad: The Boundaries of Germanness*, ed. Krista O'Donnell et al. (Ann Arbor, MI: University of Michigan Press, 2005), 17–39.

[47] James Casteel, "The Politics of Diaspora: Russian German Émigré Activists in Interwar Germany," in *German Diasporic Experiences: Identity, Migration, and Loss*, ed. Mathias Schulze, James M. Skidmore, David G. John, Grit Liebscher, and Sebastian Siebel-Achenbach (Waterloo: Wilfrid Laurier University Press, 2008), 120.

[48] See Peter Letkemann, "Mennonite Refugee Camps in Germany, 1921–1951: Part I – Lager Lechfeld," *Mennonite Historian* 38, no. 3 (2012): 1–2.

interpretation.[49] In this regard, the German government echoed Soviet administrators who encouraged local officials to define kulaks on a "case-by-case" basis and not "mechanically" or "formally."[50]

Mennonites in the Soviet Union were a special source of consternation for the Foreign Office since they did not cultivate a relationship with Germany. One report filed by a German diplomat in Kharkiv, Ukraine on April 1, 1925, expressed admiration for Mennonites' ability to resist Soviet integration but registered skepticism about their dependability since they "are not politically loyal."[51] This assessment may have been due to the fact that Mennonites eschewed participation in the Soviet Union's schemes to organize its population under national labels. In 1924, the Bolshevik government helped nationalize the country's German speakers by establishing the Volga German Autonomous Soviet Socialist Republic. Yet Mennonites eschewed this organization in favor of their own economic unions.[52] German consular officials in the Soviet Union balanced the perception that the Soviet Union's Mennonites were of German stock with the reality that they were ambivalent about their nationality.

Officials at the German embassy in Moscow were therefore quite aware of the difficulties faced by *Auslandsdeutsche* living in the Soviet Union, but they were at loggerheads among themselves over how to proceed. In the spring of 1929, Auhagen visited Mennonite colonists in Ukraine and Crimea. He was an early proponent of German intervention. In a report filed on May 26, 1929, Auhagen stated, "If the system [of collectivization] remains as it is, it is my conviction that Germanness in the colonies of southern Ukraine and Crimea will face hopeless economic impoverishment, moral decay, and their [the colonies'] eventual destruction."[53] In contrast, German minister Herbert von Dirksen was against intervention

[49] Sammartino, *The Impossible Border: Germany and the East 1914–1922* (Ithaca, NY: Cornell University Press, 2010), 109.

[50] A. S. Kiselev, State Archives of the Russian Federation f. 1235, op. 74, d. 427, 1. 109. Quoted in Alexopoulos, *Stalin's Outcasts*, 48.

[51] On an optimistic note, the report concluded that Mennonites were "harmless nonetheless." See "1 April 1925," R67278, PA AA, 4. Internal reports at the Foreign Office reveal that the government also kept tabs on Mennonite colonies in Canada, Mexico, and Paraguay. See for example R67257 and R67278, PA AA.

[52] Martin, "Russian Mennonite Encounter," 19–20.

[53] Otto Auhagen, *Die Schicksalswende des Russlanddeutschen Bauerntum in den Jahren 1927–1930* (Leipzig: Hirzel, 1942), 43. See also Christoph Mick, *Sowjetische Propaganda, Fünfjahrplan, und deutsche Rußlandpolitik 1928–1932* (Stuttgart: Franz Steiner, 1995), 335.

because it lacked a clear geopolitical incentive. In an August 1, 1929 report, Dirksen claimed the German government could help some German speakers, but helping all would be like trying "to fill a bottomless pit."[54] Dirksen lamented that the refugees would have to go to the Americas, where they would be settled in a "chess board order that endangered the preservation of Germanness."[55] Dirksen also noted that helping Germans in the Soviet Union carried the threat of exacerbating tensions in other European theaters with German-speaking populations, such as southern Tyrol.[56] He concluded that aiding prospective German migrants would cost the government a great deal without benefiting Germany.

When Dirksen returned to Germany for holidays and health treatments, his position was filled by Director of Eastern Affairs Fritz Adalbert Ernst von Twardowski.[57] The embassy's negative attitude toward the refugees changed after Twardowski sent Auhagen to investigate the refugees' living conditions in mid-October. Auhagen was a shrewd civil servant who was familiar with the Soviet system. He brought with him reporters from the *Hamburger Nachrichten*, *Kölnische Zeitung*, *Chicago Daily News*, *Christian Science Monitor*, and the *International News Service*.[58] Between October 11 and October 18, 1929, Auhagen filed several reports on the Mennonite camps and Mennonites' place of origin.[59] He estimated about 700,000 to 800,000 German speakers wished to emigrate "as fast as possible."[60]

Persuaded by Auhagen and Unruh – a member of the 1921 Russian Mennonite study commission and the German Mennonite representative to BiN – that the refugees' passage to Canada was assured (it was not), the German government permitted a limited number of refugees to enter Germany.[61] On October 15, the Germans dispatched diplomat Carl

---

[54] Herbert von Dirksen, "Lage der deutschen Kolonisten in der UdSSR," August 1, 1929, R83850, K480945, PA AA.

[55] Ibid., K480947.   [56] Ibid., K480946.

[57] Twardowski remained at this post until November.

[58] Mick, *Sowjetische Propaganda*, 357; Auhagen, *Schicksalswende*, 49 ff.

[59] Erwin Warkentin, "Germany's Diplomatic Efforts During the 1929 Mennonite Immigration Crisis," *Mennonite Historian* 31, no. 3 (2005), 4–5, 8 and "Mennonites Before Moscow: The Notes of Dr. Otto Auhagen," *Journal of Mennonite Studies* 26 (2008): 201–20.

[60] Auhagen, "Memorandum by Auhagen," October 18, 1929.

[61] Unruh made this claim based on the fact that many refugees held prepaid tickets bought for them by Canadian relatives, though the tickets did not guarantee Canadian naturalization. H. Dyck, *Weimar Germany and Soviet Russia 1926–1933*, 165–66.

Dienstmann to Moscow to meet with Soviet diplomat Boris Shtein and accept them.[62] In the preceding months, the Soviets had granted some Swedish-speaking individuals the ability to immigrate to Sweden. Dienstmann's mission was to ask for a similar privilege on behalf of the German government.[63] The Soviet Foreign Ministry responded in the affirmative and promised to cooperate as long as the Germans did not publicize their demands.[64]

On October 18, 1929, the Politburo issued a resolution, signed by Joseph Stalin, which stated that the government did not object to the emigration of Mennonite refugees.[65] The next day, N. J. Raivid, of the Second Western Department of the Soviet Foreign Ministry, relayed a message to N. N. Krestinsky, one of the regime's plenipotentiary representatives in Germany, that it was a good way for the Soviet Union to rid itself of kulaks.[66] On October 29, 1929, the first group of 323 refugees left Moscow for Leningrad. They were transferred to a steamer and arrived in Kiel, Germany on November 3.[67] Before they left, the refugees' military escorts confiscated their money and valuables. According to one source, a Soviet official laconically told the Mennonites, "You came to Russia naked and we will send you forth naked."[68]

The proposal worked for both governments and it appeared that the whole situation could be resolved through high-level negotiations. Then on October 30, the German consulate in Montreal informed Berlin that the Canadian government could not commit to accepting refugees.[69] Meanwhile, a second refugee transport left Moscow for Leningrad on October 31.[70] Now the German government faced a decision. It could drop the matter, avoid the financial burden of caring for the refugees, and risk provoking the wrath of the German press or it could accept the

---

[62] Neufeldt, "Flight to Moscow," 40. [63] Savin, "1929 Emigration," 47. [64] Ibid.

[65] *Etnokonfessiia v soveiskom gosudarstve. Mennonity Sibiri v 1920–1980-e gg Annotirovannyi sbornik arkhivnykh dokumentov I materialov. Izbrannye dokumenty.* Compiled by A. I. Savin (Novosibirsk-Saint Petersburg: n.p., 2006), 320–21. Quoted in Savin, "1929 Emigration," 47.

[66] Savin, "1929 Emigration," 48.

[67] Peter Letkemann, "Mennonite Refugee Camps in Germany, 1921–1951: Part II – Lager Mölln," *Mennonite Historian* 38, no. 4 (2012): 1–2 and 10, 1.

[68] Donald Day, "Russia Blocks Ruined German Farmers' Flight: 'Naked You Came, Naked You Go,' Says Moscow," *Chicago Daily Tribune,* November 4, 1929, 19.

[69] Trautmann, "Memorandum by Trautmann," November 25, 1929. Neufeldt dates the Canadian decision to October 28. See "Flight to Moscow," 41.

[70] This group remained in Leningrad until it was allowed to continue to Germany on November 29. See Letkemann, "Part II – Lager Mölln," 2.

refugees, bear the costs of their support, and reap favorable publicity for its sympathetic treatment of *Auslandsdeutsche*.

The refugees appeared as an item on President Paul von Hindenburg's cabinet minutes on November 9, and this instigated a debate about what the German government owed German speakers in the Soviet Union.[71] Interestingly, there was no discussion about the historic or contemporary connections the refugees had to the German state. Cabinet officials accepted that the refugees were German farmers so the very idea that Germans were being abused in the Soviet Union precluded any debate as to what constituted Germanness and whether these particular refugees were Germans. Foreign minister Julius Curtius suggested that if the German state did not help these "countrymen" then Germany's international prestige might suffer.[72] Abandoning the refugees would define the limits of Germany's foreign policy and perhaps its impotency when it came to protecting Germans abroad. A more skeptical official by the name of Planck invoked the refugee movement of 1919, when German-speaking individuals "returning" from the Soviet Union swamped Germany's borders, and proposed that Germany simply buy the refugees return tickets to Siberia under the auspices of the Red Cross.[73]

For a time, the German government entertained the idea of settling Mennonites in Prussia, where they would serve as a bulwark against the country's eastern neighbors and lessen the country's reliance on Polish farmworkers. Auhagen made a similar proposition in an October 13 letter to the Reichsminister für Ernährung und Landwirtschaft (Government Minister for Food and Agriculture) by noting that these "precious elements" would "be very suitable material as East Prussian settlers."[74] Now Reichstag representatives from the Deutsche Demokratische Partei (German Democratic Party, DDP), the Deutsche Volkspartei (German People's Party, DVP), and the Deutsche Zentrumspartei (Center Party, Z), adopted this line at

---

[71] "Sitzung des Reichsministeriums aus der Niederschrift über die Ministerbesprechung," November 9, 1929, R43 I/141, vol. 1, L196168, Bundesarchiv (hereafter, BA) Berlin-Lichterfelde, Germany.

[72] Julius Curtius, "Memorandum by Curtius," November 6, 1929, R29275, E160292. See also Twardowski, "Memorandum by Twardowski," November 11, 1929, GFM 33/4538: L192411, NA.

[73] "Rückführung deutschstämmiger Kolonisten aus Rußland," R43 I/141, vol. 1, L196156-L196158, BA.

[74] Auhagen, *Schicksalswende*, 54–55.

a meeting of party leaders on November 14.[75] Cabinet minutes indicate the representatives felt that "East Prussia and eastern Germany in general could undoubtedly accept a great number of settlers."[76] Yet twelve days later, the Zentralorgan der Deutschen Bauernschaft (Central Organ of the German Farmers' Association) tendered the dissenting position that it was impossible to resettle the refugees without spending a great deal of time and money. According to the association, "The Russian peasant families live on grain production and it is quite clear that they would never find a living on German soil in today's competitive conditions." It argued that accepting even a small number of *Rückwanderer* (return migrants) would only be possible if refugees took low-level positions as farmhands.[77]

The idealism of settling the refugees in Germany gave way to more practical considerations when the cabinet decided to *temporarily* accept refugees until a permanent host country could be found. The government granted refugees "letters of identification" instead of German citizenship, which allowed the regime to publicly demonstrate its support for the refugees while ensuring that they would not remain in Germany.[78] Based on a quota of 13,000 individuals, the cabinet earmarked up to 6,000,000 reichsmark for their transportation and housing.[79] Within days of this decision, the government established the Reichskommissar für die Deutschrussen Hilfe (Government Commission for Aid to German Russians) under the auspices of the Minister of the Interior.[80]

---

[75] "Niederschrift über eine Parteiführerbesprechung am Donnerstag der 14 Nov 1929 nachm. 5 Uhr im Reichskanzlerhause," R43 I/141, vol. 1, L196193, BA. The representatives were Erich Koch-Weser (DDP), Albert Zapf (DVP) and Johannes Bell (Z). The eastern settlement option was disseminated through government circles but was never officially pursued. For example, in January 1930 the secretary for the Imperial Colonial Office wrote to the Society for German Settlement and Migration that refugees would "constitute a very valuable part of the colonization of the nationally and racially endangered parts of the country." See "Entschließung," R43 I/141, vol. 1, L196247–L196248, BA.

[76] "Niederschrift über eine Parteiführerbesprechung."

[77] "Russlandbauern als deutsche Siedler," November 26, 1929, R43 I/141, vol. 1, L196231, 115, BA.

[78] [Walter?] de Haas "Memorandum by de Haas," November 11, 1929, GFM 33/4538: L192408, NA.

[79] "Sitzung des Reichsministeriums," November 18, 1929, R43 I/141, vol. 1, L196228, BA. The German Treasury later reduced the amount to 3.5 million reichsmark. See Neufeldt, "Flight to Moscow," 43.

[80] "Maßnahmen zu Gunsten der aus Rußland abwandernden deutschstämmigen Bauern," 28 November, 1929," R43 I/141, vol. 1, L196233, BA.

Even with this ad hoc solution in place, a month was to pass before further transports would be allowed to leave the Soviet Union, and during this time the refugees' designation as *Auslandsdeutsche* remained useful for German propaganda. Perhaps due more to the publicity surrounding the refugees than the acuteness of their plight or the size of their group, Hindenburg proclaimed that it was essential to care for these "unfortunate farmers of the German race."[81] Hindenburg also stated that the DVP and the Reichspartei des deutschen Mittelstandes (Reich Party of the German Middle Class, WP) stood ready to help.[82] As honorary president of the German Red Cross, he "directed a heartfelt plea to all Germans in[side] and out[side] of Germany each according to his abilities to contribute help to their German kinsmen."[83] In a symbolic act of solidarity with *Auslandsdeutsche*, Hindenburg donated 200,000 reichsmark from his discretionary presidential budget to the cause.[84] He also promised to write a thank-you note to anyone who donated 1,000 reichsmark or more to the effort.[85] The initiative was a natural extension of the country's domestic and international insecurities and identified the German state with an abstract, transnational Germanness. It appeared to have all the makings of a publicity coup, but it provoked more turmoil than the government anticipated.

PRESS PROBLEMS

Hindenburg's proposal came at the end of a turbulent year and it was met with a cacophony of responses. The year 1929 brought the tenth anniversary of the contentious Treaty of Versailles, and the New York stock market crash in October only deepened Germany's political and economic woes. The refugee situation splashed across the country's newspapers as an issue that could divide or unite Germany, and it quickly morphed into a debate about what the German nation and state owed *Auslandsdeutsche*. Outside Germany, the international press seized on the story to reaffirm conventional wisdom that states should protect their nations. The refugees were meaningful because they were malleable.

---

[81] "Memorandum to Dr. Pünder," November 12, 1929, R43 I/141, vol. 1, L196164, BA.
[82] "WTB," GFM 33/4538: L192399, NA. The Reichspartei des deutschen Mittelstandes replaced the Wirtschaftspartei des deutschen Mittelstandes, which existed from 1920 to 1925, though it retained the Wirtschaftspartei abbreviation, WP.
[83] Ibid.　　[84] "Memorandum to Dr. Pünder," L196164.
[85] Neufeldt, "Flight to Moscow," 43.

By early November, the refugees were being given top billing in a range of international news outlets. Perhaps at no other point in history had a group of Mennonites achieved such notoriety. Publications cast Mennonites in various molds, including "foreign settlers" living in Russia, "sober and industrious farmers," "peasant families," "a peaceful sect," and "fair-haired ... colonists," but they were always "Germans."[86] An editorial in the *Chicago Tribune* opined "The suffering of the Mennonites has met with a prompt if unavailing response from Germans, who have not ceased to regard these Russian peasants as Germans despite centuries of physical and political separation."[87] Halfway around the globe the story resonated with a *Times of India* reader, Ardeshir Edalji Bengali, who saw in the Mennonite refugees a warning against an independent, communistic India. In Bengali's view, the Mennonites "are a Christian Sect with almost Buddhistic tenets of non-violence ... They ought to prove betimes a warning to my countrymen."[88] The specifics of the Mennonites – their particular history, faith, and culture – meant little and their story could symbolize anything from romantic nationalism, to the threat of Bolshevism, to the hypocrisy of a government that cared more about *Auslandsdeutsche* than about poor Germans in Germany. The fact that most refugees were from a relatively unknown religious confession made the story even more pliable.

In Germany, the fractured Weimar press exhibited a stark difference of opinions about the refugees and about *Auslandsdeutsche* in general. Coverage of the Soviet Union's German-speaking communities was a critical topic in the press during the 1920s, especially when it became clear that the Soviet government was targeting German-speaking citizens for grain requisitions and disenfranchisement.[89] Outlets ranging from the center-left *Dresdner Neuesten Nachrichten* to the far-right *Völkische Kurier* advanced interpretations of what *Auslandsdeutsche* meant to Germany, but generally portrayed them as sturdy, hardworking, and

---

[86] Walter Duranty, "Mennonite Exodus Disturbs Russia," *New York Times*, November 10, 1929, E48; "5,300 Russians Going to Canada Reach Kiel," *New York Times*, November 5, 1929, 7; Donald Day, "Russia Blocks Ruined German Farmers' Flight" *Chicago Daily Tribune*, November 4, 1929, 19; "German Farmers of Siberia," *Manchester Guardian*, November 11, 1929, 12. Foreign Office memos generally referred to the Mennonites as a distinct group, regardless of what was written in the press.

[87] "The Plight of the Mennonites," *Chicago Daily Tribune*, November 27, 1929, 12.

[88] Ardeshir Edalji Bengali, "A Russian Model. Warning to People of India," *The Times of India*, January 9, 1930, 3.

[89] H. Dyck states that the German press "reacted with a volcanic anti-Soviet campaign" to the refugees' situation; *Weimar Germany and Soviet Russia 1926–1933*, 162–63.

resilient. On a more existential level, the refugees symbolized German insecurities about the country's reduced borders, the spread of communism, and the country's tenuous social and economic connections abroad.[90] Germans were concerned about the refugees but they were also concerned about what those refugees' plight meant for themselves.

From the fascist right, the Nazi paper *Völkischer Beobachter* used the refugees to articulate some of the most strident claims about German racial solidarity. Between November 1929 and January 1930, the paper published no fewer than fifteen articles on the refugees. Editor Arthur Rosenberg and other contributors attacked the Soviet regime with articles such as "The German Peasantry in Russia, a Parable of the Incompetence of the Parasitic Moscow Government," and waxed melodramatic about Russia's Germans who preserved their German culture "more than some communities within the German state's own borders."[91] Unsurprisingly, the National Socialists ignored the refugees' nonviolent religious beliefs, using them simply as a platform for deriding the "so-called" German embassy and its inability to save "blood comrades" from the "Mongoloid" flood.[92]

On the other end of the political spectrum, Germany's communist press used the situation to position itself as the defender of Germany's working class. On November 14, *Rote Fahne*, the official KPD organ, acquired photographs of a memorandum supposedly written by Auhagen on August 1, 1929.[93] It ran a front-page article (accompanied by numerous exclamation points) excoriating the German government for interfering in the Soviet Union's domestic politics and stealing bread from Germany's proletariat to feed kulak outlaws.[94] Importantly, the nationalist and communist presses both tacitly agreed that the Mennonites were

---

[90] Casteel, "Russian Germans," 450–52.

[91] "6000 deutsche Bauern mit Verbannung nach Sibirien bedroht," *Völkischer Beobachter* (Munich), November 12, 1929, 5.

[92] "Das deutsche Bauernsterben in Sowjetrussland," *Völkischer Beobachter* (Munich), November 24 and 25, 1929, 1.

[93] The official document bears Dirksen's name. "Die Not der Deutschen in der USSR ein entlarvter Wahlschwindel!" *Rote Fahne* (Berlin), November 14, 1929, 1. It was later claimed that the source of the leak was an official named Zarske "with a pretty bad reputation" who worked in the German immigration office and employed a communist typist. See Trautmann, "Memorandum by Trautmann," November 16, 1929, GFM 33/4538: L192359, NA.

[94] "Die Not der Deutschen," *Rote Fahne* (Berlin). See also, "Millionen für die kulaken – Nichts für die deutschen werktätigen Massen," *Rote Fahne* (Berlin), December 1, 1929, 3.

prosperous German farmers and their religious peculiarities were inconsequential.

After the publication of the *Rote Fahne* article, the KPD seized on the hypocrisy of the government's support for "kulak immigration" to Germany by claiming that many of their country's poorer farmers were simultaneously being forced to immigrate to other countries.[95] They articulated their disgust in a Reichstag interpellation, which read:

The decision of the German government to carry out a relief operation for known Russian kulaks who, in their fanatical struggle against the socialization of agriculture and the construction of socialism in Soviet Russia, desire to emigrate from the Soviet Union is an unprecedented interference of capitalist Germany in the internal affairs of the Russian workers' state.[96]

The sentiments expressed in *Völkischer Beobachter* and *Rote Fahne* strike at the paradox of what it meant for the Weimar Republic to help *Auslandsdeutsche*. On one hand, the KPD argued for the integrity of state borders, at least until the international triumph of communism. On the other, the *Völkischer Beobachter* argued for a borderless understanding of Germanness, at least until the German state could expand enough to include all Germans.

Yet in 1929, the annexation of Eastern Europe by the German state was simply one nationalist fantasy among many. There is no teleology connecting German nationalist aims in 1929 and German tanks rolling through the Soviet countryside twelve years later. Rather, the Germanness imagined by most late-Weimar Germans, including the government, would be established through connections, not conquest. *Auslandsdeutsche* represented a global web of cultural and economic nodes that could potentially be united and guided by the German nation state. *Auslandsdeutsche* were vital to Germany not as potential residents but as landowners and economic contacts abroad.[97] As a result, the government was relatively unenthusiastic about aiding poor farmers in Germany, but monitored and supported *Auslandsdeutsche*.

After the *Rote Fahne* exposé, the German embassy begged the country's dailies to cool their polemics about the Soviet regime, but it found itself under siege.[98] Led by the center-right *Kölnische Zeitung* and

---

[95] *Verhandlungen des Reichstags: IV Wahlperiode 1928*, vol. 426 (Berlin: Reichsdruckerei, 1930), 3308.
[96] Ibid.   [97] Reagin, "German Brigadoon?" 254.
[98] Twardowski, "Memorandum by Twardowski," November 19, 1929, GFM 33/4538: L192334 and L192387, NA.

Dresdner Neueste Nachrichten, journalists accused Dirksen of dereliction of duty owing to his health treatments in Germany.[99] By November 25, one Soviet official named Litwinow complained to Dirksen that he "lamented" the attitude of the German press whose "violent language had made a favorable situation very difficult."[100] Other Kremlin authorities were growing exasperated by the German government's inability to find a host country. On November 17, Twardowski informed Germany's Foreign Office that the Soviet Joint State Political Directorate (OGPU) had already arrested over 1,000 men.[101]

Time was running out for the refugees, including the Neufeld family. Soon after arriving in the Moscow suburb of Kljasma in mid-November, the family was visited by the OGPU. State officials took father K. A. and the oldest son, Heinrich, to a makeshift jail in the basement of a nearby school.[102] After being incarcerated for several days, the men were allowed to leave with the stipulation that they would return to Siberia within forty-eight hours.[103] Yet once freed, the family moved to a new Moscow suburb. During this time, two of the older children, Marie and Peter, commuted daily to Moscow, where they were told by the German embassy that their family would receive documentation at their former address in Kljasma. Risking discovery, the Neufeld family returned to Kljasma. A few nights later – while K. A. and Heinrich hid outside in the snow – the family was again visited by the OGPU. To their bewilderment, they were informed that they could leave the country.[104]

On November 18, Hindenburg's cabinet bypassed budget committee approval and sanctioned the use of state funds to accept refugees.[105] The decision came too late for some. Within a week, about 8,000 colonists had been brusquely returned to their villages or exiled to labor camps.[106] Refugees who evaded OGPU agents and possessed the required money and papers were transported to Germany by train between November 29

[99] Dirksen, "Memorandum to Schubert," November 30, 1929, Person 2782, Dirksen, PA AA.
[100] Dirksen, "Memorandum," November 25, 1929, GFM 33/4538: L192317, NA. This was likely Minister Maxim Litwinow, who organized the Litwinow Pact in February 1929.
[101] Twardowski, "Memorandum by Twardowski," November 18, 1929, R29275, E160358–E160359, PA AA.
[102] Neufeld, *Flucht aus dem Paradies*, 44. [103] Ibid., 97. [104] Ibid., 109–14.
[105] "Sitzung des Reichsministeriums," November 18, 1929, L196228.
[106] Dyck, *Weimar Germany*, 172; "Letter from H. S. Bender to Maxim Litwinow, People's Commissar for Foreign Affairs of the U.S.S.R.," June 16, 1930, CMBC, Immigration Movement I, Series 1, A. General Correspondence 1923–1946, vol. 1181, 122, MHC.

FIGURE 2.3 Refugee feeding station on the train platform in Riga, Latvia, 1929. Photo used courtesy of Mennonite Historical Library, Goshen (IN) College

and December 9.[107] The total number transported to Germany stood at 5,671. Of these, 3,885 were Mennonites, 1,260 were Lutherans, 468 were Catholics, 51 were Baptists, and 7 were Adventists (Fig. 2.3).[108]

By the end of 1929, the Soviet Union no longer entertained the possibility of a mass, legal departure of German-speaking kulaks. The costs in time, money, and diplomatic wrangling made the option impossible. Perhaps the decision was ideological as much as it was practical. Stalin's 1924 plan to establish socialism in one country confined communism's universal mandate to specific geographic parameters. Allowing unrepentant kulaks to leave the country gave the regime's mortal enemies a chance to escape justice and history itself. The Soviet Union's German-language paper *Deutsche Zentralzeitung* had already predicted the kulaks' fate when it gleefully announced in mid-November 1929 that the kulak "is sentenced to death."[109] The only options were internal exile or physical

---

[107] Letkemann, "Part II – Lager Mölln," 2.
[108] Neufeldt, "Flight to Moscow," 43. See also Abschrift II B 63361/17.2, SA.II.1404, 53, MLA.
[109] *Der Deutschen Zentralzeitung*, November 13, 1929. Quoted in Twardowski, "Twardowski to Trautmann," November 19, 1929, GFM 33/4538: L192349, NA; "Lage der deutschen Kolonisten und der Landwirtschaft in der UdSSR," December 18, 1929, GFM 33/4538: L192271–L192272, NA.

destruction. The Soviet government energetically pursued both well into the 1930s.[110]

REFUGE FOR THE REFUGEES

The Mennonite refugees entered the divisive atmosphere of late-Weimar Germany with little understanding that they sat at the nexus of competing opinions about *Auslandsdeutsche*. They initially arrived in Camp Hammerstein, Germany (now Czerne, Poland) where they found temporary housing in five abandoned army barracks. Some were also sent to Prenzlau, Germany after a measles epidemic broke out in the Hammerstein camp. Eventually, all of the refugees were consolidated at a vacant military academy in Mölln, Germany. While they waited for a host country to open its doors, representatives from BiN in Germany and the MCC in the United States visited them to evaluate their Germanness and Mennoniteness. Their assessments indicate that both agencies used the situation to promote different brands of national and religious solidarity.[111] The former viewed the refugees as their national and religious brethren, victimized by a foreign, atheist power. The latter viewed them as members of a global confession of Mennonites. Both needed to convince their constituencies that helping the refugees was a meaningful enterprise. Yet to do this, they had to represent the refugees as essentially similar to Germans in Germany and Mennonites in the United States.

Though BiN was primarily an evangelical Christian organization, it was sponsored by a wide range of associations from across the religious and political spectrum including the Red Cross, the German Caritas Association, the Hauptausschuss für Arbeiterwohlfahrt (Steering Committee for the Workers' Welfare Association), and the Zentralwohlfahrtsstelle der deutschen Juden (Central Welfare Office of German Jews) among others.[112] Until the Nazis seized power in

---

[110] See Sheila Fitzpatrick, *Everyday Stalinism: Ordinary Life in Extraordinary Times* (New York: Oxford University Press, 1999), 122ff.

[111] Mennonite aid organizations including the CMBC, Hollandsch Doopsgezind Emigranten Bureau (Dutch Mennonite Emigration Office), and the German Mennonite relief organization Christenpflicht (Christian's Duty) played smaller roles in coordinating and financing the refugees.

[112] "Memorandum to Hermann Müller," January 22, 1930, R43 I/141, vol., 1, L196245–L196246, BA. See also "Bericht über die Gründungssitzung des Evangelischen Hilfsausschusses Brüder in Not," November 22, 1929, Church Archives, Box 13, Stadtarchiv Mölln, Germany (hereafter, SAM).

1933 – after which the organization was repurposed as a supplier of "Hitler aid" to the Soviet Union – the organization's ecumenism implied that all of these groups were equally German.

Both BiN and local Germans greeted the new arrivals as long-lost brethren. It was the Christmas season, so refugees were presented with fir boughs, flower garlands, and a large banner of the German Reich at the Hammerstein camp. Major D. Fuchs gave a welcome speech and called them Germany's "disposed and scattered children." The speech was followed by a meal served on linen-covered tables.[113] Refugees were also given sweets and a "practical gift."[114] Residents near the camps invited refugees to their houses for Christmas dinners and celebrations. Deeply moved, refugee H. J. Willms wrote that while the refugees "had become no better than slaves in Russia, here they were treated as fully-fledged fellow countrymen."[115] The refugees had lost their homeland in Russia but discovered a new one in Germany (Fig. 2.4).

Although the refugees looked and spoke German, they did not think as such, at least according to their hosts. One of the best ways of reeducating the refugees was to make them aware of German political life. To this end, a contingent of nationalist students from Berlin visited the Prenzlau camp.[116] The students lectured the refugees on the greatness of the German nation and held discussion groups in order to bring the insecurities of Germany's 1918 Revolution "nearer to the farmers." Subsequent topics including "10 years rebuilding," "Germany as a world trading power," and "German agriculture," affirmed that the Mennonites were a part of the German nation and would remain connected to Germany no matter where they resettled.[117] Yet Mennonites' sense of German unity was checked by aggressive confrontations with German communists who wished to debate them on Soviet domestic policy. These encounters often

---

[113] Quoted in Willms, *At the Gates of Moscow*, 96.

[114] "Bericht über die Sitzung das Evang. Hilfsausschusses "Brüder in Not," January 9, 1930, SAM, 5.

[115] Willms, *At the Gates of Moscow*, 96.

[116] Grant Grams, *German Emigration to Canada and the Support of Its Deutschtum During the Weimar Republic* (New York: Peter Lang, 2001), 289; Siegfried Kraft, *Die rußlanddeutschen Flüchtlinge des Jahres 1929/1930 und ihre Aufnahme im Deutschen Reich: Eine Untersuchung über die Gründe der Massenflucht der deutschen Bauern und ein Beitrag zur Kenntnis der Behandlung volksdeutscher Fragen im Weimarer Zwischenreich*, Inaugural Dissertation zur Erlangung der Doktorwürde einer Hohen Philosophischen Fakultät der Martin Luther-Universität Halle-Wittenberg (Halle: Eduard Klinz Buchdruck-Werkstätte, 1939), 62.

[117] Kraft, *Die rußlanddeutschen Flüchtlinge*, 62–63.

FIGURE 2.4 Christmas celebration for the refugees in Hammerstein, Germany, 1929. Used with permission, Mennonite Archival Image Database (MAID), https://archives.mhsc.ca/ Photo ID: CA CMBS NP015-01-13

degenerated into shouting matches, with the communists accusing Mennonites of being "murderers of the working people." Others threw rocks over the camp's fences, hoping to strike a passerby. According to Willms, many of the refugees "could not understand why these Communists ... were allowed to roam the streets freely."[118]

Beyond the camp walls, BiN advertised the suffering of the refugees as a concern for all patriotic Germans.[119] While the refugees were still in the Soviet Union, the Evangelischen Preßverband (Evangelical Press Association) initiated a propaganda campaign in the country's papers.[120] In BiN's first press release, dated November 12, 1929, the organization exclaimed "a catastrophe has broken out against Germans abroad ... the fate of one German affects every German!" It aroused pathos in its readers by recalling memories of Germany's hunger years during the First World War. The article assured readers that the Mennonites' ancestors had immigrated to Russia centuries ago but they "retained their German style, language, and customs."[121] Drawing on recent events, an imagined national history, and a curated set of cultural features, BiN effectively cast the refugees as authentic Germans and made it clear that Germany's state borders were less important than the German nation's transnational ties.

In addition to the press campaign, BiN sponsored public performances and church services to raise awareness for the cause. One event featured a presentation on the refugees followed by a performance of the twelfth-century liturgical drama *Ludus de Antichristo* (*Play About the Antichrist*), which narrates the story of a shadowy political figure who brings the nations of the world under his diabolical spell and heralds the end of history.[122] The metaphorical connection between Stalin's Soviet Union and the performance was surely not lost on the audience. The efforts of BiN, in conjunction with a willing German government, raised public awareness and nearly 900,000 reichsmark.[123] The Verein für das

---

[118] Willms, *At the Gates of Moscow*, 102.

[119] Pastors in the Hamburg area also helped spread the word. See "Pastor Bestmann to Pastor Bruns," January 27, 1930, Church Archives Box 11, SAM.

[120] "Bericht über die Gründungssitzung," Church Archives, Box 13, SAM, 2; "Bericht über bisher veranlasste Hilfsmassnahmen für die deutsch-russischen Auswanderer," December 7, 1929, Church Archives, Box 13, SAM, 2.

[121] "Aufruf zugunsten der aus Rußland ausgewanderten deutschstämmigen Bauern," December 11, 1929, R43 I/141, vol. 1, L196174, BA.

[122] Ibid., "Rotes Kreuz von Berlin Büro des Vorsitzenden an die Reichskanzler," December 4, 1929, R43 I/141, vol. 1, L196235, 128, BA.

[123] Neufeldt, "Flight to Moscow," 43.

Deutschtum im Ausland (Association for Germandom Abroad, VDA),
which was the country's premier overseas cultural organization, also
contributed to the effort by donating quantities of food, clothing, toys,
books, and school materials in the hope that the refugees would retain
their Germanness when they left Germany.[124]

While BiN drew public attention to the refugees' situation and saw to
their immediate needs, the MCC researched new countries where they
could perpetuate their Mennoniteness. After the First World War,
a handful of US Mennonites founded the MCC on an ad hoc basis to
provide famine relief for Russia's Mennonites.[125] Yet even this modest
organizational achievement represented an unprecedented commitment
on behalf of the United States' Mennonite population. At a meeting in
Chicago on December 11, 1929, a group of several Mennonite leaders
paved the way for a more financially sustained and bureaucratically
sophisticated commitment to relief.[126] The executive committee consisted
of Peter C. Hiebert (chairman), Harold S. Bender (secretary), Levi
Mumaw (secretary-treasurer), Maxwell H. Kratz, and Orie O. Miller.[127]
A study committee composed of Bender, Hiebert, and Kratz was also
formed for the purpose of locating a host country for the refugees.[128]
Their guiding Bible passage was Galatians 6:10, "Therefore ... let us do
good to all people, especially to those who belong to the family of
believers."[129] The MCC not only wished to include other US
Mennonites in their "family," but also Mennonites around the world.

Not all Mennonites agreed with this vision of solidarity, especially
within the United States' largest conference, the (old) Mennonite Church
(MC). The MC's congregations were located principally in the mid-Atlantic
and Great Lakes regions of the United States and across the border in
eastern Canada. Bishops – who in many ways resembled Mennonite
Ältesten in the Russian milieu – dominated the conference's leadership
structure and were skeptical of broad-based organizations. In 1924,
Bender regretfully informed Christian Neff, moderator of the first

[124] Ibid., Grams, *German Emigration to Canada*, 287.
[125] F. H. Epp, *Mennonites in Canada, 1920–1940: A People's Struggle for Survival* (Toronto: Macmillan of Canada, 1982), 36–37.
[126] "Tentative Report of the Findings of the Refugee Colonization Study Committee," IX-3-2 Paraguayan Immigration 1/1, MCCA. Prior to the meeting, the Committee extended an open invitation to all Mennonite conferences that wished to participate. See "Chicago Meeting of the Central Committee," *Mennonite*, January 2, 1930, 1.
[127] "Tentative Report," 1.
[128] "Chicago Meeting of the Central Committee," *Mennonite*, January 2, 1930, 1.
[129] New International Version.

Mennonite World Conference in Basel, Switzerland, that the MC would not participate in the event, stating "They [MC leaders] especially take exception to the idea of a Mennonite World Union in which believing and unbelieving Mennonites would be united."[130] In fact, when the MCC's original mandate for helping starving Russians drew to a close in 1925, the MC withdrew its support and called for the organization to be disbanded.

Mennonite intellectuals were the torchbearers of Mennonite ecumenicism and none shone brighter during the early twentieth century than the young, dashing Professor H. S. Bender at Goshen College in Goshen, Indiana. Although individuals at Mennonite schools and colleges assumed that there was an essential Mennonite unity, they were often at pains to define it with precision. Bender would spend most of his life trying. Born in 1897, and educated at Goshen College, Princeton University, and the University of Heidelberg, Bender was a polymath scholar and administrator who preferred to do many things tolerably rather than a few things thoroughly. Bender wrote or edited scores of books, pamphlets, and articles on the history and theology of the Mennonites including his seminal 1944 *The Anabaptist Vision*, which projected the goals of the sixteenth-century Anabaptist movement onto twentieth-century Mennonites. He was the founding editor of the scholarly journal *Mennonite Quarterly Review* (1927–) and lead editor of the *Mennonite Encyclopedia* (four volumes, 1955–1959). Bender was also a dominant institutional presence. At his death in 1960, he held fourteen administrative positions. It is not an overstatement to say that during the twentieth century, his interpretation of Mennoniteness infused the entire North American Mennonite church.[131] Along with D. Toews in Canada, Bender stood at the forefront of a generation of North American Mennonites that viewed conference-level administration as the principle mode of Mennonite organization. In 1929, at the age of thirty-two, the precocious Bender cut his teeth on promoting the confession's global unity via the refugee situation. However, he had no direct experience with relief work, he possessed no understanding of international diplomacy, and his US sensibilities were at odds with those of his Russian-born charges.

---

[130] H. S. Bender, "Liebe Bruder," June 24, 1924. Quoted in John A. Lapp and Ed van Straten, "Mennonite World Conference 1925–2000: From Euro-American Conference to Worldwide Communion," *Mennonite Quarterly Review* 76, no. 1 (2003): 14.

[131] For Bender's biography, see Albert N. Keim, *Harold S. Bender, 1897–1962* (Scottdale, PA: Herald Press, 1997).

Nevertheless, he maintained the belief that "American know-how," when directed by the hand of God, could fix any problem.

THE CANADIAN OPTION

Canada appeared to be the most expedient and desirable option for German and Mennonite authorities because the CMBC had already helped several thousand Mennonites migrate from the Soviet Union in the preceding decade. Yet by 1929, the country had begun restricting immigration from non-preferred Eastern European countries.[132] Moreover, Canada's provincial leaders were skeptical that Mennonites made good Canadians. With anti-German attitudes waning ten years after the First World War, and separatist Mennonites safely out of sight in their Latin American enclaves, associative Mennonites who favored renewed Mennonite immigration from Russia recast the confession's constituency as German Canadians who had always prioritized their allegiance to Canada. Already in March 1929, D. Toews and an interfaith committee responded to Canada's tightening immigration laws by joining together to promote the value of "German" immigration to the country. D. Toews did not deny Russian Mennonites' Mennoniteness, but he did emphasize their Germanness, which was apparently more expedient for catching the ears of government authorities than focusing on their religious distinctions. Working with the German Catholic Immigration Board and the Lutheran Immigration Board, the collective asked the Dominion government to consider granting special treatment to German-speaking immigrants. The petition stated,

Germans residing in non-preferred countries are technically called nationals of their respective country. They are, however, in every sense of the word German. While they readily become assimilated with the Anglo-Saxon race, they have consistently refused to assume the civilization of the non-preferred countries. In practice, therefore, it is not correct to call a German from Russia a Russian.[133]

It was unclear what sort of social, cultural, or biological qualities allowed a "German" to resist the influence of non-preferred countries while quickly acculturating to "Anglo-Saxon culture." It was also unclear whether the new group's religious beliefs would impede its Canadization – an issue that western provinces had hoped to resolve with the public-

---

[132] Gerald Tulchinsky, *Canada's Jews: A People's History* (Toronto: University of Toronto Press, 2008), 233.
[133] "Statement to Hon. Robert F. Forke," March 6, 1929.

school controversy. To this end, the Mennonite Agricultural Committee of Saskatchewan averred that the refugees would hold their religious and national identifications in tandem, contending "If there have been some of the old-time Mennonites who had taken a separate position with regard to the school question, this question is settled as much as we know … Can you Honored Sirs, understand that when in a meeting or by our children at home, the song "O Canada," is sung, that not only the lips but also the hearts of us older ones are singing too?"[134] In their assessment, *real* Mennonites accepted Canadization, though it again remained unclear why they would be patriotic to Canada and not to Russia or Germany.

There were a few federal Canadian authorities at the Ministry of Immigration and Colonization, including Minister Robert Forke, Deputy Minister William Egan, and Assistant Deputy Minister Frederick C. Blair, who were interested in helping the refugees.[135] Correspondences between the Ministry of Immigration and the CMBC indicate that the Dominion deferred the issue to the provinces and would go along with the plan as long as a province accepted the refugees.[136] Saskatchewan was singled out as the best location for settlement since the head office of the CMBC was located in Rosthern.

Saskatchewan's premier James T. M. Anderson refused to cooperate with the Ministry since he considered Mennonites and Doukhobers to be inimical to the province's best interests. Anderson gained an unfavorable impression of both confessions during his years as a teacher and school inspector in Manitoba and Saskatchewan.[137] When asked whether he would allow Mennonites to settle in Saskatchewan in November 1929, Anderson expressed skepticism, "I have just recently obtained

[134] "To the Government of Saskatchewan," n.d., CMBC, Immigration Movement I, c. Organizations, Individuals and Transactions related to Immigration and Relief, 1923–1946, vol. 1269, 598, MHC.

[135] Blair went on to become the Director of Canada's Immigration Branch and was responsible for Canada's closed-door policy during the interwar years. See Tulchinsky, *Canada's Jews*, 231–33.

[136] D. Toews, "Letter to J. T. M. Anderson," May 13, 1930, CMBC, Immigration Movement I, c. Organizations, Individuals, and Transactions related to Immigration and Relief, 1923–1946, vol. 1269, 597, MHC.

[137] Patrick Kyba, "Anderson, James Thomas Milton (1878–1946)," *The Encyclopedia of Saskatchewan*, https://esask.uregina.ca/entry/anderson_james_thomas_milton_1878-1946.jsp, last accessed August 4, 2019; John McLaren, "Creating 'Slaves of Satan' or 'New Canadians'? The Law, Education, and the Socialization of Doukhobor Children, 1911–1935," in *Essays in the History of Canadian Law: British Columbia and the Yukon*, ed. Hamar Foster and John McLaren (Toronto: University of Toronto Press, 1995), 359.

information to the effect that in one locality there are at least sixty children running around in a Mennonite village with absolutely no public school facilities."[138] To the dismay of the CMBC, Anderson reasoned that all Mennonites were the same no matter if they lived in Canada or in Russia.

Coincidentally, during a conference with D. Toews and members of the Saskatchewan Parliament, Premier Anderson received a telegram from a group of Saskatchewan Mennonites that read, "We are not in favor of the immigration of Mennonites from Europe and we cannot house any as we have plenty of our own Canadian Mennonites to help."[139] The group was likely referring to the Mennonites from the Soviet Union who had already arrived in Saskatchewan over the past ten years. Though the authors' exact motives are unclear, what is certain is that some of Canada's Mennonites had met their limit of confessional charity. Obviously, this was embarrassing for D. Toews, who was trying to convince the provincial government that Canada's Mennonites were unified in their support of immigration.

Other premiers were similarly unwilling to accept the refugees. Manitoba unofficially indicated that it would be able to accept 250 families but only after March 1, 1930. Meanwhile, Alberta's premier J. E. Brownlee wished to put off his decision until after the June 1930 election.[140] By the end of November, the worsening global economy, growing unemployment, gridlock between the federal government and the provinces, and an overarching fear of public opinion put an end to the prospects of large-scale Canadian immigration. Despite the CMBC's attempts to define the confession as an assembly of loyal Canadians who happened to speak German and happened to be Mennonites, conventional wisdom dictated that the Mennonites were a diverse cast of characters, some of whom were not dependable citizens.

---

[138] "Premier Talks on Refugee Question," *Saskatoon Star Phoenix*, November 7, 1929, 13.

[139] "Mennonite Refugees Are Not Wanted by Fellow Countrymen," newspaper clipping, CMBC, Immigration Movement I, c. Organizations, Individuals and Transactions related to Immigration and Relief, 1923–1946, vol. 1270, 606, MHC. The clipping likely referred to the Dalmeny, Saskatchewan Mennonites. See Epp, *Mennonite Exodus: The Rescue and Resettlement of the Russian Mennonites Since the Communist Revolution* (Altona, MB: Canadian Mennonite Relief and Immigration Council, 1962), 247; Neufeldt, "Flight to Moscow," 42.

[140] Epp, *Mennonite Exodus*, 247–8; "Memorandum," November 13, 1929, GFM 33/4538: L192391, NA.

FOUNDING FERNHEIM

As most western countries raised their immigration gates at the end of 1929, the choice came down to Brazil or Paraguay.[141] Both counties were amenable to white, German-speaking colonies that would incorporate new land into their agricultural sectors, a strategy that dovetailed with the Weimar government's interest in German economic expansion in Latin America.[142] The Germans, including Unruh and some of the refugees, were "very taken with the idea" of a Brazilian settlement since there were already about 600,000 German speakers living in the country – 58,000 of whom had arrived in the preceding decade.[143] The country also had an immigration representative, Colonel Gaelzer-Netto, stationed in Brazil, and the settlement firm Hanseatische Kolonisationsgesellschaft (Hanseatic Colonization Society) was positioned to settle the refugees near Germans living in Santa Catarina.[144] A Mennonite settlement in Brazil promised a higher likelihood that the refugees would preserve their Germanness and establish trade relations with Germany.

Due to the mounting costs of quartering the group, the German government relocated nearly a fourth of the refugees – including most of the Catholics, Lutherans, and about 1,200 amenable Mennonites – to Santa Catarina, Brazil in the first two months of 1930.[145] The initiative was part of a shift in the Foreign Office's thinking about German settlements in Latin America, which privileged group settlement above individual migration. In association with the Foreign Office, the Gesellschaft für Siedlung im Ausland (Society for Settlement Abroad), and the Gesellschaft für Wirtschaftliche Studien in Übersee (Society for Economic Studies Overseas), subsequent German-speaking colonies were established in Paraná, including the Kolonie Rolândia, which was composed of landless Germans.[146]

---

[141] Brazil initially reacted coolly to the proposal due to its ongoing coffee crisis but it eventually consented to settlement. "Memorandum by Pistor," December 10, 1929, R43 I/141, vol. 1, L196235, 134, BA.

[142] For a detailed discussion of Weimar policy vis-à-vis Latin America, see Rinke, *"Der letzte freie Kontinent." Deutsche Lateinamerikapolitik im Zeichen transnationaler Beziehungen, 1918–1933*, vols. 1 and 2 (Stuttgart: Hans-Dieter Heinz Akademischer Verlag, 1996).

[143] "In Nachstehenden," November 13, 1929, GMF 33/4538: L192397, NA; "Tentative Report"; and Nikolaus Barbian, *Auswärtige Kulturpolitik und "Auslandsdeutsche" in Lateinamerika 1949–1973* (Wiesbaden: Springer, 2013), 76.

[144] "In Nachstehenden," L192394, NA.

[145] Epp, *Mennonites in Canada 1920–1940*, 322; Neufeldt, "Flight to Moscow," 44; Thiesen, *Mennonite and Nazi?* 47.

[146] Barbian, *Auswärtige Kulturpolitik und "Auslandsdeutsche,"* 76–77.

The MCC was disturbed by the Brazilian option because the country did not offer conscientious objection to military service, which it thought was essential for preserving the refugees' Mennoniteness. It also feared the refugees would be absorbed by the country's German-speaking population or integrated into Brazilian society.[147] The MCC preferred a Chaco settlement due to the religious guarantees enshrined in the Paraguayan *Privilegium* and because the refugees could settle adjacent to the Menno Colony.[148] It therefore requested a delay in transports until mid-February and worked to make a Chaco settlement feasible.[149] Glad that another organization would assume the financial and logistical burdens of transportation and settlement, the German government obliged.

A second MCC meeting was convened on January 25, 1930.[150] At this assembly, a study commission presented various materials regarding South American – and especially Paraguayan – immigration, including a report by John B. Faust, US consul in Asunción, a field report from two Mennonite missionaries in Argentina, and a statement from the Menno Colony.[151] Through speaking engagements and Mennonite publications, the MCC also set about trying to raise $100,000 USD (about $1,472,000 USD in 2019) from conferences and churches to transport and settle the group.[152]

The MCC dispatched Bender to Germany to steer refugees toward Paraguay, yet according to Bender's biographer, Albert N. Keim, it was "most difficult" to convince them "since they all wanted to go to Canada."[153] Like a traveling salesman, Bender visited the camps promoting the Chaco. In a letter to his friend Noah Oyer he recalled, "Now you can imagine the sort of speech I made, in a language I do not master on

---

[147] Neufeldt, "Flight to Moscow," 44; "Tentative Report."

[148] Epp, *Mennonite Exodus*, 258–59; *Mennonites in Canada 1920–1940*, 322–23.

[149] "Tentative Report."

[150] This meeting drew representatives from the MC, the GC, Mennonite Brethren Church, Lancaster Conference (Mennonite Church), and Krimmer Mennonite Brethren. The Evangelical Mennonite (Defenseless) Church joined the organization in 1930. Bender and Elmer Neufeld, "Mennonite Central Committee (International)," *Global Anabaptist Mennonite Encyclopedia Online*, last modified April 13, 2014, http://gameo .org/index.php?title=Mennonite_Central_Committee_%28International%29, last accessed June 7, 2018.

[151] Epp, *Mennonite Exodus*, 258–59.

[152] Ibid., 259. The inflation adjustment was made with the Bureau of Labor Statistics (CPI) Inflation Calculator, www.bls.gov/data/inflation_calculator.htm, last accessed August 8, 2019.

[153] Keim, *Harold S. Bender*, 209.

a subject on which I am ill-informed."[154] Despite such handicaps, Bender and some of the refugees' prominent members persuaded about 270 families to choose Paraguay.[155] While still in Germany, the refugees organized themselves into eight villages of about twenty-five families per village to streamline the move. Like the Menno Colony, each village would be laid out in a *Strassendorf* arrangement.[156] Colonists drew lots for their homesteads in order to reduce factionalism and to establish solidarity at the colony level.[157]

Simultaneously, the MCC arranged the purchase of 135,000 hectares of land from the Corporación Paraguaya, adjacent to the Menno Colony.[158] Each family was allotted forty hectares, a pair of oxen, a cow with a calf, twelve chickens, a rooster, seed grain, and food worth $50 USD (about $736 USD in 2019). Including the transportation debt, each family owed a total of $1,500 USD (about $22,080 USD in 2019), with all families in a village mutually signing for each other.[159] The MCC would collect the money over the next ten years and distribute it to the German government and the Corporación Paraguaya.[160]

Between February 1930 and August 1931, 1,572 Mennonite refugees left Germany for the Chaco. The rest either joined the Brazilian contingent, remained in Germany due to health issues, or found their way to Canada as individual families. The majority of Paraguayan-bound Mennonites arrived at Puerto Casado in the early months of 1930. Their transatlantic journey was followed by an approximately 2,000-km boat ride up the Paraná and Paraguay Rivers and a 200-km journey inland to an undefined patch of undeveloped land. The whole trip took about two and a half months.[161] According to the North American Mennonite

---

[154] "H. S. Bender to Noah Oyer," April 29, 1930, f. 2, b. 1, H. S. Bender papers, Archives of the Mennonite Church (hereafter, AMC). Quoted in Keim, *Harold S. Bender*, 210.

[155] Bender, "Die Einwanderung nach Paraguay," *Bericht über die Mennonitische Welt-Hilfs-Konferenz vom 31. August bis 3. September 1930*, ed. Christian Neff (Karlsruhe, Germany: Heinrich Schneider, 1930), 122.

[156] P. Klassen, *The Mennonites in Paraguay Volume 1*, 188; C. J. Dyck, P. Klassen, and Gundolf Niebuhr, "Fernheim Colony (Boquerón Department, Paraguay)," *Global Anabaptist Mennonite Encyclopedia Online*, last modified 2009, http://gameo.org/index.php?title=Fernheim_Colony_(Boquer%C3%B3n_Department,_Paraguay)&oldid=143401, last accessed June 7, 2018.

[157] Ibid., 188. [158] Ibid., 182.

[159] Bender, "Einwanderung nach Paraguay," 123. The inflation adjustment was made with the Bureau of Labor Statistics (CPI) Inflation Calculator, www.bls.gov/data/inflation_calculator.htm, last accessed August 8, 2019.

[160] Ibid., 123.

[161] Letkemann, "Part II – Lager Mölln," 10; Thiesen, *Mennonite and Nazi?* 76.

publication *Gospel Herald*, the refugees originated from forty-six separate villages, scattered across Russia and Ukraine, and were now brought together to form the Fernheim Colony, a little northwest of the Menno Colony.[162] Upon their arrival, the group elected Franz Heinrich to be the colony's first *Oberschulze* and each village chose a *Schulze*.[163] They also established the town of Filadelfia as a central location for their common undertakings, which eventually included a hospital, warehouse, economic cooperative, and printing press.[164]

The word "Fernheim" means "distant home" and it remained distant in every sense: It was distant from their homes in the Soviet Union, distant from their imagined national brethren in Germany, and distant from the MCC in the United States. The colony, therefore, resembled home much less than it did a preserve, since German and Mennonite officials hoped the refugees would perpetuate their Germanness or Mennoniteness in this isolated location. Yet they also remained globally connected. The MCC representatives painted a picture of the refugees as part of a global community of Mennonite brethren. Writing for the publication *Gospel Herald*, Bender referred to the refugees as hardworking and industrious. They were farmers with large families, similar to the North American Mennonites from whom he was soliciting aid.[165] Bender insisted that the refugees were not "pauperized by their experience" but were "clean, attractive, [and] active."[166] His assessment resembles the glowing descriptions of communities of *Auslandsdeutsche* in German nationalist propaganda that "reassured German readers about the essential Germanness of such qualities as cleanliness, order, and well-organized household management . . . even in isolated German settlements in Russia."[167] In the MCC's eyes, three things were certain: The world's Mennonites shared

[162] Levi Mumaw, "Relief Notes," *Gospel Herald*, April 24, 1930. According to the same article, forty-one families came from Siberia: five from Omsk, thirty from Slavgorod, one from Omur (Amur?), and one from Pavlodar. Ten families came from Ukraine, three from Orenburg, two from Saratov, two from Samara, one from Crimea, one from Donbuss, and one from Ufa.

[163] C. J. Dyck and P. Klassen, "Filadelfia (Fernheim Colony, Boquerón Department, Paraguay)," *Global Anabaptist Mennonite Encyclopedia Online*, last modified April 23, 2014, http://gameo.org/index.php?title=Filadelfia_(Fernheim_Colony, _Boquer%C3%B3n_Department,_Paraguay)&oldid=121054, last accessed June 7, 2018.

[164] Ibid.

[165] "Our Russian Refugee Brethren in Germany," *Gospel Herald*, May 29, 1930, 14.

[166] Ibid.   [167] Reagin, "German Brigadoon?" 258.

essential qualities, the time of Mennonite communal autonomy was over, and a new era of interdependence was at hand.

The arrival of the refugees in Paraguay made news among South America's German speakers, whose alleged spokespeople welcomed them as members of the German nation. Upon arriving in Buenos Aires, the German consular secretary in Argentina and a representative of the *Deutsche La Plata Zeitung* greeted the group. The paper carried the story of these "men, women, and children – people of our language and our blood" who "have heart and real culture."[168] Colonists were equally complimentary toward the German state. According to the paper, one refugee reported that the group's respite in Germany was a "rediscovery" of their German culture and that "the whole of Germany is one lovely garden."[169] Continuing up the Paraná River, the German Minister to Paraguay, Rudolf von Bülow, received the visitors in Asunción.[170] To the refugees, it appeared as though their national ties as *Auslandsdeutsche* extended around the globe.[171] In 1931, Unruh reminded the colonists, "Please continue to keep in mind that the eyes of the world – especially the eyes of us Germans – are upon you. If you succeed in proving that the Chaco can be colonized, this will be of great importance to future emigrants from Germany."[172] The refugees therefore maintained an ongoing significance in North America as Mennonites and in Germany as Germans.

NEW BORDERS, OLD PROBLEMS

The refugees would not find peace in the Chaco because Paraguay and Bolivia had their own ideas about what the refugees represented, either as partners or as usurpers in their nation-building schemes. On the heels of the Moscow contingent, a second group of Mennonite refugees from Russia arrived in the Chaco via Harbin, China in 1932.[173] Their arrival provoked

---

[168] "Die Ankunft der dritten Gruppe deutscher Flüchtlinge aus Sibirien," *Deutsche La Plata Zeitung* (Argentina), June 5, 1930, Buenos Aires 67A (Mennoniten-Einwanderung nach Paraguay), Shelf 48, Carton 2439, PA AA.

[169] Ibid.

[170] Ibid. For a refugee's perspective on the trip, see "Johann Jakob Funk to Pastor Bruns," April 23, 1930, Church Archive Box 14, SAM.

[171] Ibid.

[172] "Letter from Unruh," October 7, 1931. Quoted in P. Klassen, *The Mennonites in Paraguay Volume 1*, 74.

[173] League of Nations, "Refugees in China. Communication from the Delegates of Paraguay to the League of Nations-Annex 1972," *League of Nations Official Journal* 13, no. 7 (1932):1339. See also a report written by Rudolf von Bülow about his meeting with

a diplomatic clash between the countries that helped pave the way for the Chaco War (1932–1935). As early as March 1930, the German Foreign Office was anticipating the geopolitical dangers of Mennonite settlement in the region. One consular report states, "Mennonite leaders [from the MCC] have insisted, despite these warnings on following through with the settlement."[174] A few months later, Bender sanguinely predicted that the border problem would be solved peacefully.[175] Paradoxically, by settling the refugees in Paraguay to help them maintain their Mennoniteness (including the tenet of nonviolence) the MCC placed the refugees in the middle of a war zone.[176] Thus, the broader meanings ascribed to the refugees trumped even their physical security.

Bolivia and Paraguay each viewed the Chaco as part of its national territories, and their claims were equally flimsy. During the 1920s, Bolivia established a series of small forts in the region while Paraguay pressed forward with Mennonite colonization. Thus, by fleeing the nationalized territories of Canada (the Menno Colony) and Russia (the Fernheim Colony), Mennonites contributed to the nationalization of central South America. What is remarkable about the situation is that neither the Bolivian nor Paraguayan governments had much to do with actually settling the Mennonites. Both colonies settled on private land held by an Argentine company, days away from the nearest Bolivian or Paraguay municipality. Most Menno colonists retained their Canadian citizenship (in the event that they would have to return) and saw to their own municipal administration. In contrast, most Fernheim refugees from the Soviet Union held no citizenship and were financially supported by the MCC and the German government. The dispute nevertheless sheds light on the countries' shared perception that whoever claimed to administer the Mennonites literally administered the Chaco.

Like the Moscow refugees, the Harbin group of refugees were displaced by Stalin's war against kulaks. Instead of fleeing east, they fled south and west. In late 1928, a Mennonite couple named Johann H. Friesen and

---

MCC representative Gerhard G. Hiebert in "Russische Mennoniten im Chaco," April 6, 1931, Buenos Aires 67A (Mennoniten-Einwanderung nach Paraguay), Shelf 48, Carton 2439, PA AA.

[174] Freytag, "Transport deutschrussischer Flüchtlinge nach Paraguay," March 18, 1930, Buenos Aires 67A (Mennoniten-Einwanderung nach Paraguay), Shelf 48, Carton 2439, PA AA, 7.

[175] Bender, "Die Einwanderung nach Paraguay," 118.

[176] The settlement of Mennonite refugees in the Chaco was not the sole cause of the outbreak of hostilities, but their presence certainly did not ameliorate the situation.

Margaretha Funk Klassen were the first among many Mennonites to escape the Soviet Union across the frozen Amur River into China.[177] Over the next three years, others followed their path so that by the end of 1931 there were nearly 1,000 German-speaking refugees in Harbin.[178] They initially approached the Canadian embassy for help, but the country refused to admit "Chinese" immigrants.[179] Eventually, the MCC intervened on their behalf. At a League of Nations council meeting in September 1931, Paraguay granted them asylum. The German delegate present at the meeting, Count Johann Heinrich Graf von Bernstorff, applauded the country's offer to help these unfortunate *Auslandsdeutsche*, a diplomatic move that appeared to benefit both governments.[180]

The Bolivian government responded with a sharply worded statement to the League's secretary-general in December 1931 warning that his government "would be sorry if foreign refugees depending on unreliable information, were to infringe the laws of the [Bolivian] Republic."[181] Though a few hundred people may have been of little direct consequence to the Chaco's balance of power, there were reports floating around international diplomatic circles that approximately 100,000 Soviet refugees were awaiting relocation. Bolivia feared that Paraguay might use the refugees as a humanitarian ruse to gain hegemony in the Chaco.[182]

In April 1932, the Bolivian consulate in Le Havre, France was alarmed to learn that nearly 400 Mennonite refugees had arrived at the city's port from China and would soon embark for South America on the steamer

---

[177] Robert L. Klassen, "Harbin (Heilongjiang, China) Refugees," *Global Anabaptist Mennonite Encyclopedia Online*, last modified, August 23, 2013, http://gameo.org/index.php?title=Harbin_(Heilongjiang,_China)_Refugees&oldid=95103, last accessed June 7, 2018; Walter Quiring, "The Colonization of the German Mennonites from Russia in the Paraguayan Chaco," *Mennonite Quarterly Review* 8, no. 2 (1934): 70–71. See also Jubiläumskomitee der Harbiner Gruppe, *Die Flucht über den Amur: ein Zeugnis von Gottvertrauen und Mut* (Filadelfia: Jubiläumskomitee der Harbiner Gruppe, 2007).

[178] The majority were Mennonites, but there were also other Protestants and Catholics who made the journey. See Quiring, "The Colonization of the German Mennonites," 62–72, 71–72.

[179] R. Klassen, "Harbin (Heilongjiang, China) Refugees," *Global Anabaptist Mennonite Encyclopedia Online*.

[180] Ibid. Other individuals went to the United States and Brazil. Paraguay's proposal was adopted by the council at its sixty-fifth session on September 29, 1931. See also League of Nations, "Refugees in China."

[181] League of Nations, "Refugees in China."   [182] Ibid.

Groix without Bolivia's approval.[183] This was unacceptable for the
Bolivians since the refugees did not possess Bolivian visas. Two hours
before the ship weighed anchor, the desperate official boarded the ship
and halted its departure on the grounds that the Mennonites required
Bolivian papers in order to enter the region.[184] A German senior civil
servant, Dr. Ernst Kundt, was traveling with the Mennonites during this
"unpleasant stage" of the journey and mediated between the Mennonites
(who wanted rest from their long journey) the Bolivian official (who
declared the Mennonites' journey illegal), and the shipping line (that
wished to remain punctual).[185] After tense negotiations, the ship was
allowed to leave, with every Mennonite holding both Paraguayan and
Bolivian visas.[186] The Bolivian government also declared that in the future
they would not allow immigration to the Chaco unless it was administered
by Bolivia.[187]

When the Paraguayan government learned of the incident a few days
later, it broke off diplomatic relations with Bolivia and sent a message (via
the embassy in Paris) to the Groix protesting the Bolivian visa and the
shipping line's indifference.[188] Bolivia retaliated by breaking off diplomatic relations with Paraguay. A short while later, German, French, and
Dutch Mennonites sent letters of appreciation to the Paraguayan embassy
thanking them for the country's generous support and assuring the
Paraguayans that neither they nor the refugees wished to take part in
such "political" dealings. The Harbin Mennonites arrived in the Chaco

---

[183] Some accounts erroneously claim the ship's name was *Croix*, though *Menno-Blatt* and
contemporary German government accounts indicate that the name was *Groix*. The
group traveled by ship from Harbin, China, to Marseilles, France via the Red Sea. They
passed through France by train to the port of Le Havre, where they boarded a ship that
took them to Buenos Aires. From here, they continued up the Paraguay River to Puerto
Casado. "Reisebericht der 1. Harbiner Gruppe," *Menno-Blatt* (Fernheim, Paraguay),
June 1932, 3–4; Ernst Kundt, "Reisebericht Paris-Le Havre, 1. Bis 7. April 1932,"
R127518, 5–7, PA AA. Secondary sources on the migration include G. Ratzlaff, "Die
paraguayischen Mennoniten in der nationalen Politik," *Jahrbuch für Geschichte und
Kultur der Mennoniten in Paraguay* 5 (2004): 59–91; Quiring, "The Colonization of the
German Mennonites."

[184] G. Ratzlaff, "Die paraguayischen Mennoniten," 70–71.

[185] Kundt, "Reisebericht," 5–7; Bergfeld, "Bericht Nummer 58, Anspruch der bolivischen
Regierung auf Erteilung von Sichtvermerken für Reisende nach dem Großen Chaco,"
April 5, 1932, R78861 (Politik 3), PA AA.

[186] Kundt, "Reisebericht," 6.

[187] G. Ratzlaff, *Cristianos Evangélicos en la Guerra del Chaco 1932–1935* (Asunción:
Gerhard Ratzlaff, 2008), 32. See also G. Ratzlaff, "Die paraguayischen Mennoniten,"
70–71.

[188] Ibid. Also see Kundt, "Reisebericht," 7.

on May 12, 1932. Along with a few families from Poland that came in 1930, the colony now stood at 17 villages with a population of 2,015 people.[189] These new arrivals settled alongside their coreligionists in the Fernheim Colony as the region descended into war.

The preceding theatrics demonstrate that the nationalist paradigm though which both Bolivia and Paraguay viewed the space of the Chaco – and energetically pursued or denied immigration to it – had little bearing on the Chaco's actual administration, which rested with the Corporación Paraguaya and the Mennonites.[190] Both countries' clumsy handling of the situation shows that their understanding of territorial sovereignty was confined more to the realms of bureaucracy and imagination than infrastructure and reality. Neither Bolivia nor Paraguay knew how they would exploit the Chaco, but they perceived that the Mennonite colonies were essential to that enterprise. It was for this reason that the Paraguayan government extended the generous conditions of the Menno Colony *Privilegium* to the Fernheim group. In 1930, Bolivia granted the colonies a similar *Privilegium* – though they had not asked for it – which ensured its respect for Mennonite autonomy in the event of war.[191] The Mennonites' identifications as Canadians, Russians, and religious dissidents were less significant to both governments than the fact that they were white, German-speaking colonists. To both countries, the Mennonites were "emissaries of progress" that would establish dominion over the wilderness.[192]

Hannah Arendt argues that stateless individuals during the interwar years were "superfluous."[193] This may have been true in a legal sense, but the era's politicians, press, and society did not ignore interwar refugees. Despite their presumed physical superfluity, refugees suffered from

---

[189] "Ankunft der 1. harbiner Gruppe," *Menno-Blatt*, May 1932, 6; C. J. Dyck and P. Klassen, "Filadelfia (Fernheim Colony, Boquerón Department, Paraguay)," *Global Anabaptist Mennonite Encyclopedia Online*.

[190] The Corporación Paraguaya was the same corporation that administered the purchase of lands from the Carlos Casado S. A. on behalf of the Menno Colony colonists during the 1920s.

[191] The guarantee was titled "Decreto Supremo de 27 de Marzo de 1930 – Se concede autorización a las familias menonitas y otras de índole análoga para establecerse en los terrenes baldíos del Chaco y oriente del país," in Humberto Delgado Llano, *Complementos de la Legislacion Integral del Ramo de Colonizacion 1928–1935* (La Paz: Intendencia General de Guerra, 1938).

[192] Sigfrido Gross Brown, *Las Colonias Menonitas en el Chaco* (Asunción: Imprenta Nacional, 1934), 1.

[193] Hannah Arendt, *The Origins of Totalitarianism*, new ed. (New York: Harcourt, Brace, Jovanovich, 1973), 296.

a surfeit of meanings. Depending on who was speaking for (or against) them, refugees were heroes, criminals, victims, or scapegoats. They could be assigned a variety of nationalities depending on where they originated, where they lived, what they spoke, and what they looked like. Their religious and class statuses were equally malleable.

Government, press, and aid agency personnel imbued the Mennonite refugees with a range of meanings, but they had to make them fit into existing categories of understanding. Soviet leaders encouraged village councils to transpose communist class categories into myriad local vernaculars. The German government and press exploited conventional wisdom about *Auslandsdeutsche* to cast the Mennonites as a long-lost tribe of Germans, since their ancestors had left Central Europe over a century before. The organization BiN used similar nationalist themes, but tinged their appeals with religious pathos. Canada assumed that the Mennonites were religious dissidents, while Brazil and Paraguay viewed them as hardy pioneers. In the United States, the MCC called on North American Mennonites to view the refugees as religious brethren. They wanted the refugees to create a new homeland in the Americas as their own ancestors had done in the preceding centuries.[194] Each entity identified the refugees differently in order to clarify who belonged and did not belong to their imagined national or religious communities and to unify their constituencies around a shared goal. What the refugees represented meant more than who they actually were: a small and disparate set of individuals.

The Moscow refugees' shrewd entreaties and the Harbin refugees' daring escape unquestionably demonstrate that they were not powerless. At least initially, most refugee groups are disorganized and inarticulate. Competing external voices quickly filled the void. Certainly, their most pressing shared concern was finding a new home, but it remained unclear whether they would do it alone or as a group. Like most refugees, their ties to each other were fragmented even as external groups saw within them a purity that did not exist. David McCreedy states, "Oppressed people have no obligation to act in ways that outside observers find interesting or appropriate. They seek instead to protect themselves and their families, to survive and to keep intact as much of their world as possible."[195] This is exactly what Mennonite refugees like the Neufeld family did. They had

---

[194] According to the editor of *Mennonite*, "The future of Mennonitism lies in the new world." See "Editorial," *Mennonite*, October 31, 1929, 3.

[195] David McCreedy, *Rural Guatemala, 1760–1940* (Stanford, CA: Stanford University Press, 1994), 10.

little idea what a kulak was, they did not feel especially loyal to a transnational community, and they did not particularly care to resettle in South America. Yet they quickly had to decide whether they wished to remain a part of this local community and their broader "imagined communities" in Germany and North America.[196] If so, they had to establish the terms under which they would remain united and create an intelligible story about their unity, a process that took over a decade to resolve.

---

[196] Benedict Anderson, *Imagined Communities: Reflections on the Origins and Spread of Nationalism* (London: Verso, 1983).

3

Troubled Tribes in the Promised Land (1930–1939)

The Menno Colony drivers stood at the "Kilometer 145" train depot looking like otherworldly peasants. They wore torn clothes, straw hats, wooden clogs, and leather sun goggles. The latter protected their eyes from the glare of the Chaco's windswept flatlands. The depot was the last stop on the narrow-gage railroad extending from the river port town of Puerto Casado into the vast wilderness. The drivers were paid by the MCC to take the Fernheim Colony refugees to their new land, which was a three-day trek through the bush. The first refugee transport actually arrived at Puerto Casado on Good Friday, but the refugees were forced to wait, since the Menno Colony drivers refused to pick them up over the Easter holiday. The refugees – though poor, dirty, and tired – wore suits and dress shoes. Men sported mustaches and women wore cloche hats – fashions incongruous with the Menno Colony Mennonites' bib overalls and boots. They also preferred to speak "cultured" High German in contrast to the Menno Colony's *Plautdietsch*, which Menno Colony residents referred to simply as "Mennonite."[1] The two groups appeared to come from different worlds, and they did.

The initial meeting between the Menno Colony migrants and the Fernheim Colony refugees allowed both groups to assess the changes that had developed between them during the previous fifty years. Among the Menno Colony Mennonites, there were about eighty people who had actually been born in Russia before the 1870s mass migration to Canada. They remembered the schism between those who left the country

[1] See Amos Swartzentruber, "Mennonites in Paraguay: VI. 'Their Churches and Schools,'" *Gospel Herald*, October 31, 1929, 629.

for Canada's prairies as a defining moment when "true believers" voluntarily chose the hardships of pioneer life over acquiescing to worldly governance. Naturally, the Menno Colony Mennonites were guarded during their interactions with the refugees, viewing them as cosmopolitan, demanding, impractical, and theologically modern. In return, Fernheim Mennonites viewed the Menno Colony as backward, isolated, and intellectually dull. In time, these suspicions solidified into a general coolness between the groups.[2] Clearly, the intervening decades had deepened and expanded the differences between their religious beliefs, cultural assumptions, ideas about Mennoniteness, and articulations of an overarching Mennonite narrative.

Since both groups were Mennonite, outsiders such as the MCC and the German and Paraguayan governments hoped that the colonies would cooperate and build their settlements together. Indeed, the fact that they settled in the same area at nearly the same time seemed to anticipate an age of greater Mennonite cooperation, German solidarity, and Paraguayan consolidation of the Chaco. Yet as Menno colonists would have surely pointed out, such an assumption either presumes to know God's inscrutable will or imposes a nationalist metanarrative on the world. The colonies were vastly different from each other and from the confident expectations of outsides.

Owing to their separate pasts in Canada and Russia and the circumstances of their group formation – as voluntary migrants and as refugees – this chapter shows that the colonies held different interpretations of the Chaco and their purpose within it. The Menno colonists possessed an older, more unified, and more coherent group narrative. They viewed their migration as a path that sincere Christians had to follow and the space of the Chaco as a temporary haven from outside entities where they could stand their ground. Owing to the Fernheim Colony's formation out of a group of disparate refugees, colonists were at odds over creating a shared narrative and searched for ways to endow the Chaco with existential meaning – by settling the land, aiding the Paraguayan government, and joining with the MCC to convert indigenous people to Christianity. This chapter compares the colonies using three lenses: (1) their encounters with the natural environment, (2) their actions during the Chaco War, and (3) their interactions with indigenous peoples after the

---

[2] Martin W. Friesen, *New Homeland in the Chaco Wilderness*, 2nd ed., trans. Jake Balzer (Loma Plata, Paraguay: Cooperativa Chortitzer Limited, 1997), 404–5, 408–11.

war. Each lens helps us understand how the colonies interpreted their material and moral imperatives in the Chaco.

Narratives necessarily assume a few standard shapes in order to relate a specific meaning or moral; otherwise they would simply entail a value-neutral series of events – a chronicle, so to speak. When humans tell stories, they select events that they deem to be important, connect them (however incongruent they may seem), and use analogies that make the interpretation reasonable. Sometimes the audience is private, sometimes it is public. Sometimes analogies are scientific or historical; sometimes they are mythical. Quite often events are chosen that emphasize the narrator's desired conclusion rather than a normative consensus of what is important (if this is even possible). Yet for all the bewildering variety of events and analogies one may use to create a narrative, the contours of its plot will inevitably share much in common with others. Narratives form arcs and their most common outcomes are either happy (comic) or unfortunate (tragic).

Both colonies used biblical analogies to shape their evolving narratives. The Menno colonists typically drew on stories with a comic plot progression, which takes the narrative shape of a U.[3] *Ältester* M. C. Friesen's 1927 farewell sermon in Osterwick, Canada is a good example. In Jeremiah 51, those who were faithful to the Lord fled from Babylon's hubris and sin, whereupon the Lord "brought about [their] vindication" and they declared "the work of the Lord" in Zion.[4] Menno Colony individuals used this type of Bible story to cast themselves as heroic (though humble) nomads who resisted the temptation to comply with earthly authorities, endured the physical and moral tests of immigration, and were rewarded by God. Their most powerful moments of "groupness" occurred when outsiders tested their internal resolve to remain separate from society. These moments were subsequently incorporated into their group narrative as plot points, or climaxes, that affirmed unity and continuity.[5]

In contrast, the Fernheim colonists initially interpreted their flight and resettlement as a tragedy and used biblical stories of exile to describe their experience. A tragedy takes the shape of an inverted U, which rises to a dramatic turning point before plummeting to

---

[3] Northrop Frye, *The Great Code: The Bible and Literature*, ed. Alvin A. Lee (Toronto: University of Toronto Press, Scholarly Publishing Division, 2006), 190.

[4] Jeremiah 51:10 (ESV).

[5] Rogers Brubaker, *Ethnicity Without Groups* (Cambridge, MA: Harvard University Press, 2004), 12.

disaster.[6] Fernheim Colony's constituent families experienced prosperity in Russia before the Soviet government robbed them of their livelihoods and compelled them to rely on the goodwill of others. This formative and unwanted moment of "groupness" was instigated from without, and pride would make it difficult to embrace from within. Consequently, the Fernheim colonists faced the existential dilemma of transforming their individual tragedies into a shared narrative – perhaps one with a comic twist that would reveal a reason for their suffering and a direction for the future. One of their most compelling options was to instigate moments of "groupness" that could connect them to the narratives of larger national and religious communities such as Paraguay, Germany, and the MCC. Thus, the Fernheim Colony's search for narrative meaning was altogether more urgent and contentious than that of the Menno colonists, as the former strove to keep their settlement from disintegrating.

THE GRAN CHACO

William Cronon explains that rival narratives of an event – in this case, displacement and resettlement – produce different understandings of the relationship between humans and the natural environment.[7] This insight is applicable to the colonies' interpretation of the physical space of the Chaco. When the Menno and Fernheim colonists migrated, the transition represented either an upward or downward sweep of their collective narratives. The colonists' pasts – as voluntary migrants and as refugees – were inextricably bound to their impressions of the Chaco and each group imbued the new environment with different meanings that were mediated by the Bible and resonated with their present conditions.

Menno Colony leaders viewed their colony as the living extension of the early, nomadic Christian church. Their relocation to Paraguay was a single step in a multigenerational journey of faith. Church leaders' "theology of migration" was not especially concerned with the church's geographical movement across space – from a "worse space" to a "better space." Rather, the act of migrating was how God's people remained holy across time and space, toward the

---

[6] Frye, *Great Code*, 197.
[7] See William Cronon, "A Place for Stories: Nature, History, and Narrative," *Journal of American History* 78, no. 4 (1992): 1347–76.

"Promised Land" of heaven.[8] Leaders, therefore, did not proclaim the space of the Chaco to be sacred. They simply argued that it was a good place to maintain their religious worldview and the integrity of their *Gemeinden*. According to Calvin Redekop, the Menno Colony "chose the Chaco, not as the *summum bonum*, but as one of the best options for achieving their objectives – namely, avoiding further internal corruption from contact with a society that was imposing its values on them."[9] In short, it was the journey that was sacred, not the land.

Menno colonists therefore used the environment to comment on their path as Christian nomads. Generally speaking, the land was a practical challenge to be conquered through hard work and faith. One colonist referred to as "Mrs. (Jacob) Ginter," speculated that if the colony's agricultural endeavors fared poorly and if the leaders became disappointed "then we will move on."[10] Another believed that the land would be whatever individual colonists made of it: "To one person the Chaco appears to become fateful; the other person, however, sees traces of God's grace in it and stumps happily forward."[11] An early arrival, preacher J. W. Sawatzky, wrote that the group saw a rainbow while they were camped at Puerto Casado and proclaimed it to be "God's wonderful sign of union with Noah," for Noah had fashioned his boat at God's command without knowing where it would take him.[12] The Russian steppes had been difficult to settle, the Canadian prairies had been difficult to settle, and so colonists expected nothing less from another of God's tests. The Chaco was no "Garden of Eden," but the Menno Colony venture was infused with a positive and directional religious meaning from the start.

---

[8] Titus F. Guenther, "Theology of Migration: The Ältesten Reflect," *Journal of Mennonite Studies* 18 (2000): 173.

[9] Calvin Redekop, *Strangers Become Neighbors: Mennonite and Indigenous Relations in the Paraguayan Chaco* (Scottdale, PA: Herald Press, 1980), 90.

[10] Reprinted letter dated February 1928 from Mrs. (Jacob) Ginter titled "Nothing Grows in the Chaco," Martin W. Friesen, *Canadian Mennonites Conquer a Wilderness: The Beginning and Development of the Menno Colony First Mennonite Settlement in South America,* trans. Christel Wiebe (Loma Plata, Paraguay: Historical Committee of the Menno Colony, 2009), 34.

[11] Reprinted report from A. B. Toews of Weidenfeld titled "Dark Mood in the Desolate Bush Wilderness – We Will Die Here," quoted in ibid., 58.

[12] Reprinted letter dated January 5, 1927 from J. W. Sawatzky to M. C. Friesen titled "Encountered Everything Good," in M. W. Friesen, *Canadian Mennonites,* 29.

Menno colonists' occupations and intellectual proclivities, and the distance between their villages kept them from speculating too much on the larger meanings of the Chaco's environment. Most were farmers, so letters and reports to relatives in Canada reveal an emphasis on practical matters such as crop yields, water, and weather. Moreover, the Menno Colony did not establish a newspaper that could have provided a forum for intellectual discussion.[13] News, gossip, and ideas spread through sporadic contact between villages and weekly, biweekly, or monthly village church services – depending on whether a preacher was available.[14] The isolation of some villagers was so acute that if they wanted to visit another village for Sunday services, they had to depart Saturday night.[15]

For some, the transition to the new environment was too much. Colonists grumbled that the 1921 delegation had misled them by promising bountiful grain harvests, based on incomplete information. During the expedition, the delegation planted a test plot of wheat, which was their staple crop in Russia and Canada. The plot represented more than an agricultural experiment since wheat production was the economic barometer of the colony's ability to transplant their farm culture to a new land. Apparently, the wheat grew one foot during the month that the delegates were scouting the Chaco, which portended an easy agrarian transition.[16] Yet the auspicious test plot was merely the product of a few timely rains and colonists soon discovered that large-scale wheat cultivation was futile.

Death and desertion plagued the colony in the first years of its existence. Within 18 months, 163 had people died (including 96 children). Another 323 returned to Canada.[17] Abram A. Braun wrote that "Many [colonists] are like the disbelieving Thomas: they want to see first and only then believe."[18] Gerhard D. Klassen had a more negative assessment,

[13] Menno colonists intermittently shared their impressions with the *Steinbach Post* (Steinbach, Canada). The paper was a forum for conservative-minded Mennonites in North and South America.

[14] Swartzentruber, "Churches and Schools," 629.   [15] Ibid.

[16] M. W. Friesen, *New Homeland*, 98.

[17] There is a discrepancy with these numbers. See Burt Klassen, "Puerto Casado – 16 Monate Wartzeit an der Tür zum Chacoinneren," *Jahrbuch für Geschichte und Kultur der Mennoniten in Paraguay* 13 (2012): 7–30, 13; Alfred Neufeld, "The Mennonite Experience in Paraguay: The Congregational and Theological Experience," *Conrad Grebel Review* 27, no. 1 (2009): 6; G. Ratzlaff, *Ein Leib, viele Glieder: die mennonitischen Gemeinden in Paraguay: vielfältige Gemeinde, kämpfende Gemeinde, begnadete Gemeinde* (Asunción: Gemeindekomittee-Asociación Evangélica Mennonita del Paraguay, 2001), 55–56.

[18] Reprinted letter dated April 1927 from Abram A. Braun titled "The People Don't Have Enough to Do," in M. W. Friesen, *Canadian Mennonites*, 30.

writing to his siblings in Canada, "If a change doesn't happen soon, I don't know what will come of this … we have less than nothing here … Please, send me my birth certificate and passport. I think I will need it yet."[19] Ginter simply stated, "Everything dries up. Everybody gets diarrhea here. Humans get maggots alive."[20] Yet those who complained did not think that the land was cursed. Nor did they believe that God was punishing them. Rather, they directed their grievances at colony leaders. Acrimony between those who stayed and those who returned to Canada spilled across the pages of the Canadian newspaper *Steinbach Post* during the late 1920s. One unnamed returnee bitterly complained about the colony's self-righteousness and – regarding colonists' maintenance of their *Plautdietsch* dialect – taunted them that they should not start speaking Spanish, since "The enemy [Satan] will sow his weeds there [in Paraguay] as well as here [in Canada]."[21] Menno Colony Mennonites retaliated by calling leavers "bondbreakers."[22] Canada may have been a moral desert, but the Chaco represented the real thing: desolate and unproductive (Fig. 3.1).

Fernheim colonists encountered the space of the Chaco much like the Menno colonists, but the former found it more difficult to situate the new environment within a shared cosmology. The Chaco was not simply an agricultural challenge that they had prepared themselves to overcome, but an unwanted destiny that was thrust upon each individual colonist by some dimly understood earthly or supernatural power. Most had wanted to go to Canada. Johann Ediger, a homeopathic doctor who was contracted by McRoberts to serve the colonists, recorded "It makes me sick to see and hear again and again how people try to curry the favor of the Canadian government, as if it were a matter of getting into the Promised Land."[23] The Fernheim colonists were also less prepared for farming than their Menno Colony neighbors since they counted among their ranks

[19] Reprinted letter dated January 4, 1927 from Gerhard D. Klassen to siblings titled "I Don't Know What Will Come of This," quoted in ibid., 30.

[20] Ibid., 34.

[21] *Steinbach Post* (Canada), March 5, 1930, quoted in M. W. Friesen, *New Homeland*, 263.

[22] Royden Loewen, *Village Among Nations: "Canadian" Mennonites in a Transnational World, 1916–2006* (Toronto: University of Toronto Press, 2013), 69.

[23] Letter from Ediger to Unruh, April 6, 1920. Quoted in Peter P. Klassen, *The Mennonites in Paraguay Volume 1: Kingdom of God and Kingdom of This World*, trans. by Gunther H. Schmitt (Filadelfia, Paraguay: Peter P. Klassen, 2003), 84. Ediger was a Russian-born Mennonite living in Germany when McRoberts contacted him about providing health-care for the Menno Colony. See Uwe S. Friesen and Rudolf Dyck, "Ediger, Johann," *Lexikon der Mennoniten in Paraguay*, 117–18.

FIGURE 3.1 Hauling water in Menno Colony, n.d. Samuel McRoberts photo collection 713-BK4-161, Mennonite Heritage Archives

a number of professionals and educators.[24] Some families lacked a father and were dependent on the labor of the children and the goodwill of the MCC.

The Fernheim Colony's nascent churches found it difficult to supply a unified or coherent explanation of the colonists' fate. From the

---

[24] Peter Rahn, "Was fehlt uns? – und wie kann uns geholfen werden?" *Menno-Blatt* (Fernheim, Paraguay), May 1931, 3–4.

beginning, colonists were not inclined to organize under the direct leadership of an *Ältester* but instead created individual congregations, organized under the egalitarian conference structures imported from Russia. The first was the Brüdergemeinde, which was established by Isaak I. Braun on June 9, 1930. The Brüdergemeinde represented the colony's largest church and claimed 1,023 members (434 baptized). In 1860s Russia, the Brüdergemeinde parted with the larger Mennonitengemeinde owing to the former's emphasis on mission work, personal repentance from sin, and the conversion experience. The second-largest church was the Mennonitengemeinde. Preacher Johann Bergmann convened the church on June 22, 1930, but Peter P. Klassen notes that it suffered from indecisive leadership until 1936, when the Russian-born preacher and teacher Abraham Harder relocated from Germany to Fernheim. The Mennonitengemeinde attempted to reconstruct its previous traditions but it also incorporated new practices, such as allowing women to partake in congregational discussions. By 1932, it included 816 members (355 baptized). The third was the Evangelisch-Mennonitische Bruderschaft (Evangelical-Mennonite Brethren, Allianzgemeinde). In many respects, the Allianzgemeinde was theologically similar to the Brüdergemeinde, but their paths eventually diverged in the Paraguayan context over the issue of Nazism. Organized by Nikolai Wiebe in August 1930, it had grown to 116 members (62 baptized) by 1933.[25]

Fernheim colonists were more theologically eclectic and progressive than their Menno Colony counterparts. Fernheim's population was composed of individuals from various congregations across the Soviet Union, and Siberia, in particular, was more dynamic than the confession's established strongholds in southern Russia. During the late nineteenth century, Russia's Mennonites were influenced by various strains of radical Protestantism that swept across the country. During the early twentieth century, they were introduced to European educational and religious developments including the dispensational paradigm of history and the pietistic and Moravian movements.[26] Moreover, during their sojourn in

---

[25] These numbers are imprecise due to the number of deaths and births during the first years of settlement. For a description of each conference including membership numbers, see Walter Quiring, *Deutsche erschliessen den Chaco* (Karlsruhe, Germany: Heinrich Schneider, 1936), 191–202. For a later account including the names of conference leaders, see P. Klassen, *The Mennonites in Paraguay Volume 1*, 305 ff.

[26] A. Neufeld, "Congregational and Theological," 16. See also Harry Loewen, "Intellectual Developments Among the Mennonites 1880–1917," *Journal of Mennonite Studies* 8 (1990): 90–93.

Germany, the refugees interacted with a variety of Baptist, Catholic, and Lutheran refugees, camp staff, and visitors.

Environmental-related factors contributing to their interpretation of the Chaco included inadequate housing, medical care, and livestock management. Living in poorly sealed tents, with a meager diet and scarce water supplies, Fernheim colonists were soon beset with malnutrition and disease. Typhoid fever hit the colony in 1930.[27] From Schoenbrunn alone, the disease had claimed a total of 32 out of 127 people within a few months.[28] Allianzgemeinde leader N. Wiebe indicated the depth of the crisis in March 1930:

Even on Sunday we had to make coffins and dig graves, instead of going to church … In one tent the tablecloth was still on the table. Beds were in the tent as well as outside – but the 6 previously healthy members of the Harms family who had lived there – had left forever. I looked across the street and saw a different sight. An elderly lady was sitting in her tent alone. Her three adult children had died.[29]

The situation remained grim for months. In December, Wilhelm Klassen reported, "Several men were constantly on the lookout for bottle trees for coffins."[30]

The Chaco's wildlife was also deadly. Puma and jaguar attacks were common until colonists began using patrols and strychnine.[31] Foxes stole chickens, locusts ravished scanty fields, wasps and poisonous snakes bit curious children and, according to Fernheim resident Gerhard Schartner, Paraguayan cattle often ran away, which caused their owners to incur debts for animals that died in the bush.[32]

The Chaco's lack of water and extreme weather also caused misery. The dry season lasted from June to September, but rainfall was unpredictable the rest of the year. Viable freshwater wells were difficult to find and maintain since their sandy walls collapsed and threatened to bury workers alive.[33] Strong winds brought downpours that flooded the tent-dwellers,

---

[27] Wilhelm Klassen, "Painful Paths," in *The Schoenbrunn Chronicles*, comps. Agnes Balzer and Liselotte Dueck, trans. Henry and Esther Regehr (Waterloo: Sweetwater Books, 2009), 34; Johann Regehr, "Death in Schoenbrunn," in *The Schoenbrunn Chronicles*, 39.

[28] W. Klassen, "Painful Paths," 34.

[29] "Letter from Nikolai Wiebe to Harold S. Bender," March 5, 1931. Quoted in P. Klassen, *The Mennonites in Paraguay Volume 1*, 78.

[30] W. Klassen, "Tiefe Wege," *Menno-Blatt* (Fernheim, Paraguay), December 1930, 2–4.

[31] Frieda Balzer, "Brush with Terror," in *Schoenbrunn Chronicles*, 65–66.

[32] Jakob Unger, "Aus der Natur unserer neuen Heimat," *Menno-Blatt* (Fernheim, Paraguay) August 1933, 3; P. Klassen, *The Mennonites in Paraguay Volume 1*, 77.

[33] P. Klassen, *The Mennonites in Paraguay Volume 1*, 77.

FIGURE 3.2 Fernheim Colony family outside their tent in the Chaco, 1930. Note the "bottle tree" in front. The tree's interior can be used for stuffing mattresses, the wood is useful for making buckets and trays, and the bark can be used for rope. Photo used courtesy of Mennonite Historical Library, Goshen (IN) College

or dust storms that covered everything with a fine yellow silt.[34] Temperatures regularly exceeded forty degrees Celsius during the summer, and winter temperatures sometimes fell below freezing. Colonists huddled in their Siberian coats and hung blankets over the doors to conserve the heat from their small wood-burning stoves.[35] For many colonists, the Chaco embodied its designation as the "green hell," a term popularized by Luis Bazoberry's 1936 film about the Chaco War, since the region appeared completely hostile and beyond control (Fig. 3.2).

In this harsh context, Fernheim colonists ascribed multiple and contrasting religious and environmental meanings to the Chaco. Though Fernheimers were conditioned to pursue broad-level cooperation in Russia, they nevertheless exhibited a great deal of diversity in their theological reflections. Some believed that God had blessed them with a new

[34] W. Klassen, "Tiefe Wege."
[35] According to Nikolai Siemens, it was not the level of the mercury in the thermostat that caused the most misery but the relentlessness of the heat. See "Muss es im Chaco immer heiß sein?" *Menno-Blatt* (Fernheim, Paraguay), July 1931, 3–4.

homeland. Others thought that their true homeland was still in Russia. Still others believed that God had sent them to this wild location for the difficult – though ultimately constructive – purpose of spreading Christianity. Some viewed it as an interminable prison sentence. The diversity of opinions indicates that they were not unified in their interpretation of the new land.

The Fernheim Colony's impressions of the Chaco are best observed in the pages of the colony's newspaper *Menno-Blatt,* which started as a four-page monthly in 1930. The paper's masthead suggests the dawning of new day in the Chaco through tremendous physical toil: A blazing sun bears down on a faceless pioneer driving a team of oxen across a barren expanse. To the right stands an unruly agave plant, to the left stands a wooden cross that is nearly obscured by a prickly pear. This was the Chaco as the colony's supporters viewed it: defiant and scorching but with the possibility of redemption through hard work and Christian faith.[36]

The wilderness was an obvious and visceral metaphor for Fernheim colonists.[37] Biblical concepts of exile and wandering in the wilderness were recurring themes for Fernheim colonists and indicate the general paradigm through which Fernheim Mennonites viewed the territory. In fact, some individuals compared the "Red Gate" over the train track on their way out of the Soviet Union to the Red Sea through which the Israelites had passed on their way out of Egypt.[38] Yet was the Chaco a "Sinai Desert" through which they must wander, or was it a "Promised Land" where they would remain forever? In a letter to Bender dated November 22, 1930, H. B. Friesen compared the attitudes of the Israelites on their journey through the Siani with that of the Fernheim colonists, writing that "One is now better able to understand the whole nature of the complaining, dissatisfaction and loss of courage ... and the fact that God had to punish them so often."[39] Two years later, Abraham Löewen of Kleefeld advanced a similar theme in his article "Ten Golden

---

[36] The masthead was designed by a Mennonite artist living in Germany by the name of Hans Legiehn. For more on the history of *Menno-Blatt,* see A. Neufeld, "Nikolai Siemens: Ein Wanderer zwischen Welten," *Jahrbuch für Geschichte und Kultur der Mennoniten in Paraguay* 6 (2005): 91–113, 94.

[37] See M. W. Friesen, *New Homeland,* 406.

[38] Helmuth Isaak, *Your Faith Will Sustain You, and You Will Prevail,* trans. Jack Thiessen (Norderstedt, Germany: Books on Demand, 2014), 7.

[39] "Letter from H. B. Friesen to Harold S. Bender." Quoted in P. Klassen, *The Mennonites in Paraguay Volume 1,* 79.

Rules for the Citizens of Fernheim Colony."[40] His first commandment was that colonists must remember their suffering in Moscow and, since "fortune favors the brave," he concluded that the Fernheim colonists should "let it also be known in the Chaco wilderness that you are a Mennonite."[41] Other biblical stories were similarly useful. A 1933 front-page *Menno-Blatt* article written by Johann Schellenberg meditated on the biblical patriarch Noah's faithfulness to God in the face of extreme hardship. Another front-page column published in February 1935 spoke of Noah's "lonely wandering" before the flood destroyed the wicked of the earth.[42] Others believed that God had actually sanctified the colonists' destruction by ceding control of their fate to Satan. Apparently, enough believed that Satan was responsible for their fate to warrant a rebuke by colonist Jacob Wall.[43] Wall argued that they had no proof that Satan controlled their destiny, and so it was the Lord who had led them to this place of misery. The colony's early years were "a time of bitter testing, a time when we could scarcely understand our Father in heaven."[44]

In any case, life in the Chaco was hard and pessimistic attitudes prevailed. Writing under the pseudonym "Dark Glasses" (likely a play on the phrase "rose-tinted glasses"), one cynical colonist stated, "Our new homeland is difficult ... Almost every tree and bush is full of thorns ... the roses fail here."[45] Another colonist wrote to his brother-in-law in Russia that "The heat is intolerable ... if you still have potatoes to eat, thank God ... We don't have any."[46] A female colonist simply stated that she would rather live in a chicken coop in Russia than in a tent in the Chaco.[47] Though *Menno-Blatt* bound the colony together as a forum for public commiseration, and letters abroad tied the colony to its overseas supporters, the newspaper's content also cast a glaring light on the settlement's inability to coalesce around a shared meaning.

[40] Abraham Löewen, "Zehn goldene Regeln für den Bürger der Kolonie Fernheim," *Menno-Blatt* (Fernheim, Paraguay), March/April 1932, 4. Löewen was the Colony's bookkeeper. See John D. Thiesen, "The Mennonite Encounter with National Socialism in Latin America, 1933–1944," *Journal of Mennonite Studies* 12 (1994): 108.

[41] Abraham Löewen, "Zehn goldene Regeln."

[42] "Gehorsam," *Menno-Blatt* (Fernheim, Paraguay), February 1935, 1.

[43] Jacob Wall, "Erntedankfest," *Menno-Blatt* (Fernheim, Paraguay), June 1932, 1.

[44] Quoted in Friedrich (Fritz) Kliewer, "The Mennonites of Paraguay," *Mennonite Quarterly Review* 11, no. 1 (1937): 94.

[45] Dunkle Brille (pseudonym), "Grauer Alltag," *Menno-Blatt* (Fernheim, Paraguay), October 1935, 5.

[46] Quoted in P. Klassen, *The Mennonites in Paraguay Volume 1*, 80.   [47] Ibid., 80.

While the Menno and Fernheim Colonies struggled to maintain their presence in the Chaco, the Paraguayan government looked on the venture as Manifest Destiny on the cheap. The Mennonite colonists were central actors in an upward-sweeping nationalist narrative of economic development and environmental management. One detailed government report written in 1934 on behalf of the Ministry of Agriculture stated, "There one sees it, hand on the plow, furrows as emissaries of progress opening up fertile ground for the country's economy. Noble fruits sprout from their fields!"[48] By contrast, average Paraguayans were less interested in the role that Mennonites would play in developing "their" Chaco since the territory was widely considered to be a wasteland.[49] Before the Chaco War, the idea of the Chaco as an incorporated part of country was more of a dream than a reality.

Competing impressions of the Chaco indicate that neither the Menno Colony nor the Fernheim Colony nor the Paraguayan government shared a common interpretation of the space. Menno Colony Mennonites viewed the Chaco as a place where they could recreate their local culture until the next plot twist sent them packing. Pessimistic Fernheimers believed that the Chaco was a prison, while optimists argued that God wanted them to create a garden in the wilderness. Paraguayans saw the Chaco either as a no-man's-land or as the nation's final frontier. Combined, such impressions indicate that the Chaco was not only a borderland between two states – Bolivia and Paraguay – but a liminal and malleable area in the minds of its colonizers. The critical years of the Chaco War would imbue the space with increasingly nationalist meanings even as the colonies renegotiated their relationships with the Paraguayan and Bolivian governments.

THE CHACO WAR

The late-nineteenth- and early-twentieth-century experiment in establishing firm bonds between territories, states, and nations extended to the world's most isolated regions and entailed some of its poorest governments gambling their country's meager resources to achieve this objective.

[48] Sigfrido (Sigifredo) Gross Brown, *Las Colonias Menonitas en el Chaco* (Asunción: Imprenta Nacional, 1934), 1.
[49] On the various ways the Chaco was imagined by Paraguayans see the chapter "Comparing Eastern and Western Paraguay: Scientific Nationalism," in Bridget María Chesterton, *Grandchildren of Solano López: Frontier and Nation in Paraguay, 1904–1936* (Albuquerque, NM: University of New Mexico Press, 2013).

The Chaco War was one such venture. For Bolivia and Paraguay, the Chaco was a blank slate upon which would be written the future of their countries. The war tested Paraguay's respect for Mennonite military exemption, and both warring countries' respect for Mennonite neutrality. For the Mennonites, the war required them to choose how they would engage the two governments and tested their ability to preserve their communities in the face of violence. These tests, in turn, reaffirmed their collective narratives: the Menno Colony as an independent and privileged unit and the Fernheim Colony as a collection of thankful and pragmatic survivors.

The Menno colonists incorporated the war into their collective narrative by maintaining a position of privileged separatism. They provided only relatively little support to the Paraguayan military personnel stationed near their colony. In contrast, the Fernheim colonists used the war to test, and perhaps affirm, a narrative of colonial and national solidarity and worked closely with the Paraguayan military for several reasons: (1) The war was an opportunity to generate much-needed income; (2) they were thankful that the country had accepted them as refugees; and (3) they were familiar with government cooperation and viewed national affinities as a normal feature of the modern world.

The Fernheim Colony initiated friendly relations with the Paraguayan government soon after their arrival. In February 1932, several of the colony's teachers were invited to the presidential palace to meet with President Dr. José Patricio Guggiari.[50] Entering the palace, the delegation passed a contingent of Marines, clad in white, with their arms at their sides. The pomp and circumstance of the occasion impressed the Mennonites.[51] Writing in *Menno-Blatt*, Fernheim schoolteacher Friedrich Kliewer noted the "joyful message" that the president wanted Mennonites to furnish Paraguayan soldiers with food, supplies, and horses and he assured colonists "of the government's best goodwill."[52] A few months later, German Minister to Paraguay Rudolf von Bülow received a second group of Fernheim leaders in the capital. After the

---

[50] A full report of the meeting is recorded in Friedrich Kliewer, "Empfang beim Präsidenten von Paraguay [part 1]," *Menno-Blatt* (Fernheim, Paraguay), March/April 1932, 4.

[51] Ibid.

[52] Friedrich Kliewer, "Empfang beim Präsidenten von Paraguay [Part 2]," *Menno-Blatt* (Fernheim, Paraguay), May 1932, 2.

meeting, the Paraguayan government offered the Mennonites a tour of the country's new battleship, which they gladly accepted.[53]

Menno Colony was more limited in its contact with the Paraguayan government, and its representatives did not accompany the Fernheim contingents to Asunción in 1932. The Menno Colony conducted business in the capital only when absolutely necessary. For instance, on February 5, 1931, Menno Colony representative J. J. Priesz visited the German legation and complained to Bülow about various robberies committed by Paraguayan troops stationed in the Chaco. The interaction was a natural extension of separatist Mennonites' history of capitalizing on their Germanness when it was advantageous and dismissing it when it was not. Owing to the Menno Colony's "cultural connections" to Germany, Bülow arranged a meeting with President Guggiari to discuss the issue, and served as translator because the colonists had not yet mastered Spanish.[54] Thus, the Menno colonists leveraged their status as German speakers to gain an audience with the Paraguayan president, whom they asked to help maintain Menno Colony's separation from Paraguay's only presence in the region.

Between 1929 and 1932 Bolivia and Paraguay careened toward conflict and the Mennonite colonies found themselves occupying its geographic and discursive "ground zero."[55] Bolivian officials were alarmed at the Paraguayan governments' ongoing promotion of Mennonite immigration, while rumors spread through the Paraguayan press that "German-speaking officers" from the Menno Colony were leading Bolivian patrols through the Chaco.[56] The rumors were unfounded; yet it is true that the Mennonites' presence indirectly exacerbated an already tense situation. Ultimately, a combination of factors – the failure of an international

---

[53] N. Siemens, "In Asunción," *Menno-Blatt* (Fernheim, Paraguay), September 1932, 2. Bülow apparently met with Fernheim leaders quite frequently, having greeted them upon their arrival in Paraguay and meeting with them again in early 1931. For a record of this meeting, see Bülow, "Russische Mennoniten im Chaco," PA AA.

[54] Bülow, "Kanadische Mennoniten," February 5, 1931, 48, Buenos Aires 67A (Mennoniten-Einwanderung nach Paraguay), Shelf 48, Carton 2439, PA AA.

[55] The dispute gained the attention of international actors including the Pan American League and the League of Nations. See League of Nations, "Dispute Between Bolivia and Paraguay-Annex 1099 and 1099(a)," *League of Nations Official Journal* 10, no. 1 (1929): 253–56; "Documentation Concerning the Dispute Between Bolivia and Paraguay," *League of Nations Official Journal* 10, no. 2 (1929): 264–74.

[56] The rumors were likely aroused by the knowledge that an ex-German general named Hans Kundt led the Bolivian armed forces. See Bülow, "Bericht Nr. 37. Inhalt: Paraguayisch-bolivianischer Grenzstreit," February 18, 1929, 3," R78859 (Politik 3), PA AA. For more on Kundt, see Farcau, 87.

solution, economic insecurities caused by the Great Depression, the polemics of each country's press, and the shared belief that nations must have clear borders – propelled Bolivia and Paraguay into Latin America's bloodiest twentieth-century international conflict. It cost the lives of about 90,000–100,000 combatants, disrupted the lives of untold numbers of indigenous people, and jeopardized the survival of both Mennonite colonies.[57]

By mid-1932, the two states were engaged in a full-fledged war. Much of the initial fighting was centered west of Puerto Casado and immediately south of the Mennonites.[58] The Bolivians were positioned to the southwest of the colonies and the Paraguayans were stationed at Isla Po'i, a few kilometers southeast of Menno Colony's "capital" Sommerfeld (later renamed Loma Plata).[59] The Fernheim Colony was closest to the front and most in danger of being taken or destroyed. *Menno-Blatt* reports that individuals living in the village of Schoenbrunn witnessed a Bolivian military aircraft graze the colony's western border. Another Bolivian biplane – perhaps confusing the colony's capital of Filadelfia for a Paraguayan encampment – strafed a group of people on the town's main street and put five rounds through a metal roof.[60]

A few days later, the Paraguayan government threatened a mass evacuation of the colonies, likely because the Bolivians had captured four of Paraguay's forts in as many days.[61] For the Fernheim Mennonites, this development invoked a specter of death and violence that seemed to follow them wherever they went. Considering the prospect of war waged on colony soil, N. Siemens stated "Before the mind's eye serious images appeared" of desolate Russian villages and endless refugee trains.[62] The only thing left to do, suggested N. Siemens, was to pray

---

[57] Matthew Hughes, "Logistics and the Chaco War: Bolivia Versus Paraguay, 1932–1935," *Journal of Military History* 69, no. 2 (2005): 412.

[58] M. Hughes, "Logistics and the Chaco War," 420–21.

[59] Gerhard Ratzlaff, *Zwischen den Fronten: Mennoniten und andere evangelische Christen im Chacokrieg 1932–1935* (Asunción: Gerhard Ratzlaff, 2009), 37.

[60] N. Siemens, "Gewitterwolken am politischen Horizont," *Menno-Blatt* (Fernheim, Paraguay), August 1932, 1–2.

[61] Alejandro Quesada, *The Chaco War 1932–95: South America's Greatest War* (Oxford: Osprey Publishing, 2011).

[62] N. Siemens, "Gewitterwolken am politischen Horizont," *Menno-Blatt* (Fernheim, Paraguay), August 1932, 1–2. N. Siemens also drew on Johann Wolfgang von Goethe ("From the spirits that I called Sir, deliver me!") to provide a literary interpretation of the situation. See Siemens, "Krieg und Kriegsopfer," *Menno-Blatt* (Fernheim, Paraguay), October 1932, 3.

and wait. Their prayers were answered when unseasonal rains stalled the Bolivians' advance.

Bolivian forces briefly occupied the colonies in September 1932 during the Battle of Boquerón, indicating the colonies' strategic importance, but also suggesting the impotency of both countries' military administration. At the start of the battle, a detachment of Bolivian soldiers approached the Fernheim Colony border and accosted three Mennonite brothers who were searching for reeds. The soldiers asked the youths for the location of Fort Guajó. One boy knew the outpost so the soldiers took him captive, gave him a horse, and forced him to lead the way. He led them down a narrow path to a small hut with a straw roof.[63] The leader of the detachment, a Lieutenant Suárez, proceeded to storm the hut and, upon finding it empty, noted in his field book that the position was captured. The detachment then rode their horses into the dusty Mennonite village of Schönwiese, on the eastern side of Fernheim Colony. Here, the lieutenant issued a statement to the undoubtedly surprised mayor Heinrich Dürksen. It affirmed Bolivia's sovereignty over the colonies and guaranteed Mennonites' special privileges under the laws of Bolivia but it warned residents that helping Paraguay would cause the Bolivian army to "punish any treachery."[64] The soldiers left, presumably satisfied that Bolivia now "possessed" the colonies.

Soon thereafter, Paraguay repulsed the Bolivian advance at Boquerón and the Mennonites' interaction with the Paraguayan government became much closer. Paraguayan leaders viewed the colonies as a valuable source of medical aid and transportation, and a critical link in their tenuous supply chain from the Paraguayan River to the front. They also tended to view both colonies as a single unit that could be ordered to comply with their requests. Yet the colonies responded differently to Paraguay's war plans. While the Menno Colony equivocated, Fernheim colonists committed to ongoing aid.[65]

The Menno Colony were largely indifferent to Paraguayan war aims but they were not indifferent to the physical and ideological risks of war. Colonists feared that their fields and homes would be destroyed and that infantrymen might transmit their violent attitudes to the colony's youth. In August 1932, one individual helped a Paraguayan detachment recover

---

[63] Hans Dueck, "Prisoner in the Chaco War," in *Schoenbrunn Chronicles*, 57.
[64] Quoted in G. Ratzlaff, *Christianos Evangélicos*, 33. See also G. Ratzlaff, *Zwischen den Fronten*, 33–34; Hans Dueck, "Prisoner in the Chaco War," 57.
[65] G. Ratzlaff, *Zwischen den Fronten*, 41.

supplies from the Carayá military post, located near the colony. When he returned, the man received a sharp rebuke from colony leaders for his "military service."[66] After the incident, Menno Colony leaders refused to allow members to aid either army and declined Paraguayan government contracts for men and materiel. It is unclear how individual colonists felt about the leadership's refusal of military contracts, but the fact that there is but one reported violation of the decision testifies that it was not a large enough issue to cause colony-wide unrest or overturn the colony's leadership.

In late 1932, a more serious request was handed down by Paraguayan authorities. On October 6, the colonies received word from Lieutenant Colonel José Félix Estigarribia that they must supply the Paraguayan army with sixty wagons, oxen, and drivers (forty from the Menno Colony and twenty from the Fernheim Colony) to transport supplies from "Km 145" to Isla Po'i. Menno Colony leaders immediately convened a meeting and drafted a short letter to Estigarribia. In the letter, they thanked God that Paraguay acquitted them from military service but affirmed that they would not aid the Paraguayan military under any circumstances.[67] A few days later Estigarribia clarified that his message was not a request, but an order. The wagons and oxen would be due on October 14, at 4 p.m. at Hoffnungsfeld.[68]

The following day, Menno Colony leaders convened a second meeting in the village of Osterwick, to which all male members were invited. During the meeting, it was determined that M. C. Friesen and Isaak K. Fehr, would meet with Estigarribia personally. In the meantime, they sent another message to Estigarribia stating that the colony would do everything it its power to serve the (non-military) economic development of the country but they could not violate the dictates of their conscious on behalf of the military. After Estigarribia received the leaders at his camp, the colony were granted their exemption.[69]

A curious encounter happened when the Mennonite delegates returned to the colony. According to the American *Literary Digest*, an Argentine journalist encountered them on the road. It is unclear which individuals the reporter spoke to, but he stated that the Mennonites had met with

---

[66] Ibid., 29–30.

[67] "Kolonie Menno to Estigarribia," October 6, 1932, Binder 15, Archivo Colonia Menno (hereafter, ACM), Loma Plata, Paraguay.

[68] "Chacokrieg-Nach Aufzeichnungen des AB Toews," Binder 15, ACM. See also G. Ratzlaff, *Zwischen den Fronten*, 25–26.

[69] G. Ratzlaff, *Zwischen den Fronten*, 26.

Estigarribia to "offer their humble contribution to the defense of Paraguay."[70] The correspondent noted that the Mennonites fled to the Chaco to escape human warfare and instead launch a "peaceful war with the wilderness." However, their interest in defending the Paraguayan nation state was apparently stronger still. The correspondent opined "it is touching to see these farmers ... unacquainted as yet with the Spanish language, identifying themselves with the Paraguayan cause."[71] The reporter failed to see the differences between the Mennonite groups and assumed that they were both patriotically enlisted in Paraguay's military gamble.

Not long after, a new dispatch requested that colonists bake bread for the Paraguayan forces. It would be paid work and the government agreed to supply Mennonite families with flour. Menno Colony leaders convened a meeting on October 21, to discuss the issue. Over the protests of many, they agreed that the colony would provide foodstuffs and limited aid to soldiers – especially the sick and wounded – out of Christian charity.[72] In their exchanges with military authorities, Menno Colony Mennonites reacted quickly and decisively, drawing a firm line between their interests and those of the military.

The Fernheim Colony also convened a meeting after Estigarribia issued his demand for wagons and oxen. Many opinions were voiced about how the colony should act, but the discussion revolved around three general points: (1) the experiences of their forefathers dealing with Russian authorities (2) the biblical injunction found in Romans 13 that commands Christians to obey government authorities and pay their taxes, and (3) the role of their "special privileges" in relation to their civic duties. After much debate, the group agreed that it was wrong to deny the government's request since they enjoyed the benefits of Paraguayan citizenship and their religious privileges.[73] They were thankful to the Paraguayan government for accepting them as refugees and now they wished to perform their duties as citizens. Like Canada's associative Mennonites, the

---

[70] It is possible that Fernheim delegates accompanied M. C. Friesen and Fehr to the meeting. "The Blond Men of the Chaco," *The Literary Digest* (New York), April 1, 1933, 27.

[71] Ibid.

[72] "Chacokrieg-Nach Aufzeichnungen des AB Toews." See also "Brotbacken fuer das Militaer, Protokoll 29 November 1932," Binder 15, ACM; G. Ratzlaff, *Zwischen den Fronten*, 27.

[73] Four preachers from the Fernheim Colony attended the Menno Colony discussion – which took place the next day – though the latter's decision to request Estigarribia's exemption did not affect the Fernheimers' decision. See N. Siemens, "Krieg und Kriegsopfer," 4.

Fernheim colonists believed that they should play an active role in the political life of their host country.

The Fernheim Mennonites were a major asset to the Paraguayan military. They tended wounded soldiers and transported Bolivian prisoners of war.[74] By January of 1933, the hospital and village schools were overflowing with wounded soldiers. Perhaps the most critical assistance they provided to Paraguay was supplying soldiers with nutriment (sweet potatoes, beans, bread, honey, and eggs) so the army could maintain a constant presence in the Chaco.[75] During the dry months, surface water was negligible and Mennonite villages supplied fresh water.[76] During the wet months, flash floods made supply roads impassable and the Paraguayan army had to abandon their trucks and commission Mennonites' wagon transports.[77] The mutuality between the Fernheim Colony and the Paraguayan Army eventually became so close that a joint church service was held at Lichtfelde in 1935 (Fig. 3.3).[78]

As the public voice of the Fernheim Colony, *Menno-Blatt* affirmed colonists' solidarity with Paraguay. One article noted that a great number of wounded soldiers passed through the colony on a daily basis but they were "polite and modest" compared to Russian soldiers during the Bolshevik Revolution.[79] A 1933 report from a P. Klassen of Rosenort (not the author P. Klassen) mentions, "there remains much to be desired," in the soldiers' conduct but he compared the troops favorably to his understanding of how "Cossacks" treated Germans when they invaded East Prussia during the First World War.[80] The authors asserted the goodness of Paraguay's military, but also withheld from criticizing Paraguay's enemy, Bolivia. Their focus on Russia suggests that the authors were chiefly interested in advancing a narrative that compared their previous (worse) homeland to their new (better) homeland. The second

---

[74] G. Ratzlaff, *Zwischen den Fronten*, 40–41.

[75] For a sense of how much food the Paraguayan military needed, in December 1935 the army ordered 30,000 eggs so that each soldier at the front could receive a Christmas cake. See Paul Janzen, "Weihnacht – Hochbetrieb," *Menno-Blatt* (Fernheim, Paraguay), January 1935, 5.

[76] The army sometimes brought the Fernheim Colony to the brink of water shortages. See N. Siemens, "Noch weiter Gewitterwolken," *Menno-Blatt* (Fernheim, Paraguay), September 1932, 3–4.

[77] G. Ratzlaff, *Zwischen den Fronten*, 40.

[78] N. Siemens, "Spanischer Gottesdienst in Lichtfelde," *Menno-Blatt* (Fernheim, Paraguay), May 1935, 3.

[79] Gerhard F[?], *Menno-Blatt* (Fernheim, Paraguay), August 1932, 2.

[80] P. Klassen, "Bericht aus Rosenort," *Menno-Blatt* (Fernheim, Paraguay), February 1933, 2–3.

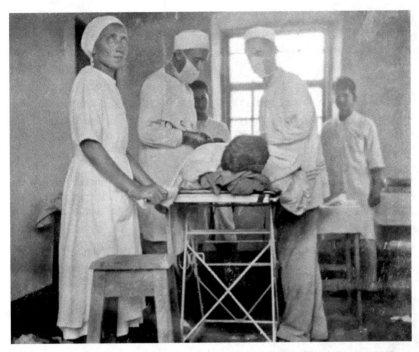

FIGURE 3.3 Performing surgery on a wounded soldier in Fernheim Colony during the Chaco War. To the left is Suse Isaac; n.d. Source: Archivo Colonia Fernheim

author's analogy to Prussians during the First World War likewise suggests an affinity with Germany. Altogether, *Menno-Blatt* affirmed that Fernheimers were loyal Paraguayan citizens even as their experiences in Russia echoed in their minds.

Sometimes Mennonite/Paraguayan relations were too close, but colonists usually blamed individual transgressors and not the Paraguayan government. For instance, a young woman from Halbstadt, Menno Colony reportedly had a romantic affair with a Paraguayan officer before her parents forcibly relocated her to a distant village.[81] Colony historian Uwe S. Friesen circumspectly notes this "liaison," but there was a darker side to the presence of troops in the colonies. In Blumengart (Menno

---

[81] Literature – Mennonite or otherwise – on civilian/military liaisons during the Chaco War is sparse. Uwe S. Friesen, "Der Erschließungsprozess des Gran Chaco seit dem Späten 19. Jahrhundert," *Jahrbuch für Geschichte und Kultur der Mennoniten in Paraguay* 14 (2013): 62.

Colony), colonist Franz Funk wrote of a "soldier plague," after infantry-men shot villagers' cattle, cut off hunks of meat, and left the carcasses.[82] Another report stated that soldiers broke into Mennonite houses at night to molest women and girls.[83] The Fernheim Colony also experienced the reckless terror of soldiers when two women (one heavily pregnant) were molested in their homes and a third was molested on her way to the train station.[84] Such troubling reports culminated in a "horrible murder" in the village of Chortitz (Menno Colony) on February 1, 1934.[85] Colonist F. Funk stated,

> three soldiers seized Abram Giesbrecht's daughter, with whom they undertook their nefarious mischief ... After the neighbors had freed the girl, the soldiers began firing at the Mennonites ... whereby Abram F. Giesbrecht was unluckily hit by a bullet, killing him right on the spot.[86]

Despite the transgressions, colonists did not blame Paraguay's govern-ment for the misconduct of its soldiers. F. Funk reports the soldiers who had shot at Giesbrecht received "their just reward," which came at the hands of the prison guard or the firing squad.[87]

The war clearly demonstrated to Asunción that the settlements held different ideas about how they imagined their role vis-à-vis the state. The Menno Colony was amenable to indirect state-building but kept its dis-tance. Fernheim colonists were more intentionally patriotic and showed signs that they had begun to merge their narrative with that of the Paraguayan state. In 1934, a lawyer named Dr. Sigfrido (or Sigifredo) Gross Brown visited both settlements and submitted a report to the government outlining the colonies' administration and economy.[88] He did not disparage the Menno Colony, but he reserved his highest praise for the Fernheim Colony. Referring to the latter, Brown glowed "the Russian colonist is hospitable and generous," and better able to cope with the privations of war, due to their experiences in Soviet Russia.[89] Their past, according to Brown, made them more responsive to Paraguay's military authorities and its nationalist goals.[90] It was quite clear to Brown that the

---

[82] Franz Funk, "Colonia Menno, Paraguay," *Steinbach Post* (Canada), March 23, 1933, 4. From a collection of newspaper clippings compiled by Andrea Dyck and R. Loewen.

[83] Ibid.

[84] Additional transgressions committed against colonists and their property are recorded in the letter "An den Herrn Oberschulzen," Cabinet 7A, Archivo Colonia Fernheim (here-after, ACF), Filadelfia, Paraguay.

[85] F. Funk, "Colonia Menno, Paraguay," 6.   [86] Ibid.   [87] Ibid.

[88] Gross Brown, *Las Colonias Menonitas*, 43.   [89] Ibid., 20.   [90] Ibid., 19.

Fernheim colonists were better Paraguayans than their Menno Colony neighbors.[91]

The Chaco War ended with an armistice and peace negotiations in June 1935, though the peace treaty would not be concluded until 1938. Fernheim Mennonites received the news on Pentecost Sunday, when two military cars arrived from Trebol. Mennonites and soldiers flooded the streets of Filadelfia, their cheers vying with each other in patriotic fervor. The July issue of *Menno-Blatt* included a picture of the Paraguayan flag and the contributor nimbly combined German and Paraguayan patriotism with the words "Hail to thee in Victor's Crown" (the unofficial national anthem of the defunct German Empire) printed above the flag and "¡Viva! Republica del Paraguay" printed over the flag. The author explained what the colors of Paraguay's flag meant – blue for justice, white for peace, and red for freedom – and elaborated that Paraguayan freedom was "not as it was preached to us in Soviet Russia, but a real one."[92]

A month later, N. Siemens and the Fernheim Colony *Oberschulze* J. Siemens visited President Ayala in Asunción to offer their congratulations.[93] In his greeting to the president, J. Siemens stated, "At the same time we thank you that through your mediation, and the thoughtfulness of the high command in the Chaco, we got along well with the Paraguayan military."[94] N. Siemens's report in *Menno-Blatt* marveled that they had freely entered the presidential palace without being questioned and had left assured that the colony would be compensated for any property damage sustained as a result of the war.[95]

The Menno colonists were less enthusiastic than the Fernheimers about maintaining relations with Asunción.[96] After the war, Jacob A. Braun, the

---

[91] The German Foreign Service closely followed the war and Fernheim Colony's "very good relations" with Paraguay. See Erhard Graf von Wedel, "Betr. Gespräch mit dem Staatspräsidenten, Asunción," August 20, 1935," R79816 (Politik 25), PA AA. See also Bülow, "Bericht Nr. 194 Inhalt: Paraguayisch-bolivianischer Grenzstreit," August 6, 1932," R78861 (Politik 3), PA AA; Ernst Kundt, "Aufzeichnung, betreffend den Chaco-Konflikt zwischen Bolivien und Paraguay und die mennonitischen Kolonien im Chaco," August 4, 1932, Band 1a, R127502. PA AA.

[92] "Gemeinnutz vor Eigennutz!" *Menno-Blatt* (Fernheim, Paraguay), July 1935, 5.

[93] N. Siemens, "Unterhaltendes, Nach Asunción," *Menno-Blatt* (Fernheim, Paraguay), August 1935, 4–6. Eusebio Ayala occupied the presidency twice, from 1921 to 1923 and again from 1932 to 1936. In the interim, Eligio Ayala occupied the office from 1923 to 1924 and again from 1924 to 1928.

[94] Ibid., 5.   [95] Ibid.

[96] G. Ratzlaff, *Zwischen den Fronten*, 42; Jacob A. Braun, *Im Gedenken an jene Zeit: Mitteilungen zur Entstehungsgeschichte der Kolonie Menno* (Loma Plata, Paraguay: Jakob a. Braun, [2001?]), 93–94.

first *Oberschulze* of the Menno Colony, paid a visit to President Ayala but it was business, and not patriotism, that guided his mission. In his meeting, J. A. Braun reported that there were a number of outstanding invoices for products that his colony had delivered to the army.[97] With apparent kindness, the president promised to clear the matter up immediately. J. A. Braun then visited the finance minister, who issued him a check on the spot.[98] Menno Colony had helped Paraguayan soldiers for humanitarian reasons but they had little interest in congratulating the government for its military prowess.

Menno Colony's leadership thought that aiding the Paraguayan government could drag members of their colony toward the enticements of greater material prosperity and the negative influences of "worldly" soldiers. The war was simply a new test of their fidelity to an ancient narrative. Yet Fernheim colonists were willing to aid the Paraguayan army because they had worked with governments before and wanted to thank the country that welcomed them as refugees. Fernheim colonists originated from communities in the Russian Empire that had cooperated with the Tsar in the 1870s and attempted to establish a modus vivendi with the Soviets in the 1920s. This post-1870s cooperative spirit was not confined to peacetime. Mennonites aided Russia during the Russo-Turkish War (1877–1878) and the Russo-Japanese War (1904–1905) by establishing field hospitals and contributing hundreds of thousands of rubles of material aid to soldiers. The First World War and the Russian Civil War likewise saw Mennonite men aiding, and in a few instances, even fighting on behalf of the Germans and Whites (i.e. groups that opposed Communism). [99] Moreover, when they left the Soviet Union, the refugees were aided by Germany, Brüder in Not, and the MCC, each of which presupposed that individuals fit within national and religious rubrics. Altogether, the Chaco War brought into sharp relief the distance between the colonies.

THE CHACO PEOPLE

The Bolivian and Paraguayan governments hoped that war would determine who would give the space of the Chaco a national meaning. Yet it

---

[97] G. Ratzlaff, "Die paraguayischen Mennoniten in der nationalen Politik," *Jahrbuch für Geschichte und Kultur der Mennoniten in Paraguay* 5 (2004), 73–74.

[98] J. A. Braun, *Im Gedenken an jene Zeit*, 93–94.

[99] John B. Toews, "The Origins and Activities of the Mennonite Selbstschutz in the Ukraine (1918–1919)," *Mennonite Quarterly Review* 46 (1972): 11, 17–19.

was the Mennonites and their daily mediation with indigenous peoples that ultimately determined the Chaco's social trajectory. Each colony took a different approach. Fernheim colonists played an active role in the region's transformation. They created a missionary agency that served as a social and economic conduit between indigenous people and Asunción. The initiative complimented a worldview that presupposed the gathering together of the world's people within nation states and under the banner of Christianity. Alternately, the Menno Colony limited its contact with indigenous people to contracted and seasonal labor and did not wish to become an indigenous conduit to the capital or cultivate indigenous Christianity in the Chaco. Doing so would make them active participants in the modernization of the Paraguayan nation state, which was a situation that they wished to avoid.

The Fernheim Mennonites used missionary activity as a way to give meaning to their collective venture since it let them recast their exile from Russia as a divine mandate. After all, what better reason was there to travel to a remote wilderness halfway around the world if not to redeem people to the Lord and thereby redeem themselves from their past? Missionary work was an ideal venture because it could be interpreted in different though complimentary ways. Some Fernheimers believed that God had led them to the Chaco to save indigenous souls, while others viewed the initiative as a way for the colony to improve its relationship with the government. Still others believed that missionary activity would benefit both the Mennonites and Paraguayan society. Finally, a few individuals saw the venture as a way to introduce German culture to a benighted population. None of these opinions were immediately accepted by the settlement, but the debate surrounding them indicates that the Fernheim colonists viewed missionary activity as beneficial for group unity. By establishing a missionary organization, the colony affirmed their place in a Christian narrative of saving souls for Christ, a Paraguayan narrative of state citizenship, and a German narrative of national culture, thereby endowing the venture with both spiritual and earthly mandates.

Conversely, the Menno colonists were not interested in spreading the gospel because they did not see themselves as part of an international Christian community or as working at the behest of the Paraguayan government. Colonists believed that it was enough to live the example of the early church instead of convincing others to do the same. According to M. C. Friesen, "before [the Menno Colony] lies a large field of activity," not of missionary work but a place "where we can operate unhindered by the world."[100] Menno Colony would eventually increase its contact with indigenous people to the point of sponsoring its own missionary organization, but this development took two decades. Initially, missionary work was inimical to the Menno Colony narrative but crucial to that of the Fernheim Colony.

Menno Colony's contact with Paraguay's indigenous population began in 1921 when members of the exploratory delegation made contact with several Enlhit communities.[101] The meeting represented the third time on three continents in less than 150 years that Mennonites sought indigenous lands confiscated by state authorities: The first had occurred in 1789 when Mennonites settled the Nogaitsi-dominated Russian steppe, the second in the 1870s when Canada displaced Métis in Manitoba, and the third was underway in 1921 when the delegates surveyed the Chaco.[102] Mennonite colonizers did not recognize indigenous people as legitimate proprietors of the land, because the Lord sanctified Christian dominion over nature, and the state granted Mennonite colonial expansion. Thus, the Menno colonists had two requests after the 1921 expedition. The first was to have the railroad extended from the Paraguayan River to their settlement. The second was to have indigenous people removed from the land, as had been done in Canada in the 1870s.[103] Neither request had materialized by the time the migrants arrived. Informal contact with indigenous people therefore remained a constant feature of colony life. Sometimes Enlhit individuals brought the colonists logs and food, or raided Mennonite crops and tents for food and luxuries.[104] Colony members used indigenous people as guides and laborers. One report filed by

[100] Quoted in Heinrich Ratzlaff, *Ältester Martin C. Friesen: Ein Mann, den Gott brauchen konnte* (Loma Plata, Paraguay: Geschichtskomitee der Kolonie Menno, 2006), 102.

[101] The Enlhit were the most prominent group of indigenous people on the land. They belonged to the Maskoy peoples, who had settled along the upper Paraguay River toward the end of the nineteenth century. For a description of indigenous groups, see René D. Harder Horst, *The Stroessner Regime and Indigenous Resistance in Paraguay* (Tallahassee, FL: University Press of Florida, 2007), 14.

[102] E. K. Francis, *In Search of Utopia: The Mennonites in Manitoba* (Glencoe, IL: Free Press, 1955), 19; Donovan Giesbrecht, "Metis, Mennonites and the 'Unsettled Prairie,' 1874–1896," *Journal of Mennonite Studies* 19 (2001): 104.

[103] M. W. Friesen, "Chaco Mission (Paraguay)," *Global Anabaptist Mennonite Encyclopedia Online*, last modified, August 20, 2013, http://gameo.org/index.php?title=Chaco_Mission_(Paraguay)&oldid=86629, last accessed June 7, 2018; M. W. Friesen, *New Homeland*, 99.

[104] Cornelius T. Sawatzky, "The Bolivians Are Here!" quoted in M. W. Friesen, *Canadian Mennonites*, 64; M. W. Friesen, *New Homeland*, 340; Redekop, *Strangers Become Neighbors*, 49.

a Corporación Paraguaya employee stated that tensions often developed between the groups: "We worked Indians as long as possible but there was always friction between the Mennonites and them. One day at noon it almost came to blows."[105] Generally speaking, colonists did not consider sustained contact with indigenous groups to be desirable, though they certainly benefited from their local knowledge and cheap labor.[106]

The Menno Colony's separatism upheld a firm distinction between their congregations and outsiders – be they Russians, Canadians, or Enlhit. Yet individual colony members believed in the general goodness of missionary activity and some donated money to evangelical causes, but they did not participate in such ventures collectively. In the early 1970s, Menno Colony missionary Bernhard W. Toews recalled a debate about mission work among members of his congregation that took place during the 1920s.[107] Some individuals believed that it was good for Christians to translate the Bible into new languages and preach the gospel in an "unsophisticated" way, but it was not right to forcefully convert "heathens." Others rejected all missionary activity as a "Pharisee-like undertaking" that was self-aggrandizing and prideful.[108] It was not until 1952 that the Menno Colony began underwriting missionary activity among indigenous people, and it is possible that this would not have materialized had not the physical proximity of Menno Colony and Enlhit people been so great.[109] Thus, during the first years of settlement it was the combined influence of the Chaco War and the Fernheim Mennonites that decisively entwined indigenous and Mennonite groups.

The Chaco War displaced thousands of indigenous Ayoreode, Chané, Enlhit, Enenlhit, Guaraní, Nivaklé, and Tapieté peoples.[110] Each group had a unique relationship with the Bolivian and Paraguayan governments and with each of the other groups. For instance, some groups, including the Guaraní and Tapieté, collaborated with Paraguayan military personnel.[111] Meanwhile, the Chané were often in conflict with the Guaraní and joined with the Bolivians as they advanced south.[112] The

[105] J. N. McRoberts, Jr., "Brethren in Need [Field Report], December 1, 1930," Corporacíon Paraguay Correspondence Joseph McRoberts, January 1928–June 1931, IX-3-3 Paraguayan Immigration 1920–1933 (1/19), MCCA.

[106] Peter P. Klassen, *The Mennonites in Paraguay Volume 2: Encounter with Indians and Paraguayans*, trans. Gunther H. Schmitt (Filadelfia, Paraguay: Peter P. Klassen, 2002), 65; Gross Brown, *Las Colonias Menonitas*, 13.

[107] Bernhard W. Toews, "The Church and Mission," quoted in M. W. Friesen, *Canadian Mennonites*, 81–82.

[108] Ibid.   [109] Ibid.   [110] Harder Horst, *The Stroessner Regime*, 18.

[111] P. Klassen, *The Mennonites in Paraguay Volume 2*, 76.   [112] Ibid., 76–77.

Nivaklé were initially pressed into military service by the Bolivian government but abandoned their ranks. In response, the Bolivians engaged a group of Oblate priests from Germany to settle them. Of course, the priests had their own designs for converting the Nivaklé people to Catholicism.[113] Altogether, the war transformed indigenous communities, generally to their detriment. Displaced indigenous men entered the labor market to work in local industries, including Mennonite farming operations, while women and children sold handicrafts and begged.

All Mennonites were willing to use indigenous labor, but it was the Fernheim Colony that viewed the labor market as a mission field. During the late nineteenth century, Mennonitengemeinde and Brüdergemeinde churches sent missionaries to India and the Dutch East Indies, though their work was terminated after the Bolshevik Revolution. P. Klassen observes continuity between this mission work and the Fernheim initiative to evangelize to indigenous people.[114] In both instances, it tended to be the evangelically minded Brüdergemeinde who led the way. P. Klassen maintains that, as a result of the colony's lack of unity the Brüdergemeinde agitation for missionary work was accepted in other Mennonite congregations as a valuable joint enterprise.[115] Of the various indigenous groups, the Enlhit and the Nivaklé entered into the most sustained contact with Mennonites through the Fernheim missionary initiative Licht den Indianern! (Light to the Indians!).[116]

The seeds for Fernheim missionary activity were planted as early as 1932 but it was not until February 1935 that the Fernheim Colony's Kommission für kirchliche Angelegenheiten (Commission for Church Affairs, KfK) sent a document outlining Mennonite missionary plans to the Paraguayan government. The Colony's *Oberschulze*, J. Siemens, and three KfK members signed it: Johann Teichgräf, N. Wiebe, and Gerhard Isaak.[117] The petition stated that the Mennonites wished to "tie these savages to the soil, to gradually educate them into useful citizens of the Paraguayan state." It also noted that the committee had already made progress in this direction by establishing relations with an Indian cacique who had brought his group to settle on Mennonite land, west of the village of Friedensfeld.[118]

---

[113] Ibid., 72.   [114] Ibid., 143.   [115] Ibid., 139.

[116] The organization's name officially contained an exclamation point.

[117] "Zur Indianermission im Chaco Paraguay," *Menno-Blatt* (Fernheim, Paraguay), October 1935, 3.

[118] Ibid.

Menno-Blatt embraced the missionary initiative. From 1935 to 1936, the paper published nearly twenty articles on indigenous groups in the area. The reports and opinions combined detailed ethnographic information – food, clothing, and social structures – with a conviction that Mennonites should improve the spiritual and economic lives of these people. Writing for *Menno-Blatt*, N. Siemens reported in May 1935 that he had traveled with some Paraguayan military "friends" for 18 days and more than 1,000 kilometers in order to inspect the western Chaco. Along the way, he visited the Nivaklé and wrote positively, if patronizingly, of their culture and customs.[119] The next edition of *Menno-Blatt* focused on indigenous people near the colonies, with N. Siemens reporting that about 5,000 Guaraní war refugees had arrived at Fort Toledo, about 35 km from Filadelfia.[120] The article was followed by a report that Lieutenant Ortiz, Paraguayan military police chief and son-in-law of General Estigarribia, had visited N. Siemens and invited him to inspect the military barracks where the Guaraní were located. N. Siemens noted that although the Guaraní were poor, they were friendly and hardworking.[121]

Licht den Indianern! was established on September 13, 1935.[122] Initially, there were six Enlhit families enrolled in the program. They were required to build their own adobe huts and cultivate their own one-hectare plots of land. The mission station was located near Yalve Sanga, about 35 km southeast of Filadelfia.[123] The KfK was charged with administering the new mission through an elected committee of representatives from the Fernheim villages.[124] Additionally, there were ninety-seven *Missionsfreunden* (mission friends) who lent support to the project.[125]

[119] P. Klassen, *The Mennonites in Paraguay Volume 2*, 71; N. Siemens, "Zum Pilcomayo," *Menno-Blatt* (Fernheim, Paraguay), May 1935, 4–5.

[120] P. Klassen, *The Mennonites in Paraguay Volume 2*, 75–76; N. Siemens, "Neue Nachbarn. Guarani-Indianer," *Menno-Blatt* (Fernheim, Paraguay), June 1935, 3; N. Siemens, "Ein Besuch bei den Guaranies," *Menno-Blatt* (Fernheim, Paraguay), July 1935, 3.

[121] N. Siemens, "Ein Besuch."   [122] "Zur Indianermission."

[123] Redekop, *Strangers Become Neighbors*, 142.

[124] "Zur Indianermission." Committee members from the Mennonitengemeinde included Jakob Martens (Waldesruh), Jakob Dürksen (Schönwiese), and Franz Wiens (Schönwiese). Committee members from the Allianzgemeinde included Nikolai Wiebe (Schönwiese) and Johann Käthler (Friedensruh). Committee members from the Brüdergemeinde included Gerhard Isaak (Waldesruh), Kornelius Voth (Waldesruh), and Johann Schellenberg (Auhagen).

[125] G. G., "Missionsfest in Gnadenheim," *Menno-Blatt* (Fernheim, Paraguay), September 1935, 2.

To raise awareness, the colony held a *Missionsfest* (mission festival). Mission friends donated sundry articles such as horse bridles, chairs, brooms, and bedding for a fundraising auction.[126] Additional support came from contributions within Paraguay and abroad (especially North America), contributions from the Paraguayan government, and projected income from the planned mission economy.[127] The mission's four goals were:

1) Introduce Indians to the living God and give them instruction in Christian doctrine according to the Holy Scriptures.
2) Raise the spiritual level of the Indians through their children's education and instruction about a morally pure, Christian family life.
3) Educate the Indians in regard to hygiene.
4) Educate the Indians in economic and cultural spheres, as well as educate them to be loyal, helpful, and hardworking citizens of the Paraguayan state.[128]

The Paraguayan government was interested in Mennonite missionary activity for the purpose of turning indigenous people into state citizens and confining them to permanent settlements.[129] During the 1930s, Paraguayan/indigenous relations was marked by the Liberal government's attempt to integrate indigenous people into the national fabric, even as it continued to exoticize them in the nation's mythology. Licht den Indianern! soon became the focal point of contact between indigenous groups and modern systems – including the cash economy and standardized education – that drew (or compelled) the Chaco's indigenous population into Paraguayan society.[130] Ironically, the Menno Colony's neighbors, the Fernheimers, were the harbingers of Paraguay's "educational state" in the Chaco in that they promoted a foreign culture and national citizenship to a "benighted" population.[131] The Menno colonists

---

[126] Ibid.

[127] Apparently, the organization believed the best way to learn about the Lord was through physical labor.

[128] "Statut für den Missionsbund 'Licht den Indianern!'" *Menno-Blatt* (Fernheim, Paraguay), October 1935, 4.

[129] Harder Horst, *The Stroessner Regime*, 49.

[130] Informal accounts suggest that Mennonite treatment of indigenous people was not especially exploitative. According to one indigenous person: "Mennonites pay more, make us work less, and do not beat us," in comparison to Paraguayans. Quoted in ibid.

[131] See Bruce Curtis, *Building the Educational State: Canada, West, 1836–1871* (London, ON: Falmer, 1988).

left Canada to escape this paradigm but it stood once again at their doorstep, giving them all the more reason to remain suspicious of the Fernheim Colony's modern inclinations.

Settling Enlhit permanently in one location – to say nothing of convincing them to embrace a Paraguayan or Christian identification – was a daunting task. Indigenous traditions remained strong. Puberty festivals held in faraway villages drew indigenous people away from the settlement for extended periods and the missionaries' education programs were met with indifference.[132] It would be fifteen years before the first Enlhit people were baptized as Christians. It was consequently not the popularity – or even the viability – of missionary activity that maintained Fernheim Colony's interest in the venture. Rather, it served as a unifying force for the colony and offered a ready explanation for their traumatic displacement from Russia. If they remained in the Chaco, colonists believed that it would have to be for something greater than simply owning a piece of land or preserving their Mennoniteness.

Colonists could interpret the missionary enterprise in many ways and each interpretation provided a different trajectory for the colony's evolving collective narrative as Mennonites, Christians, and *Auslandsdeutsche*. Despite this range of interpretations, the colonists' goal remained the same: deciphering the colony's place in the Lord's divine plan or in the modern zeitgeist that would legitimate their arbitrary settlement in South America. In the February 1935 issue of *Menno-Blatt*, A. Kröker connected the presence of indigenous people in the Chaco to the Fernheim Colony's religious trajectory. Kröker wrote a sensational account of an indigenous celebration that included dancing, evil spirits, and alcohol, each of which was enough to disturb any Mennonite observer. Kröker concluded his report by admonishing his fellow Mennonites that:

We have been here for quite a few years and what have we done? We do not know the duration of our sojourn in the Chaco. If our time should unexpectedly and quickly expire and we have done nothing for these poor – what would Jesus say to that?[133]

With this statement, Kröker invoked Jesus's parable of the Minas by arguing that Fernheim colonists should be ashamed that they had not done more to evangelize to indigenous people given the resources (in this

---

[132] Redekop, *Strangers Become Neighbors*, 142–43.
[133] A. Kröker, "Indianer='Penj-Penj.' 'Was würde Jesus dazu sagen'?" *Menno-Blatt* (Fernheim, Paraguay), February 1935, 3–4.

case, time) at their disposal.[134] Even if they eventually moved to a different country, the possibility should not inhibit them from following the will of the Lord while in Paraguay.

Departing from Kröker's impression that Mennonites might not remain in the Chaco, missionary Giesbrecht believed that the establishment of the Fernheim Colony was part of God's plan to expand the global reach of Christianity. Giesbrecht was a member of the Brüdergemeinde.[135] In 1937 he moved with his family to Yalve Sanga, which was the mission station for Licht den Indianern! Along with Abram Ratzlaff and Abram Unger, Giesbrecht was one of the first Fernheimers to devote his life to settling and evangelizing the Enlhit.[136] In a 1936 article for *Menno-Blatt*, Giesbrecht noted that some pessimistic colonists had attacked the missionaries' goals and deemed them unlikely to succeed based on cultural, racial, and spiritual grounds (going so far as to call those goals "stupid") but asserted that those who supported the mission would be paid back in "blessings with interest."[137] Years later, during a 1972 interview with Redekop, Giesbrecht stated, "It came to us that God had sent us to this strange and difficult land for a purpose. God has provided us with a challenge to do something about the miserable condition of these 'wild' people."[138] Giesbrecht interpreted the movement of Fernheim colonists to Paraguay as an unforeseen but sanctified act of God.

One of the colony's most influential voices, a schoolteacher by the name of Friedrich Kliewer, also believed God had given the Fernheim Colony a heavenly mandate to help the indigenous population, but he conflated it with an equally zealous promotion of German culture. Kliewer was a Mennonite who voluntarily accompanied the Fernheim refugees from Germany to Paraguay in 1930. Before and after a period of graduate study in Germany (1934–39), he oversaw the colony's schools and was a frequent contributor to *Menno-Blatt*. In May 1935, Kliewer submitted an article titled "Our purpose and our assignment in Paraguay," which argued, "There must be a reason why we settled

---

[134] The parable of the minas is found in Luke 19: 11–27 (ESV).
[135] G. Ratzlaff, "Giesbrecht, Gerhard Benjamin (1906–1977)," *Global Anabaptist Mennonite Encyclopedia Online*, last modified August 20, 2013, http://gameo.org/index .php?title=Giesbrecht,_Gerhard_Benjamin_(1906–1977)&oldid=87831, last accessed June 7, 2018.
[136] Ibid.
[137] Gerhard Giesbrecht, "Teure Missionsfreunde," *Menno-Blatt* (Fernheim, Paraguay), September 1936, 3.
[138] Redekop, *Strangers Become Neighbors*, 142.

among heathen tribes." He viewed the arrival of Mennonites as serendipitous, for without "the timely and powerful influence of the gospel, these magnificent people could easily be ruined by alcoholism and sexual promiscuity."[139] Thus, the loss experienced by the refugees when they were forced to flee Russia was actually a blessing in disguise since they had "saved" another group of people in South America.

The bulk of Kliewer's article, however, focused on the role that the Fernheimers' Germanness played in their missionary activities. In fact, Kliewer stressed that it was not the colony's Mennonite features that made the colony special. Rather, it was their identity as Christians and their German culture, which portended great things for the settlement. He argued that since it was impossible for all German-speaking individuals to live within the present borders of Germany, Mennonites in the meantime "blessed" the lands they inhabited through their cultural values and economic prowess. Kliewer believed so much in the colony's mandate to edify the indigenous people that he wished to create a protected area for "our Lenguas" (Enlhit) that would remove the Paraguayan government's role in indigenous affairs.[140]

Also writing from Germany, Mennonite scholar Walter Quiring encouraged the Fernheimers to Christianize indigenous peoples along German-Christian lines, but warned colonists not to mix too closely with indigenous people. Quiring was born in the large Mennonite settlement of Chortitza, Russia in 1893 but moved to the Orenburg Mennonite settlement in Siberia in 1905. In 1921, he fled to Germany with his wife, Maria Friesen, and his infant son, Manfred. Quiring earned a doctorate from the University of Munich in 1927 and supported himself by working in a private school that was owned by a wealthy Jewish family. During the 1930s he joined the Nazi Party, wrote two books on the Chaco Mennonites, took up work with the Deutsches Ausland Institut (German Foreign Institute, DAI), and changed his name from the biblically derived "Jakob" to the more German-sounding "Walter." At the DAI, he crafted propaganda that advocated the return of *Auslandsdeutsche* to a German-controlled Eastern Europe. He also participated in some of the population exchanges after the signing of the 1939 Molotov–Ribbentrop Pact.[141] Quiring visited the Mennonite colonies in

---

[139] Friedrich Kliewer, "Unsere Aufgaben in Paraguay," *Menno-Blatt* (Fernheim, Paraguay), May 1935, 1–2.

[140] Ibid.

[141] Ted D. Regehr, "Quiring, Walter (1893–1983)," *Global Anabaptist Mennonite Encyclopedia Online*, last modified August 23, 2013, http://gameo.org/index.php?title=Quiring,_Walter_(1893–1983)&oldid=96151, last accessed June 7, 2018.

Brazil and Paraguay and consequently felt entitled to offer the Fernheim settlers guidance on their venture.[142] Arguing along more secular lines than Kliewer, Quiring viewed the Fernheim Colony as a great experiment that would test the superiority of German Christian culture.

In response to a *Menno-Blatt* article titled "Fernheimer Proletariat," which suggested that the Fernheim Colony could use indigenous people in their workforce, Quiring penned an article titled "Masters and Servants" that criticized the suggestion as sowing the seeds of future destruction. Quiring argued that choosing this path would reproduce the same inequalities between Mennonites and indigenous people that had existed between Mennonites and their Russian neighbors before the Bolshevik Revolution. "The time for cheap labor," according to Quiring, "is irrevocably past." Mennonites must approach their indigenous neighbors not as "masters" – as other white people had done – but through the equitable medium of German Christian culture. He lamented that the "childlike naïve Indians" of the Chaco have already been corrupted by distrust, selfishness, and alcohol, "which is unfortunately available in Fernheim." Quiring then outlined his solution to the "Indian problem." Mennonites would serve as a model for indigenous improvement but they must remain detached – for to mix with them would be *Blutschande* (blood disgrace).[143] Quiring approved of missionary work as a path to unity, but he felt the venture should reflect the colony's reputed German – and not necessarily Christian – qualities.

Licht den Indianern! was a focal point of unity since it provided Fernheimers with an existential meaning that connected colonists to their local neighbors, the Paraguayan government, and overseas supporters. Altogether, the Fernheim Colony's consensus that the venture was important and necessary – despite its early shortcomings – promised a much-needed resolution to the colony's open-ended group narrative as refugees in a foreign land (Fig. 3.4).

Throughout the 1930s and early 1940s, Menno Colony Mennonites viewed the Fernheim Colony's mission work with varying degrees of admiration and suspicion. However, the establishment of a second

---

[142] The 1,245 Mennonite refugees who migrated to Brazil from Germany established two colonies named Auhagen and Witmarsum (after the birthplace of Menno Simons) in Santa Catarina. Due to the isolation of both groups, there was not much communication between the Fernheim Colony and these settlements. On the Brazilian Mennonite settlement see John D. Thiesen, *Mennonite and Nazi? Attitudes Among Mennonite Colonists in Latin America, 1933–1945* (Kitchener, ON: Pandora Press), 1999.

[143] Quiring, "Herren und Knechte," *Menno-Blatt* (Fernheim, Paraguay), March 1935, 3.

FIGURE 3.4 Early meeting with the Enlhit near Schoenbrunn, Fernheim Colony. To the far left appears to be Julius Legiehn. To the far right appears to be Franz Heinrichs. The former was a schoolteacher and the latter was the colony's business agent in Asunción. Both men also served terms as the Fernheim Colony *Oberschulze*. May 1931. Source: Archivo Colonia Fernheim

Menno Colony settlement in 1949, named South Menno, coincided with the movement of Enlhit toward the Menno colonists. Three years later, a South Menno resident named Johann M. Funk began working among the Enlhit in the village of Schoenbrunn on his own initiative. In 1955, the North Menno colonist B. W. Toews began similar work near Sommerfeld (Loma Plata). According to these men, they did not start from a position of wanting to proselytize to indigenous people but rather it was indigenous people living near the colony who wished to enroll their children in Mennonite schools. In this roundabout way, the Menno Colony began influencing the religious lives of indigenous people.[144]

Latter-day church historians reinterpreted the Menno Colony's indifference to missionary activity. In the 1920s, the Canadian public-school issue was the most obvious reason for relocating to Paraguay, but God's inscrutable will eventually revealed a greater purpose. *Oberschulze*

---

[144] P. Klassen, *The Mennonites in Paraguay Volume 2*, 157–58.

J. A. Braun noted that by migrating to the Chaco, Menno Colony Mennonites followed the biblical commandment found in Matthew 24:14 that Christians should be a (passive?) witness to all nations.[145] Heinrich Ratzlaff likewise argued that God led the colony to the Chaco to witness to indigenous people.[146] We could dismiss these accounts as reading present interpretations onto past events, but this does not explain why the Menno Colony initially resisted missionary work and why the Fernheim Colony embraced it. Missionary work – and the external attachments that it entailed – was unimportant (and even inimical) to the Menno Colony's collective narrative during the first twenty years of settlement. Biblical mandates were no doubt *part* of the reason why the Menno Colony eventually began witnessing to indigenous people, but it was not a primary goal of the colony's leadership until at least the late 1950s.

The Menno and Fernheim Colonies held different interpretations of their local environment, which affected their nascent collective narratives of life in Paraguay and their relationships to each other, indigenous people, the Paraguayan government, and Germany. The voluntary migrants of Menno Colony were mostly in consensus about their collective narrative as a people on the move and their reasons for settling in the Chaco. Apart from the families who returned to Canada during the initial years of settlement, the Menno colonists endured frontier hardships because they were fulfilling a reoccurring "plot point" in a collective narrative about God's people. God's chosen people followed God's call no matter where it took them: from the Israelites' forty-year excursion through the Sinai Desert to Jesus's forty-day trial in the Judean Desert; from their ancestors' 2,000-km trek from Danzig to southern Russia to their 10,000-km journey from southern Russia to Manitoba. Mythology and history blended into a cyclical and seamless plot. The Menno Colony's collective narrative was likewise flexible enough to incorporate new situations but firm enough to slot those situations into preexisting interpretative categories. As unexpected as the Chaco War was for the colony, it revealed a new instance whereby the community's integrity was threatened by outside forces. Even though the conflict imperiled colonists' physical existence, it reaffirmed divisions between themselves and "the world." Moreover, had the colonists settled in land without an indigenous population, they might not have

---

[145] Braun, *Im Gedenken an jene Zeit*, 17–18.
[146] See H. Ratzlaff, *Ältester Martin C. Friesen*, 103.

incorporated missionary activity into their group narrative, since they only did so after years of interaction and consideration. In sum, the colony's interpretation of their movements fit into a broader "comedic" narrative structure of persecution, migration, hardship, and restoration, but it was elastic enough to assimilate new events and "revelations" that infused the narrative with fresh imperatives.

Fernheim Colony's refugees were more heterogeneous than Menno Colony's voluntary migrants since they were thrust together by fate rather than by choice. As a result, their initial attempts to forge a shared narrative about the Chaco were tenuous and outwardly focused. Fernheim colonists' individual tragedies of exile from Russia did not magically transform into a collective, comic resolution when they disembarked at "Kilometer 145" (as the MCC had facilely hoped), but persisted during the first decade of settlement as they tried to figure out what their shared beginning actually *was*. Amidst colonists' initial fears of disintegration or annihilation, a range of narrative possibilities emerged: Perhaps the Chaco was a test of their faith. Perhaps it was a punishment that would redeem them to the Lord. Perhaps they were destined to achieve some greater good on account of their Mennoniteness, Christianity, Paraguayan citizenship, or Germanness. Unlike the Menno Colony, the Chaco was not a place where they could recreate a set of shared convictions, but a place that needed to be endowed with a heavenly or temporal mandate that would bind them together. The narrative possibilities advanced by colonists during the early years of settlement were therefore charged with emotion, since each suggested a shared destiny for the colony as a whole. According to Edward Said,

> without at least a sense of a beginning, nothing can really be done, much less ended [in this case, the colonists' individual tragedies of exile] ... And the more crowded and confused a field appears, the more a beginning, fictional or not, seems imperative. A beginning gives us the chance to do work that compensates us for the tumbling disorder of brute reality that will not settle down.[147]

As the colonists struggled forward, they created new meanings for the Chaco, some of which complemented each other while others were difficult to reconcile.

---

[147] Edward Said, "Beginnings," in *Narrative Dynamics: Essay on Time, Plot, Closure, and Frames*, ed. Brian Richardson (Columbus, OH: Ohio State University Press, 2002), 165.

Both settlements initially drew on past experiences to interpret present realities, but they increasingly drew on their experiences in the Chaco until it became difficult to tell which ideas and sentiments they had brought with them and which they had developed locally. In time, the "break" of resettlement was smoothed and their past and present contexts merged – like metronomes moving at different tempos that suddenly come into phase – but this took a great deal of time and stress and it was never predictable.

4

Mennonite (Di)Visions (1930–1939)

The Second Mennonite World Conference was held at the stately Friedrich Wilhelm Schutzenhaus in the Free City of Danzig from August 30 to September 3, 1930. It was entitled "Mennonite World Help." The conference brought together leaders from Mennonite aid agencies in Canada, France, Germany, the Netherlands, Poland, and the United States. The bulk of the meeting dealt with the Mennonite refugees who had been sent to South America and Mennonites who remained in the Soviet Union. The conference's first session was dedicated to a lecture on Mennonite mutual aid in the past, which lent a sense of historic continuity to the event. The second session entailed reports on what was being done to aid Russian Mennonites in the present, and the third focused on the necessity of Mennonite cooperation in the future.[1] As claimed by Bender, the MCC's representative, the meeting was billed as a World Conference because they wished to gather "as wide attendance of the general membership as possible, in order to increase the interest and participation in the relief … of the refugees."[2] Along with his promotion of Mennonite religious solidarity, the charismatic Bender shared an ambitious vision of the Paraguayan Chaco as a place where the MCC

could easily accommodate all of the Mennonites in the world … [the MCC] had a vague notion of a future state of Mennonites where, if possible, all Russian

[1] "Einladung zur Mennonitischen Welt-Hilfs-Konferenz," CMBC, Immigration Movement I, a. General Correspondence 1923–1946, vol. 1184, David Toews 1923–1930, MHC.
[2] Bender, "Report III, June 25, 1930," CMBC, Immigration Movement I, a. General Correspondence 1923–1946, vol. 1175, Mennonite Central Committee 1929–1941, MHC.

Mennonites would be able to reestablish and develop their life and culture within a context of unrestricted freedom. Another particular advantage of the Paraguayan Chaco in regard to culture is the fact that there exists no culture in that area at all. So there is no danger that the Mennonites and their German culture will perish in a foreign culture. The *Mennoniten-Völklein* [Mennonite subnation] can continue to exist in Paraguay with its culture and faith under the most favorable conditions possible.[3]

What caused Bender to make this bold pronouncement, particularly in light of the Mennonites' historic disunity and emphasis on the separation of church and state? Clearly, the MCC aspired to something greater than mere relief work. They hoped that the refugees (and perhaps all Mennonites) could somehow live unmolested by un-Mennonite ideologies. Most strikingly, Bender suggests that Mennonites in North America and Europe should initiate an almost Zionist experiment to solve the problem of Mennonite persecution by obtaining territory that was not yet completely under the jurisdiction of a nation state – territory that possessed "no culture." In fact, a month before the conference, Bender confided to his friend Oyer, "We old Mennonites are somewhat like the Jews, it seems to me. We are almost a race, as well as a Church."[4]

In Bender's view, the confession's religious security and spiritual prosperity would not be achieved through cultural isolation and perpetual movement, as Mennonites had attempted in the past. Rather, it would be achieved by establishing secure and permanent Mennonite enclaves that held a curated set of religious principles and were willing to cooperate with governments and the broader church. In contrast to the Paraguayan government's plan for the Mennonite colonies to serve as a national outpost in the Chaco, and the German government's plan for the Fernheim Colony to enhance its economic and political connections to *Auslandsdeutsche* in Latin America, Bender viewed the colonies as an opportunity to create a Mennonite territory that was theologically and organizationally connected to a global Mennonite confession. In the MCC's evolving philosophy of Mennonite unity, this linkage was based upon Mennonites sharing a few, definitive tenets – such as mutual aid and the primacy of nonviolence – that could be historically justified and concisely articulated to individuals outside the faith. In short, Bender

---

[3] Harold S. Bender, "Die Einwanderung nach Paraguay," in *Bericht über die Mennonitische Welt-Hilfs-Konferenz vom 31. August bis 3. September 1930*, ed. Christian Neff (Karlsruhe: Heinrich Schneider, 1930), 121–22.

[4] "Harold S. Bender to Noah Oyer," July 14, 1930, f. 1, b. 2, H. S. Bender papers, AMC. Quoted in Keim, 210.

advanced something akin to a nationalist Mennonite narrative; a normative definition of what Mennoniteness was in the past, present, and future. Yet there were competing interpretations of the "Mennonite nation" and how it could sustain itself in the modern world. For instance, Mennonite intellectuals in Germany and Canada advanced notions that Mennonites should fuse their narrative with a German nationalist narrative as a *Völklein*, and thereby remain secure under the tutelage of a recognized nation state.[5]

Paraguay's Mennonites took center stage in these debates since they served as petri dishes for Mennonite unity. Yet the experiment was not without danger. Owing to their isolation in the Chaco, the colonies inspired fear that constituents would lose their Mennonite or German-Mennonite heritage or refuse to join a Mennonite or German-Mennonite nation. The term "Mennonite," as this chapter will demonstrate, represented more than a religious confession during the interwar years, and stood alongside other nascent nationalisms vying to win the loyalties of an often-indifferent constituency.

Potential nations need land, administration, propaganda, and money if they are to become states. During the 1930s, the MCC mushroomed from a small group of individuals who resettled a limited number of Russia's Mennonites into a major Paraguayan landowner that developed a sophisticated bureaucracy to manage its activities, corresponded with governments on four continents, created a propaganda arm to legitimate it, and – most importantly – solicited donations – a sort-of voluntary tax – from its constitutes to make it all happen.[6]

In spite of the MCC's evolving ambitions, unity in the Chaco remained elusive. The Menno Colony was at first ignorant of, and then indifferent to, even the most perfunctory goals of the MCC. It was also embroiled in its own administrative disputes and had little interest in bonding with Mennonites elsewhere. From their side, the Fernheim colonists were grateful for the MCC's help but they soon became suspicious of the organization's motives as "good Samaritans" who also served as "tax collectors" for their travel debt. Moreover, the divisions between and within the colonies undermined the chances of any possible unity between them.

---

[5] The concept of Mennonites representing a *Völklein* was convincing since it reaffirmed Mennonites' place as the "children" of a paternalistic state.

[6] Ironically, according to an October 13, 1929 *Chicago Daily News* article written by Junius B. Wood and titled "Mennonite State," the Menno Colony was already a "practically autonomous state." IX-3-3 Paraguayan Immigration 1920–1933, Corporación Paraguaya, Publicity 1929 (1/12), MCCA.

Still, the MCC hoped that their sponsorship of the Mennonite refugees –
and their contact with coreligionists in the Menno Colony – would serve
as a model for a united and cooperative spirit among Mennonites in the
Americas and around the world. The MCC reckoned that through its
financial aid and frequent visitations – and trusting in the homogenizing
bent of history – it could instill its version of Mennoniteness on the
colonies.

NEW NARRATIVES FOR A DIVIDED "NATION"

Divisions between the world's Mennonite communities were theological, organizational, cultural, and historical. Theologically and organizationally, the MCC stood in marked contrast to separatist Mennonites in
North and South America. Titus F. Guenther – whose parents were part
of the Menno Colony migration – argues that conservative Mennonite
leaders are best understood as holding a practical view of Christianity
that was "pastoral biblical" rather than theological and abstract.[7]
J. Denny Weaver echoes this analysis by noting that Bergthal *Ältester*
G. Wiebe believed that the church was "defined and reinforced by
a lifestyle rather than by an explicitly biblical and theological
rationale."[8] This lifestyle meshed with an "integrated worldview," that
cannot be parsed into religious and secular spheres since "integration
was not so much that of a theological outlook as it was an understanding
of the visible church."[9] When leaders ventured into biblical interpretation they focused on passages that emphasized orthopraxy (right acting)
rather than orthodoxy (right teaching), since the fundamental point of
Christianity was to live a righteous life, rather than understand,
abstractly, what righteousness is.[10]

By contrast, Bender was one of the first individuals to propose
a universal Mennonite theology. His interpretation of Mennonite "essentials" defined twentieth-century Mennoniteness in North America and
beyond. Bender emphasized orthopraxy, but he was especially sensitive
to how it would be taught, understood, and made intelligible to non-
Mennonites. He was not an *Ältester* – a humble shepherd with both eyes

---

[7] See Titus F. Guenther, "Theology of Migration: The Ältesten Reflect," *Journal of
Mennonite Studies* 18 (2000): 164–65.
[8] J. Denny Weaver, *Keeping Salvation Ethical: Mennonite and Amish Atonement Theology
in the Late Nineteenth Century* (Scottdale, PA: Herald Press, 1997), 78.
[9] Ibid.   [10] Guenther, "Theology of Migration," 165.

trained on his own sheep – but an intellectual who was prepared to formulate and describe (and prescribe) similarities among the entire Mennonite flock. Bender's theology revolved around three principles, which are recorded in his *Anabaptist Vision*. The first urged Mennonites to replicate the person of Christ within themselves by following Jesus' example as closely as possible.[11] His second focus was on the church. True Anabaptism (and true Christianity), Bender argued, exists in tension with "the world." The church should not attempt to overthrow or impose itself on the existing social order, since this would compromise its members' commitment to discipleship. Rather it should work through or around the existing social order to advance God's kingdom. Proceeding from these concepts is the idea of nonresistance to violence, or the "peace position," which Bender believed stood at the center of individual and collective Christian action. This idea draws on the example of Christ's renunciation of earthly power and his willingness to die at the hands of state authorities.[12] Bender believed that the global Mennonite Church should set aside their local differences and unite under this core set of principles.

Bender did not think he was creating a new vision of the church; he believed that he had recovered an old one. If one could return to the original sixteenth-century source of Anabaptism, so he thought, the twentieth-century church's latent unity would be properly revealed. In this regard, he fit into an academic climate of the 1930s that was attenuated to discovering historical "essences" through rigorous (albeit selective) scholarship – for example, the "essence" of nationality, the "essence" of a time period, or the "essence" of a particular environment.[13] Bender's goal was to discover the historical essence (i.e. essentials) of Anabaptism. It would not be achieved through mysticism, but through research. In this regard, Bender represented the leading edge of a confession in the midst of building a common past. His early writings – including a dissertation on the early Anabaptist leader Conrad Grebel (1935), a biography of Menno Simons (1936), and the book *Mennonite Origins in Europe* (1942) – testify to this aim. For Bender, it was a given that all Mennonites shared a common origin in Anabaptism and were at some point persecuted for their beliefs. All that was needed was to document and memorialize this

---

[11] Harold S. Bender, *The Anabaptist Vision* (Scottdale, PA: Herald Press, 1944), 33.

[12] Ibid., 31.

[13] John S. Oyer, "The Anabaptist Vision," *Global Anabaptist Mennonite Encyclopedia Online*, last modified January 18, 2015, http://gameo.org/index.php?title=The_Anabaptist_Vision&oldid=130434, last accessed June 7, 2018.

shared story so the world's Mennonites could be inspired and united by it. It is important to note that – at least early in his career – Bender did not look to biblical sources for spiritual inspiration, as the early Anabaptist leaders had done. Rather, he recast the contemporary Mennonite Church as a continuation of the sixteenth-century Anabaptist movement, which depended on history and culture as much as spirituality and faith.[14]

In Bender's analysis, the Mennonites enjoyed a spiritual golden age in the sixteenth century. Now after a 400-year dark age of dispersion, twentieth-century Mennonites were on the cusp of a religious reawakening.[15] This mimetic narrative arc placed the modern Mennonite Church on an epic upward trajectory that would find its resolution in unity. Surely this was what Bender had in mind when he wrote an open letter in the inaugural issue of *Mennonite Quarterly Review* entitled "To the youth of the Mennonite Church." It stated, "The Golden Age of the Mennonite Church is not past; it is just ahead ... The coming generation in the Mennonite Church is being given a carefully built, well-knit, efficient organization of activities."[16] Like so many nationalist thinkers of the interwar era, Bender placed his faith in the youth and the institutions that his generation would create for them. The coming generation was poised to inaugurate a new epoch of Mennonite cooperation that would resurrect the essence of the Anabaptist movement and perhaps supersede it. His feelings on rediscovering his people's special path are strikingly similar to the concerns of early twentieth-century nationalist intellectuals in Europe. For instance, Timothy Snyder's *Reconstruction of Nations: Poland, Ukraine, Lithuania, Belarus, 1569–1999*, shows how late-nineteenth- and early-twentieth-century Lithuanian historians refurbished "an imagined Grand Duchy that fit their present predicament" and conceptualized a new periodization of their national history "in which the medieval was glorious and the early modern was shameful."[17] By rediscovering and documenting this

---

[14] Later in his career, Bender looked to the Bible to inform his mission but, according to his biographer Albert Keim, his exegesis was always oriented to current events. See Albert N. Keim, *Harold S. Bender, 1897–1962* (Scottdale, PA: Herald Press, 1997), 500.

[15] See Rodney J. Sawatsky, *History and Ideology: American Mennonite Identity Definition Through History* (Kitchener, ON: Pandora Press, 2005).

[16] Bender, "To the Youth of the Mennonite Church," *Mennonite Quarterly Review* 1, no. 1 (1927), n.p.

[17] Timothy Snyder, *Reconstruction of Nations: Poland, Ukraine, Lithuania, Belarus, 1569–1999* (New Haven, CT: Yale University Press, 2003), 32, 34.

fractured past, nationalist historians provided a historical reason for contemporary disunity and a logical argument that it should be rectified.

Bender and the MCC hoped that a unified version of Mennoniteness could also make the confession legible to governments and outsiders – a problem that Ewert and D. Toews had encountered in their negotiations with Canadian authorities. This "public relations" aspect would streamline Mennonite interactions with non-Mennonites and overturn the prevailing, negative understanding of the Anabaptist movement, from which the Mennonites had arisen. Until the twentieth century, Mennonites were often conflated with sensational branches of Anabaptism that arose during the German Peasants' War of 1525 and the bizarre and brutal Münster Rebellion of 1534–1535. The latter was led by the messianic leaders Jan Matthijsz (Matthys) van Haarlem and Jan Beukelszoon (van Leiden), who occupied Münster, proclaimed it the "New Jerusalem," and – among other eccentricities – pursued polygamy and a "community of goods."[18] Thus, in November 1929, when the Moscow refugee crisis splashed across the world's headlines, Bender was chagrined to read a *New York Times* editorial that argued, "the Mennonites in their time were good revolutionists – they were closely connected with the Anabaptists and through them with the Peasants' War of 1525, the greatest rural uprising in the history of Europe."[19] Bender responded that the *Times*'s "conception of the Mennonites and Anabaptists is the traditional one based on the historiography of their enemies and has now been completely invalidated by modern scholarship."[20] In reality, sixteenth-century Anabaptism was a motley assemblage of individuals that participated in the Peasants' War, Münsterites, Dutch dissidents, and Bender's preferred subjects, the Swiss Brethren.[21] Bender and the MCC wished to once and for all define the Mennonite faith and clarify – for insiders and outsiders alike – that its associative wing represented the purest modern form of Anabaptism.

Later Mennonite historians, such as the Canadian F. H. Epp, championed the unity and standardization proposed by interwar Mennonite

[18] C. Krahn, Nanne van der Zijpp, and James M. Stayer, "Münster Anabaptists," *Global Anabaptist Mennonite Encyclopedia Online*, last modified December 18, 2017, http://gameo.org/index.php?title=M%C3%BCnster_Anabaptists&oldid=145911, last accessed June 7, 2018.

[19] "Editorial on Mennonites," *New York Times*, December 6, 1929, 26.

[20] Bender, "H. S. Bender on History of Mennonites," *New York Times*, December 11, 1929, 28.

[21] For a discussion of various forms of Anabaptism, see J. Stayer, Werner O. Packull, and Klaus Deppermann, "From Monogenesis to Polygenesis: The Historical Discussion of Anabaptist Origins," *Mennonite Quarterly Review* 49, no. 2 (1975): 83–121.

intellectuals and followed Bender in painting a picture of inevitable confessional consolidation over sectarian separation.[22] Yet even on this point,
F. H. Epp and other Mennonite intellectuals in Canada were wary that
"international" Mennonite organizations, such as the MCC, had
a decidedly American flavor, which threatened other national
Mennonite cultures. Writing in 1977, F. H. Epp argued "Since it is
American institutions playing the international role, there is a strong
tendency both within and without America to equate the two. By that
equation American institutions become the institutional incarnation of
the universal church." Later, he quipped, "What Americans call trans-
cending nationalism, looks like an expanding nationalism from the other
side."[23] Thus, Mennonite intellectuals were often as divided over their
proposed units of confederation – either nationally or internationally – as
the locally focused *Ältesten* and separatist Mennonites that they wished to
displace.

Bender was not alone in his interwar vision of Mennonite fraternity. The era was a cauldron of ideas concerning the confession's
perceived group identity. The notion of global Mennonite unity had
existed at least since the 1880s, when Mennonite intellectuals living in
Germany and the Netherlands promoted the idea that the Mennonite
diaspora was a German nation in miniature owing to both groups'
stereotypical proclivity for hard work, honesty, husbandry, and migration. This brand of confessional nationalism found its locus in the
heady   atmosphere   of   the   late-nineteenth-century   German
Kulturkampf, which pitted a secularizing German state against its
citizens' religious convictions. Rather than assimilating to the new
imperative, religious groups seized the moment to articulate why
their constituents embodied the essence of Germanness. Germany's
Mennonites embraced the challenge with gusto.[24] Abandoning their
historic separation from society and the principle of nonviolence in the
face of new mandatory conscription legislation, they favored
a narrative arc that positioned Mennonites as sixteenth-century

---

[22] F. H. Epp criticizes the "rivalry, jealousy, suspicion and mistrust," that pervaded North
American Mennonite circles during these years in *Mennonite Exodus: The Rescue and
Resettlement of the Russian Mennonites Since the Communist Revolution* (Altona, MB:
Canadian Mennonite Relief and Immigration Council, 1962), 158.

[23] F. H. Epp, *Mennonite Peoplehood: A Plea for New Initiatives* (Waterloo: Conrad Press,
1977), 14–15, 75–84.

[24] Benjamin W. Goossen, *Chosen Nation: Mennonites and Germany in a Global Era*
(Princeton, NJ: Princeton University Press, 2017), 46, 49.

pathbreakers for German Protestantism.[25] As a prelude to Bender's future scholarship, Mennonite "activists" in Germany skillfully traced the confession's lineage back to the New Testament and through a succession of "Old-Evangelical Churches," which challenged the Pope and set the stage for the Reformation.[26] The Mennonite Church was a *German* church and like pre-unification Germany, Mennonites were a geographically dispersed yet essentially united community.[27] Advocates of this narrative of German Mennoniteness called for a reawakening of the confession through the formation of a nationwide conference, titled the Union of Mennonite Congregations in the German Empire. Founded in Berlin in 1886, the organization hoped to set aside minor issues (like nonviolence) in its bid to unite Germany's Mennonites and perhaps all Mennonites around the world. As in North America, Mennonite unity in Germany was a hard sell.[28] Yet by the 1930s, Germany's Mennonites had unified around the notion that they were perhaps the *most* German confession: they advocated the complete separation of church and state (per the *Kulturkampf*), laid claim to a remarkable military service record during the First World War, and their diasporic brethren abroad were some of the most tenacious carriers of German culture and Aryan characteristics in all of Germandom. In light of German Mennonites' slow but steady accommodation to the state and all Mennonites' mercurial biblical exegesis, it is entirely unsurprising that Germany's Mennonites so easily adapted their theology to National Socialism's bellicose program.

Owing to the Soviet regime's persecution of its German-speaking minority, some of the most fantastic plans for Mennonite unification were generated by Mennonites in Germany and Canada who had recently emigrated from Russia. These individuals imagined that Russia's Mennonites exemplified the persecution of *Auslandsdeutsche* and found a great deal to like in Germany's ascendant Nazi Party. They were not

---

[25] On the transition of Mennonite nonviolence from a major tenet to a minor one in *fin-de-siècle* Germany see ibid., 90–93. On Mennonites and the draft in late-nineteenth-century Germany see Mark Jantzen, *Mennonite German Soldiers: Nation, Religion, and Family in the Prussian East, 1772–1880* (South Bend, IN: University of Notre Dame Press), 2010.

[26] Goossen, *Chosen Nation*, 58–61.

[27] For example, see Samuel Cramer, "Internationales Mennonitenthum," *Mennonitische Blätter*, May 1902, 39–40.

[28] According to Goossen, only seventeen of seventy-one congregations joined the Union in 1886. *Chosen Nation*, 15.

alone. James Casteel notes that there were tens of thousands of Russian German émigrés who fled the Soviet Union during the interwar years and "generated new narratives of common German identity between Russian Germans and Germans in the Reich ... In these narratives, war and revolution figured as shared moments of victimization by internal and external enemies of Germanness."[29] Mennonite refugees shared similar reference points with the broader Russian-German diaspora regarding their place in the German firmament. Yet because of their distinct history and religious culture, pro-German Mennonites were initially less focused on Germany as a perceived "homeland." In their creative visions of the Mennonite diaspora's future, pro-German Mennonites tended to alternate between Mennonite and German poles of identification and plans for a Mennonite or German-Mennonite state solution.

The groundwork for a Mennonite state had already been laid in Tsarist Russia when the government "officially recognized a single, non-religious Mennonite identity." State officials "affirmed – indeed, they effectively created – a distinct people by bureaucracy."[30] As Francis states, this policy "was directly responsible for the transformation of this group of German Mennonites into something like a new ethnic unit."[31] Thus, Russia's Mennonites did not necessarily need their German-born brethren to inspire nationalist fantasies. Sentimental about the lost "Russian Commonwealth," Canadian Mennonite author, Arnold Dyck, wrote frequently and positively of a *Mennostaat* (Mennonite state) in both his fiction and personal letters throughout the 1940s and 1950s.[32] A specific scheme was proposed by a Nazi-sympathizing Mennonite living in Canada during the interwar years named J. J. Hildebrand. His plan involved the creation of a *Mennostaat* in Australia. J. J. Hildebrand had been a leader among the Mennonites of Siberia and remained a prolific writer on contemporary and historical issues after he moved to Canada in

[29] James E. Casteel, "The Politics of Diaspora: Russian German Émigré Activists in Interwar Germany," in *German Diasporic Experiences: Identity, Migration, and Loss*, ed. Mathias Schulze, James M. Skidmore, David G. John, Grit Liebscher, and Sebastian Siebel-Achenbach, 117–29 (Waterloo: Wilfrid Laurier University Press, 2008), 117.

[30] Robert Zacharias, *Rewriting the Break Event: Memories and Migration in Canadian Literature* (Winnipeg: University of Manitoba Press, 2013), 52.

[31] E. K. Francis, *Interethnic Relations: An Essay in Sociological Theory* (New York: Elsevier, 1976), 172.

[32] Zacharias provides a detailed analysis of Arnold Dyck's fiction in *Rewriting the Break Event*.

1924. His plan called for 400,000 Mennonites (presumably *all* Mennonites) to settle Australia's Northern Territory, where they could create an autonomous republic.[33] The settlement would have its own government (popular democracy), national language (High or Low German), official currency (the Menno Gulden), and a blue, green, and white flag with a white dove holding a palm leaf in its beak.[34] Though the Australian government summarily rejected J. J. Hildebrand's petition, the refusal did not keep him from pressing for Mennonite unity and the creation of a Mennonite state.[35] The Canadian Mennonite writer and Nazi supporter J. P. Dyck advanced a different vision of Mennonite unity that relied less on the establishment of a permanent territory and more on transnational economic cooperation, similar to what the Weimar and Nazi governments hoped to achieve with *Auslandsdeutsche* in Latin America. J. P. Dyck proposed the creation of a Mennonite "free-trade area" that would connect Mennonite communities via a global economic partnership.[36] J. P. Dyck's proposal promised Mennonite economic self-sufficiency in the midst of the Great Depression. The Russian-born Mennonite Nazi Walter Quiring was less interested in Mennonite autonomy and economic interdependence. He feared the racial and cultural assimilation that already threatened Mennonites living in North America and championed Paraguay as the Russian Mennonites' best and last chance to live out their German-Mennonite destiny.[37] Along similar lines, the Russian Mennonite-cum-Nazi propagandist and SS leader Heinrich Hayo Schröder hoped that Russian-born Mennonites would renew their ties with Germany by establishing 100 new settlements within the Reich according to the traditional colony structure of their settlements in Russia.[38] This plan would fulfill Mennonites' destiny as a *Völklein* within the Nazi state's larger *Volksgemeinschaft*.

Mennonites in North America and recent emigrants from Russia were guided by different sets of assumptions owing to their distinct cultures and histories. While the majority of Russia's Mennonites had arrived in the

---

[33] James Urry gives an account of J. J. Hildebrand's life and work in his article "*Mennostaat for the Mennovolk?* Mennonite Immigrant Fantasies in Canada in the 1930s," *Journal of Mennonite Studies* 14 (1996): 65–80. See also the J. J. Hildebrand papers, Mennonite Heritage Centre Archives, Winnipeg, Manitoba, Volumes 2821, 3308, 3481–84.

[34] Urry, "*Mennostaat for the Mennovolk?*" 65.

[35] J. J. Hildebrand proposed Angola and Dutch New Guinea as alternate locations. Ironically, J. J. Hildebrand worked against Mennonite unity by establishing his own aid organization in direct competition with D. Toews's CMBC named "Mennonite Immigration Aid." Urry, "*Mennostaat for the Mennovolk?*" 67.

[36] Urry, "*Mennostaat for the Mennovolk?*" 73.   [37] Ibid.   [38] Ibid., 72.

Black Sea region from north-central Europe and during a few key periods
in the late eighteenth and early nineteenth centuries, North American
Mennonites were more diverse, having arrived on the continent from
multiple locations over the course of 250 years. Individual congregations
traced their roots back to various locales in Switzerland, France, the
Netherlands, Germany, and Russia, each with its own political and cultural contexts. They had separate traditions – and spoke different dialects.
Consequently, unifiers such as Bender tended toward a creedal understanding of Mennoniteness that promoted shared beliefs originating in the
Anabaptist movement over a shared migration story or a shared ethnic
profile. Many North American Mennonites, in fact, considered their
"German" heritage to be less important than their American identification. Moreover, Mennonites in Russia were forbidden to proselytize to
their Orthodox neighbors, which may have led them to conflate religion,
culture, and race, while North American Mennonites had no such restric-
tions placed on evangelism.

Bender was not a Nazi and his creedal vision of Mennonite unity stood
in marked contrast to strategies that treated Mennonites as a group
defined solely by culture or race. Yet the territorial, social, and cultural
ambitions outlined by Russian-German Mennonite dreamers are not far
from Bender's plan of establishing a "state of Mennonites," that possessed
a "German culture," and was religiously and financially connected to
a community that extended around the globe.[39] They are also similar to
contemporaneous debates in interwar American Jewish circles about the
destiny of their European coreligionists. While some Zionists advanced
the idea of a permanent settlement in Palestine, others – including the
American-based Jewish Joint Distribution Committee (JDC, established
in 1915) – proposed establishing Jewish settlements in a piecemeal fashion
throughout the world, from the plains of northern Crimea to the jungles of
the Dominican Republic, that would serve as bastions of Jewishness in
a hostile world.[40] Nationalist paradigms and fantastic solutions for territorial insecurities were not only the domain of governments who wished
to solve a "German Question" or "Jewish Question" during the interwar
years, but had seeped into the organizational ideals of a wide range of
religious groups.

---

[39] Bender, "Einwanderung nach Paraguay," 121–22.
[40] Allen Wells, *Tropical Zion: General Trujillo, FDR, and the Jews of Sosua* (Durham, NC:
Duke University Press, 2009), 44 ff.

Bender's evolving set of Mennonite essentials as recorded in his *Anabaptist Vision*, and the MCC's ecumenical activities in the Chaco were amplified by a burgeoning North American Mennonite press, which bypassed local leadership and reached members in their homes. Anderson observes that "reading a newspaper is like reading a novel whose author has abandoned any thought of a coherent plot."[41] By reading the daily (or weekly, or monthly) news, individuals cannot help but imagine themselves within larger narratives unfurling through "homogenous, empty time" (i.e. "blank pages" in an unfinished "book").[42] Coherent or not, newspapers are an essential feature of modern nationalism since they promote a common language, a shared interpretation of events, and provide the rough fodder for national stories of development or decline. At the time, North American Mennonite journalists portrayed the Mennonite Church as a house with many rooms. Some were smaller, more isolated, and perhaps not exposed to as much ecumenical "light," but they were all – or should be – connected to each other. US-based publications such as *Gospel Herald* and *Mennonite* regularly ran stories about the importance of Mennonites joining confessional activities. For instance, an editorial for *Mennonite* argued "Mergers are common and in many instances necessary to the welfare of those becoming parties to them. If the Mennonite church is to live ... the first important step to be taken is for its numerous branches to find a way whereby they may become one."[43] In the eyes of Mennonite newspapers, the modern world demanded consolidation and interdependence. Mennonite publications in the United States therefore embraced the Fernheim Colony as fellow Mennonites, and encouraged readers to support the settlement. As early as October 10, 1929, *Mennonite* printed a front-page article, written by Toews, on the mounting crisis in the Soviet Union.[44] The publication also criticized Mennonites who did not see the refugees as their confessional brothers. One article stated, "The next best blessing after rendering help should be the drawing together into closer fellowship of the numerous bodies that call themselves Mennonites but jealously maintain separate organizations."[45] It is interesting to note that

---

[41] Benedict Anderson, *Imagined Communities: Reflections on the Origins and Spread of Nationalism* (London: Verso, 1983), 33, n. 54.
[42] Ibid. [43] "Editorial," *Mennonite*, March 13, 1930, 3.
[44] "A Plea for Help," *Mennonite*, October 10, 1929, 1.
[45] "Editorial," *Mennonite*, December 19, 1929, 3. *Mennonite* carried frequent articles on the desirability of a unified Mennonite set of principles. See, for example, "The Need for a Creed," *Mennonite*, March 27, 1930, 6.

in Paraguay it was the nationally minded Fernheim colonists who began publishing *Menno-Blatt* almost immediately after their arrival, while their antinationalist neighbors in Menno Colony did not.

Though the MCC's solicitations for aid were initially successful, donations began to dry up in the summer of 1930. In his "Relief Notes" section, Levi Mumaw reported that it was only by carrying over money from previous contributions that the MCC could sustain its work.[46] The situation remained urgent well into the fall, with Mumaw reporting in October 1930 that the MCC needed $132,500 USD (about $2,021,324 USD in 2019) to cover the refugees' expenses but only had $83,225 USD (about $1,269,620 USD in 2019) in its coffers.[47] The funding difficulties could partly have been due to the deepening economic depression, but the 100,000-plus individuals living in Canada and the United States who called themselves "Mennonites" could have raised the funds at less than a dollar per individual. A little over a month later the organization raised a further $5,000 USD (about $78,171 USD in 2019), even as its expenses rose by about the same amount.[48] North American Mennonites traditionally supported relief work on an ad hoc basis, but there was little historical precedent for indefinite giving to humanitarian initiatives.

As noble as Bender's unifying vision may have appeared to his colleagues in North America, it certainly did not resonate with Paraguay's Mennonites. The MCC's growing precision about what constituted universal Mennonite essentials clashed with the Menno colonists' belief that the Mennonite Church existed at the local level. The organization's optimistic tenor also clashed with that of the Fernheim refugees, who were scraping by in a foreign land.[49] P. Klassen suggests that Bender's stance, including his focus on the "peace position," was less central to the Fernheim colonists than reestablishing the "Mennonite commonwealth" that colonists had known in Russia. Bender's speech at the 1930 Mennonite World Conference, however, appeared to reconcile both the MCC's and the Fernheim Colony's positions through the notion that the

---

[46] Mumaw, "Relief Notes," *Mennonite*, October 2, 1930, 4.

[47] Mumaw, "Relief Notes," *Mennonite*, October 30, 1930, 7. The inflation adjustment was made with the Bureau of Labor Statistics (CPI) Inflation Calculator, www.bls.gov/data/inflation_calculator.htm, last accessed August 8, 2019.

[48] Mumaw, "Relief Notes," *Mennonite*, December 11, 1930, 3. The inflation adjustment was made with the Bureau of Labor Statistics (CPI) Inflation Calculator, www.bls.gov/data/inflation_calculator.htm, last accessed August 8, 2019.

[49] See P. Klassen, "Die Rolle des Mennonitischen Zentralkomitees (MCC) in den Konflikten der Mennonitenkolonien in Paraguay," *Jahrbuch für Geschichte und Kultur der Mennoniten in Paraguay* 2 (2001): 35–58, 39–40.

colony could create a nonviolent "state of Mennonites" in the Chaco that was autonomous from the secular nation states that dominated the geopolitical order. Yet appearances proved to be deceptive, even as Bender and the MCC pressed forward with making the Chaco colonies a microcosm of Mennonite collaboration.

Given the range of ideas and practices concerning Mennonite organization that were current during the interwar period, there was nothing to suggest that Bender and the MCC's unifying goals could actually be achieved. In 1929, on the eve of the refugee crisis, the Mennonite publication *Gospel Herald* lamented, "In America there are more than a dozen sects who have branched off from the Mennonite Church (to say nothing about further subdivisions in some of these branches)."[50] It would take a well-organized and well-funded transnational church to bring these groups together, bond with Mennonites around the world, and realize Bender's ambitions – perhaps something more akin to the fifteenth-century Catholic Church than the boisterous and disorderly Anabaptist movement from whence his confession arose. United States Mennonite intellectuals' quest to unite the country's – and eventually the world's – Mennonites consequently arose less from historical precedent and more from modern preoccupations: standardization, homogenization, and associational networks. Like the JDC and the Armenian Relief Society (established in 1910), the MCC's leaders believed that if Mennonitism were to remain viable in a Wilsonian world of international cooperation, then they must establish institutions and promote homogenized convictions that transcended local particularities. Anticipating the flood of Second World War–era Mennonite books on conscientious objection to military service and personal nonviolence – ideals that held important but variable roles in Mennonite history – Mennonite intellectuals in North America increasingly viewed the acceptance of a discrete set of convictions as the litmus test for confessional membership. Other particularities – private schooling, refusing to vote, and the desirability of a government *Privilegium*, and so on – were decidedly less important.

DISCOVERING INDIFFERENCE

The Menno Colony initially found itself in a somewhat unwelcome position regarding the MCC's vision of international Mennonite cooperation. Bender stated in his World Conference speech that one of Paraguay's main

---

[50] "The Mennonites," *Gospel Herald*, September 19, 1929, 1.

advantages was the fact that there were already Mennonites living in the Chaco who, presumably, would help the refugees out of a sense of fraternal sympathy.[51] Yet the reason why Bender even knew about the Menno Colony in the first place was not because the colony had initiated contact with the MCC, but rather because two MCC representatives visited the colony in an unsolicited attempt to see if it needed the MCC's help. Ironically, it was the MCC's attempt to aid the Menno Colony that provoked the organization to request the colony's help in resettling the refugees, a task that the latter had little interest in doing.

When MCC representatives visited the Menno Colony they encountered a type of Mennoniteness that looked very different from what they were familiar with. In late 1928, various newspapers in North America and Europe began running articles about a group of "distressed" Canadian Mennonites who were living in the Chaco. One US report stated, "hunger and sickness are snatching away these pioneers, making help urgent."[52] In Germany, *Völkischer Beobachter* tied the Menno Colony's suffering to the perceived persecution of Germans worldwide with an article titled, "The Drama of the Slaves in the Chaco: the largest private landowners in the world as modern slave owners – gruesome fate for Mennonites attracted to the country – the exploitation and destruction revealed – who will intervene?"[53] Alarmed at these reports, MCC leader O. Miller contacted two missionaries – an American named T. K. Hershey and a Canadian named Amos Swartzentruber – who were both stationed in Argentina, to investigate the situation and, if necessary, volunteer their help.[54]

Hershey sent a series of letters to the Menno Colony, asking them for information about their colony and inquiring about a possible visit.[55] His

---

[51] Bender, "Einwanderung nach Paraguay," 119.

[52] *Philadelphia Enquirer*, December 13, 1928.

[53] The author was Bruno Fricke, founder of Paraguay's Nazi association. "Das Drama der Sklaven im Chaco: Der größte Private Grundbesitzer der Welt als moderner Sklavenhalter – Grauenhaftes Schicksal der ins Land gelockten Mennoniten – Der Ausbeutung und Vernichtung preisgegeben – Wer schreitet ein?" *Völkischer Beobachter* (Munich), August 22, 1929. This article was forwarded to the MCC by a Corporación Paraguaya employee who, in turn, received it from a Mennonite by the name of Priesz (perhaps Jacob B. Pries of the Bergthaler (West Reserve) Menno Colony colonists). See J. M. Vebber, "Corporación Paraguaya [Field Report] December 2, 1929," IX-3-3 Paraguayan Immigration 1920–1933, Corporación Paraguaya, Publicity 1929 (1/ 12), MCCA.

[54] Martin W. Friesen, *New Homeland in the Chaco Wilderness*, 2nd ed., trans. Jake Balzer (Loma Plata, Paraguay: Cooperativa Chortitzer Limited, 1997), 335.

[55] Ibid., 335–37.

first letter, written August 10, 1928, announced, "I do not know any of you" but assured the colonists that "the motives for our visit are entirely Christian."[56] Having received no response by December 1928, Hershey's second letter (this time written in German) stated:

As you will notice from the letterhead, we are Mennonites, Mennonite ministers. Our churches in the USA and Canada have sent us here to Argentina to preach the gospel to the people living in darkness. Lately, we have repeatedly received inquiries from the USA and Canada regarding how the people in the Chaco of Paraguay are doing . . . We are getting no connection with you . . . The churches of North America have only your best in mind. They have already proved that by their relief work in Russia some years earlier. We would like you to answer the following questions:

1) How do you find the new country and the weather there?
2) How are our brethren doing there and how many are there?
3) Would you welcome us if we visited you?
4) Which is the best time to come there . . . ?
5) We are waiting for your reply.
P. S. In what language do you preach in your church, English or German?[57]

Since the Menno Colony Mennonites had left Canada, in part, to separate themselves from associative Mennonites, it must have come as a surprise to colony leader M. C. Friesen when he received this letter early in 1929. According to M. W. Friesen (the son of *Ältester* M. C. Friesen), the record does not indicate whether his father responded to Hershey's solicitations, but eventually Hershey and Swartzentruber's curiosity was so great that they embarked on a trip to the colony in February 1929 to discover this lost tribe of Mennonites.[58]

Hershey and Swartzentruber's report took the form of an ethnographic survey of an unfamiliar people. The missionaries were most interested in the Menno Colony's farming operations and their religious customs. After a brief description of the "aboriginals" who "live very simply," built "their huts of sticks," and went "almost entirely naked," Hershey exclaimed that "these hardworking Mennonites" were "creating

---

[56] Quoted in ibid., 336.   [57] Letter reprinted in ibid., 337.
[58] M. W. Friesen was born in Grunthal, Canada in 1912 and was the Menno Colony's most prominent historian. For more on M. W. Friesen, see Susan Huebert, "Friesen, Martin W. (1912–2000)," *Global Anabaptist Mennonite Encyclopedia Online*, last modified August 23, 2013, http://gameo.org/index.php?title=Friesen,_Martin_W._(1912–2000) &oldid=94752, last accessed June 7, 2018. See also, Uwe Friesen, "Martin W. Friesen: Ein Leben im Dienste der Gemeinschaft," *Jahrbuch für Geschichte und Kultur der Mennoniten in Paraguay* 5 (2005): 53–90.

a beautiful landscape of cultivation" and outlined their ambitious build-ing plans.[59] Their description of a colony worship service, conducted in "real German," as opposed to colonists' everyday *Plautdietsch*, was par-ticularly detailed and indicated that it was much different (and more tedious) than services that they were familiar with.

Their services were conducted in the following order: First, the singing of two hymns (all their hymns have from 5 to 12 long verses) with an old time slow tune. After this the minister ... got up and pulling a bundle of papers out of his pocket began to read off his sermon which consisted of 28 pages foolscap of very small script. During the reading of the sermon – which took over an hour – the congregation knelt down twice for prayer but nobody prayed audibly ... It was very tiresome to sit for over two hours on benches without backs in very hot weather and a good many of the listeners fell asleep for the last half of the meeting.[60]

The feelings of familiarity and foreignness experienced by the North American visitors bear a striking resemblance to those found in an 1871 account of a Dutch Mennonite woman named Antje Brons who sponsored a missionary trip to Mennonite communities in Alsace and Lorraine after the regions were absorbed into the German Empire. Reporting back to Brons, one visiting preacher described a group that had maintained the outer vestiges of Mennoniteness (despite being surrounded by Catholics!) but were spiritually dead. Like the missionaries' impressions of the Menno Colony colonists, the rustic Mennonites of Alsace and Lorraine were simple, sincere, and suspiciously antiquated.[61]

The missionaries' report also bears a resemblance to the accounts of German tourists and researchers who visited settlements of *Auslandsdeutsche* – sometimes referred to as "language islands" – in foreign lands wishing to locate an authentic and primitive Germanness within far-flung *Auslandsdeutsche* communities. Especially during the interwar years, German visitors to Africa, Latin America, and Eastern Europe made special note of *Auslandsdeutsche* crafts, guilds, and farming practices.[62] They were filled with condescending admiration for their

[59] The report from Hershey's journal is reprinted in M. W. Friesen, *New Homeland*, 346–48.

[60] Amos Swartzentruber, "Mennonites in Paraguay: VI. 'Their Churches and Schools,'" *Gospel Herald*, October 31, 1929, Some Mennonite groups considered the singing of melodies to be prideful.

[61] See Goossen, "Into a Great Nation: Mennonites and Nationalism in Imperial Germany, 1871–1900" (honors history thesis, Swarthmore College, 2013), 21–22.

[62] Nancy R. Reagin, "German Brigadoon? Domesticity and Metropolitan Perceptions of Auslandsdeutschen in Southwest Africa and Eastern Europe," in *The Heimat Abroad:*

archaic practices and odd dialects, even as visitors noted the presumed superiority of settlers' "German" houses in contrast to native inhabitants' primitive "huts."[63] The Mennonite missionaries' paper trail followed the same trajectory as Germans' accounts of *Auslandsdeutsche*, since their report was first filed with a central organization, the MCC, and then disseminated by various Mennonite publications, including *Gospel Herald*.[64] In the German context, articles on German-speaking communities were collected and broadcast by publications such as *Auslandsdeutsche* and *Volksdeutsche*.[65] The effects of this journalism on readers invoked a kaleidoscope of "authentic" features that often had as much to do with language or religion as they did with class, occupation, environment, and the amount of time the community had existed. It was therefore often as confusing as it was exhilarating to "discover" these lost brethren.

Menno Colony Mennonites appear to have welcomed the visitors into their homes – though Swartzentruber marked the aloofness of the colony's bishop, deacon, and ministers: "We were introduced to them but that was about all the conversation we had."[66] The missionaries did not ask the Menno colonists to change their language, alter their education system, or forsake their version of Christianity, yet Menno Colony leaders were likely suspicious of the missionaries' motives and perhaps this was for good reason. As the Mennonite refugee situation grew desperate in late 1929, the MCC repurposed Hershey and Swartzentruber's impromptu relief trip as a serendipitous reconnaissance mission for finding the refugees a new home.

Yet after the refugees arrived in Paraguay in mid-1930, the Menno Colony did not go out of its way to express solidarity with the MCC or donate its time and labor to the cause. Resembling the tensions between older German-speaking communities in Paraguay's La Plata region and German-speaking immigrants who arrived after the First World War, there were few similarities between the groups to forecast a shared future.

The Boundaries of Germanness, ed. Krista O'Donnell, Renate Bridenthal, and Nancy Reagin (Ann Arbor, MI: University of Michigan Press, 2005), 255.

[63] Ibid., 250.

[64] For the initial report, see T. K. Hershey and Swartzentruber, "Report of Condition of Mennonites in Paraguay," *Gospel Herald*, May 16, 1929, 147–48. Subsequent reports were printed as "Mennonites in Paraguay," and ranged from September 19, 1929–October 31, 1929.

[65] Reagin, "German Brigadoon?" 253–54.

[66] Swartzentruber, "Churches and Schools," 629.

The Menno Colony expected the Fernheim Colony to remain a separate settlement. According to M. W. Friesen, colony leaders believed that "the Russians should and would take care of themselves."[67] It did not matter to them if the MCC thought the refugees were Mennonites because the Menno Colony's leadership did not care about Mennonite unity. *They* were Mennonites and that was all that mattered.

FERNHEIM'S FIRST EXODUS

When Bender traveled to Germany to coordinate the refugee transports to Paraguay in early 1930, another MCC representative named Gerhard G. Hiebert was simultaneously dispatched to Paraguay to greet the arrivals. G. Hiebert was an experienced refugee worker, having scouted settlement possibilities in Mexico and coordinated the distribution of tractors among Mennonites in the Soviet Union during the early 1920s.[68] He regarded the Fernheim Mennonites as coreligionists as long as they were duly appreciative of the MCC's wisdom and effort. Yet when a group of colonists attempted to carve out an alternate destiny by establishing a new settlement, G. Hiebert was confounded and angered by their lack of trust in the MCC's good intentions. Thus, the MCC marked the Fernheim colonists as troublesome because they did not share its vision of Mennonite unity under its leadership, even as Fernheim colonists began to suspect that the MCC had ulterior motives for bringing them to the Chaco.

Personality differences quickly emerged between G. Hiebert and the colonists. Gundolf Niebuhr states that G. Hiebert was a "sober and factual man" whose partisanship and diplomatic ignorance quickly got him into trouble.[69] The Fernheimers also saw him as distinctly American and under the protection of "Uncle Sam."[70] One Corporación Paraguaya employee, J. N. McRoberts Jr., who was stationed at the neighboring Menno Colony, reported to his superiors in New York that G. "Hiebert was the wrong man to have come here" after hearing much "gossip and

---

[67] M. W. Friesen, *New Homeland*, 405.   [68] F. H. Epp, *Mennonite Exodus*, 59, 163, 259.
[69] Niebuhr, "Hiebert, Gerhard G.," in Ratzlaff et al. (eds.), *Lexikon der Mennoniten in Paraguay* (Asunción: Verein für Geschichte und Kultur der Mennoniten in Paraguay, 2009), 203.
[70] Nikolai Siemens, "November – Auhagen – Unruh – Hiebert," *Menno-Blatt* (Fernheim, Paraguay), November 1932, 2–3.

tales" from another Corporación employee, Mr. Norén, who was stationed at the Fernheim Colony.[71]

Personality conflicts aside, the atmosphere was ripe for confrontation between the MCC and the Fernheim Colony. Even before the move, colonists viewed South America as a less desirable option than North America. They were also nervous about the land agreements that they signed in Germany, which were based solely on the MCC's positive reports. Upon the colonists' arrival in the Chaco, they were disappointed in the "preparations" made by the Corporación Paraguaya, which amounted to little more than a small clearing, a shed, and a well with a high alkaline content.[72] The timing of the colonists' arrival exacerbated their concerns since most arrived in the Southern Hemisphere's autumn and had to wait six months to plant crops. Though the refugees were glad to be free from Bolshevik persecution, they now had to pay for travel expenses and land in a country that they had not necessarily chosen.

Within a few months, some Fernheimers were fed up with the venture. According to McRoberts Jr., all of the Fernheim colonists, with the exception of the small "Polish" contingent of voluntary migrants, wished to leave.[73] They were especially unhappy about the price that they were charged for land and the quality of livestock supplied by the Corporación Paraguaya, since eighty-three head of cattle died soon after their delivery. What made the situation even more frustrating was that there was free land available near the port city of Concepción with direct access to the railroad.[74] The only advantage to living in the Chaco as far as the colonists could tell was its isolation, which most did not care for anyway. They blamed the MCC for promising them good, inexpensive land and delivering an overpriced wilderness. One colonist wrote that they were "sold to South America like sheep" and that "We are dealing with an organization of Mennonites, in which everyone cheats as much as he can."[75] These

---

[71] J. N. McRoberts, Jr., "Corporación Paraguaya [Field Report], December 1, 1930," Corporación Paraguay Correspondence Joseph McRoberts, January 1928–June 1931, IX-3-3 Paraguayan Immigration 1920–1933 (1/19), MCCA.

[72] John D. Unruh, *In the Name of Christ: A History of the Mennonite Central Committee and Its Service 1920–1951* (Scottdale, PA: Herald Press, 1952), 27.

[73] McRoberts, Jr., "Corporación Paraguaya [Field Report], December 1, 1930," Corporación Paraguay Correspondence Joseph McRoberts, January 1928–June 1931, IX-3-3 Paraguayan Immigration 1920–1933 (1/19), MCCA.

[74] J. D. Unruh, *In the Name of Christ*, 28.

[75] Quoted in Peter P. Klassen, *Mennonites in Paraguay Volume 1: Kingdom of God and Kingdom of This World*, trans. Gunther H. Schmitt (Filadelfia, Paraguay: Peter P. Klassen, 2003), 80.

complaints soon reached Mennonite publications in North America. Mumaw's "Relief Notes" column reported that "we have here a busy man [G. Hiebert], and when not given full support by those under his care he is not able to do things not under his control, it is very easy for some one to write to a friend on the spur of the moment and make complaint. We trust our people in the homeland [North America] will give due consideration to such possibilities and not to take too seriously any such rumors or letters."[76] Casting itself as an impartial authority, the MCC projected an air of calmness in the midst of a situation that was spinning out of control. By November 13, 1930, Mumaw was happy to report, "in general the people are resigned to their lot."[77] In reality, they were not.

On October 31, 1930, the colony held a general assembly and commissioned Gerhard Isaak and Kornelius Langemann to scout for land in eastern Paraguay. The reasons were (1) that the Chaco's climate is "unhealthy for Europeans," (2) the lack of markets for their goods, (3) the "exorbitant" price of land, and (4) their "intolerable dependence" on the Corporación Paraguaya.[78] They left in January 1931. The scouts first visited Asunción and held a private meeting with the president who, when told of how much the colonists had paid for their land, reportedly exclaimed, "That is a crime!"[79] While the scouts were on their trip, T. K. Hershey returned to the colony in order to help G. Hiebert dissuade colonists from moving.[80] Both individuals reminded colonists' that the MCC would not provide money for a second settlement, which gave them reason to pause. A serendipitous rain and cooler weather also helped change colonists' minds prior to the scouts' return.[81]

When Isaak and Langemann returned to Fernheim in late February, G. Hiebert and Hershey immediately convened a private meeting with them. The MCC representatives especially chastised Langemann for going behind the MCC's back to look for a new settlement. According to Langemann, G. Hiebert denounced him as an agitator and as a communist, shouting "No one wants to leave the Chaco except you!"[82] G. Hiebert's anger was understandable. A mass movement would vastly complicate the MCC's position since it stood as the

---

[76] Mumaw, "Relief Notes," *Mennonite*, July 31, 1930, 5.
[77] Mumaw, "Relief Notes," *Mennonite*, November 13, 1930, 5.
[78] Quoted in P. Klassen, *Mennonites in Paraguay Volume 1*, 87. See also Walter Quiring, *Deutsche erschliessen den Chaco* (Karlsruhe, Germany: Heinrich Schneider, 1936), 152.
[79] P. Klassen, *Mennonites in Paraguay Volume 1*, 94.
[80] J. D. Unruh, *In the Name of Christ*, 28.
[81] P. Klassen, *Mennonites in Paraguay Volume 1*, 87.   [82] Ibid., 87–88.

guarantor of the colony's travel debt to Germany and land debt to the Corporación Paraguaya. The last thing the MCC wished to do was liquidate its Chaco holdings, find someone to buy them, and help the disgruntled colonists purchase unsurveyed land elsewhere.

A second meeting was held on February 28, 1931, which drew a clear line between colonists who wanted to abandon the venture and those who were willing to stay. Isaak and Langemann's report appeared as the last item on the agenda and someone had changed the title from "Report by the Committee to Seek Land" to "Report about a Study Tour to Improve Knowledge about the Land."[83] At the meeting, the majority of the colonists decided to remain in the Chaco. At this point, Langemann and his followers felt deceived by the MCC and disowned by their fellow colonists. Writing years later, Langemann maintained that colony leaders were cowed by the MCC and the change in the agenda did not reflect a change in colonists' interest toward moving. Langemann also criticized his co-delegate, Isaak, for remaining silent during the debate in order to save his position as a preacher. Not too long after the meeting, Langemann and about twenty-five families left the colony. They initially settled alongside German-speaking families in Horqueta, near Concepción, but here too they experienced tension with their neighbors, and established a new settlement named Neuhoffnung.[84] Their exodus signaled to the remaining colonists that leaving was viable, though it would require them to sell their Chaco property at a pittance, alienate them from their coreligionists, and expose them to the possibility of financial ruin without the MCC safety net.

Langemann's new settlement struggled to survive. Within a year they were writing letters to former refugee camp employees in Germany asking for used clothes and Christmas presents. Unruh caught word of the solicitations and forwarded one to Bender stating, "This is a letter that disloyal settlers sent to Mr. Reimann. Now they are begging."[85] Writing to another associate in Germany, Unruh stated, "These people have a bad conscience . . . Don't you agree that these [Mennonite] committees have to

---

[83] Ibid., 87.

[84] Joseph Winfield Fretz, *Immigrant Group Settlement in Paraguay: A Study in the Sociology of Colonization* (North Newton, KS: Bethel College, 1962), 39. See also J. D. Unruh, *In the Name of Christ*, 28; Rudolf Dyck, "Neuhoffnung bei Horqueta," *Lexikon der Mennoniten in Paraguay*, 314.

[85] B. H. Unruh, "Letter to H. S. Bender," n.d. Quoted in P. Klassen, *Mennonites in Paraguay Volume 1*, 89.

remain firm[?] We have to maintain order in this business."[86] In response
to the disgruntled Fernheim colonists who remained, Unruh admonished,
"You fled out of Russia. We did not ask you to do that. We helped you
here to the limits of our resources – in fact beyond our resources ... We
cannot let you yell at us and scold us."[87] For their part, Hershey and
G. Hiebert believed that if the Menno Colony could survive, then the
Fernheim Colony could too. Its members needed to work together, trust
the MCC, and pray for better days.

The MCC successfully deterred a mass departure from Fernheim,
but the stage was set for further disputes between the organization
and the colonists. On T. K. Hershey's recommendation, G. Hiebert
was relieved of his position in the fall of 1931, and the decision
appeared to have a calming effect on the colony.[88] A letter dated
October 3, 1931, from the colony's *Oberschulze* Franz Heinrichs to
Unruh confidently (if prematurely) reported, "Many of those who
griped initially, now admit that they did wrong and wish that they
could take their words back."[89] Nevertheless, individuals and families
continued to trickle out of the colony and settled on the fertile land
around Concepción or migrated south to work for German individuals and companies in the capital. By 1936 a total of thirty-six
families had left the colony and by 1938 there were about sixty
Mennonite individuals living in Asunción.[90]

Generally speaking, the Fernheim Mennonites were grateful for the
MCC's help, but found the organization's worldview and personalities
to be alienating. Most of the MCC's leaders, such as H. Bender,
O. Miller, P. Hiebert, Mumaw, and Kratz were English-speaking
Mennonites from well-established communities in the United States.
Like associative-minded Mennonites in Canada, they were among the
first generation of Mennonites in North America to believe that
Mennoniteness could exist comfortably in the modern world. They
held a positive view of American democracy and "know-how," and an
"unquestioning confidence that it was both possible and right to enjoy
the fruits of US citizenship while preserving Mennonite culture and

---

[86] B. H. Unruh, "Letter to Pastor Handiges," October 9, 1932. Quoted in ibid., 89.
[87] B. H. Unruh, September 3, 1931. Quoted in P. Klassen, *Mennonites in Paraguay Volume 1*, 80.
[88] Niebuhr, "Hiebert, Gerhard G.," 203.
[89] Quoted in P. Klassen, *Mennonites in Paraguay Volume 1*, 81.
[90] Ibid., 89; Harold S. Bender, "With the Mennonite Refugee Colonies in Brazil and Paraguay: A Personal Narrative," *Mennonite Quarterly Review* 13, no. 1 (1939): 65.

religious heritage."[91] By the early 1940s, Bender believed that Anabaptism and Western democracy were inseparable since "there can be no question but that the great principles of freedom of conscience, separation of church and state, and voluntarism in religion, so basic in US Protestantism and so essential to democracy, ultimately are derived from the Anabaptists of the Reformation period."[92] Energized equally by Anabaptist history and the modern zeitgeist of freedom and equality, they wished to extend their bourgeoning historical, theological, and political gospel to the ends of the (Mennonite) earth.

By contrast, most Fernheim colonists came from German-speaking frontier settlements in Siberia. They were unfamiliar with the North American church and they had only met a few MCC delegates in person – one of whom was the hard-edged G. Hiebert. They were skeptical about the MCC's effusive optimism about the future, having witnessed firsthand the terrors of communism and the political turmoil of late-Weimar Germany. It also did not help that the MCC's newspaper reports and internal memoranda spoke of the refugees patronizingly as poor brethren whom they had been entrusted to protect. The MCC did not simply wish to help the Fernheim Colony, but to cultivate them into model Mennonites who shared their optimistic vision.

Outsiders offered reassurances throughout the 1930s but they were cold comfort to the Fernheim colonists who saw their crops fail, children die, and others abandon the venture. Between 1930 and 1932, colonists remained tied to the land mostly by a lack of money to move elsewhere, the authoritarian injunctions of their sponsors, their fledgling leadership, and whatever group pressure optimistic colonists could muster. One positive voice in the colony was *Menno-Blatt* editor N. Siemens. A year after G. Hiebert departed the colony, N. Siemens published a front-page article titled "November – Auhagen – Unruh – Hiebert." The article focused on the help that each individual had provided the colony during the month of November in the three preceding years: German diplomat Otto Auhagen (1929), Benjamin H. Unruh (1930), and G. Hiebert (1931). N. Siemens reminded his readers that G. Hiebert could have remained in the United States instead of volunteering in Paraguay. He also recounted several stories about G. Hiebert's aid to the colony including one instance where he slept overnight in a storage barn to protect the colony's supplies,

---

[91] James C. Juhnke, *A People of Two Kingdoms* (Newton, KS: Faith and Life Press, 1975), 67.
[92] Bender, *The Anabaptist Vision*, 4.

and ended up getting involved in a shootout with would-be thieves.[93]
N. Siemens served as a bridge from the Chaco to North America and
Germany throughout the decade, sometimes to his own detriment.
In a December 1938 letter to Bender, N. Siemens gloomily reported,
"I have tried to stay entirely on the side of the Fernheim Colony and to
influence our people to remain faithful to the Colony ... as a result, I have
been besmirched ... and some have canceled their subscriptions [to
Menno-Blatt] out of spite."[94]

The years 1932 and 1933 saw an upturn in the colony's morale
and economic situation and Fernheim colonists' thoughts returned to
planting crops and improving their land. A March 12, 1932, meeting
between the MCC's Executive Committee and H. G. Norman of the
Corporación Paraguaya resulted in a reduction of the price of colonists' land from $8.00 USD to $3.00 USD per acre.[95] In May 1932,
the first group of refugees from Harbin, China arrived in the colony,
which provided a boost in morale. The new arrivals brought word of
Mennonites who were still living in the Soviet Union and Fernheim
residents showed the newcomers how to survive in the new environment. A few months later, the Chaco War brought lucrative government contracts and the influx of soldiers provided a steady revenue
stream for the cash-strapped colonists. For the time being, it
appeared to many colonists that the situation between themselves,
the Corporación Paraguaya, and the MCC might work out after all
(Fig. 4.1).

Thus, the Fernheim Colony's initial months of settlement were not only
defined by local, material struggles – poor health, poor weather, and poor
livestock – but by a transnational, existential struggle over what the
venture meant to the MCC and the colonists. The MCC entertained the
false hope that there was a Mennonite essence that transcended the
vagaries of time and space and would ease relations between itself and
the two Chaco colonies. Yet its representatives were astonished to learn
that a shared sense of mutuality would have to be created and not
discovered. Strangely, the MCC looked to the Menno Colony as
a model of unity and perseverance even though its religious life was
strikingly anachronistic in comparison to the one the MCC hoped to
build. For their part, the Fernheim colonists simply wanted productive

[93] N. Siemens, "November – Auhagen – Unruh – Hiebert," 2–3.
[94] Quoted in P. Klassen, *Mennonites in Paraguay Volume 1*, 86.
[95] J. D. Unruh, *In the Name of Christ*, 29.

FIGURE 4.1 Benjamin H. Unruh and H. S. Bender. Circa 1930. Photo used courtesy of Mennonite Historical Library, Goshen (IN) College

land with good transportation links at a cheap price but the MCC frustratingly delivered unproductive, isolated, and expensive acreage. Colonists therefore possessed a tenuous notion that they should remain together and remained on the lookout for more satisfying conclusions to their tribulations elsewhere.

A COLONY DIVIDED

The Menno Colony marked the early 1930s as a time of internal struggle between its constituent churches and paid little attention to its Fernheim neighbors or the MCC. While the Fernheim colonists were divided at all levels over their commitment to remaining in the colony, the Menno Colony contended with church-level factionalism. Far from reaching out to its Fernheim neighbors and unifying with an imagined global church – as the MCC had hoped it would – the Menno Colony undermined and eventually destroyed its own administrative structure.

Before the Menno Colony Mennonites left Canada, its leaders were more concerned with the colony's religious organization than its managerial and economic apparatus. One settlement leader regretted that they had not considered administration issues before arriving in Paraguay because they had believed that they simply needed to follow the biblical mandate to "seek first the kingdom of God and his righteousness, and all these things will be added to you."[96] Soon after their arrival, however, inequalities developed between a small group who had a large amount of money and power and a larger group who did not.

The origins of the conflict can be traced to June 19, 1928, a year and a half after the first colonists arrived in the Chaco. On this date, Menno Colony leaders convened a joint assembly of the three *Gemeinden* at Puerto Casado in order to reestablish the Fürsorge-Komitee, which had administered the group's affairs while still in Canada. It would now be tasked with establishing "a civic-social government" that would, among other things, oversee colonization of the Chaco, promote commerce, and administer mortgages and loans.[97] Earlier, some of the delegates of the smaller Sommerfelder (West Reserve) and the Bergthaler (Saskatchewan) groups had met with a lawyer in Asunción to draw up a set of documents outlining the settlement's leadership and jurisdiction. They decided that each colony – irrespective of size – should have equal voting rights in the colony's administration. Apparently, the Chortitzer (East Reserve) delegates were not at the Asunción meeting and did not examine the documents until the June 1928 meeting. The Chortitzer (East Reserve) group represented about 80 percent of the Menno Colony settlers, including

---

[96] Matthew 6:33 (ESV); M. W. Friesen, *New Homeland*, 419.
[97] The colony's representatives were M. C. Friesen and Abraham A. Braun from the Chortitza (East Reserve), Isaak K. Fehr and Bernhard F. Penner from the Sommerfeld (West Reserve), and Peter Peters and Cornelius H. Wiebe from the Bergthal (Saskatchewan) group. M. W. Friesen, *New Homeland*, 422–24.

many of the poorer colonists. According to M. W. Friesen, the Chortitzer (East Reserve) delegates balked at the equal voting clause during the meeting but apparently let the matter drop in order to avoid controversy.[98] By 1932, the clause had opened up a large rift between the Chortitzer (East Reserve) group and the other colonists. Among other things, Chortitzer (East Reserve) colonists wished to buy cattle and expand their farming operations on credit, but they were voted down. In January, there was a general meeting between the three groups to settle the issue, but it ended in what M. W. Friesen described as an "indulgence in altercations."[99] Additional Fürsorge-Komitee meetings were held throughout 1932 to find a modus vivendi, but neither side was willing to compromise.

The Chaco War temporarily relegated the issue to the background, but as the conflict wound down in 1934, the Chortitzer (East Reserve) representative J. A. Braun arranged an audience with President Ayala to discuss the colony's problems. At the September meeting between the Chortitzer (East Reserve) delegates and the president, the delegates enumerated the difficulties that they were experiencing with their coreligionists in the Sommerfelder (West Reserve) and Bergthaler (Saskatchewan) groups. Apparently, the president listened to their complaints, and their request for him to moderate the dispute, but refrained from entangling himself in the issue. The next month, Sommerfelder (West Reserve) and Bergthaler (Saskatchewan) representatives likewise called on the president to listen as they aired their side of the story. Exasperated with both groups, the president admonished the Mennonites that there was enough discord in Paraguay already and that Paraguayans believed Mennonites to be a model of unity and cooperation. Ironically, Ayala's statements revealed that he thought the antinationalist Menno Colony made a good metaphor for Paraguayan national unity. Two more meetings between the president and the Chortitzer (East Reserve) group followed in 1935 and 1936. Now claiming the support of 90 percent of the colony, the Chortitzer (East Reserve) Mennonites broke from the Fürsorge-Komitee and created a separate organization in 1936 named the Chortitzer Komitee, which effectively undermined the Fürsorge-Komitee's authority.[100]

The fact that the Menno Colony Mennonites asked the president of the country to arbitrate the conflict reveals how the colonists understood their relationship to each other and the state. They had initially tried to work out the problem among themselves, along the lines of Matthew 5:25

---

[98] Ibid.   [99] Ibid., 428.   [100] Ibid., 435–37.

where Jesus admonishes his followers to resolve problems with each other before seeking out government authorities. After this approach failed, Menno Colony representatives did not ask their Fernheim coreligionists or the MCC to help settle the problem. God's kingdom on earth (i.e. their settlement) did not extend outward to engage other self-professed Christians but was manifested through a direct relationship with heaven. The Menno Colony was therefore mostly indifferent to opinions of their Mennonite coreligionists. They also did not try to resolve the dispute through the country's legal system – as Paraguayan citizens may have done – but appealed directly to the Solomonic president of the country because they viewed themselves as subjects of God, in the first instance, and of a king (or president), in the second. Like their ancestors in Canada and Russia, the Mennonites of Menno Colony viewed their settlement as an autonomous unit, separate from other Mennonite groups and existing outside the normal framework of citizenship.

FERNHEIM'S SECOND EXODUS

In 1936, the MCC encountered another impediment to its authority and its uniting goals. While the Menno Colony struggled to resolve its administrative crisis, new tensions arose in the Fernheim Colony. The harvests of 1933 and 1934 were satisfactory, but drought and grasshoppers demolished the colony's yields in 1935 and 1936. Colonists were forced to buy imported food and live off credit from the colony's economic cooperative. In 1935, the colony's *Oberschulze*, J. Siemens, was placed in charge of mediating debt repayments between the colonists and the MCC, a decision that placed more power in the hands of the colony but also made its administration the focal point for bitter colonists.[101] By 1936, the drought was so bad that the Paraguayan River was practically unnavigable and the colony risked starvation.[102] Colonists were desperate and turned once again to thoughts of migration. They were nevertheless unable to do so because the MCC had request the Paraguayan Port Authority at Puerto Casado to refuse ticket sales to any Fernheim Mennonite who did not have written permission from the colony office.[103] They felt trapped. Within this atmosphere of crisis, the MCC

---

[101] Niebuhr, "Siemens, Jakob Wilhelm," *Lexikon der Mennoniten in Paraguay*, 387.
[102] John D. Thiesen, *Mennonite and Nazi? Attitudes Among Mennonite Colonists in Latin America, 1933–1945* (Kitchener, ON: Pandora Press, 1999), 111.
[103] P. Klassen, "Die Rolle des Mennonitischen Zentralkomitees," 43.

sought to buy the Corporación Paraguaya, a move that would consolidate its economic control over both colonies' land debts and the corporation's residual Chaco holdings. Yet Mennonite control of the corporation came at a price for the Fernheim colonists, who would have to consent to a set of "Mennonite principles" that ideologically bound them to the North Americans. The MCC desired Mennonite unity, but on their own terms. Like national elites imposing shared identifications and narratives on their populations in Europe and across the world, the MCC determined that it would forge the colonists' identity, not the colonists themselves.

As pests and drought devastated the Fernheim Colony's crops for the second year in a row, its leaders wrote to delegates at the 1936 Mennonite World Conference in Amsterdam that the colony was in a "panic" and debt restructuring was necessary in order to avoid a mass exodus.[104] The MCC responded by sending MCC executive secretary O. Miller to Paraguay in December 1936 to calm the colonists' fears and investigate the purchase of the Corporación Paraguaya from its North American owners. The prospect of buying the corporation was made possible by the death of investment banker Edward Robinette in 1935. Robinette was the business associate of Samuel McRoberts, and owned a 65 percent controlling interest in the corporation.[105] Buying out both shareholders would mean that: (1) The MCC would be the primary debtor to both the Menno and the Fernheim Colonies; (2) it could restructure land repayments on a more generous schedule; (3) it would be the principal landowner of nearly 121,405 additional hectares of Chaco wilderness; and (4) it would allow Fernheim Mennonites who wished to leave the colony to do so in a regulated fashion.[106] Though the MCC was formed on a purely ad hoc basis in 1920 to provide aid to starving Mennonites in the Soviet Union, it was now a permanent institution with tangible assets. As a result, it was not acting alone but in the name of a constituency that supported its mission and wanted accountability for its actions. The MCC therefore not only felt pressure from the Fernheim Colony to make the

[104] Fernheim Colony writers included KfK director and Allianzgemeinde leader, Nikolai Wiebe; Brüdergemeinde leader, Gerhard Isaak; Mennonitengemeinde leader, Johann Teichgräf; *Oberschulze*, Jakob Siemens; and school administrator, Abraham Harder. See Harder et al., "An die Mennonitische Weltkonferenz in Holland," in *Der Allgemeine Kongress der Mennoniten gehalten in Amsterdam, Elspeet, Witmarsum (Holland) 29. Juni bis 3. Juli 1936*, ed. D. Christian Neff (Karlsruhe, Germany: Heinrich Schneider, 1936), 83.

[105] P. Klassen, *Mennonites in Paraguay Volume 1*, 95.

[106] Ibid.; J. D. Unruh, *In the Name of Christ*, 31–32.

deal work, but also from North American Mennonites who funded the operation and wanted to see a payoff on their investment.

O. Miller convened a series of meetings with colony and corporation representatives in January 1937. At these meetings, he realized that a number of colonists wanted to completely cut their ties to the MCC and that two distinct groups had solidified within the Fernheim Colony: the *Bleibende* (individuals who wanted to stay in the Chaco) and the *Abwanderer* (individuals who wished to find new land elsewhere).[107]

Meanwhile, MCC representatives moved forward with purchase negotiations. The MCC would solicit $25,000 USD (about $446,298 USD in 2019) from North American Mennonites for an upfront payment and pay the remaining $32,500 USD (about $580,187 USD in 2019) within one year.[108] On February 13, 1937, the MCC, McRoberts, and the Robinette heirs agreed to the final terms and signed the papers. Now the MCC was the sole debt collector for land owned by both Mennonite colonies.[109] In addition to the land debt, the Fernheim Colony also owed the MCC $175,000 (about $3,124,085 USD in 2019) for supplies and relocation expenses.[110] A few months later, the MCC was incorporated as a charitable organization "to have perpetual existence by its corporate name," while the Corporación Paraguaya was reorganized to include two US citizens, O. Miller and M. Kratz; one Paraguayan, Dr. Garaj; and two Fernheim colonists, Franz Heinrichs and Heinz Krupp (Krupp was later replaced by Abram Loewen).[111] Menno Colony was not represented in the corporation's administration.

The Menno Colony appears to have viewed the MCC's purchase of the Corporación Paraguaya strictly as a land deal; one debtor was as good as another and it did not matter if it was a Mennonite organization or not. The buyout came in the middle of the colony's administration dispute and so it appears to have been a minor event for the Menno colonists. In general, one gets a sense from the literature that the land debt mattered very little in relation to the colony's internal power struggles, since it

[107] P. Klassen, *Mennonites in Paraguay Volume 1*, 91.

[108] J. D. Unruh, *In the Name of Christ*, 33. The inflation adjustment was made with the Bureau of Labor Statistics (CPI) Inflation Calculator, www.bls.gov/data/inflation_calculator.htm, last accessed August 8, 2019.

[109] Ibid., 31–32.

[110] Fernheim and Menno colonists were individually responsible for paying these debts. Three fourths of the Menno Colony debt was guaranteed by the church. See ibid., 34–35. The inflation adjustment was made with the Bureau of Labor Statistics (CPI) Inflation Calculator, www.bls.gov/data/inflation_calculator.htm, last accessed August 8, 2019.

[111] J. D. Unruh, *In the Name of Christ*, 35–36; Thiesen, *Mennonite and Nazi?* 114.

receives little mention in the colony's official histories. J. A. Braun, who was the first leader of the Chortitzer Komitee, only spends half of a page in his memoir *Im Gedenken an jene Zeit* discussing the acquisition, and he is not sure whether it happened in 1936 or 1937. M. W. Friesen's 474-page history of the settlement *New Homeland in the Chaco Wilderness* includes two brief sentences on the Menno Colony's role in the purchase. Likewise, Abram W. Hiebert and Jacob T. Friesen's exhaustive history of the Menno Colony's administrative and economic organization only provides a short section on the colony's relationship with the MCC during the transition.[112] The difficulties between the MCC and the Fernheim Colony appear to have not affected the Menno colonists, and the sale of the Corporación Paraguaya to the MCC provoked neither fear nor relief (Fig. 4.2).

FIGURE 4.2 Family photograph enclosed with September 4, 1935 letter from H. B. Toews to Samuel McRoberts, Menno Colony, Paraguay. "September 4, 1935. Dear Sir McRoberts, New York. I am sending you a picture of my famaly [*sic*] an [*sic*] my house, which we build ourselfs [*sic*] in the Chaco Paraguayo Colonia Menno Waldheim No. 2. Best wisches [*sic*] to you and your family from my famaly [*sic*]. These shade trees are 4 years old. H. B. Toews, Colonia Menno, Paraguayo." Photo used courtesy of Mennonite Historical Library, Goshen (IN) College

[112] See Abram W. Hiebert and Jacob T. Friesen, *Eine bewegte Geschichte ... die zu uns spricht: Materialien zur Entwicklungsgeschichte der Kolonie Menno: Ein Beitrag zur 75. Gedenkfeier* (Asunción, Paraguay: Chortitzer Komitee, Colonia Menno, 2002).

The MCC's purchase of the Corporación Paraguaya represented something momentous for the organization since it was the fullest realization of Bender's idea of creating a Mennonite republic in Paraguay. Religion and culture were indispensable factors in bringing about this situation, and the MCC believed that their maintenance would determine the colony's success. In fact, the MCC's sixth point in its contract with Fernheim Colony included the statement, "Since the maintenance of *Mennonitentum* [Mennoniteness] is an essential element in this agreement, both sides mutually commit to establishing the colony Fernheim as a pure Mennonite Colony and to maintain Mennonite principles as such."[113] Though it was unclear from the document the exact nature of these "principles," it *was* clear that they would not be created by the Fernheim Colony nor adapted from the Menno Colony, but handed down by the North Americans, who increasingly positioned themselves as spokespeople for the global Mennonite Church.

The purchase ameliorated some of the Fernheim colonists' concerns about debt repayments, but others remained steadfast in their plan to leave. Out of the colony's 384 landowners, 206 wished to abandon the colony at the end of 1936 and 140 maintained this position after the MCC had purchased the Corporación Paraguaya.[114] The *Abwanderer* contingent sent out land scouts in early 1937 to look for acreage in eastern Paraguay. They also asked the Paraguayan government if they could retain their Mennonite privileges if they left Fernheim Colony, since there was a rumor that the privileges would only be recognized in the Chaco. By July 1937, the *Abwanderer* received word that their privileges were guaranteed throughout Paraguay and that two German-speaking individuals named Arthur and Wilhelm Strauch wished to sell them land near Rosario on the Paraguayan River.

In July 1937, about 750 people, representing over one third of the colonists, left the Fernheim Colony for 6,879 hectares of mixed jungle and grassland in eastern Paraguay, which they named Friesland, after the area of Holland where their forefathers had originated.[115] The new

---

[113] Quoted in P. Klassen, "Die Rolle des Mennonitischen Zentralkomitees," 46.

[114] P. Klassen, *Mennonites in Paraguay Volume 1*, 96.

[115] The exact number is debatable. Beate Penner claims there were 750 individuals, Alfred Fast and G. Ratzlaff claim 748, and Thiesen (via Friedrich Kliewer) claims 706. See Penner, "Friesland," *Lexikon der Mennoniten in Paraguay*, 166; A. Fast and G. Ratzlaff, "Friesland Colony (San Pedro Department, Paraguay)," *Global Anabaptist Mennonite Encyclopedia Online*, last modified November 20, 2016, http://gameo.org/index.php?titl e=Friesland_Colony_(San_Pedro_Department,_Paraguay)&oldid=91825, last accessed

colony included many of the Fernheim Colony's wealthier families, though it did not include many of its leaders, and its population was divided between Mennonitengemeinde and Brüdergemeinde congregants.[116] Writing to *Oberschulze* J. Siemens from Germany, Unruh sarcastically quipped, "You could have run a grand colonization program together. Why are you separating? After all, God saved you from persecution together."[117] Friesland Colony's newly elected *Oberschulze* Heinrich Rempel answered Unruh's rhetorical question by claiming the main cause of the split had less to do with climate and economic difficulties than with the Fernheim Colony's administration. In his view, 90 percent of the Friesland colonists would have remained in the Fernheim Colony if the latter's leadership had been less strict and had allowed private trade (instead of conducting all business through the colony's cooperative). Rempel also claimed that the MCC's representatives were out of touch with the colonists and unwilling to devise a creative solution.[118]

Yet economic opportunities and hostility to the MCC were likely not the only reasons for colonists' dissatisfaction. A large number of *Abwanderer* supported closer ties to Nazi Germany since they were hedging their bets that they could eventually "return" to their German "homeland." This is verified by a 1938 report from the German legation in Asunción, which noted that the Friesland settlers were more aligned to the Nazi cause than either the Menno or Fernheim Colonies.[119] Tellingly, there were no *Abwanderer* from the Allianzgemeinde, a church that was firmly against ties to Nazi Germany. This circumstance suggests an ideological motive for the departure in addition to an economic and administrative one, but this will be taken up in subsequent chapters. On a narrative level, colonists did not necessarily see the "togetherness" of their salvation as lasting indefinitely. Their flight to the Chaco was a tragic conclusion to their story in Russia, but it did not necessarily portend the beginning of a unified story in South America. Their community of fate, made possible by the German government and helped along by the MCC,

---

June 7, 2018; Thiesen, *Mennonite and Nazi*, 112; Friedrich Kliewer, "Die Mennoniten-Kolonie Friesland in Ostparaguay," *Mennonitische Geschichtsblätter* (Emden, Germany) 3 (1938): 58. See also P. Klassen, *Mennonites in Paraguay Volume 1*, 97.

[116] A. Fast and G. Ratzlaff, "Friesland Colony"; Thiesen, *Mennonite and Nazi?* 112.

[117] B. H. Unruh to Jakob Siemens, August 10, 1937. Quoted in P. Klassen, *Mennonites in Paraguay Volume 1*, 98.

[118] P. Klassen, *Mennonites in Paraguay Volume 1*, 97; Thiesen, *Mennonite and Nazi?* 98.

[119] Dr. Hans Karl Paul Eduard Büsing, "Nr. 371, 2 Durchdrucke," R127972e, PA AA.

needed more than either entity's money or well-wishes to survive. It needed a shared story that could only be manifested from within.

MCC representative P. Hiebert arrived in Fernheim from the United States in July 1937, just as the dissatisfied colonists were packing their bags for Friesland. He was upset. P. Hiebert lauded the *Bleibende* for believing that God had ordained the Chaco as a Mennonite refuge, and excoriated the *Abwanderer* for not recognizing God's hand in the matter. He also suggested that the latter were influenced by communist ideology while in Russia and were simply pretending to be martyrs.[120] This was the second MCC representative to accuse Fernheim colonists of being communist sympathizers. After all, it was easier to accuse the *Abwanderer* of ideological subterfuge than to admit that the Chaco made a poor setting for destitute agriculturalists or acknowledge variations between the MCC's and the colonists' conceptions of Mennoniteness. P. Hiebert believed that dissention in the colony betrayed not only the MCC but the Mennonite faith in general. In drawing the Fernheim Colony into a global community of Mennonites, the MCC wished to transform Russian Mennonites into North American–style Mennonites, which was a cultural undertaking as much as a humanitarian or religious one. As with other state-centered nationalist initiatives, the confession's faith and future were not egalitarian and open-ended but united and linear. Any other Mennonite trajectory was heretical.

"THESE ARE [NOT] MY PEOPLE"

Bender's first visit to the Paraguayan colonies came eight years after his bold proclamation that the MCC wished to create a "Mennonite state" in the Chaco. Before his trip, Bender clung to a vision that the Mennonite colonies in Paraguay should be a stronghold of a pure Mennonite faith. Like interwar German ethnographers who were disappointed when they encountered the bricolage of *Auslandsdeutsche* in Eastern Europe, and resembling the JDC, which was unable to sustain its wartime settlement of 757 refugees in Sosúa, Dominican Republic, Bender regretfully noted "I wish it were possible to speak of the Mennonites of Paraguay as one united body, but alas, this is not the case," for what he encountered was

---

[120] Peter C. Hiebert, *Mitteilungen von der Reise nach Süd-Amerika* (Hillsboro, KS: Mennonite Brethren Publishing House, n.d.), 64; J. D. Unruh, *In the Name of Christ*, 38.

a situation that was far more complex.[121] Unsurprisingly, his report reveals that he considered himself to be a qualified judge of the colonies' Mennoniteness and even ranked them on a scale, with individuals closest to the MCC receiving the best marks.

When Bender's plane touched down in Asunción he was greeted by former Fernheim Mennonites who were living in the capital, and J. A. Braun of the Menno Colony, who happened to be in Asunción on business. Bender's impression of the Asunción Mennonites was largely unfavorable owing to their worldliness. He concluded "it is difficult to maintain high ideals of faith and life in the midst of the destructive influences of the city, where the low standards of life, which are so common in Paraguay find their full expression." Nevertheless, he was happy to learn that "an attempt is made to hold the group together by holding services Sunday afternoons in the German church."[122] For Bender, "urban Mennonite" was a contradiction in terms and portended the eventual disintegration of the faith. Compact, rural settlements, similar in form to the ones prescribed by Germany's overseas associations, were Bender's ideal since they kept Mennonites close to each other and close to the land.

Traveling north to the Chaco, Bender spent a few days visiting the Menno Colony *Ältester* M. C. Friesen, whom he described as an "able man, determined to maintain uncompromisingly the principles of his group, and evidently succeeding in doing so." Bender was impressed with the material progress the colony had made, though he unfavorably describes the people as "very conservative" and desiring "little contact with others."[123] He had nothing to report on their religious life, but instead pressed on to the Fernheim Colony.

When Bender visited the Fernheim Colony, he describes it as "the most important and most interesting of all the Mennonite groups" in Paraguay because it "represents the great relief project which was undertaken in 1930 by the Mennonite Central Committee."[124] Skirting the edge of solipsism, Bender wrote that the colonists are "anxious to prove worthy of their privileges and blessings" on account of their salvation from the Soviet Union, and therefore "anxious for fellowship with the Mennonites of North America."[125] Apparently, the reason why the Fernheim Colony

---

[121] Bender, "With the Mennonite Refugee Colonies," 66. On the Sosúa colony, see Wells, *Tropical Zion.*
[122] Bender, "With the Mennonite Refugee Colonies," 65.   [123] Ibid., 66.
[124] Ibid., 66–67.   [125] Ibid., 69.

was "interesting" was because some of its members wished to draw closer to North American Mennonites. Bender was coy about the colony's difficulties, opaquely noting that "not everything is as it ought to be, but there is no need to enter into details here." He reassured his North American audience that the Fernheimers "have maintained a staunch Mennonitism thus far ... including the principle of complete nonresistance," which he increasingly viewed as the litmus test of true Mennoniteness, but was a more ambiguous tenet for colonists whose lives had been defined by war for the past twenty years. Bender admitted that "there are good reasons why most of us from North America would not want to exchange [places] with them," but concluded that the Fernheim Colony was a "paradise" and "the best organized, the most prosperous, and spiritually the soundest Mennonite colony in Paraguay."[126]

Bender had a preexisting ideal of what Mennoniteness looked like and tried his best to discover this phenotype among the Mennonites of Paraguay. Playing the role of Goldilocks, he maintained that the Asunción Mennonites were too liberal, and the Menno Colony Mennonites were too conservative, but the Fernheim Mennonites were "just right," even though the preceding eight years had witnessed two major departures that had provoked bitter disputes and reduced the colony's population by over one third.[127] Yet the colonists' associative inclinations, agrarian circumstances, and high level of education helped them resemble North American Mennonites more than the other groups and, by extension, Bender's Mennonite ideal.

In spite of the MCC's desire for Mennonite cooperation, the interwar years witnessed continued theological and cultural divisions between this organization and the colonists. The source of the tension came down to each entity's collective narrative and its articulation of Mennoniteness. Secure in its local conception of Mennoniteness, the Menno Colony was indifferent to outsiders' appraisals of their settlement. Their Mennoniteness positioned the colony in a binary relationship with God and a binary relationship with "the world." They did not consider themselves to be members of a transnational confession or nation, so the settlement did not worry about how outsiders viewed their faith, much less concern themselves with advancing a vision of "the" Mennonite Church.

---

[126] Ibid., 67, 69.   [127] Ibid., 67.

On the other hand, the fate of the Fernheim Colony was intertwined with the MCC, but they were far from sharing a similar vision of the future with the organization because they were so deeply divided among themselves. After all, they had made their decision to flee the Soviet Union as individuals and families, not as a group. As the Fernheim Colony moved from one crisis to another, their fractured identifications not only inhibited the MCC's projected future of unity and cooperation but the colony's own ability to see themselves as a united group.

For its part, the MCC undertook the daunting task of transporting the Fernheim refugees, covering their debts, and purchasing the Corporación Paraguaya because they believed that Paraguay held the promise of a new Mennonite homeland, far from the incursions of hostile governments and the terrors of invading armies. Amidst a cacophony of voices that proposed various destinies for the colonists, the MCC pressed forward with linking the colonists' narrative to an emerging North American–style Mennoniteness, which alternately agitated and angered the Fernheimers. Attendant to this project were the inevitable consequences of institution-building: quarterly reports, standards of accountability, cost–benefit analyses, propaganda, and a sustainable cash flow. Thus, the MCC reckoned with the difficulties of cajoling the Fernheim Colony into accepting its vision of Mennoniteness while maintaining an upbeat story of its successes to an expectant North American constituency.

On a broader level, the decades of the 1920s and 1930s were an unprecedented time of both interconnection and conflict among Mennonites worldwide. Concepts of nation, state, and race that were a prominent feature in the writings of Mennonites such as J. P. Dyck, J. J. Hildebrand, and Quiring figured into these debates, especially among the nearly 30,000 Mennonites who arrived in the Americas from the Soviet Union. As Hitler's "New Germany" unfolded into a world-encompassing vision of German solidarity, the Mennonites of the Paraguayan Chaco stood at a crossroads between their religious identity as Mennonites and their purported national identity as Germans.

5

Peanuts for the Führer (1933–1939)

Among the millions of reichsmarks' worth of gifts lavished on Hermann Göring and Emmi Sonnenmann at their April 11, 1935, wedding in Berlin was a bag of peanuts from the Fernheim Colony, Paraguay.[1] A report in *Menno-Blatt* announced that the newlyweds were "particularly pleased" by the modest gift and that an additional 1,500 kg of the colony's peanuts were distributed to VDA supporters throughout Germany. In fact, the head of the VDA, Hans Steinacher, was sufficiently impressed by the shipment to pen a letter extolling the colonists' commitment to the German *Volk* as inspiration for "new work, with double force . . . [for] the benefit of our great German people."[2]

Two years later, a lecturer at the University of Kiel, Dr. Herbert Wilhelmy, visited the Menno and Fernheim colonies to investigate how closely Paraguay's *Auslandsdeutsche* aligned with the global ambitions of Hitler's "New Germany."[3] Wilhelmy was unimpressed by both groups. As *Volksdeutsche* (ethnic Germans without German citizenship), they certainly did not measure up to the *Reichsdeutsche* (individuals with German citizenship) that he visited on his ethnographic tour of Paraguay. Wilhelmy saw little difference between the colonies and

---

[1] Samuel W. Mitcham, *The Rise of the Wehrmacht: The German Armed Forces and World War II*, vol. 1 (Westport, CT: Praeger, 2008), 91; Peter Hildebrand, "Über unsere Erdnusssendung," *Menno-Blatt* (Filadelfia, Paraguay), September 1935, 4–5.

[2] Hildebrand, "Über unsere Erdnusssendung."

[3] Dr. H.[erbert] Wilhelmy, "Bericht über eine [?] mit Unterstützung der Albrecht-Penk-Stiftung – Berlin, der Deutschen Forschungsgemeinschaft und der Hänel-Stiftung – Kiel durch geführten kolonialgeographischen Forschungsreise nach Südamerika" (26. VI.1936 – 8.IV.1937), R127972d, PA AA, 71–79, 73.

damned them both as hopelessly religious. Moreover, his detailed report warned that they maintained a deceitful "Jewish" culture that was embarrassing to the Reich.[4]

How did Mennonite-grown peanuts end up in the mouth of one of Hitler's closest confidants? Why did Wilhelmy look upon Paraguay's Mennonites as degenerate religious fanatics? Why was the Fernheim Colony inspired by the Nazi movement while their Menno Colony neighbors were not?

This chapter demonstrates that the reason for the colonies' different interpretations of Nazism stems from their specific migration histories – as voluntary migrants and as refugees – and the degree to which the VDA and local Nazi "interpreters" successfully merged the story of National Socialism with their communal narratives. Although the Menno and Fernheim colonies ostensibly shared much in common, they developed widely different interpretations of Nazism. The voluntary migrants of Menno Colony used their local religious solidarity to reject (trans) National Socialism. Their restricted vision of community was an end in itself and had no national or transnational corollary. In contrast, the refugees of Fernheim Colony viewed (trans)National Socialism as a possible vehicle for communal unity. In their view, communal unity was the highest form of *völkisch* (nationalist) unity and Christian cooperation underpinned *völkisch* cooperation.[5] Nazi proponents in Germany, for their part, bore a striking resemblance to MCC representatives who used the colonies to promote a transnational version of Mennoniteness: They wished to use the colonies to foster (trans) National Socialism but were ambivalent toward, if not hostile to, the local realities when they witnessed them firsthand.

By using the phrase "(trans)National Socialism," I draw attention to the Nazi Party's goal of integrating *Auslandsdeutsche* into the *Volksgemeinschaft* no matter where they physically resided.[6] During the interwar years, Nazism

---

[4] Ibid., 77.

[5] It is difficult to find an English corollary for the word *völkisch*. Generally speaking, it may be rendered as "nationalist," but in the Nazi era it carried militant and exclusionary overtones. In general, I agree with Egbert Klautke who states "all composites that include the German term *Volk* or the adjective *völkisch* are potentially misleading in English translation." See *The Mind of the Nation: Völkerpsychologie in Germany, 1851–1955* (New York: Berghahn, 2013), 7.

[6] Along similar lines, Norbert Götz employs the phrase "supranational conceptualization" of *Volksgemeinschaft* to describe the phenomenon and compares it with national and subnational conceptions. See "German-Speaking People and German Heritage: Nazi Germany and the Problem of Volksgemeinschaft," in *The Heimat Abroad: The*

operated primarily as a nationalist movement in Central Europe that prioritized expanding Germany's national borders on behalf of the *Volksgemeinschaft*. Yet it also operated as a transnational movement that disregarded borders in its quest to unearth members of the *Volksgemeinschaft* elsewhere. Thus, the *Volksgemeinschaft* was located within the territory of an expanding German state, but was connected to hundreds of Germans living in non-German territories around the world. The party may have argued confidently that its *Lebensraum* objectives would eventually unite all Germans within a single realm, but its appeals to *Auslandsdeutsche* displayed insecurities that Germans living abroad may actually understand themselves to be members of other cultures and societies. The term (trans)National Socialism emphasizes the value that the Nazi movement placed on incorporating *Auslandsdeutsche* into the German nation, while revealing the inherent contradiction between the concept of transnationalism and the territorial aims of a regime bent on creating a "Greater German Reich."

Interwar *völkisch* organizations such as the DAI and especially the VDA – which more than doubled in size to more than 2,000,000 members between 1925 and 1929 – advanced strident claims that the German government should help all members of the German *Volk*, no matter where they resided.[7] In one book, published in conjunction with the Weimar Republic's Reichswanderungsamt (Migration Office) in 1923, the VDA conceded that although there "is no period in which the boundaries of nation and state overlapped completely," the "deepening of a [national] state of consciousness" among *Auslandsdeutsche* could transform Germany into a "world power." An "alertness" of Germany's global connections "forms the spirit and cultural community of all Germans!"[8] With a fillip from the ascendant Nazi Party, this mandate extended to even the most remote *Auslandsdeutsche* communities.

Boundaries of Germanness, ed. Krista O'Donnell, Renate Bridenthal, and Nancy Reagin (Ann Arbor, MI: University of Michigan Press, 2005), 58–82.

[7] On the DAI and VDA mandates see Grant Grams, *German Emigration to Canada and the Support of Its Deutschtum During the Weimar Republic* (New York: Peter Lang, 2001), 7–14. See also Nancy R. Reagin, "German Brigadoon? Domesticity and Metropolitan Perceptions of Auslandsdeutschen in Southwest Africa and Eastern Europe." In *The Heimat Abroad: The Boundaries of Germanness*, ed. Krista O'Donnell, Renate Bridenthal, and Nancy Reagin, 248–88 (Ann Arbor, MI: University of Michigan Press, 2005), 253–54.

[8] Friedrich Flierl, "Die Ausbreitung des deutschen Volkes," in *Deutsche im Ausland – im Auftrage des Reichswanderungsamtes und in Verbindung mit dem Verein für das Deutschtum im Ausland*, ed. Friedrich Wilhelm Mohr and Walter von Hauff (Breslau, Germany: F. Hirt, 1923): 1, 17.

Germany's governments and *völkisch* organizations had, for a long time, fantasized about maintaining connections to Latin America's *Auslandsdeutsche*. Brazilianist Glen Goodman writes, "Imperial, Weimar and Nazi governments had each imagined ... *Auslandsdeutsche* ... variously as cultural and economic footholds in a developing region, as possible advocates for German interests abroad, or even as founts of a true and uncorrupted ur-Germanness."[9] Latin America's *Auslandsdeutsche* population was an especially attractive target for homeland solidarity owing to the presence of prewar German networks, the likelihood of German speakers retaining their culture (in comparison with individuals in North America), and its growing size.[10] In fact, between 1919 and 1930, about 130,000 *Reichsdeutsche* arrived in the region. Paraguay especially saw an increase in German speakers after the war. According to Stefan Rinke, it overtook Chile for third place behind Argentina and Brazil.[11]

Latin America's German-speaking residents were incredibly heterogeneous.[12] They were urban and rural; atheistic and religious; working-class, middle-class, and wealthy; and they had emigrated as individuals, families, and groups from states across the Northern Hemisphere: Austria-Hungary, Canada, Switzerland, the pre-1871 German Confederation's constituent realms, Russia, and Germany itself. Some had lived in Latin America for decades while others were recent arrivals. Some romanticized the Kaiserreich, others lamented the passing of the Weimar Republic, supported the rise of the Nazis, or were waiting

---

[9] Glen Goodman, "The Enduring Politics of German-Brazilian Ethnicity," *German History* 33, no. 3 (2015): 423–38, 423.

[10] Albrecht von Gleich, *Germany and Latin America, Memorandum RM-5523-RC* (Santa Monica, CA: RAND Corporation, 1968), 7.

[11] Stefan Rinke, "German Migration to Latin America," in *Germany and the Americas: Culture, Politics, and History, a Multidisciplinary Encyclopedia*, vol. 1, ed. Thomas Adam (Santa Barbara, Denver, Oxford: ABC CLIO, 2005). 29. For German immigration statistics to Latin America, see Walther L. Bernecker and Thomas Fischer, "Deutsche in Lateinamerika," in *Deutsche im Ausland, Fremde in Deutschland: Migration in Geschichte und Gegenwart*, ed. Klaus Bade (Munich: C. H. Beck, 1992), 197–200; Hartmut Bickelmann, *Deutsche Überseeauswanderung in der Weimarer Zeit* (Wiesbaden: Steiner, 1980); Albrecht von Gleich, *Germany and Latin America, Memorandum RM-5523-RC* (Santa Monica, CA: RAND Corporation, 1968), 5–10; Rinke, "German Migration to Latin America," 291–412.

[12] H. Glenn Penny, "Latin American Connections: Recent Work on German Interactions with Latin America," *Central European History* 46, no. 2 (2013): 370–71. See also Dirk Hoerder, "The German-Language Diasporas: A Survey, Critique, and Interpretation," *Diaspora* 11, no. 1 (2002): 31–32.

for the triumph of global communism. Some individuals could claim Reichsdeutsch status while others – including the majority of Paraguay's Mennonites – could only claim the "second-class" designation of *Volksdeutsche*, which kept them from officially participating in the Nazi Party or freely returning to Germany. Despite all of these handicaps, optimistic observers in Germany believed that Latin America's *Auslandsdeutsche* had nation-building potential.[13]

Guiding the continent's *Auslandsdeutsche* was nevertheless akin to herding cats. Local concerns trumped national ones and the Third Reich's long-term ambitions remained unclear. The Nazi Party's underfunded and overextended Auslandsorganisation (Foreign Organization, AO) leaned on local Nazi syndicates to control *Reichsdeutsche* activities abroad, but as Dirk Hoerder argues, it is hard to speak of a unified German "community" in any national context in Latin America.[14] Aligning the region's *Volksdeutsche* with Nazi aims was even more difficult. One succinct report by Hermann von Freeden, a *Regierungsrat* (senior civil servant) in the government's Reichsstelle für das Auswanderungswesen (Emigration Office) stated, "colonization in the northern part of South America can be characterized in a few words. The old German colonies of Pomerania in Espirito Santo, the colony Tovar in Venezuela and the old settlements in Peru Oxapampa and Pozuzo stagnate."[15] Continuing south, the report included mixed impressions of state-, railroad-, charity-, and

---

[13] Although there is a paucity of fine-grained studies of the Nazi movement's effects on local German cultures in Latin America, there is a surfeit of national-level studies. Exceptions include Bernd Breunig, *Die Deutsche Rolandwanderung (1932–1938): Soziologische Analyse in historischer, wirtschaftlicher und politischer Sicht, mit einem Geleitwort von Johannes Schauff* (Munich: Nymphenburger, 1983); Jürgen Buchenau, *Tools of Progress: A German Merchant Family in Mexico City, 1865–Present* (Albuquerque, NM: University of New Mexico Press, 2004); and Peter Johann Mainka, *Roland und Rolândia Gründungs – und Frühgeschichte einer Deutschen Kolonie in Brasilien (1932–1944/45)* (São Paulo: Cultura Acadêmica/Instituto Maritus-Staden, 2008). A good starting point for national-level surveys is the list footnoted in Penny's "Latin American Connections," 364, n. 10. See, especially, Hartmut Fröschle's edited collection, *Die Deutschen in Lateinamerika: Schicksal und Leistung* (Basel: Horst Erdmann, 1979). Notable for its breadth and depth on the topic of German-speaking exiles in Latin America during the Nazi period is Patrik von zur Mühlen, *Fluchtziel Lateinamerika: Die deutsche Emigration 1933–1945: Politische Aktivitäten und soziokulturelle Integration* (Bonn: Neue Gesellschaft, 1988).

[14] Hoerder, "German-Language Diasporas," 31.

[15] Hermann von Freeden, "Kolonisatorische Erfahrungen aus der Nachkriegszeit," *Archiv für Wanderungswesen und Auslandkunde: Studien und Mitteilungen zur Wanderungsbewegung der Kulturvölker* 4, no. 4 (1933/1934): 1.

capitalist-sponsored colonies in the Southern Cone, with the latter category receiving praise for its economic potential.[16] Freeden had firsthand experience working with *Auslandsdeutsche* when he established the Kolonie Rolândia for landless Germans in Brazil during the early 1930s and was predisposed to favor group settlements with direct connections to Germany.[17] In a subsequent publication Freeden concluded, "spontaneous settlement, a settlement without organic connections to the mother country, its people and its national needs, is a loss and a waste of national resources."[18] By Freeden's criteria, the Menno Colony was an "amateur colony," the Fernheim Colony was a "charity colony," and neither possessed "organic connections" to Germany. Freeden's analysis was not the only opinion informing the Nazi Party's view of *Auslandsdeutsche*, but it indicates that just beneath AO's and VDA's optimism lurked the hidden realities of localism.

Alon Confino nevertheless indicates the means by which *Auslandsdeutsche* could imagine their membership in the *Volksgemeinschaft*. In his study of German collective memory, Confino shows that individuals belonging to imperial Germany's Heimat movement interpreted the "nation as a local metaphor" whereby local and national identifications became mutually reinforcing concepts.[19] In particular, he shows how Heimatlers reframed local histories to create a template for interpreting Germany's national history and narrative.[20] Interwar *Auslandsdeutsche* who aspired to a place in the *Volksgemeinschaft* could likewise reframe the development of their local or communal histories as a revelation of national solidarity with Nazi Germany. This insight helps explain Hermann Rüdiger's argument in the widely read 1935 *Das Buch vom deutschen Volkstum* (*The Book of German National Character*) that Mennonite colonies who were scattered across the world and maintained their Germanness could "serve as an

---

[16] Ibid., 7.

[17] Pedro Moreira, "Juden aus dem deutschsprachigen Kulturraum in Brasilien: Ein Überblick," in *Das Kulturerbe deutschsprachiger Juden: Eine Spurensuche in den Ursprungs*, ed. Elke-Vera Kotowaski (Berlin, Germany: Walter De Gruyter, 2015), 426.

[18] Hermann von Freeden, "Über die Möglichkeiten der Kolonisation für die Weisse Rasse in der Tropischen Zone," in *Comptes rendus du Congrès International de Geographie Amsterdam* (Leiden, Netherlands: E. J. Brill, 1938), 118.

[19] Alon Confino, *The Nation as a Local Metaphor: Wurttemberg, Imperial Germany, and National Memory, 1871–1918* (Chapel Hill, NC: University of North Carolina Press, 1997).

[20] Ibid., 137.

allegory for the entire fate of Germandom" since they maintained their German language and culture but lacked broader organization.[21] In his view, Mennonite communities were the perfect local, yet transnational, metaphor for the *Volk*.

During the 1930s, the Fernheim Colony searched for ways to build a shared story by (more or less) working with US Mennonites. Yet key Fernheim leaders were increasingly inspired by the Nazi concept of a German *Volksgemeinschaft* and viewed the Nazi narrative of a broken German nation – unified and redeemed through *völkisch* solidarity – as a ready-made analogy for the colony's struggle. Fernheim colonists had little hope that they could live inside the German state, but they believed that maintaining a connection to the country that had sheltered them as refugees promised to validate their local cohesion. Even as the MCC wove both colonies into a narrative of transnational Mennonite solidarity, Nazi interpreters – led by schoolteachers Kliewer and Julius Legiehn and nursed by Quiring and Unruh in Germany – wove the colonies into a narrative of transnational German solidarity. To this end, Kliewer and his supporters organized a Nazi-style *Jugendbund* (youth group), curried the VDA's attention, and argued with their coreligionists in Menno Colony.

The loans and optimism afforded by the MCC's American representatives were now in direct competition with a well-oiled *völkisch* publicity machine that seemed more relevant to the Fernheimers' specific history and context. Saddled with the task of handling the colony's debts, the nascent MCC had little time and few resources to influence the colony's religious and educational culture. Unlike the VDA, the MCC did not possess a German-language propaganda arsenal and teaching English to a German-speaking colony in a Spanish-speaking country was admittedly pointless. Hence, Fernheim Mennonites looked more to the VDA, an organization to whom they were sentimentally indebted, than to the MCC, an organization to whom they were monetarily indebted. The MCC's sincere but nervous creditors were no match for the VDA's propaganda, which made Nazi Germany appear strong, compassionate, and hopeful of the future. It would not be until the early 1940s that the MCC would have enough resources, staff, and motivation to challenge the VDA's pan-Germanist promises.

---

[21] Hermann Rüdiger, "Zahl und Verbreitung des deutschen Volkes," in Paul Gauß, *Das Buch vom deutschen Volkstum: Wesen, Lebensraum, Schicksal* (Leipzig: F. A. Brockhaus, 1935), 4.

The VDA's pro-*Auslandsdeutsche*, anti-communist sentiments were obviously attractive to the Fernheim Mennonites, but the Nazi movement's appeal went deeper still. Upon their baptism in Imperial Russia, Fernheim colonists would have recited the words "we experience the great emotion and sacred obligation of gratitude that unites us with our dear Russian fatherland ... [so] we should pray both in our public services and in our private chambers for our fatherland and our emperor."[22] The Fernheimers' affection for the tsar had been extinguished by the Bolsheviks but their historic reverence for monarchical rule predisposed them to view Hitler the Führer as a kind of German-Christian sovereign. According to Abraham Friesen, the "Mennonite addiction to autocratic rule was a long-standing one."[23] Before the Russian Revolution, Russia's Mennonites proclaimed their loyalty to the crown but by the 1920s, Heinrich J. Braun recalled "we had been awakened out of our blissful childhood slumber to a national consciousness; the result was that we suddenly felt ourselves lonesome and God-forsaken, no longer having any contact with Germany."[24] On a practical level, German-speaking communities across Latin America, including the Fernheim Mennonites, "instrumentalized" the term *Auslandsdeutsche* to serve local purposes and secure a range of economic and cultural privileges from Germany.[25] Fernheim Mennonites were enamored of Nazi Germany less because they wished to serve as a fifth column in Latin America, and more because Nazi Germany appeared to have a benevolent and benign interest in them.

[22] The commentary was written by David H. Epp, a Mennonite preacher, historian, editor of the newspaper *Botschafter*, and chairman of the Russian KfK. See "*Kurze Erklärungen und Erläuterungen zum Katechismus der christlichen, taufgesinnten Gemeinden, so Mennoniten genannt werden*," trans. Al Reimer (Odessa: A. Schultze, 1897; 2nd ed., Klaterinoslav: D. H. Epp, 1899; Canadian reprint of 1899 ed., Rosthern: Dietrich Epp Verlag, 1941), 176–79. Quoted in James Urry, *Mennonites, Politics, and Peoplehood: Europe-Russia-Canada 1525–1980* (Winnipeg: University of Manitoba Press, 2006), 108.

[23] Abraham Friesen, *In Defense of Privilege: Russian Mennonites and the State Before and During World War I* (Winnipeg: Kindred Productions, 2006), 201.

[24] Ibid., 276. Incidentally, after Braun escaped Russia for Canada in 1921, he funded a 1924 research trip to Paraguay to investigate settlement possibilities for Russia's Mennonites. See S. Huebert and Helmut Huebert, "Braun, Heinrich Jakob (1873–1946)," *Global Anabaptist Mennonite Encyclopedia Online*, last modified August 23, 2013, http://gameo.org/index.php?title=Braun,_Heinrich_Jakob_(1873–1946), last accessed June 7, 2018.

[25] Penny, "Latin American Connections," 376. Penny bases this observation on Hoerder, "German-Language Diasporas."

Naturally, the Menno Colony did not share this worldview. The analogies they drew on to describe their situation centered on the resigned but confident acceptance of God's mandate to flee from expanding states. The nationalism embedded in "Russification," "Canadization," and now "Nazification" symbolized hubris and evil. Thus, the Menno Colony flatly refused to participate in *völkisch* activities. They did not view Hitler as a potential leader since they were already "subjects" of a country that guaranteed their *Privilegium*. They saw within German propaganda and the VDA's "free" aid a new manifestation of an old menace to graft foreign identifications on their colony and educate their youth along national lines. Altogether, the Fernheim Colony refashioned a national narrative as a local narrative, while the Menno Colony used their local narrative to reject a national narrative.

THE JUGENDBUND INFLUENCE

In December 1931, about a month after the divisive MCC representative G. Hiebert had left the Fernheim Colony, German Minister Bülow, toured the Mennonite settlements.[26] It was the first time he had made the trip, since the Menno Colony did not seek his counsel when they immigrated in 1926–1927. Bülow was impressed by the colonies' cleanliness and the fact that they had given their villages German names. Nevertheless, he was disappointed that the groups were not socially unified. The relationship between the two was "clouded" due to the ideological differences between the Menno Colony's "simple farmers" and Fernheim's more educated settlers.[27] Bülow was the first German representative to visit the colonies and he set the tone for subsequent German interpretations. The two settlements held a great deal of cultural potential, but the Menno Colony's religious peculiarities and the Fernheim's internal conflicts threatened to keep them separated and to undermine a connection to Germany.

Fernheim colonists who hoped to change Bülow's mind started where so many other nationalists did: by "educating" youth about their Germanness. Between 1932 and 1933, a series of events provoked the Fernheim Colony to strengthen its attachment to the Nazi movement via

---

[26] Bülow, "Bericht Nr. 184, Asunción," December 17, 1931, Buenos Aires 67A (Mennoniten-Einwanderung nach Paraguay), Shelf 48, Carton 2439, PA AA. Incidentally, Bülow had briefly met Hiebert earlier in the year to discuss land prices. Bülow's wife also made the trip to gain a better understanding of Mennonite women's concerns, though her notes are not in the report.

[27] Ibid.

a Jugendbund. According to Kliewer, the rowdy behavior of a few of the colony's youths inspired him and Legiehn to form the group. Despite the local nature of the problem, Kliewer believed that it should be solved with a nationalist solution, one that would simultaneously promote obedience to authority and bring the colony into sustained contact with (trans) National Socialism. The plan was especially appealing because a Jugendbund was a ready-made organizational template for *völkisch* unity – a franchise so to speak – complete with its own activities, songs, and rituals. Yet the goal was not to create little Storm Troopers who would defend the Nazi state, but to adopt the strategies of the Hitlerjugend (Nazi Youth) to suit the colony's local needs and adapt a national narrative to suit the colony's local one.

The origins of the insubordination are unclear but it appears to have stemmed from the colony's lack of opportunities for young people and colony leaders' inability to maintain control. According to Kliewer, about twenty of Fernheim's young men were employed at a Casado-owned agricultural station at Palo Santo, which was located about 90 km east of the colony. Kliewer avers that within a few months the group was engaged in a variety of "intolerable excesses."[28] Colony records show that the KfK discussed the situation in November 1932. They were especially disturbed that "individuals [at the station] behave very badly, especially because they were mocking God's Word."[29] Ultimately, the youths' actions embarrassed the Fernheim Colony's *Oberschulze* enough that he requested that the offenders be fired from the station.[30]

The young men brought their disorderly conduct with them back to the colony. According to Kliewer, it climaxed during an Easter gathering at Rosenort, when the men engaged in "extreme misbehavior" of an undisclosed nature. In Kliewer's telling, the behavior required "energetic [disciplinary] action" by colony leaders, who meted out "penalties" to the "rioters."[31] Yet a public hearing in Filadelfia apparently ended with leaders being embarrassed in the eyes of the broader community.[32] It is

---

[28] Friedrich Kliewer, "Mennonite Young People's Work in the Paraguayan Chaco," *Mennonite Quarterly Review* 11, no. 2 (1937): 121.
[29] "Protokoll einer K. F. K.-Sitzung," November 14, 1932, ACF.   [30] Ibid.
[31] The festival was variously reported as a youth-sponsored "Chacofest" or a "chacrafest." The latter is a mixed Spanish and German expression for a farmworker celebration. See Kliewer, "Mennonite Young People's Work," 121; Walter Quiring, *Deutsche erschliessen den Chaco* (Karlsruhe, Germany: Heinrich Schneider, 1936), 182–83; John D. Thiesen, *Mennonite and Nazi? Attitudes Among Mennonite Colonists in Latin America, 1933–1945* (Kitchener, ON: Pandora Press, 1999), f. 19, 264.
[32] Thiesen, *Mennonite and Nazi?* 80.

possible that the discord was exacerbated by the fact that colonists held different ideas about parenting, youth culture, and their obligations to colony leaders and Casado. Shortly thereafter, Kliewer and Legiehn seized the opportunity to find a solution to juvenile idleness and disobedience through a nationalistic youth group.

Kliewer and Legiehn seemed suited for the job because they were relatively young schoolteachers. Born in 1905, Kliewer grew up as part of the German-speaking minority in Deutsch-Wymysle, Russia (now Nowe Wymyśle, Poland). From 1926 to 1930, he attended a teacher-training school in Łódź Poland, where he absorbed a German-nationalist teaching philosophy promulgated by the Deutsche Schulverein's (German School Association) regional base in Bydgoszcz. He was also familiar with VDA materials aimed at *Auslandsdeutsche* and brought this knowledge with him to Paraguay. At the age of twenty-five, he arrived in the Chaco with his parents and siblings as part of the small Polish-Mennonite contingent that accompanied the refugees to Paraguay.[33] Legiehn, a slight man with a shy face, was born in Ukraine in 1899. At age thirty-one, he arrived in the Chaco as part of the Moscow refugee group.[34] He settled with his wife and three children in the village of Schönwiese. Naturally, the schoolteachers viewed the question of youth delinquency as the result of bad education. From Kliewer's perspective, the root of the problem concerned the "communist schools" that colony youths had attended in the Soviet Union.[35] Although the disturbances were unsystematic and coarse, Kliewer saw them as part of an ideological problem that required an ideological solution – their "reeducation" from "communist" delinquency to *völkisch* good behavior.[36]

Coincidentally, German Mennonite scholar Walter Quiring was conducting research in the Fernheim Colony during the first half of 1933.[37]

---

[33] Robert Foth, *Global Anabaptist Mennonite Encyclopedia Online*, "Deutsch-Wymysle (Poland)," last modified September 14, 2014, http://gameo.org/index.php?title=Deutsch-Wymysle_(Masovian_Voivodeship,_Poland), last accessed June 7, 2018; Jakob Warkentin, "Kliewer, Frederich," *Lexikon der Mennoniten in Paraguay*, 244–45; Kurt Daniel Stahl, "Zwischen Volkstumspflege, Nationalsozialismus und Mennonitentum, unveröffentlichte wissenschaftliche" (Jena: Wissenschaftliche Hausarbeit zur Ersten Staatsprüfung für das Lehramt an Gymnasien im Fach Geschichte, Universität Jena, 2007), 35.

[34] Thiesen, *Mennonite and Nazi?* 80.

[35] Like MCC leaders' communist accusations, this charge should perhaps be taken with a grain of salt. "Communist" may simply have been the worst bad word that Kliewer could call them.

[36] Kliewer, "Mennonite Young People's Work," 121.

[37] "Verschiedenes," *Menno-Blatt* (Fernheim, Paraguay), May 1933, 6.

He was born in Russia in 1893, fled to Germany in 1921, received a doctorate from the University of Munich in 1927, and "was an early and ardent supporter and propagandist of the National Socialist government."[38] Quiring was quite knowledgeable about Germany's political situation and highly esteemed by the colonists. More than their Menno Colony neighbors, the Fernheim Colony wished to stay abreast of political developments in the broader world, particularly as they related to Germany and Russia. Quiring relayed his knowledge of the Nazi movement to a curious KfK at some point in the fall of 1933.[39] His information inspired the committee to draft a resolution in which the colonists proclaimed their Germanness to Unruh in Germany and the German legation in Asunción.[40]

The Fernheim colonists also wanted to make their enthusiasm for the Nazi's political victories known to the German government in Berlin. They thought the party's ascendency portended great things not only for the German nation, themselves included, but also for Christianity and the geopolitical balance of power. On May 18, 1933 – about the same time as Quiring's return to Germany – one of the settlement's Brüdergemeinde preachers, Gerhard Isaak, spoke enthusiastically at a colony meeting about Germany's "national awakening."[41] His speech led the settlement's leaders – *Oberschulze* David Löwen and KfK leader N. Wiebe – to write a letter to Berlin expressing their "excitement" over the country's "new direction."[42] With apparent serendipity, Germany had "discovered" its true direction within National Socialism – its mission as a nation – at the same time the Fernheim Colony was beginning its own mission in South America. Speaking on behalf of the Fernheim Colony, and perhaps even the Menno Colony, the letter stated,

We German Mennonites of the Paraguayan Chaco follow the events in our dear motherland and experience in spirit the national awakening of the German people.

---

[38] T. Regehr, "Quiring, Walter (1893–1983)," *Global Anabaptist Mennonite Encyclopedia Online.*

[39] Thiesen, *Mennonite and Nazi?* 81.

[40] "KfK minutes," May 9, 1933, Center for Mennonite Brethren Studies (hereafter, CMBS), Fresno Pacific University, Fresno, California. Cited in Thiesen, *Mennonite and Nazi?* 79.

[41] "Die Mennonitensiedlungen des paraguayischen Chaco und die nationale Erhebung in Deutschland," *Menno-Blatt* (Fernheim, Paraguay), June 1933, 2.

[42] Ibid. N. Wiebe's title was "Geistlicher Vorstand." He was the chairman of the colony's pastors and the leader of Fernheim colony's Allianzgemeinde, though this group would later distance themselves from the *völkisch* cause. The letter was reprinted in the "Paraguay" column of the Deutsches Ausland Institut's *Kalender des Auslanddeutschtums 1934* (Stuttgart), 16, no. 21 (1933): 542–43.

We are pleased that after a long time a German government stands at the head of the nation, freely and openly professing God as the ruler of the world, which can lead our enslaved and battered people to new heights.[43]

The letter went on to praise the new government's stance against communism and criticize the Weimar government's tolerance of this "ruinous" ideology. Although the money and logistics that saved the Fernheimers had come from the Weimar government, colonists saw greater continuity between Weimar-era organizations that broadcasted an anti-Weimar narrative and the ascendant Nazi regime. Fernheim's civic and religious administrators viewed the Nazi stance against communism as a "mighty deed," and as a result felt "most closely associated with [it]." It concluded by declaring the Fernheim Colony's "loyalty to the German people, to which we belong . . . without forgetting that we are loyal citizens of our Paraguayan fatherland."[44] The colonists affirmed their German nationality but they also affirmed that they were loyal to the state in which they resided. This position was common among the world's *Auslandsdeutsche* communities but it is likely that the Fernheim Colony were particularly adamant in their support of the new government because of its clear position against the Soviet Union.

The letter's enthusiastic tone suggests that the authors viewed the ascension of a new government as unequivocally good for *Auslandsdeutsche*. It emphasizes the unity of the German people – an important value for a colony beset by the Chaco War and struggling to maintain group cohesion – and conflates the colonists' suffering at the hands of the Soviet government with the perceived suffering of "enslaved and battered" Germans elsewhere in the world. Altogether, the Fernheim colonists viewed the Nazi Party as an improvement for the German nation state and Germans living abroad.

It is possible that Quiring's pro-Nazi sympathies inspired Kliewer and Legiehn to form the Jugendbund.[45] The initial organizational meeting in 1933 attracted members of all three of Fernheim's Mennonite churches – Allianzgemeinde, Brüdergemeinde, and Mennonitengemeinde – who all agreed that the Jugendbund should be a joint project. At a second conference in August 1933, Kliewer was nominated as the *Bundesleiter* (group leader), Peter Klassen was named the *Vertreter* (deputy leader), and Legiehn held the position of *Schriftführer* (secretary). The assembly christened the Jugendbund the Deutsche-Mennonitischen Jugendbund der

[43] "Mennonitensiedlungen."   [44] Ibid.
[45] "Verschiedenes," *Menno-Blatt* (Fernheim, Paraguay), May 1933, 6.

Kolonie Fernheim (German Mennonite Young People's Federation of Fernheim Colony).[46] Notably, no one from the Menno Colony participated in the gathering.

In the weeks following the August meeting, Kliewer was chagrined to learn that membership was flagging in some villages and that many of the "elder brethren did not understand the purposes and goals of the work and unjustly attributed various undesirable intentions to the new organization."[47] Recognizing a public relations problem, Kliewer convened a colony-wide youth meeting in the village of Waldesruh in October 1933, which was perhaps the first general, non-holiday celebration held in the settlement. The *Jugendfest* (youth fest), as it was called, was better planned than the August meeting and included "flowers and other festival materials"; fresh baked biscuits, coffee, and tea; a tent that could accommodate 700 people; and a raised platform with the conference's motto "Forward, upward, homeward!" written above it.[48] The gathering climaxed in a group rendition of the Jugendbund's official song, "Aufruf zum Kampf" ("Call to Arms"), which apparently did not provoke censure from religious leaders. As the Nazi Party in Germany was simultaneously inventing its own traditions through public spectacles and festivals, Fernheim Colony's Jugendbund leaders recognized the value of orchestrated performances that galvanized the community.

Apparently, the celebration proceeded so smoothly that the Jugendbund gained the approval of colony leaders, though they continued to monitor the group's leadership meetings. By the end of the year, the Jugendbund claimed 350 participants from 13 of the colony's 17 villages.[49] The Jugendbund's activities highlight the type of organization that Kliewer and his associates wished to build, which intermingled religious and *völkisch* elements. The group appeared to take its cues from the Hitlerjugend, which had itself been named the Jugendbund from 1922 to 1923. Its work revolved around weekly village-level meetings, organized hikes, bonfires, and field trips. The first meeting of the month concerned Bible devotions and prayer. The second meeting entailed studying and discussing Mennonite history (likely in the context of German history). The third focused on the "development of Germany in the past and in the present." The fourth meeting centered on teaching the youths about good manners and music. Whenever there were five weeks in a month, the last

---

[46] Kliewer, "Aus der Jugendarbeit in der Kolonie Fernheim," *Menno-Blatt* (Fernheim, Paraguay), October 1933, 1.
[47] Kliewer, "Mennonite Young People's Work," 122.   [48] Ibid., 123.   [49] Ibid., 125.

meeting was devoted to learning German folk songs since – according to Kliewer – the youth "had no common treasury of songs." Of course, this statement overlooked the religious hymns that they certainly shared.[50] The Fernheim Mennonites' support for the "New Germany" was therefore not confined to a few giddy months of excitement. It was carried forth through an ongoing dialogue between Unruh, Quiring, Kliewer, Legiehn, and the colony's civic and religious leaders about how Fernheim Colony's *Völklein* fit in to the larger *Volksgemeinschaft*. Yet the Jugendbund was initially more interested in *völkisch* activities for local, cultural, reasons than in the Nazi Party's legislative, racial, or military imperatives.

The Bible was recognized by the colony's churches as the definitive source of God's guidance and so the Jugendbund and the concept of a Mennoniten-*Völklein* had to make theological sense. Jugendbund leaders professed that they were not trying to undermine the colony's Mennonite faith, but they viewed it more as a cultural tradition than as a living connection. Legiehn clarified the point when he claimed that the youth group advocated the "biblical Christianity" of their ancestors but made no mention of applying it to contemporary life.[51] Rather, the Jugendbund wished to celebrate the colony's German nationality, which they felt was more relevant to the times. In a circuitous way, Legiehn tied the "wonderful diversity" of clans, nations, and languages expressed in Genesis 10:4–5, to Mennonites and other present-day Germans discovering their national "ennoblement."[52] The Bible's unfolding narrative of Christian peoplehood was unfurling before their eyes as German peoplehood. In Russia, God blessed Mennonites for their faith. Now God blessed them for their Germanness. Kliewer and Legiehn earnestly hoped that the Fernheim Colony – and especially its youths – would embrace their national identity and thereby achieve religious *and* national harmony.

Unruh, who saw the confession's destiny as entwined with the Nazi state, helped guide the Fernheim Colony's "recovery" of its Germanness and vouched for its authenticity to the Nazi regime. During the 1930s, he was the principal interlocutor between Germany's Mennonites, the Fernheim Colony, the VDA, and the German government (to whom the

---

[50] Ibid., 127–28.
[51] Julius Legiehn, "Unser Jugendbund," *Menno-Blatt* (Fernheim, Paraguay), August 1934, 3–4.
[52] Ibid.

colonists still owed money). Unruh welcomed the Nazi rise to power since he believed that Hitler was a deeply religious man who revered agrarian communities like the Mennonites. In fact, Unruh subscribed to the notion that the Mennonite diaspora was diametrically opposed to the Jewish diaspora, insofar as Mennonites were racially pure Aryans dispersed throughout the world.[53]

As the Nazis rose to power in 1933, Unruh and most of Germany's Mennonites viewed the party as a welcome change from the Weimar Republic. Many of Germany's Mennonite communities were located in the southwest and northeast regions of imperial Germany – areas that were cut off from Weimar Germany by mapmakers at the 1919 Paris Peace Conference. Added to this was the perception that the Weimar government was soft on the Soviets and a more assertive German government could help Mennonite brethren in Eastern Europe. Accordingly, the Conference of East and West Prussian Mennonite Congregations wrote to Hitler stating their "deepest thanks for the mighty revolution, which God has granted our nation through your energy."[54] Of course, the Nazi Party of 1933 looked different from the Nazi Party of 1939, or 1942–1943 (the high tide of genocide), but Mennonites joined the organization, apparently with few compunctions, throughout the 1930s. Writing in 1939, Bender noted, "I have been told that in Eastern Prussia at first the party made its progress largely on the basis of Mennonite participation."[55] Though perhaps an overstatement there was some truth to his claim. Individuals with Mennonite connections were found at all levels of government, particularly in eastern Germany. Despite some initial fears that the confession would be conglomerated into a Nazified Protestant Church, average Mennonites' interest in the party was robust. By the mid-1930s, Germany's Mennonite youth association and its periodical, the *Mennonitische Jugendwarte*, regularly promoted *völkisch* positions. In fact, simply being Mennonite was considered racially patriotic to the regime since it emerged through Nazi race science that Mennonites'

---

[53] On Mennonites as "Anti-Jews" see Benjamin W. Goossen, *Chosen Nation: Mennonites and Germany in a Global Era* (Princeton, NJ: Princeton University Press, 2017), 136–46. Unruh had a face-to-face meeting with Heinrich Himmler on New Year's Eve, 1942 at which time they discussed the desolation of Ukraine's population and its replacement with Mennonite colonists. See Goossen, *Chosen Nation*, 147–50.

[54] Translated and quoted in Goossen, *Chosen Nation*, 123.

[55] Harold S. Bender, "Church and State in Mennonite History," *Mennonite Quarterly Review* 13, no. 2 (1939): 83–103, 91.

proclivity for endogamy made them "purer" than average Aryans, particularly in regard to their communities abroad.[56]

The drift toward Nazism by Germany's Mennonites was uncontested, unsurprising, and represented the final step in the confession's move toward embracing German nationalism and the German nation-state.[57] The country's Mennonites had aligned themselves with German nation-building as far back as the 1870s when most decided to trade military service for citizenship. As in the Russian Empire during this same decade, hundreds of separatist Mennonites left Germany for the Americas, while their erstwhile brethren incorporated themselves into German society.[58] In defense of their choice to accept National Socialism, Germany's Mennonite publications argued that Nazism was good for Christianity since it would once and for all separate the spheres of church and state. In a surprising twist on Anabaptist ecclesiology, German Mennonites argued that "the proper separation of religion and politics, the separation between state and church (but please not between *Volk* and church!) that is so hotly contested [in these times] was realized some four-hundred years ago in our founding principles."[59] Mennonite bodies not only epitomized Aryan purity, but their confessional history epitomized one of the highest ideals of religion under the Nazi government, namely that the former does not influence or critique the latter. As North American Mennonites advanced a set of Mennonite principles that highlighted Anabaptism's "historic" proclivity for democracy – thus legitimating their place in American society – German Mennonites viewed their confession as the harbinger of Germany's separation of church and state, which legitimated their place in the *Volksgemeinschaft*.

---

[56] Goossen, *Chosen Nation*, 131.

[57] Concerning military service, its acceptance "was widely endorsed, and was mentioned in many articles in various Mennonite periodicals." See Diether Götz Lichdi, "National Socialism (Nazism) (Germany)," *Global Anabaptist Mennonite Encyclopedia Online*, last modified May 23, 2014, https://gameo.org/index.php?title=National_Socialism_(Nazism)_(Germany), last accessed June 7, 2018.

[58] Goossen, *Chosen Nation*, 7–12.

[59] Ernst Fellmann, "Warum und wozu Jugendarbeit?" *Mennonitische Jugendwarte* (Elbing, Germany), 3 (1936), 72. Quoted in James Irvin Lichti, *Houses on the Sand? Pacifist Denominations in Nazi Germany* (New York: Peter Lang, 2008), 42. Pastors Gustav Kraemer and Horst Quiring made similar observations in Mennonite publications throughout the 1930s. See Kraemer, *Wir und unsere Volksgemeinschaft 1938* (Crefeld, Germany: Crefeld Mennonitengemeinde, 1938), 15; Quiring, "Kirche, Volk und Staat in mennonitischer Sicht," *Mennonitische Jugendwarte* 5 (1937): 106–7. Also see Fritz Hege, "Das Täufertum in der Reformationszeit," *Mennonitische Jugendwarte* 2 (1935): 52.

Colonists looked to Mennonites in Germany to understand their national identity at the same time that Germany's Mennonites were aligning themselves with the strident ideology of the new regime. For example, an August 1933 issue of *Menno-Blatt* included an announcement that a recent Kuratoriumssitzung (conference of Mennonite leaders) in Germany had decided to drop an affirmation of nonviolence from their statement of faith.[60] Marked by its elasticity, the style of Mennoniteness emanating from Germany suggested that Mennonites could retain their familiar *personal* religious story – birth, salvation, death, and deliverance – while giving them a *collective* political story that was tied to the *Volk*. Accordingly, Fernheim's *völkisch* activists argued that overt expressions of Mennonite faith were best left to individuals' private lives, or at most the lives of the colony's *separate* churches. The colony's *collective* identification was best represented by its Germanness, since it was arguably the one thing that all colonists shared in common (other than their unfortunate status as refugees).

In July 1934, the Jugendbund was permitted to launch a two-page *Menno-Blatt* insert titled *Kämpfende Jugend* (*Fighting Youth*) with the encouragement of Unruh and other friends of the group. The first page of each issue typically contained an inspirational or didactic message that encouraged young readers to be virtuous, obey authority, and sustain the fight against evil. The second page included announcements, such as information on the group's past and future meetings. The paper's name was an ironic choice considering the confession's ostensible emphasis on nonviolence. It is unclear how much resistance there was to the bellicose title, but Kliewer argued that the paper inspired youth to fight against their individualistic pride, "'for Christ and our German Mennonite people,' that is our slogan!" Editor N. Siemens likewise deemed it appropriate because the youth were not using physical weapons but were battling "for nonviolence as defined by Jesus Christ." N. Siemens also took the opportunity to encourage German and North American Mennonites to accept the paper as a gift that would connect the Fernheim youth to their friends abroad.[61]

As the mouthpiece of the Jugendbund, the paper articulated a narrative of Mennoniteness that erased the line between "Mennonite" and

---

[60] "Verschiedenes," *Menno-Blatt* (Fernheim, Paraguay), August 1933, 6.
[61] Nikolai Siemens, "Kämpfende Jugend," *Kämpfende Jugend* (Fernheim, Paraguay), July 1934, 1.

"German" and blurred the line between spiritual and earthly "friends" and "enemies." In one article dated February 1935, Quiring proclaimed "for the first time a light has awakened Mennonite youths from the idle notion that *Auslandsdeutsche* Mennonites are Dutch or Russian Mennonites! – We are Germans!"[62] Quiring also motivated his readers to refrain from incorporating Spanish into their daily speech by arguing that Mennonites do not speak a "mutilated Dutch," but a pure and recognized form of Low German that they should sustain and be proud of.[63] In general, *Kämpfende Jugend* contained more fighting words in support of Germanness than in support of Mennoniteness. Apparently, this articulation of Mennoniteness and its history was well received by the colony since the youth insert became a reoccurring feature in *Menno-Blatt*.

Menno-Blatt and *Kämpfende Jugend* were not the only publications floating around the Fernheim Colony. Colonists also subscribed to Mennonite and German newspapers that debated Mennonite and *Auslandsdeutsche* loyalty to Germany. Already by 1932, the colony was receiving sixty-four copies of the *Mennonitische Rundschau* and fifteen of *Der Bote*, which were both published in Canada.[64] The Fernheim Colony held another thirty-five subscriptions to the German Mennonite paper *Dein Reich komme* and forty-eight subscriptions to *La Plata Post*, which was the weekly edition of the pro-Nazi *Deutsche La Plata Zeitung* published in Buenos Aires.[65] The colony also received copies of Paraguay's leading pro-Nazi German-language newspapers *Deutsche Zeitung für Paraguay* and *Deutsche Warte*, which regularly carried announcements from the Fernheim Colony, including a full-page article on the Mennonite colonies authored by Legiehn.[66] It may have also received copies of *Deutsche Post aus dem Osten*, whose mandate was to mobilize "Russian Germandom in all the world and to join it to the German *Muttervolk* under the leadership of Adolf Hitler."[67] In the main, the German papers were staunchly pro-Nazi while the Mennonite papers

---

[62] Walter (Jakob) Quiring, "Kampf dem Fremdwort!" *Kämpfende Jugend* (Fernheim, Paraguay), February 1935, 1.

[63] Ibid.

[64] The former was established in 1880 to serve the Russian Mennonite diaspora in Canada Russia, and the United States. The latter was established by and for the Mennonites who had left Russia in the 1920s. Thiesen, *Mennonite and Nazi?* 88.

[65] Ibid.

[66] Julius Legiehn, "Die Mennoniten im Chaco von Paraguay," *Deutsche Warte* (Asunción), July 15, 1937, 56.

[67] "An unsere Leser und Freunde!" *Deutsche Zeitung für Paraguay* (Asunción), Eingehende Korrespondenz (amtliche) 1933, Cabinet 11B, ACF. On *Deutsche Post aus dem Osten* see

expressed both pro- and anti-Nazi sentiments. Importantly, the publications informed colonists that they belonged to overlapping national and transnational communities including other German-speaking Mennonites, the Russian Mennonite diaspora, *Auslandsdeutsche*, and Paraguay's own German-speaking minority. Holding these affiliations in equilibrium would become increasingly difficult as the German-based VDA insinuated itself in the colony's schools and the MCC began drawing a line between nonviolent Mennoniteness and an increasingly truculent Nazi Germany.

During the early 1930s, the Jugendbund gave form to National Socialism's function as a symbol of *völkisch* unity. The colony's *völkisch* activists – Kliewer and Legiehn foremost among them – hoped to peg the colony's local narrative to a larger Nazi narrative that promised strength through solidarity. *Kämpfende Jugend* likewise attempted to tie the colony's youths to its allies in Germany, such as Unruh and Quiring. Kliewer and Legiehn were successful because they did not violate the colony's local religious culture. Rather, they rhetorically made *völkisch* pride the epitome of Mennoniteness. Although Bülow had had little confidence in 1931 that the Fernheim Mennonites could be an asset to Germany, within a few years the colony's *völkisch* supporters laid claim to a popular youth group and a publication that identified itself with the aims of the Nazi state. By mid-decade, the notion that the Fernheim Colony was as German outpost was taken for granted both in the Chaco and in Germany.

THE VDA INFLUENCE

Under the Nazi regime, the VDA's foreign connections and its voluminous cultural and educational materials were repurposed as vectors for overseas propaganda. Like the CMBC and the MCC in North America, the VDA assumed that nodes of similar people who shared essential qualities could be found across the world and should remain connected to each other. The

---

Renate Bridenthal, "Germans from Russia: The Political Network of a Double Diaspora," in *The Heimat Abroad: The Boundaries of Germanness*, ed. Krista O'Donnell, Renate Bridenthal, and Nancy Reagin (Ann Arbor, MI: University of Michigan Press, 2005), 196; James E. Casteel, "The Politics of Diaspora: Russian German Émigré Activists in Interwar Germany," in *German Diasporic Experiences: Identity, Migration, and Loss*, ed. Mathias Schulze, James M. Skidmore, David G. John, Grit Liebscher, and Sebastian Siebel-Achenbach, 117–29 (Waterloo: Wilfrid Laurier University Press, 2008), 121.

organization's first contact with the Fernheim colonists occurred during their sojourn in Germany, when the VDA provided refugees with food, clothing, and other supplies. Now the VDA looked on the compact, agrarian colony in the heart of South America as a strategic economic and cultural connection that should strengthen its bond to the "homeland."[68]

On August 5, 1934 – at the height of the Jugendbund's success – Kliewer left the Fernheim Colony for Germany to pursue a doctorate in pedagogy at the University of Marburg.[69] The trip, his tuition, and the costs of finding a substitute teacher were covered by the VDA with Unruh's assistance.[70] By now, Unruh was working closely with the Nazi Party, so much so that when the Gestapo later reflected on his work, it considered him to be an "old member" of the party who had "succeeded in recruiting numberless [German] Mennonites for National Socialism."[71] In Fernheim, those means entailed gaining control of the schools by tapping Russian Mennonite Peter Hildebrand to assume Kliewer's duties and supplying the colony with VDA education material.[72] P. Hildebrand may have been blessed by the VDA but he was not as skilled as Kliewer at translating Nazism into a local vernacular. Rather, he ushered in more controversy than cooperation, which allowed doubt to seep into colonists' hope that the *völkisch* movement was a panacea for disunity.

P. Hildebrand was born in Imperial Russia in 1906 and trained as a teacher before he fled the country for Harbin, China in 1930. Here, he took up work teaching German-speaking refugees while attempting to immigrate to Canada, Mexico, or the United States. After those attempts failed, he was granted permission to live in Germany. Before P. Hildebrand and his wife Susie Penner moved to Paraguay in 1934, he became associated with the Nazis' Sturmabteilung (SS) and various

---

[68] Grams, *German Emigration to Canada*, 287.

[69] His dissertation was titled "Die deutsche Volksgruppe in Paraguay. Eine siedlungs-geschichtliche, volkskundliche und volkpolitische Untersuchung (The German minority in Paraguay. A settlement history, folkloric, and national political investigation)." See Warkentin, "Kliewer, Friedrich," *Lexikon der Mennoniten in Paraguay*, 244–45.

[70] Thiesen, *Mennonite and Nazi?* 85.

[71] "Berlin Gestapo to Dr. Karl Götz, Stuttgart," October 2, 1942, Berlin Geheimes Staatspolizeiamt, United States National Archives/T-81/143/0181573. Quoted in Gerhard Rempel, review of *Fügungen und Führungen: Benjamin Heinrich Unruh, 1881–1959: Ein Leben im Geiste christlicher Humanität und im Dienste der Nächstenliebe*, by Heinrich B. Unruh, *Mennonite Quarterly Review* 84, no. 2 (2010): 277.

[72] Peter Hildebrand, *Odyssee wider Willen: Das Schicksal eines Auslandsdeutschen* (Oldenburg, Germany: Heinz Holzberg Verlag, 1984), 187–88.

Auslandsdeutsche organizations.[73] P. Hildebrand's years as a refugee and his gratefulness to Germany were formative experiences that led him to identify strongly with the Nazi Party's anti-communist stance.

P. Hildebrand was more nationalistic than his predecessor, Kliewer, and more knowledgeable about the Nazi Party's political goals. However, he did not experience the difficult early years of settlement and did not try to appease the colony's religious sensibilities as Kliewer had done. Nevertheless, having arrived at the high tide of Kliewer's efforts, P. Hildebrand was pleased to hear his students greet him with "Heil Hitler!" at the colony's secondary school in Schönwiese.[74] In July of 1934, he addressed a colony assembly in Filadelfia with a speech titled "Germany under the Nazi Government and the Interest for Germans Abroad." His talk focused on questions about Germany's economic recovery, the German education system, the "Jewish Question," and Hitler as a person and as a leader.[75] In addition to this news, P. Hildebrand brought with him 800 reichsmark donated by the VDA and much "equipment of great value" including 1,800 books, medicine, land survey tools, sawmill and printing press parts, and musical instruments.[76] The shipment seemed to have something for everyone including a wheelchair for "one of our legless citizens, Peter Esau."[77] In this way, the VDA gained valuable publicity as an organization that cared for colonists' specific, local needs. Importantly, the colony received copies of the elementary school textbook *Lehrplan der reichsdeutschen Grundschule* – which painted subjects such as geography and history in a patently *völkisch* hue – and an additional 250 book titles.[78] Unruh encouraged the use of the new materials and worked to acquire more donations for Fernheim's schools since it would reduce P. Hildebrand's dependence on the colony's fickle leadership.[79]

Menno Colony, for its part, interpreted the VDA's interest in the colonies as a threat to their local leadership. They possessed a clear

---

[73] Thiesen, *Mennonite and Nazi?* 85; Jakob Warkentin, "Hildebrand, Peter," *Lexikon der Mennoniten in Paraguay*, 203–4.

[74] P. Hildebrand, *Odyssee wider Willen*, 183. "Heil Hitler" was not an uncommon salutation among the Fernheim Mennonites. P. Hildebrand, Kliewer, Quiring, and Unruh often used it in their correspondences. It was also used at the end of some colony meetings.

[75] "Zum Tierschutzmann," *Menno-Blatt* (Fernheim, Paraguay), July 1934, 2, 5. "Auszüge," *Menno-Blatt* (Fernheim, Paraguay), July 1934, 5.

[76] K. Stahl, " "Zwischen Volkstumspflege, Nationalsozialismus und Mennonitentum," 36.

[77] "Verschiedenes," *Menno-Blatt*, June 1934, 6.

[78] K. Stahl, " "Zwischen Volkstumspflege, Nationalsozialismus und Mennonitentum," 36.

[79] Thiesen, *Mennonite and Nazi?* 88.

sense of their mission in Paraguay and lacked an interpreter such as Kliewer. Had they wished, the colony's leadership could have used the Nazi movement as a transnational legitimation of their authority and Germany as a lucrative destination for their agricultural products. They did not because they knew that nothing provided by a government was free. Most importantly, the VDA shared with the Manitoban and Saskatchewan governments the idea that nationalism began in the schoolhouse.[80] According to one VDA press release, "whoever has the youth, has the future; and he who has the schools, has the youth."[81] In Canada, accepting state support would have meant that they would have been required to teach uncomfortable subjects in a foreign language. Presented with another Faustian bargain, the Menno Colony remained committed to their rudimentary school materials.

Hildebrand was not satisfied with simply filling Kliewer's shoes. He wanted to prove the settlers' economic and political allegiance to Germany, even at the expense of dismissing their religious convictions, which was the Colony's point of entry into the *völkisch* movement and its only other point of solidarity. A shipment of peanuts from the colony to Germany and its propaganda potential presented an ideal opportunity. Though *Menno-Blatt* gives few logistical details, the peanuts made for a distinct and nonperishable gift to the colony's German benefactors. Most of the peanuts were distributed to the more than 5,500 VDA-sponsored school groups in Germany as a sign of goodwill between the Fernheim Colony and the "homeland." Even Adolf Hitler received a small sack. The gesture received a good deal of publicity in the German press and a flood of letters to the Fernheim Colony. One "enthusiastic" Hitlerjugend member wrote, "we love you [the Fernheim Colony] because you have also sent peanuts to our leader."[82] Peanuts were a delicious and exotic treat that carried the flavor of empire, since most of the world's peanut crop was produced in the United States and the British Empire. The idea of a "German"

[80] This idea was one of the VDA's founding tenets when it was initially established in Vienna in 1881 as the Allgemeiner Deutscher Schulverein (General German School Association). See Jonathan Kwan, "Transylvanian Saxon Politics, Hungarian State Building and the Case of the Allgemeiner Deutscher Schulverein (1881–82)," *English Historical Review* 127, no. 526 (2012): 604.

[81] "VDA Pressemitteilungen Dezember 1932," *Der VDA und die deutsche-amerikanische Press*, 5. Quoted in Grams, *German Emigration to Canada*, 13.

[82] P. Hildebrand, "Über unsere Erdnusssendung," *Menno-Blatt* (Fernheim, Paraguay), September 1935, 4–5. The DAI also maintained a pen-pal program that connected Reich Germans with Auslandsdeutsche called *Lesepaten*.

agricultural stronghold in the heart of South America therefore had both a culinary and geopolitical appeal to the Nazi government and German citizens. Yet the gift symbolized more than a suggestion that Germany could economically benefit from the colony. Though it was probably negligible from Hitler and Göring's perspective, their acceptance of the colony's peanuts validated the colonists as real Germans and as collaborators in a story of German solidarity.

The peanuts were a publicity coup, but the disruption caused by Kliewer's departure and P. Hildebrand's arrival led Fernheim's leaders to reevaluate the Jugendbund's place in the community. Thiesen argues that it created an alternate "power center" that existed outside the colony's civil, economic, and religious structures and observes that "competition among such social institutions for public influence has been a prominent theme in Russian Mennonite history."[83] The Jugendbund was a new interloper since it held its own weekly meetings and promoted an alternative group identification. In the eyes of some of the colony's pastors, Kliewer and his associates were perhaps *too* successful at unifying the colony. Despite his Mennonite background, Hildebrand was not of the colony and was therefore likely treated with more suspicion than Kliewer.

Suspicion of the Jugendbund's popularity under P. Hildebrand's leadership – though not of its *völkisch* inclinations – gained momentum in the colony throughout 1935 and 1936. Fernheim's parents favored the group's structured activities and especially those that promoted family values, but they were wary of its militant overtones. One January 1935 *Menno-Blatt* article written by a colonist obliquely mentioned the group's militant drift, but failed to explore its repercussions.[84] Minutes from a KfK meeting in Filadelfia on May 8, 1935, picked up this theme and reveal that at least one leader found "the entire movement" to be a "thoroughly unhealthy" influence.[85] Like many Germans in Germany, the KfK believed that Hitler stood above the fray of politics. It was the Nazi Party lackeys, the "little Hitlers" such as P. Hildebrand, who were to blame for

---

[83] Thiesen, *Mennonite and Nazi?* 85. See also James Urry, *None but Saints: The Transformation of Mennonite Life in Russia 1789–1889* (Winnipeg: Hyperion Press, 1989).

[84] A. Braun, "Eltern hört!" *Menno-Blatt* (Fernheim, Paraguay), January 1935, 2–3.

[85] "Protokoll einer KfK-Sitzung am 8. Mai 1935 in Philadelphia," CMBS. Quoted in Thiesen, *Mennonite and Nazi?* 92.

FIGURE 5.1 Fernheim Colony meeting hall in Filadelfia with a picture of Adolf Hitler displayed prominently at the front. The banner reads *"Gemeinnutz vor Eigennutz!"* ("Common good before self-interest!"), 1935, Mennonite Library and Archives, Bethel College, North Newton, Kansas, 2007–0189

National Socialism's ills.[86] In this way, the purity of the ideal remained intact despite its disordered reality. The KfK did not have a problem with Nazism as long as it worked to unify the colony, but they were wary when it appeared to threaten division. Ultimately, colony leaders believed that local unity was the highest form of German patriotism – notwithstanding the opinions of P. Hildebrand or the VDA (Fig. 5.1).

Despite his efforts to unite the colony under Nazism, P. Hildebrand was terminated from his position as the leader of the colony's central school in Filadelfia at the end of 1935. The action was provoked by an assembly of thirty-seven parents who were concerned that one of the school's pupils, a D. Bergmann, had stabbed another student. Parents called on the KfK to look into the issue. They also requested that the KfK review the school's

---

[86] For an account of German attitudes toward Hitler and Nazi Party bosses (i.e. the "little Hitlers"), see Ian Kershaw, *The Hitler Myth: Image and Reality in the Third Reich* (Oxford: Oxford University Press, 1987).

curriculum, including its VDA-supplied reading materials.[87] Not long after, the Hildebrands resigned from their teaching positions before they were officially dismissed. The formal reasons for P. Hildebrand's dismissal – had it been carried out – would have included charges that he did not believe in Christ, did not regularly attend church services, and had spoken disparagingly about the Mennonite faith. The KfK also accused him of arrogance, uncollegial behavior, and mockery.[88] Legiehn did not escape the fracas either. The KfK threatened to terminate his teaching position if he did not alter his political opinions too.[89] Once again, a local issue regarding disruptive youth led the KfK to reevaluate Fernheim's relationship with its external attachments. Though their displeasure was channeled through the person of P. Hildebrand, the situation indicates that Nazism did not sit well with some of Fernheim's leaders and households – not because Hitler or the *völkisch* movement were irreligious – but because some of their representatives were.

The colony's elected leaders reasoned that they did not dismiss P. Hildebrand because he was too influenced by the Nazi movement, but because he did not exhibit enough *Volkstum* (national consciousness).[90] Writing to Unruh, they accused P. Hildebrand of working against colony unity since he reported to authorities in Berlin and the German legation in Asunción that some of the colony's prominent members were anti-German. According to the KfK, P. Hildebrand's defamation of Fernheim residents would not be tolerated by a colony of Mennonites who held their Germanness in the highest regard. The letter praised God for uniting the German people under Adolf Hitler but the KfK thought that P. Hildebrand's political

---

[87] "Protokoll einer Elternversammlung in Philadelphia, Col. Fernheim zwecks Behandlung der vorliegenden Fragen unserer Zentralschule Stattgefunden," November, 5, 1935, ACF.

[88] Jakob Warkentin, "Hildebrand, Peter," *Lexikon der Mennoniten in Paraguay*, 203–4. P. Hildebrand provided his own reasons for the dismissal, including his high level of education and his production of Schiller's *Die Räuber*, which the KfK considered to be "corrupting" of the youth. See P. Hildebrand, *Odyssee wider Willen*, 185–99.

[89] It is possible that the KfK was more lenient toward Legiehn because he was the stepson of Brüdergemeinde preacher Gerhard Isaak. See Thiesen, *Mennonite and Nazi?* 101.

[90] Like other *Volk* composites, *Volkstum* is a difficult word to render in English. It implies a sense of national character or consciousness. Friedrich Ludwig Jahn developed the concept in the early nineteenth century and it was appropriated (and argued over) by members of the Nazi's *völkisch* movement a century later. See Egbert Klautke, *The Mind of the Nation: Völkerpsychologie in Germany, 1851–1955* (New York: Berghahn 2013), 124; Götz, "German-Speaking People," 65–66.

opinions were so divisive that they were anti-German.[91] In a way that recalls the religious debates over Mennoniteness and biblical exegesis that divided Mennonites in the past, the KfK felt that it was completely within their authority to determine the type of Germanness – nationalist exegesis, so to speak – that was suitable for their colony.

Unruh was furious that the KfK had fired P. Hildebrand and that the parents' committee had questioned the VDA materials. Recalling G. Hiebert's complaints about the Fernheim colonists, Unruh was annoyed that they had elevated their local concerns over the interests of their international benefactors. The colonists apparently made Nazism *too much* of a local metaphor to be useful to the nation. He responded with a letter addressed to the colony *Oberschulze* that trivialized parents' concerns over the materials. Unruh emphasized that there was "only *one* authoritative book on National Socialism": Hitler's *Mein Kampf*. Unruh was adamant that colonists should let leaders in Germany decide what they should read. Behind it all, Unruh saw, "certain Canadian circles," plotting to cast P. Hildebrand, Legiehn, and Kliewer in a bad light and disrupt the *völkisch* cause. Unruh warned the *Oberschulze* "against these international intrigues!" and closed his letter with a "Heil Hitler!"

It is unclear who belonged to Unruh's feared "Canadian circles" but it was probably not the politically recalcitrant Menno Colony colonists, who had little interest in geopolitical affairs. Like their Canadianness, Menno Colony's Germanness lacked a political edge. It was not something that they elected to participate in (no letters to Berlin here) but something that was inscribed in the daily rhythms of life such as Bible study, church, food, and other folkways. The most significant contact the Menno Colony had with the broader world came from letters exchanged with friends in Canada and the news they received through the publication *Steinbach Post*, which was published in Steinbach, Manitoba. The *Steinbach Post* reported the concerns of the 1870s group of immigrants from Russia and served as a message board for their communities in Canada, Mexico, and Paraguay. It generally avoided political commentary and struck a conservative and religious tone. In this way, the *Steinbach Post*'s readers were not so different from millions of German speakers around the world who entwined local and transnational attachments while bypassing nationalist conceptions of Germanness. German-speaking migrants created and maintained durable transcontinental

---

[91] Thiesen, *Mennonite and Nazi?* 98.

networks through chain letters, community newspapers, and self-published books, histories, genealogies, and musings, which circumvented the German state and connected individuals in Eastern Europe and the Americas. The Menno Colony, however, did not lack controversy during the 1930s. The Chaco War, the drought, and the Fürsorge-Komitee dispute of 1928–36 were major sources of tension and kept members' focus on their local context. Nevertheless, the May and June 1936 issues of *Kämpfende Jugend* contain an illuminating perspective on one Menno colonist's attitudes toward the *völkisch* movement. In these issues, Menno colonist Peter J. R. Funk debated Fernheim colonist and *völkisch* supporter P. Neufeld of Orloff on the ethics of entwining religious and *völkisch* loyalties. What is important about the exchange is that both writers use scripture to defend their opposing views on national identifications: either as an essential identification or as one possible identification among many.

In his opening gambit, P. Funk pointedly asked Jugendbund members whether they owed primary allegiance to their Germanness or to Christianity. He called on the Bible to make his point by noting that Joseph, Daniel, and David all fulfilled their duties to God without needing broader help.[92] These individuals operated independently, outside of the context of the Israelite nation. P. Funk contended that the Bible teaches Christians to trust in God alone and not in human institutions. His letter was brief but its argument reveals a clear dichotomy between sacred and secular paths: God calls his chosen people to forge a course of complete separation from broader loyalties even at the expense of persecution, which in Daniel's case meant being thrown into a den of lions by the Persians. Demonstrating the elasticity of biblical exegesis, P. Funk used individual "heroes" as an example of the Menno Colony's collective autonomy even though Menno Colony leaders generally suppressed the individualism of their constituency.

In the next issue, P. Neufeld took the opportunity to enlighten his conservative Mennonite brother on the virtues of the Jugendbund and national loyalties. He too used scripture to argue that the Jugendbund fulfilled the colony's Christian duty to shield its youth from dangerous forces.[93] P. Neufeld drew on the Apostle Paul's letters to Titus and Timothy, written at a time when Paul was trying to give direction and

[92] Peter J. R. Funk, "Kolonie Menno," *Kämpfende Jugend* (Fernheim, Paraguay), May 1936, 1.

[93] P. Neufeld, "Antwort auf den Artikel 'Kolonie Menno,'" *Kämpfende Jugend* (Fernheim, Paraguay), May 1936, 1–2.

clarity to a nascent and disorganized church. Applying their message in a modern-day context, P. Neufeld suggested that Paul would have approved of *völkisch* youth instruction since it taught children the importance of broader loyalties, including those demanded by church and state, which were both ordained by God.

P. Neufeld then challenged P. Funk on the Menno Colony's expression of Germanness. He asked: "Had they not, after all, left [Canada] to retain their German culture?"[94] With this rhetorical question, P. Neufeld suggested that P. Funk was ignorant of the real reason why they had left the country: It was not their religion but their Germanness that they wished to preserve, and it was not their local form of Germanness but the Germanness that was now revealed in the *völkisch* movement. This is also what Kliewer was getting at in his Mennonite World Conference speech of the same year; namely that the Menno colonists are part of "Germandom," even though they "rather unconsciously feel" it. Presumably, P. Neufeld wanted the Menno Colony to discover their true historic path as Christians within the Nazi movement, as had he and so many other Fernheim Mennonites.

The exchange demonstrated that the colonies had very different philosophies about God and nation that were based on their experiences as voluntary migrants and refugees. The Menno Colony was settled, stable, and chose to live in Paraguay to escape the pressures of nationalism. Alternately, the refugees of Fernheim Colony lacked communal solidarity and hoped to foster it by melding their faith with *völkisch* nationalism. On a broader level, the exchange testifies to a bourgeoning sense among Latin America's German speakers that (trans)National Socialism represented something new – and perhaps troubling – under the sun when it came to squaring transnational, national, local, and religious affinities.

Throughout 1936, Unruh and Kliewer shored up support for the *völkisch* cause in Fernheim by publishing articles and writing letters that emphasized a theological connection between National Socialism and Christianity. Yet interest in the Jugendbund flagged without a strong local advocate. By the beginning of 1937, *Kämpfende Jugend* had been downsized to a column in the *Menno-Blatt* and there were rumblings that the small Allianzgemeinde was against the *völkisch* movement altogether. Kliewer had successfully combined local and national concerns into a credible story that accounted for Christian theology and German history, but Hildebrand could not build on his successes. His overt Nazism

---

[94] Ibid.

was too aggressive and un-Christian (and therefore un-German), to a leadership committee that placed a premium on communal harmony.

VISITORS FROM THE REICH

It was within this context that the colonies played host to several high-profile German visitors including Josef Ponten, the German novelist and former colleague of Thomas Mann, and the famous African explorer Adolf Friedrich Albrecht Heinrich, Duke of Mecklenburg. The visitors' assessments of the colonies ranged from tepid approval to amused antipathy.[95] Yet the most detailed, scholarly, and damning, report on the Mennonite colonies came from Wilhelmy's pen. His early research focused on Bulgarian *Auslandsdeutsche*, but he reoriented his academic interests to South America after he met Oskar Schmieder, who was working with the Nazi regime to uncover the purported connections between geography, culture, and race.[96] Under Schmieder's supervision, Wilhelmy secured government funds from the Deutsche Forschungsgemeinschaft (German Research Council), the Albrecht-Penck-Stiftung (Albrecht Penck Foundation) of Berlin, and the Hänel-Stiftung (Hänel Foundation) of Kiel to undertake a "colonial geographic expedition" of German colonization in South America.[97] His goal was to assess the viability of German settlement in the Chaco and uncover the loyalties of Paraguayan *Auslandsdeutsche* to the Nazi cause.

Until this point, the VDA's interest in the colony had inflated colonists' sense of importance as an important node of Germanness. Yet this development correspondingly elevated colonists' sensitivity to Wilhelmy's criticisms. His report dealt a blow that laid bare the rift between colonists' self-assessment as members of the *Volk* and an external German

---

[95] Richard W. Seifert, "Bericht über die Reise nach der Mennoniten-Kolonie Fernheim mit S. H. Herzog Adolf Friedrich von Mecklenburg," February 15, 1936, R127972d, PA AA, 163–65. N. Siemens, "Dr. Josef Ponten," *Menno-Blatt* (Fernheim, Paraguay), October 1936, 6; "Ein Gesucher," "Gemeinnutz vor Eigennutz," *Menno-Blatt* (Fernheim, Paraguay), Oct. 1936, 5.

[96] Ulrike Block, "Deutsche Lateinamerikaforschung im Nationalsozialismus – Ansätze zu einer wissenschaftshistorischen Perspektive," in *Der Nationalsozialismus und Lateinamerika: Institutionen – Repräsentationen – Wissenskonstrukte I*, ed. Sandra Carreras (Berlin: Ibero-Amerikanisches Institut Preußischer Kulturbesitz, 2005), 11–12.

[97] Dr. H[erbert] Wilhelmy, Bericht über eine [?] mit Unterstützung der Albrecht-Penk-Stiftung – Berlin, der Deutschen Forschungsgemeinschaft und der Hänel-Stiftung – Kiel durch geführten kolonialgeographischen Forschungsreise nach Südamerika," (26. VI.1936 – 8.IV.1937), R127972d, PA AA, 71–79, 71.

assessment that they were religious rubes. Wilhelmy's visit is also significant for its timing. It was a long shot, but by 1937 some colonists had started to believe that a positive report from an influential German academic could improve their chances of being repatriated to Germany. A negative assessment would destroy them. Altogether, Wilhelmy's analysis – and the Fernheim Colony's reaction to it – exhibited in stark relief the problems that *Auslandsdeutsche* faced when they tried to make their Germanness intelligible to hard-line Nazis.

After the Nazi seizure of power, a small army of Reich journalists, scholars, and freelance explorers fanned out across the globe to uncover the special "genius" of Germanness worldwide. Trips combined patriotism and ideology with tourism and the thrill of adventure.[98] Before leaving Germany, they may have viewed such films as *Flüchtlinge* (*Refugees*, 1933) or *Friesennot* (*Frisians in Peril*, 1935), which highlighted the persecution and dispersion of the Soviet Union's German speakers. The latter film prominently features Mennonites taking up arms to defend themselves from Bolshevik tyranny. Closed farming settlements, like the Mennonite colonies, made especially compelling destinations since there was a perception in Germany that emigrants who settled in urban areas or scattered homesteads quickly lost their Germanness.[99] Yet what visitors found – even in closed settlements – often surprised them. Many *Auslandsdeutsche*, especially those whose ancestors had left Europe generations before, were sometimes more "foreign" in their customs and demeanor than the racially "non-Aryan" Poles, Jews, and other minorities who were well integrated into German society.

In the months preceding Wilhelmy's visit to the Fernheim Colony, he assessed the *völkisch* loyalties of fourteen German-speaking colonies in Paraguay's Alto Parana region and around Encarnación.[100] By the late 1930s, the country claimed 26,000 German speakers out of a total

---

[98] Elizabeth Harvey, "Emissaries of Nazism: German Student Travelers in Romania and Yugoslavia in the 1930s," *Österreichische Zeitschrift für Geschichtswissenschaften* 22, no. 1 (2011): 138.

[99] Thomas Lekan, "German Landscape: Local Promotion of the Heimat Abroad," in *The Heimat Abroad: The Boundaries of Germanness*, ed. Krista O'Donnell, Renate Bridenthal, and Nancy Reagin, 141–66 (Ann Arbor, MI: University of Michigan Press, 2005), 159.

[100] For a description of Wilhelmy's trip, see his coauthored publication with Oskar Schmieder, *Deutsche Akerbausiedlungen im südamerikanischen Grasland, Pampa und Gran Chaco*. Wissenschaftliche Veröffentlichungen, Neue Folge 6 (Leipzig: Deutsches Museum für Ländkunde), 1938.

population of less than 1 million.[101] Eastern Paraguay was an especially important destination because it received an influx of German immigrants after the First World War who "remained unassimilated and aloof in their new surroundings."[102] Taken as a whole, however, Paraguay's German-speaking population was composed of a mixture of *Reichsdeutsche*, "Brazilian-Germans," and to a lesser extent "Russian-Germans," "Austrian-Germans," and "Swiss." Not surprisingly, Wilhelmy notes "the greatest cultural and political unity prevails without doubt in the settlements of *Reichsdeutsche*."[103] In contrast, the colonies

> inhabited mainly by Brazilian-Germans and Russian-Germans, the overall situation is much different. The settlers know little or nothing of Germany and are only curious about major transformations in the former homeland. Supplying colonists with newspapers and other literature is almost fruitless, since a large percentage can only read or write poorly ... School and church capture the majority of the population.[104]

In an observation that foreshadowed his impressions of the Mennonite colonies, Wilhelmy concluded that the moral level of the Russian Germans gives "food for thought" for anyone trying to exert a Nazi influence.[105] They were only concerned with events in Russia and were mostly indifferent to the geopolitical issues facing their presumed national homeland.

Wilhelmy next turned his sights on the Mennonite colonies. He encountered a Menno Colony that was entirely beyond Nazi redemption, and a Fernheim Colony that tarnished the Nazi cause with their ignorant expressions of Germanness. Wilhelmy spent about a week in the Fernheim Colony – inspecting its villages, giving lectures on the "New Germany," and presenting patriotic slideshows of the bucolic German countryside. Coincidentally, his visit came on the heels of O. Miller's trip to calm Fernheim colonists' fears about land debts, the ongoing drought, and the threat that a third of its members would leave the colony and form their own settlement (the Friesland Colony). He therefore encountered a colony that, in his telling, was in the throes of crisis, with a leadership structure that would do anything to maintain its hold on the group. His observations led him to conclude that they were not loyal Germans – at

---

[101] Michael Grow, *The Good Neighbor Policy and Authoritarianism in Paraguay: United States Economic Expansion and Great Power Rivalry in Latin America During World War II* (Lawrence, KS: Regents Press of Kansas, 1998), 51.

[102] Ibid., 34.

[103] Wilhelmy, "An die Deutsche Gesandtschaft in Asuncion: Bericht über meine Reise im südlichen Paraguay," R127972d, PA AA, 69–70, 69.

[104] Ibid., 69.   [105] Ibid., 70.

least in comparison to the *Reichsdeutsche* that "met the work of the Nazis with understanding."[106] In an observation that would have made the MCC happy, Wilhelmy believed that it was not their Germanness that the Fernheim colonists wished to preserve but their abstruse Mennonite doctrines.[107]

Wilhelmy saw the world as a battleground of competing races and ideologies, and he interpreted the Fernheim migration to the Chaco as a conspiracy of the global Mennonite church. "The political and religious goal of colony leaders" was implementing "the dream of all orthodox Mennonites whether they live in Paraguay, Brazil, Canada, the USA, Holland and Switzerland," namely the creation of a Mennostaat.[108] The colonists had nearly realized this dream by securing from the Paraguayan government a set of "extraordinary privileges," which allowed their "inviolable" preachers to extend their religious authority down to the family unit.[109] To further their goals, colony leaders practiced "Pharisaism" and dishonesty by unabashedly exploiting Germany's good-will for their own benefit: "While the ignorant, but religiously fanatical farmer does not conceal his negative attitude [toward Germany], the preachers and mayors try to work with the [German] legation and consulate on friendly terms."[110]

Far from being honest Germans, let alone loyal Nazis, the colonists in Wilhelmy's eyes were more similar to the Jews who believed that they were "God's chosen people." Here he discovered another conspiracy, arguing that "Jewish history dominates the Mennonites to the last detail and by giving their people Jewish names, they outwardly align themselves with the Jewish people."[111] It is unclear exactly what Wilhelmy meant by "Jewish names" – considering that a substantial number of Germans in Germany possessed names belonging to Jews in the Bible – but he likely meant Old Testament names, such as Abraham, that were relatively uncommon among non-Jewish Germans. While the Fernheim Mennonites certainly gave their children biblical names and their identification as Germans had saved them from the Soviet Union, it was absurd to argue that there was a global conspiracy of Mennonites plotting against Germany, much less a unified sense of Mennoniteness within the colonies.

[106] Wilhelmy, "Forschungsreise nach Südamerika," 73.
[107] Ibid., 77–78"; "Fritz Kliewer to Landesleiter des VDA Landesverbandes Weser-Ems," November 18, 1937, R127972d, PA AA, 51–62, 52.
[108] Wilhelmy, "Forschungsreise nach Südamerika," 77.   [109] Ibid.   [110] Ibid., 78.
[111] Ibid., 77.

Wilhelmy's fears therefore resembled contemporaneous anxieties about spies and "fifth columns," and he perceived a vast conspiracy in a situation marked primarily by disunity on the part of the Fernheim Colony and indifference on the part of the Menno Colony. The only bright mark on his report was a suggestion that the Fernheim Colony's young people – shaped by their experiences in the Soviet Union and the Chaco War – were perhaps inclined to reject Mennonite nonresistance and accept the Nazi "*Wille zur Tat*" ("Will to action").[112] Although the colonists "appreciated" National Socialism and were "thankful" that God had created it as a bulwark against the Soviet Union, Mennonite culture was entirely unsatisfactory from the standpoint of this *reichsdeutsch* Nazi.[113]

The Fernheim Mennonites were surprised and dismayed by Wilhelmy's report because it appeared to invalidate the sincerity of their Germanness and compromise their standing with the Nazi government. In response, *Oberschulze* J. Siemens and other colony leaders wrote a letter to Unruh, who was still smoldering over P. Hildebrand's dismissal. In an impersonal and passive voice, they admitted that the colony had many "defects and disabilities" but argued that Wilhelmy simply had not spent enough time in the colony. They concluded by declaring that he was an "enemy of the Mennonites."[114] Even so, they restated their appreciation of National Socialism and were thankful to God for Hitler's leadership.

Friedrich Kliewer – who was still living in Germany – took it upon himself to mail a strongly worded rebuttal to the German Foreign Office. Kliewer's tightly spaced eleven-page document argued that the Fernheim Mennonites were mostly concerned for their German *cultural* preservation (not necessarily their religious preservation) and had proven themselves both generous and patriotic during the Chaco War – a conflict that Kliewer suggested could not have been won without their aid. Kliewer also called it "absurd" to suggest that some Mennonite religious leaders wished to create a "*Menno-Staat*" in Paraguay instead of identifying principally with the German nation state. In fact, Kliewer averred that the Menno and Fernheim colonies were "largely the same" when it came to their sentiments on "*Mennonitentum und Deutschtum*" ("Mennoniteness and Germanness"). Kliewer's trump card (though

[112] Ibid., 78–79.
[113] "Jakob Siemens, Heinrich Pauls, and Abram Loewen to B. H. Unruh," September 29, 1937, Paraguay Fernheim Colony 1937, IX-6-3 Central Correspondence, 1931–85, MCCA.
[114] "Siemens, Pauls, and Loewen to Unruh."

probably more of a guess than a fact) was that the Fernheim Mennonites "are also quite determined to send their sons to military training in the Reich."[115] Thus, Kliewer not only tried to make Nazism intelligible to the Fernheim Colony, but also tried to make the colony's brand of Germanness intelligible to a German audience.

Concerning the most serious of Wilhelmy's accusations – that the Mennonites were pro-Jewish – Kliewer stated, "Dr. Wilhelmy's statements on this issue are hurtful to every upright *Auslandsdeutsche* Mennonite."[116] According to Kliewer, the Mennonites gave their children Jewish names out of respect for the Old Testament, not out of respect for present-day Judaism. He also challenged Wilhelmy to criticize Nazi Party leaders who had biblical names.[117] Kliewer assured the Foreign Office that the Fernheim Mennonites only wished to live in peace – a peace that assured their freedom to express their faith and nationality.

Despite the great strides made by the colony toward incorporating *völkisch* Germanness into their local community, this still fell far short of the Nazi ideal. Wilhelmy's visit revealed precisely how much the Nazi interpretation of Germanness differed from local interpretations of the concept. Too much was lost in translation across so wide a geographic, philosophical, and historical terrain. Although Wilhelmy's report was mostly of an academic nature, Kliewer and the Fernheim colonists were nevertheless anxious that it reflected poorly on their settlement. It was as much of a patriotic anxiety as a practical one. From about 1935 until 1944, there was a growing impression within the colony that its members could be repatriated to Germany, if they could only obtain German citizenship.[118] Upon Kliewer's return to the colony in 1939, he set about promoting the idea that colonists could be relocated *en toto* to Germany or a German-controlled Eastern Europe. As the next chapter demonstrates, his plan only raised the colony's anxieties and expectations to a fever pitch before throwing it into chaos once more.

During the first half of the 1930s, solidarity with Nazi Germany remained elusive for the Fernheim colonists and was nonexistent for the Menno Colony. The Jugendbund, peanut shipment, VDA materials, and even the Nazi slogan hanging in Filadelfia's community building "*Gemeinnutz vor Eigennutz!*" ("Common good before self-interest!"), demonstrated the Fernheim Colony's longing to achieve local unity through the template of *völkisch* unity. Fernheim's *völkisch* contingent

---

[115] "Kliewer to Landesleiter," 55–61.   [116] Ibid., 59.   [117] Ibid., 60.
[118] Thiesen, *Mennonite and Nazi?* 135.

therefore sought to align the colony's local story of a battered but stalwart *Mennoniten-Völklein* in South America with the Nazi story of a battered but stalwart *Volksgemeinschaft* in Central Europe. The medium through which this story developed was (trans)National Socialism, which promised a borderless understanding of Germanness despite the Nazi regime's increasingly precise definitions of the concept. Yet for (trans) National Socialism to work, it needed local interpreters that could deftly weave together communal and national stories. This was increasingly difficult the further each interpreter – Kliewer, Hildebrand, and Wilhelmy – stood from the Fernheim Colony and the closer they stood to the actual Nazi Party. Ironically, what had saved the Fernheim colonists from the Soviet Union – their identification as *Auslandsdeutsche* – ended up alienating them from their German benefactors once they were settled in Paraguay, since they did not exhibit the particular type of Germanness that Nazi representatives were looking for. They "passed" as Germans in 1929, but not in 1937.

Meanwhile, the Menno Colony maintained that national allegiances unequivocally jeopardized their religious culture. They interpreted external developments through their homegrown lay biblical exegesis and their past dealings with overbearing governments. The two biggest politico-religious events for Menno Colony during the 1930s included an internal power struggle between its constituent churches and the decision to limit their aid to the Paraguayan military during the Chaco War. The former event was exclusively local until they approached the Solomon-like figure of President Ayala, and the latter had less to do with patriotism and citizenship than with their interpretation of biblical nonviolence. Compared to these immediate struggles, Nazism was little more than an afterthought. Menno colonists wanted to maintain a German culture without being labeled as Germans, and certainly not as National Socialists. Years later, when the Menno Colony created an archive of its history in Paraguay, it contained a single, slim binder on the Nazi period. Titled "Fernheim Nazis," the binder held printed and handwritten transcriptions of articles from various Mennonite publications, writings by Kliewer and other Nazi sympathizers, and a few unorganized historical commentaries on the Nazi episode. Barring a single sermon delivered by colony leader M. C. Friesen in 1944, it contained no internally generated documents.[119] In other words, the

---

[119] In contrast, the Fernheim Colony maintains a relatively large archive with extensive documentation of its Nazi past.

Menno Colony had little to remember about Nazism, and even less to say about it.

The (trans)National Socialism projected outward from the Nazi state during the 1930s was a multiuse tool that could be adopted, adapted, or ignored when it collided with bourgeoning and long-standing local narratives. Quite often, local notions of Germanness were more consistent and durable ("intractable" from a state perspective) than official interpretations that emanated from Germany. Altogether, Paraguay's Mennonites – like other German-speaking communities in Latin America – were more valuable as signifiers of (trans)National Socialism than as an actual political or military asset for the Third Reich. This situation inflated the Fernheim Colony's sense of value to the regime, but it also increased their sensitivity to Nazi criticisms and provided Kliewer with a new opportunity to assert himself as the colony's Nazi ambassador. Yet now he no longer wanted to bring Nazism to the colony; instead he wished to bring colonists to Nazi Germany.

6

Centrifugal Fantasies, Centripetal Realities
(1939–1945)

On the night of March 11, 1944, about sixty armed members of the Fernheim Colony's *völkisch* movement violently confronted several of their former compatriots over public embarrassments, sundry personal slights, and the fading hope that they could be repatriated to a German-controlled Eastern Europe. It was fifteen years since the German attaché Auhagen had discovered the motley collection of German-speaking refugees in Moscow. Now most colonists believed their true destiny could only be achieved by "returning" to Europe. The outbreak of the Second World War fueled the idea that they were not exiles forced to contrive their own fate in the Chaco. Rather, their purgatorial Southern Hemisphere sojourn augured a happy resolution in the "paradise" of a German-controlled Eastern Europe. As speculation about the Fernheim Colony's place in the "Greater German Reich" during the 1930s segued into the heady possibilities of war and finally disintegrated in Germany's defeat, the Fernheim Colony's *völkisch* movement imploded in a violent and highly local fashion that had less to do with grand notions of German solidarity than with the colony's persistent inability to achieve local unity.

The *völkisch* contingent's collapse was a small and almost comedic footnote to the broader geopolitics of the 1940s, but it caused an inordinate amount of international intrigue. The meltdown brought several MCC representatives and high-ranking Paraguayan and US officials to the Chaco, who variously feared that the colonists had drifted too far into the Nazis' orbit and too far afield of Paraguayan domestic control or US hemispheric hegemony. Perhaps never before had the US intelligence community cared so much about a group of Mennonites as it now did about the Fernheim colonists. In 1944, US Naval Intelligence detained and interrogated the MCC's O. Miller in the Panama Canal Zone on a trip to the Chaco and the director of the US Federal Bureau of Investigation, J. Edgar Hoover, issued numerous memoranda on the Fernheim situation.[1] Kliewer was one of eleven people placed on the US government's list of "individuals who should be expelled or deported from Paraguay," and Franz Heinrichs – the Fernheim Colony's business agent in Asunción – was placed on the government's "Confidential List of Unsatisfactory Consignees."[2] Quoting Hosea 8:7, Fernheim *Oberschulze* Bernhard Wall observed that the Fernheim Colony "planted wind and we reaped a storm."[3]

During the 1930s, the recurring disasters Fernheim experienced – war, drought, disease, conflict, and division – cast a dark shadow over the proposition that the colonists could remain in the Chaco. According to political scientist Michael Barckun: "Belief systems which under non-disaster conditions might be dismissed now receive sympathetic consideration ... It is small wonder that among persons so situated doctrines of imminent salvation should find such a ready acceptance."[4] By the late 1930s, many colonists began looking to Nazi Germany not as a template for local unity but as a country that could literally rescue them from the Chaco. The colonists' reevaluation of their fate and their hope for repatriation is not surprising, since the Nazis appeared fully capable of instituting their "Thousand-Year Reich" in Eastern Europe during the

---

[1] John D. Thiesen, *Mennonite and Nazi? Attitudes Among Mennonite Colonists in Latin America, 1933–1945* (Kitchener, ON: Pandora Press, 1999), 195; the bulk of Hoover's memorandums are found in Box 2727, Entry decimal file 1940–44; Box 5563 [mislabeled 5564] (862.20210–862.20210), Entry dec. file 1940–44; Box 6734, Entry dec. file 1945–49, Record Group 59, and especially Box 1, Entry UD 3090 (Paraguay U.S. Embassy, Asuncion, Supplemental Confidential General Records, 1944–1947), RG 84, National Archives at College Park (hereafter, NACP), College Park, MD.

[2] "Wesley Frost to Secretary of State," March 1, 1944, enclosed in dispatch 1860 (Asuncion 1944, 820.02 Germany), Container 10, Entry UD 3088 (Classified General Records {Confidential File} 1936–1961), RG 84, NACP; "Wesley Frost to Secretary of State," April 2, 1943, dispatch 910, Box 2727 (740.00112A EW 39/28440 to 28781A), Entry dec. file 1940–44, RG 59, NACP.

[3] P. Klassen, *Die deutsch-völkish Zeit in der Kolonie Fernheim, Chaco, Paraguay, 1943–1945: Ein Beitrag zur Geschichte der auslandsdeutschen Mennoniten während des Dritten Reiches* (Bolanden-Weierhof, Germany: Mennonitischer Geschichtsverein e.V., 1990), 81. Quoted in Gerhard Reimer, "The 'Green Hell' Becomes Home: Mennonites in Paraguay as Described in the Writings of Peter P. Klassen, A Review Essay," *Mennonite Quarterly Review* 76, no. 4 (2002): 467.

[4] Michael Barkun, *Disaster and the Millennium* (Syracuse, NY: Syracuse University, 1986), 56–57.

early years of the war. In fact, Russia's Mennonites had nearly come to an arrangement of this sort during the First World War. In 1918, after Germany and Russia signed the Treaty of Brest-Litovsk, the Molotschna and Chortitza colonies sent a delegation to Berlin to negotiate with the German government over becoming citizens of the yet-to-be-formed Ukrainian puppet state under German rule.[5] The plan came to naught after Germany's borders were redrawn at the Paris Peace Conference. Those earlier disappointments notwithstanding, some Mennonites still hoped there might be a place for them in Hitler's empire. Owing to the Mennonites' specialized agricultural skills and the fact that the German government had rescued them once before, colonists could well imagine that they might once again farm the Russian steppes.[6]

Enter Kliewer. Playing the role of a traveling salesman, he arrived from Germany in 1939 and positioned himself as an agent of the Reich who could grant the colonists German citizenship and ensure their return. Yet the story was a fairy tale, a fantasy that – if only for a short time – seemed better than the truth. Between 1937 and 1944, the Fernheim Colony shifted from understanding themselves as *Auslandsdeutsche*, to seeing themselves as potential citizens of the Third Reich, to a final realization that any understanding of their Germanness would remain grounded at the local level. Along the way, several developments thwarted the colony's repatriation narrative, not least of which was the German army's declining fortunes after 1943. Soon after Kliewer returned to the colony in 1939, his temper and divisive rhetoric split the *völkisch* movement in two, with each group appealing for recognition by Nazi Party representatives in Asunción. At about the same time, a *wehrlos* (nonresistant) group of colonists began voicing its opposition to Nazism on biblical-confessional grounds with the encouragements of the MCC. For its part, the MCC redoubled its efforts to draw the colonists into its narrative of global Mennonite unity. It dispatched representatives to the colony to streamline its finances, improve its infrastructure, provide healthcare, and monitor colonists' attitudes. Yet it was neither the *wehrlos* faction nor the

[5] See Abraham Friesen, *In Defense of Privilege: Russian Mennonites and the State Before and During World War I* (Winnipeg: Kindred Productions, 2006), 17–27. See also Frank H. Epp, *Mennonite Exodus: The Rescue and Resettlement of the Russian Mennonites Since the Communist Revolution* (Altona, MB: Canadian Mennonite Relief and Immigration Council, 1962), 30; James Urry, *Mennonites, Politics, and Peoplehood: Europe-Russia-Canada 1525–1980* (Winnipeg: University of Manitoba Press, 2006), 132, 138.

[6] Urry, *Mennonites, Politics, and Peoplehood*, 138.

MCC representatives who destroyed the *völkisch* movement. Rather, it was undone by its members' inability to impose their vision of an ideal future on the community. This chapter demonstrates that the ambiguity and rapid shifts in the Fernheim Colony's group narrative between 1937 and 1944 put colonists on edge by drawing their attention outward, toward an ideal yet uncontrollable future in a Nazi-controlled Europe. Yet as they increasingly relied on this external event for their salvation – and as the prospect of a Nazi victory grew ever more remote – the colony's *völkisch* leaders ratcheted up control over local events, which eventually overwhelmed the colony in violence.

Meanwhile, the Menno Colony carried on as it had before the war and had zero interest in relocating to Europe. To do so would have meant abandoning every position that had led them to the wilds of the Paraguayan Chaco. Moreover, they did not view Hitler as their earthly ruler because they did not subscribe to the notion of transnational German unity. In the Menno Colony's ordering of the world, if anyone represented a "father" in its members' collective consciousness, it was the representatives of the Paraguayan government who guaranteed their privileges. Oddly, and perhaps sentimentally, Menno colonists even favored the country that had precipitated their move to the Chaco over Nazi Germany. According to one 1943 confidential memo from Wesley Frost, US ambassador to Paraguay, "Sentiment about the war in Colonie Menno follows rather closely the teachings of the Mennonite Church itself, namely strictly aloofness from the affairs of the world ... However, Mr. Martin [likely Martin C. Friesen], who lives in this colony, says that in their hearts these people favor Canada and the Allied cause."[7] The Menno Colony therefore remained relatively free of ideological strife during the war years. Ironically, it may have appeared as though Menno Colony colonists exhibited a greater degree of Paraguayan patriotism, since they did not politicize their Germanness as Nazism, but it was actually the Fernheim colonists who were better citizens of the modern world, since they aspired to belong to a nation; it just happened not to be the one in which they resided.

During the early 1940s, the MCC was concerned that the Fernheim Colony was losing its Mennoniteness. In the United States, Mennonite intellectuals and their supporting institutions – colleges, seminaries, periodicals, and relief organizations – were increasingly supplanting the confession's many local expressions of Mennoniteness with a few standardized

---

[7] "Wesley Frost to Secretary of State," February 18, 1943, dispatch no. 800, Box C295, Entry dec. file 1940–44, RG 59, NACP, 1.

tenets – for example, those outlined in *Bender's Anabaptist Visions*. They especially argued that nonviolence was a foundational Mennonite principle and that it must be pursued as a political and social endeavor as much as a personal and communal one. Startled by the violence directed at their communities during the First World War, the outbreak of the Second World War prompted US Mennonites to engage their government and argue that their "unpatriotic" convictions translated into patriotic actions through voluntary service at home and abroad. One such outlet for their volunteer work was the Fernheim Colony, which unfortunately supported the Nazis. The colony's *völkisch* movement consequently presented a major problem to the MCC when the United States went to war against Germany, since it appeared that US Mennonites were using their conscientious-objector status to aid the enemy.

The German presence in Latin America during the Second World War was more than a matter of Nazi espionage intrigues and *Auslandsdeutsche* solidarity with the "homeland."[8] As discussed in the previous chapter, Latin America's German-speaking population exhibited a range of attitudes toward the Nazi regime, which did not necessarily change with the onset of war. Nevertheless, Latin America's German speakers were haphazardly monitored and highly misunderstood by both German and US authorities in the lead-up to war. Max Paul Friedman claims "The view from Berlin was equally blurred [as the view from Washington D.C.] ... Their hopes for the German expatriates [in Latin America] faintly echoed

---

[8] Historians writing on the Nazi presence in Latin America during the war typically focus on the party's disorganized political and intelligence-gathering activities. See Olaf Gaudig and Peter Veit, *Der Widerschein des Nazismus: Das Bild des Nationalsozialismus in der deutschsprachigen Presse Argentiniens, Brasiliens und Chiles 1932–1945* (Berlin: Wissenschaftlicher, 1997); Stanley Hilton, *Hitler's Secret War in South America 1939–1945* (Baton Rouge, LA: Louisiana State University Press, 1981); David P. Mowry, *German Clandestine Activities in South America in World War II* (Ft. Meade, MD: Office of Archives and History of the National Security Agency and Central Security Service, 1989); Ronald C. Newton, *The "Nazi Menace" in Argentina, 1931–1947* (Stanford, CA: Stanford University Press, 1992); Leslie B. Rout Jr. and John F. Bratzel, *The Shadow War: German Espionage and United States Counterespionage in Latin America During World War II* (Frederick, MD: University Publications of America, 1986). Particularly notable is Jürgen Müller's *Nationalsozialismus in Lateinamerika: Die Auslandsorganisation der NSDAP in Argentinien, Brasilien, Chile und Mexiko, 1931–1945* (Stuttgart: Heinz, 1997), which outlines the myriad problems faced by the AO when it tried to promote the Nazification of the region's *Reichsdeutsche*. Host states pushed back against the Organization's political influence over German-speaking minorities. See Käte Harms-Baltzer, *Die Nationalisierung der deutschen Einwanderer und ihrer Nachkommen in Brasilien als Problem der deutsch-brasilianischen Beziehungen, 1930–1938* (Berlin: Colloquium, 1970).

US fears: both sides misconstrued expressions of group solidarity and ethnic and national pride among the Germans of Latin America as a sign of their readiness to collaborate in war."[9] The unity projected by Nazi Germany onto Latin America's German speakers appeared clear from afar but was mercurial up close.

Latin America is therefore a unique setting for studying the impact of (trans)National Socialism on *Auslandsdeutsche*, because the region invited a disproportionately high level of attention from Nazi authorities and a disproportionately high level of intervention from US authorities in comparison to that which it deserved. From the German side, the Nazi regime had long written off North America's German speakers as a lost cause, while Eastern Europe's German-speaking population offered it the real possibility of physical annexation. Between these poles, Latin America held the allure of being "the last free continent" for German cultural and economic expansion, but was simultaneously impossible for the Nazi state to control or invade.[10] From the US side, the Roosevelt administration's Good Neighbor policy promised non-interference in the domestic activities of Latin American countries, yet it carried out an invasive internment and deportation program in the region, which served as a prelude to its equally intrusive Cold War machinations south of the border. Fed on a steady diet of exaggerated press coverage; inflated intelligence estimates about the Nazi presence; unreliable scoops from informants who cared more for intrigue than accuracy; a British disinformation campaign to draw the United States into the war; and reported coup attempts in Argentina (1939), Uruguay (1940), Columbia (1941), and Bolivia (1941), the Roosevelt administration readily regurgitated its fears about the western hemisphere's security in the halls of power and across the nation's headlines.[11] Accordingly, "of the nearly 100 meetings

---

[9] Max Paul Friedman, *Nazis and Good Neighbors: The United States Campaign Against the Germans of Latin America in World War II* (Cambridge, UK: Cambridge University Press, 2003), 5.

[10] The quote references Stefan Rinke's book of the same name. See also Gerhard Drekonja-Kornat, "Nationalsozialismus und Lateinamerika. Neue Kontroversen," in *Wiener Zeitschrift zur Geschichte der Neuzeit* 6, no. 2 (2006): 109–18.

[11] Friedman, *Nazis and Good Neighbors*, 52, 73. See for example J. M. Batista i Roca, "Nazi Intrigues in Latin America," *Contemporary Review*, January 1, 1941, 308–15; Carleton Beals, "Swastika over the Andes," *Harper's Monthly Magazine*, June 1, 1938, 176–86; W. L. Schurz, "The Nazis and Latin America," *Washington Post*, April 17, 1939, 9. Commentators often conflated worries about Nazism in Latin America with Benito Mussolini's idea for a fascist transatlantic Latin alliance. See Genaro Arbaiza, "Are the Americas Safe?" *Current History*, December 1, 1937, 29–34; Carleton Beals,

of the joint planning committee of the US State, Navy, and War Departments in 1939 and 1940, all but six had Latin America at the top of the agenda."[12] President Franklin Roosevelt even speculated in one of his "fireside chats" that the Nazis could mobilize Latin-American German speakers as a "fifth column" to do their bidding.[13] However, the attention US officials gave to the situation was based less on their knowledge of actual German-speaking communities in Latin America and more on propaganda emanating from Germany and the presumed impotence of Latin American governments' ability to control their populations.

Paraguay is an especially relevant context for understanding this dynamic owing to its isolation from the United States and its flirtation with fascism in the 1930s. On a political level, Paraguay was one of three countries that pointedly refused to concede to anti-German resolutions at the 1938 Pan-American Conference for hemispheric solidarity.[14] On an economic level, Paraguay produced and traded raw materials that the United States already possessed domestically, so Great Britain and Germany were more logical trade partners.[15] Altogether, "Paraguay was in fact more remote from United States influence and interest than any other Latin American nation."[16] The country was also an especially fertile context for fascist and Nazi activity during the interwar years despite the heterogeneity of its German-speaking population. Around 1930, it was the first country to claim a Nazi Party cell outside of Germany and Austria.[17] In

---

"Black Shirts in Latin America," *Current History*, November 1, 1938, 32–34; "Latin America Called Hotbed of Fascism," *Washington Post*, November 28, 1938, X4.

[12] Friedman, *Nazis and Good Neighbors*, 2.

[13] Roosevelt broadcast his concern in a fireside chat. See Russell D. Buhite and David W. Levy, eds., *FDR's Fireside Chats* (Norman, OK: University of Oklahoma Press, 1992), 192.

[14] Michael Grow, *The Good Neighbor Policy and Authoritarianism in Paraguay: United States Economic Expansion and Great Power Rivalry in Latin America During World War II* (Lawrence, KS: Regents Press of Kansas, 1998), 38.

[15] By 1938, Germany was outselling both Great Britain and the United States in Brazil and Paraguay. See ibid., 27, 30. For a broad view of German–Latin American economic relations during the Nazi era, see Reiner Pommerin, *Das Dritte Reich und Lateinamerika: Die deutsche Politik gegenüber Süd- und Mittelamerika 1939–1942* (Dusseldorf: Droste, 1977).

[16] Grow, *Good Neighbor Policy*, 52.

[17] There is a discrepancy concerning the date the organization was founded. Friedman (*Nazis and Good Neighbors*, 21) claims it was 1929 while Grow (*Good Neighbor Policy*, 52) claims it was 1931. Frank Mora and Jerry Cooney likewise use 1931 in *Paraguay and the United States: Distant Allies* (Athens, GA: University of Georgia Press, 2007), 95. Ron Young explains that in 1928, a group of Paraguayan Nazi Party

February 1936, a cadre of fascist military officers calling themselves the *Revolutionarios* overthrew the ruling Liberal government and proclaimed that their "liberating revolution in Paraguay is of the same type as the totalitarian social transformations of contemporary Europe."[18] The Revolutionarios disintegrated in less than two years, but their cause was revived with General Higinio Morínigo's assumption of the presidency in 1940. Paraguay's constitution of the same year drew heavily on twentieth-century fascist theory.[19] Enthusiasm for fascism was not confined to the Palacio de López, however. Rank-and-file military and government posts were dominated by pro-Axis nationalists.[20] As stated by Grow, "By 1939, Nazi swastikas and portraits of Hitler were being prominently displayed in German schools and business establishments throughout Paraguay," apparently without eliciting much concern from the authorities.[21] The US–Paraguayan relationship reached a low point in 1943 when the US State Department sent Avra Warren to Asunción to remove Axis diplomats. On May 1, the military faction in Morínigo's cabinet loudly condemned this "persecution of peaceful Germans."[22] Within days, however, the United States had announced an expansive assistance package to Paraguay, which brought it back into a US orbit, but mostly lined the pockets of US companies. The deal especially profited Pan-American Airlines, which subsequently brought US Mennonites to Paraguay in greater numbers and with greater speed than ever before.[23] Altogether, there was little to suggest that Paraguay's fascist activity was relevant beyond its borders, but that did not hinder US interest in the country, regardless of whether the concerned Americans were government authorities or Mennonites.

members formed an "organization center," but it was not until August 1931 that an official *Landesgruppe* (national party unit) was formed. By 1933 there were sixty-two party members in the Paraguayan Nazi Party cell, making it the third largest in South America. See "Paraguay," *World Fascism: A Historical Encyclopedia*, ed. Cyprian P. Blamires, vol. 1 (Santa Barbara, Denver, Oxford: ABC CLIO, 2006), 505.

[18] Grow, *Good Neighbor Policy*, 49.

[19] Ibid., 49–58. See also Mora and Cooney, *Paraguay and the United States*, 94–96.

[20] Grow, *Good Neighbor Policy*, 65.   [21] Ibid., 52.

[22] Telegram 179, Frost to Welles, May 3, 1942, DS834.50/24. Quoted in Grow, *Good Neighbor Policy*, 76. An assessment of pro-German attitudes in the Paraguayan government as the result of German economic activity is contained in "Wesley Frost to Secretary of State," May 20, 1943, dispatch no. 1051, Container 7, Entry UD 3088 (Classified General Records {Confidential File} 1936–1961), NACP, 2.

[23] Grow, *Good Neighbor Policy*, 76–81.

A BRIDGE TO GERMANY

In 1937, some of the colony's most strident supporters of the *völkisch* cause formed the Bund Deutscher Mennoniten in Paraguay (League of German Mennonites in Paraguay, BDMP), which would provide a focal point for the colony's repatriation dreams. The group held its first meeting in Filadelfia on February 20, 1937, and elected Julius Legiehn as chairman and N. Siemens as secretary. Preacher and teacher A. Harder consecrated the event with a prayer.[24] Within a few months, about 274 individuals had joined the BDMP out of a total estimated Fernheim population of 2,015.[25] Though the group employed military terms such as *Stützpunkt* ("outpost") in its organization structure, its activities were mostly local and entirely civilian.[26] Initially, they wished to create an archive and library, support the schools and Jugendbund, and promote German and Mennonite periodicals in the colony.[27] The BDMP and its successor organization, the Verband der Russlanddeutschen (Association of Russian Germans, VRD), also worked to strengthen the colony's ties to the German presence in Asunción and throughout Paraguay. They soon elected to join the larger Deutscher Volksbund für Paraguay (German League for Paraguay, DVfP),[28] to which they paid a third of their yearly dues (set at 60 pesos).[29] The DVfP originated during the First World War to unify Paraguay's German minority and shore up support for its language, culture, and educational institutions. After the war, it turned its attention to promoting German settlement in Paraguay. By 1939, the DVfP claimed a membership of 1,574 individuals and a year later it had

---

[24] Harder arrived from Kaiserslautern, Germany in 1935 and took up work as a preacher in the Mennonitengemeinde.

[25] Herbert Wilhelmy and Oskar Schmieder, *Deutsche Akerbausiedlungen im südamerikanischen Grasland, Pampa und Gran Chaco*, Wissenschaftliche Veröffentlichungen, Neue Folge 6 (Leipzig: Deutsches Museum für Ländkunde, 1938), 105; "Bund Deutscher Mennoniten," *Menno-Blatt* (Fernheim, Paraguay) October 1938, 5. It is likely that only adult males were allowed to join the organization. Relying on Wilhelmy's numbers (126), in February 1937, there were 384 "farm owners" (i.e. male heads of household) in the Fernheim Colony. Given the fact that most colonists made their living off the land, it is reasonable that about 50 to 70 percent of the colony's adult male population belonged to the organization.

[26] Their designation as a *Stützpunkt* aligned with the Nazi's organizational schema for local groups who supported the *völkisch* cause.

[27] Bund Deutscher Mennoniten, "Richtlinien für den 'Bund Deutscher Mennoniten in Paraguay,'" *Menno-Blatt* (Fernheim, Paraguay) March 1937, 4.

[28] It was also known in Paraguay as the "Unión Germánica."

[29] Bund Deutscher Mennoniten, "Richtlinien," *Menno-Blatt* (Fernheim, Paraguay) March 1937, 4.

reached 1,677, or about 8 percent of Paraguay's German-speaking population.[30] Its trajectory and challenges resembled that of other German organizations in interwar Latin America including the Deutsch–Chilenische Bund (German–Chilean League), the Germanische Bund für Südamerika in Brazil (Germanic League for South America in Brazil), and the Verband Deutscher Reichsangehöriger (Association of German Nationals) in Mexico.[31] In the Fernheim Colony specifically, *völkisch* activists believed that a strong connections to the DVfP was crucial for sustaining an attachment to Nazi Germany.

Interestingly, the German government's diplomatic representatives, both in Asunción and the provinces, often declined to follow Nazi Party ideology and tactics. For example, Friedrich Brixner, the Villarrica consul since 1929, was a party member but he abstained from anti-Semitic rhetoric in order to maintain peaceful relations with the resident Jews in his sector. Other consuls, such as Emil Kloss and Eugen Franck from Encarnación, Erwin Eberhardt from Villeta, and R. W. Seifert from Concepción assumed their positions before the regime came to power and declined joining the party despite official encouragements.[32] In general, before and during the war years, the diplomatic personnel sustained a balancing act of maintaining friendly relations with the Paraguayan government even at the expense of frustrating Nazis in the country and in Europe. Like the varied communities of German speakers it monitored, the Nazis' diplomatic corps was hardly the vision of solidarity that Berlin wished it to be.

In mid-1938, a little over a year after the BDMP was established, the German government's highest-ranking diplomat in the country, Dr. Hans Karl Paul Eduard Büsing, visited all three Mennonite colonies. Büsing was the fourth minister in five years to hold the post. This turnover rate attests to a turbulent era for Germany's diplomatic presence in Paraguay. After Bülow was redeployed to Calcutta in 1933, Fritz Max Weiß assumed the post for several months until Erhard Graf von Wedel replaced him. Wedel was described in Foreign Service memoranda as an "old National

[30] Translated copy of "GERMAN SOCIETY IN PARAGUAY, 25 Years 1916–1941" (862.20234/140), Box 1, Entry UD 3090 (Paraguay U.S. Embassy, Asuncion, Supplemental Confidential General Records, 1944–1947), RG 84, NACP, 9.

[31] Nikolaus Barbian, *Auswärtige Kulturpolitik und "Auslandsdeutsche" in Lateinamerika 1949–1973* (Wiesbaden: Springer, 2013), 74–75.

[32] Jan Päßler, "Kuriositäten und Wissenswertes aus Paraguays Vergangenheit," *Das Wochenblatt* (Asunción), January 22, 2012, https://wochenblatt.cc/kuriositaten-und-wissenswertes-aus-paraguays-vergangenheit-teil-8/, last accessed June 7, 2018.

Socialist," who was "very active" in the party. Yet Wedel held the position for less than three years and left amid a flurry of allegations, including one that he had maintained a homosexual liaison with a young Austrian.[33] Büsing took over in February 1937 and attempted to restore the Nazi mission in Paraguay by ascertaining who within Paraguay's German-speaking population could be relied upon and who could not. Like Bender, who had graded the Mennonite colonies on their Mennoniteness when he visited the colonies that same year, Büsing devised his own hierarchy of Mennonite Germanness. In contrast to Bender, who wrote disparagingly of urban Mennonites, Büsing reported that the Asunción Mennonites were most in line with the goals of the Nazi state.[34] Like so many other nationally minded individuals of their era, Büsing and Bender believed that individuals could be described and ranked according to their adherence to an "essence" – be it German, Mennonite, or otherwise.

Unlike previous ministers, Büsing felt it was his duty to broaden the Nazis' *Auslandsdeutsche* tent in Paraguay.[35] In his report, Büsing notes that the Fernheim colonists had warm feelings about their Germanness, but they remained "widely separated from [*Reichsdeutsche*]," and were "typical overseas Germans." Presumably, this meant that that they were more interested in their local community than the *Volksgemeinschaft*. As evidence of that self-interest, Büsing noted that the Fernheim colonists were hopeful that Hitler would conquer Ukraine so they could be wheat farmers again.[36] In his analysis, the BDMP was a weak attempt to manifest loyalty where there was only selfishness. Unsurprisingly, Büsing described the Menno Colony colonists as "cool and reserved." He reported that they remained British subjects and felt "comfortable doing so without making much use of it." Even so, he established "a loose bond"

[33] "Memorandum by R. Hess to Herr von Neurath," February 1, 1936, Erhard Graf von Wedel Personalakten 016255, PA AA. The undisclosed author who wrote the document concerning Wedel's rumored homosexuality (and an individual by the name of Berthel who passed it up the chain of command), clearly had an axe to grind against the man. See "Berthel to Kreisleiter, July 24, 1936," Erhard Graf von Wedel Personalakten 016255, PA AA. Jan Päßler of the Paraguayan *Wochenblatt* offers the perspective that Wedel was "insufficiently sympathetic" to the Nazi cause. See Jan Päßler, "Kuriositäten und Wissenswertes aus Paraguays Vergangenheit," *Das Wochenblatt* (Paraguay), last modified January 22, 2012. http://wochenblatt.cc/nachrichten/kuriositaten-und-wissenswertes-aus-paraguays-vergangenheit-teil-8/7953, last accessed June 7, 2018.
[34] Dr. Hans Karl Paul Eduard Büsing, "Nr. 371, 2 Durchdrucke," R127972e, PA AA, 164.
[35] Päßler, "Kuriositäten und Wissenswertes."
[36] Büsing, "Nr. 371, 2 Durchdrucke," 163.

with them since, after all, "it is German blood that flows in their veins."[37] Unclear as to what the colony's archaic form of Germanness actually *meant* to the Third Reich, Büsing wrote them off as a lost cause.

Büsing placed urban Mennonites and Menno Colony Mennonites at either end of his spectrum, with the Fernheim and Friesland colonists falling in between. Concerning urban and Friesland Mennonites, this makes sense because the more that individual colonists were disillusioned with the MCC's goals and left the Chaco, the more they gravitated to other solidarities. Büsing concluded his report by cynically recommending that "a degree of caution is in order concerning their [the Fernheim Colony's] joyful commitment to the Third Reich. At the moment they only have Germany, from which they can expect help and support, and they are not foolish enough to squander it."[38]

In June 1939, Kliewer and his German-born Mennonite wife, Margarete Dyck, returned to the Fernheim Colony to reinvigorate its *völkisch* movement. Having completed his doctorate studies, Kliewer was elected leader of the colony's teachers' organization and took up work with the BDMP and the Jugendbund.[39] Apparently, it was easy for him to pick up where he had left off. According to a May 27 US intelligence report by John Philips, a photographer for *Life* who had gathered "photographic material on Nazi penetration" in the colony, Fernheim regularly received news from the Berlin Haus des Rundfunks (Berlin House of Broadcasting) via a short-wave Telefunken radio. Philips likewise reported that the Fernheimers are "anti-Semitic," had a picture of Hitler on display in Filadelfia's administrative building with the slogan "*Ein Mann ein Volk*" ("one man one people"), and "in some gardens carefully made swastika designs are seen."[40] The Kliewers' arrival was preceded by the contentious election of Legiehn to the position of colony *Oberschulze*. Legiehn won the election with a two-thirds majority, but he did not begin his term until after a two-day meeting in which his political attitudes generated much controversy among Allianzgemeinde pastors.[41] The Allianzgemeinde was the colony's

---

[37] Ibid., 161–62.   [38] Ibid., 167.

[39] He also arranged shipments of "Nazi textbooks" to the colony. See "RE: FRIEDRICH KLIEWER, with aliases Fritz Kliewer, Federico Kliewer," October 5, 1945, enclosed in "John Edgar Hoover to Mr. Frederick B. Lyon," November 15, 1945, Box 6734 (862.20233/1–145 to 862.20234/12–3148), Entry dec. file 1945–49, RG 59, NACP, 4; www.menonitica.org/lexikon/?K:Kliewer%2C_Friedrich, last accessed June 7, 2018.

[40] "Findley Howard to Secretary of State," May 27, 1939, dispatch no. 859, Container 2, Entry UD 3088 (Classified General Records {Confidential File} 1936–1961), RG 84, NACP, 2–3.

[41] Thiesen, *Mennonite and Nazi?* 125.

FIGURE 6.1 A young women in the Fernheim Colony tends her swastika garden. The photographer, a US citizen named John Philips, reported to US intelligence on the colony's Nazi activity, 1939. Source: John Phillips, The LIFE Picture Collection, Getty Images

smallest denomination and the most adamant about the Mennonite tenet of nonviolence. P. Klassen observes that throughout the 1930s they were increasingly exclusive, especially after the rise of the *völkisch* movement. He ascribes their separatist attitude to their "patriarchal leadership and their uncompromising family orientation," though it also likely had to do with their minority status and opposition to the games and other amusements practiced by the Jugendbund, which they considered to be "worldly."[42] Similar in some respects to the Menno Colony colonists, its members were opposed to leaving the Chaco and worried that the colony would be impossible to maintain if their brethren abandoned them (Fig. 6.1).[43]

Although Fernheim's original *völkisch* leaders, Kliewer and Legiehn, were back in power, the intervening years had changed both men. Kliewer's time as a graduate student in Germany had made him more convinced of the Nazi cause, while Legiehn took a more cautious

---

[42] Peter P. Klassen, *The Mennonites in Paraguay Volume 1: Kingdom of God and Kingdom of This World*, trans. Gunther H. Schmitt (Filadelfia, Paraguay: Peter P. Klassen, 2003), 315.

[43] Ibid., 315–16.

approach to questions of religion and politics. Legiehn wanted to restore the community's trust in him by avoiding controversy, while Kliewer wished to provoke the colony to action.[44]

The idea of repatriation to Germany first excited colonists in 1935 when the Mennonite Nazi propagandist and SS leader Schröder promoted a scheme to bring fifty Fernheim families to Germany. Nothing came of the proposal, but after a few years Schröder and P. Hildebrand collaborated in another plan to create a traditional Russian Mennonite colony using individuals from Canada and Paraguay. Schröder falsely assured potential colonists that the German government supported his plan, which it did not. Although Schröder's actions aroused the imaginations of Fernheim's and Friesland's young people, it triggered the ire of the Reichsministerium für Ernährung und Landwirtschaft (Ministry of Food and Agriculture) and led to a series of exchanges between this agency, the Hauptamt Volksdeutsche Mittelstelle (Central Welfare Office for Ethnic Germans, VoMi),[45] the German Foreign Office, German consulates in Canada and Paraguay, the MCC, and Fernheim Colony leaders – who all agreed that the idea was "fantastic" and "utopian."[46]

Despite Schröder's failed plan, a month before the Kliewers' return the VoMi granted twenty-six young people from Friesland (twenty-one men and five women) permission to migrate to Germany for the purpose of attending agricultural school. In Unruh's view, the young people would maintain government interest in the Mennonite resettlement scheme and serve as a bridgehead for future transfers. In fact, Unruh confidently predicted that "Sooner or later, the question of the reacquisition of our settlements in Russia will be put on the order of the day."[47] The plan looked great on paper. The VoMi assured participants that they would attend classes for two years, after which they would be placed on German farms. Yet the plan changed after the participants arrived in Germany,

---

[44] This is perhaps why he resigned from his post with the BDMP at the end of 1939 and turned his responsibilities over to Kliewer. See "Bund Deutscher Mennoniten in Paraguay," *Menno-Blatt* (Fernheim, Paraguay), December 1939, 4.

[45] The VoMi absorbed the VDA's duties in July 1938, as part of Hitler's Gleichschaltung. For more on the VoMi, see Valdis O. Lumans, *Himmler's Auxiliaries: The Volksdeutsche Mittelstelle and the German National Minorities of Europe 1933–1935* (Chapel Hill, NC: University of North Carolina Press, 1993).

[46] "Betrifft: Heinrich Hayo Schröder," R127972e, PA-AA, 143–46. The entire series of exchanges runs from pages 143–54 and includes Schröder's justifications for his scheme.

[47] "Benjamin Unruh to Orie Miller, July 4, 1939, Nachlaß Benjamin Unruh, box 9, folder 48, MFS. Quoted in Benjamin W. Goossen, *Chosen Nation: Mennonites and Germany in a Global Era* (Princeton, NJ: Princeton University Press, 2017), 151.

and they were immediately hired out as farm laborers. Within a couple of years, the men had been drafted into the army, and only a few participants actually saw the inside of a classroom.[48] Of course, the difference between the VoMi plan and Schröder's scheme was that the former entailed cheap labor in exchange for third-class boat tickets while the latter required land, resources, money, and trust, which the suspicious and authoritarian government could not afford. Nevertheless, the 1939 partnership between the Friesland Mennonites and the VoMi appeared to colonists to be an auspicious development.

Kliewer had previously supported the idea of Fernheim as a German outpost in South America, but now he increasingly believed that the position was untenable. Kliewer had come of age imbibing the siege mentality of the German-speaking minority in Poland during the 1920s, so when war broke out between Germany and Poland in September 1929, he embraced the Nazis' eastern fantasies with gusto.[49] In an October 1939 letter to Quiring, Kliewer wrote that Paraguay's Mennonites were destined to fail if they remained in Paraguay, since "The decline of their cultural life cannot be stopped ... I am now of the opinion, that neither economic nor *völkisch* positions can be maintained and therefore a way out of this situation must be sought."[50] After years of drought, war, poor harvests, and inadequate medical care, death made its rounds again in early 1940 in the form of malaria and typhus. On April 29, an observer reported that twenty wagons of sick and dying colonists lined the street in front of the colony's small hospital.[51] Kliewer's initiative therefore fell on receptive ears in the Fernheim Colony, including the ears of those who did not otherwise support National Socialism.

There is no indication that the Menno Colony had an opinion on Germany's declaration of war, but the Fernheim and Friesland colonies greeted it with muted excitement.[52] As 1939 drew to a close, however, editor N. Siemens gloomily reported in *Menno-Blatt* that the colony could no longer sell cotton to Germany ("Our plans have once again been

---

[48] Thiesen, *Mennonite and Nazi?* 136.   [49] K. Stahl, 35.

[50] Quoted in Peter P. Klassen, *Die deutsch-völkish Zeit*, 56.

[51] "Nelson Litwiller to H. S. Bender," May 1, 1940, f. 69, b. 54, H. S. Bender papers, Hist. Mss. 1–278, AMC.

[52] The news reached Fernheim and Friesland via radio broadcast. See "Radioapparat für die Kolonie Friesland," R127972e, PA AA, 100–7. *Menno-Blatt* printed a column titled *"Neueste Nachrichte"* ("Latest News") based on these transmissions. For the first written war report in *Menno-Blatt*, see "Krieg in Europa!" *Menno-Blatt* (Fernheim, Paraguay), August/September 1939, 8.

thwarted.") and penned a general condemnation of war, but he refrained from blaming Germany or the Allies.[53] By this point, the Fernheim colonists – and especially those under the age of thirty – were mostly inured to war and violence. In the preceding quarter century, they had survived the First World War, the Russian Revolution and Civil War, Stalin's war against kulaks, and the Chaco War. Their lives were defined by conflict and so the renewed hostilities in Europe were less of a rupture than a continuity, and one that held the promise of opportunity.

Breaking completely with Mennonites' historic distaste for violence, some individuals, including the Kliewers and members of the BDMP, were energized by the war and the possibility of German victory. On Kliewer's first day as leader of the BDMP in November 1939, he set forth a new set of goals for the organization:

1) Mobilize nationalist forces in our colony and deploy them accordingly.
2) Mobilize our municipal administration as well as our cultural and charitable institutions such as the hospital and school.
3) Maintain communication with German organizations and their branches in Paraguay.
4) Maintain a connection with the Reich and the German legation in Paraguay.[54]

A little less than a year later, the BDMP held an anniversary celebration in Filadelfia, by which point it was clear that the BDMP's meetings regularly included readings of "Mein Kampf," lectures on political matters, and discussions of "German race questions." At least by this time, and perhaps much earlier, Nazi attitudes toward Jews and other minorities were common knowledge within colony, yet there is little evidence of exactly what this meant to its members.[55]

---

[53] N. Siemens, "Verschiedenes," *Menno-Blatt* (Fernheim, Paraguay), October 1939, 6; N. Siemens, "Friede auf Erden?!" *Menno-Blatt* (Fernheim, Paraguay), December 1939, 1.

[54] "Bund Deutscher Mennoniten in Paraguay," *Menno-Blatt* (Fernheim, Paraguay), December 1939, 4. It's unclear how large the BDMP's membership was upon Kliewer's return, but by 1942 it stood at 260 and by 1943 it was 278. See "Excerpts of statements made by Dr. Kliewer at the annual meeting of the Russo-German Association in Filadelfia, on October 18, 1942," in "MENNONITE COLONIES IN PARAGUAY – DR. FRITZ KLIEWER, WITH ALIASES," September 14, 1943, Box 1, Entry UD 3090 (Paraguay U.S. Embassy, Asuncion, Supplemental Confidential General Records, 1944–1947), RG 84, NACP, 4.

[55] "Report of the Anniversary Meeting of the Union of German Mennonites [BDMP], September 20, 1940," translated and enclosed in "Re: Dr. Fritz Kliewer, was.

By January 1940, Fernheim preachers were embroiled in a heated debate with Kliewer and M. Dyck about the pair's growing militarism. One report claimed that Kliewer was teaching students German military drills and having them sing "Wir sind Soldaten von den Reich" ("We Are Soldiers of the Reich").[56] This tension placed Kliewer and Dyck in clear opposition to the colonies' religious leadership.[57] Coincidentally, the DVfP's business manager in Asunción, Gerd von Schütz, was visiting the colony at the time. In February, *Menno-Blatt* printed an article on Schütz's impressions. Unlike Wilhelmy and Büsing, Schütz praised the Mennonites' Germanness: "German will, German tenacity, German faith has once again, as so often, repeatedly, shown that the seemingly impossible is still feasible," from the steppe to the bush.[58] Perhaps his enthusiasm was due to an awareness that the colony's *völkisch* supporters were experiencing local difficulties, or because he wished to count victories wherever he could find them among Paraguay's heterogeneous German-speaking population. Either way, Kliewer and N. Siemens traveled to the capital for news and a debriefing with Schütz at his private residence.

After the meeting with Schütz, N. Siemens experienced an abrupt change of heart concerning his role as a *völkisch* booster, which led to his decisive withdrawal from the *völkisch* movement. It is unclear exactly what transpired at the meeting, but he later claimed that he had seen the dark heart of National Socialism and no longer wished to place *Menno-Blatt* at its service.[59] From this point on, he began running articles that highlighted the biblical basis for pacifism, and mailed a request to Miller at the MCC for resources to combat the colony's *völkisch* drift. In April, N. Siemens went public with his dissatisfaction during a general meeting of the Brüdergemeinde. The Brüdergemeinde church was the largest

Asunción, Paraguay," June 18, 1944, Box 5563 [mislabeled 5564] (862.20210–862.20210), Entry dec. file 1940–44, RG 59, NACP.

[56] "G. S. Klassen to the American Embassy, April 14, 1944," reproduced in "Re: Dr. Fritz Kliewer, was. Asunción, Paraguay," June 18, 1944, Box 5563 [mislabeled 5564] (862.20210–862.20210), Entry dec. file 1940–44, RG 59, NACP, 8. G. Klassen observed these practices when he arrived in 1943.

[57] Thiesen, *Mennonite and Nazi?* 127.

[58] Gerd von Schütz, "Eindrücke in Fernheim," *Menno-Blatt* (Fernheim, Paraguay), February 1940, 4.

[59] Thiesen, *Mennonite and Nazi?* 128. Apparently, at about this same time he was offered money from "paid Germans" to sell them his printing press, which he refused to do. See "Litwiller to Bender," May 1, 1940, f. 69, b. 54, H. S. Bender papers, Hist. Mss. 1–278, AMC.

denomination in Fernheim and Friesland and contained most of the colonies' *völkisch* supporters.[60] Siemens's speech "Fernheim in Distress!" laid out the stakes as he saw them.[61] He argued that the colony had a choice between two paths: "*Volkstum*" and "*Christentum*" (Christianity). Although Germany was the colony's national "mother," she had forsaken her children by becoming a *Sonderling* (eccentric). Adding a biblical twist to the analogy, Siemens argued that the colonists were orphans who must wander the earth, according to Hebrews 13:14 "For here we have no lasting city, but we seek the city that is to come."[62] With this plea, Siemens suggested that the Fernheim Colony's collective narrative did not have an earthly conclusion – either in Paraguay or in Germany – but would only be revealed by faithfulness to God. Siemens believed that politics was a sickness that infected the colony and must be cured by a return to biblical Christianity.[63]

Perhaps inspired by Siemens's speech at the Brüdergemeinde meeting, the Allianzgemeinde submitted a statement to *Oberschulze* Legiehn in February 1940 that affirmed their commitment to remaining in the Chaco. The document was signed by all male members of the church. As quoted by P. Klassen, it read, "We believe that God prepared the way to Paraguay for us, where we can live by our beliefs and Mennonite principles, as stated in the *Privilegium* that was issued by the Paraguayan government."[64] They argued that *völkisch* activity had jeopardized the colony's integrity and that Kliewer's leadership of the schools had infused the youth with a martial spirit. To put meat on the bones of their contention, they threatened Legiehn that they would withdraw their children from the colony's school system if he did not take immediate action.[65] Weighing his odds, Legiehn declined to check the *völkisch* movement's growing strength and allowed Kliewer to maintain his position in the school. Stonewalled by the colony's leaders, N. Siemens and the Allianzgemeinde found an ally in three North American missionaries – Nelson Litwiller, Josephus W. Shank, and Elvin V. Snyder – who visited the colony from their station in Argentina in April 1940 and who shared the belief that God had ordained that the colonists remain in the Chaco. If *völkisch*

---

[60] It is of note that Unruh belonged to the Brüdergemeinde.
[61] N. Siemens, "Fernheim in Not!" f. "Paraguay Fernheim Colony 1940," IX-6–3 Central Correspondence, 1931–85, MCCA.
[62] Ibid., 6 (ESV).   [63] Ibid., 3–4.
[64] P. Klassen, *The Mennonites in Paraguay Volume 1*, 316.   [65] Ibid.

FIGURE 6.2 Fernheim students receiving pedagogic education: Peter Wolff, David Hein, Abram Harder, Hans Wiens, Margarete Kliewer, David Boschmann, Friedrich Kliewer, Peter Wiens, Heinrich Ratzlaff, Peter Derksen, 1941. Source: Archivo Colonia Fernheim

activists could garner transnational support, so too could the *wehrlos* (Fig. 6.2).

YANKEE MENNONITES

Perhaps unbeknownst to them, the missionaries were shock troops sent over in a bid to consolidate American-style Mennoniteness in the Chaco. Fully apparent to them, however, was the notion that US-style Mennoniteness was the scale against which all other interpretations of the faith should be weighed. As a non-creedal church, the "correct" interpretation of Mennoniteness always and only came down to the number of constituents swayed by a given interpretation. Conspicuously out of their element in the Fernheim Colony, the missionaries stood aghast that United States–style Mennoniteness was not manifestly true to the Fernheimers. Reporting to US Mennonite leaders after their visit, the missionaries' impressions would result in a new MCC initiative to convince Fernheimers to forfeit their repatriation fantasies. Mirroring the US assistance package to Paraguay, the MCC used material aid to bring colonists back into their orbit.

The North American missionaries worked for the MC (Bender's denomination) and arrived at the same time that the Fernheim colonists were celebrating Hitler's birthday (which happened to fall on a Sunday). Though the missionaries could overlook Kliewer and Harder's "riding pants," "high boot[s]," and "a certain amount of heel clicking," Litwiller reported that they "were simply dumbfounded" by the colony's "vociferous" support for Hitler.[66] As North American Mennonites who had come to view the principle of nonviolence as the cornerstone of Mennonite doctrine, the notion that any Mennonites were favorable toward (let alone celebratory of) the Nazi dictator seemed antithetical and bizarre. Yet from the colonists' perspective, Hitler was a decisive leader who had apparently brought peace to a quarreling German populace through his *völkisch* tactics and might even secure their own return to Europe. Both colonists and missionaries therefore viewed the colony as a local metaphor for national and global anxieties.

Tensions came to a head when the three missionaries preached sermons at a colony assembly in Filadelfia. During their speeches, they clarified the North American Mennonite position against German militarism, which provoked a coarse *völkisch* rebuttal. Snyder was second to speak, and directly addressed the issues of nonviolence and Nazism. He argued that Nazism systematically abuses power, represents totalitarian absolutism, and is determined to abolish both individual personality and Christianity. Placing quotes from Hitler's *Mein Kampf* in contrast to statements by Karl Barth, Snyder avoided emotional appeals in favor of a theological critique of Nazism.[67] His approach depersonalized the assault, but also made him appear out of touch with an audience that viewed Nazism much more personally. Obviously, Snyder's speech did not go over well with the colony's *völkisch* group. After he sat down, several young men walked out of the assembly and were followed soon thereafter by Kliewer and Harder. After they had commiserated with each other in the yard, Kliewer shouted through the open door that the sermons were an insult to Germany and would be refuted in

---

[66] "Litwiller to Bender," May 1, 1940, f. 69, b. 54, H. S. Bender papers, Hist. Mss. 1–278, AMC.

[67] "Elvin Snyder to S. C. Yoder," May 1, 1940, f. 2/13, Elvin Snyder papers, Hist. Mss. 1–113, AMC.

due time.[68] The colony's high-school students supported his reprisal with applause.[69]

After the missionaries had left, each wrote a report to a different Mennonite leader in the United States revealing their distinctly North American attitudes to faith and politics. For example, in Litwiller's letter to Bender, he stated that the missionaries encouraged the Fernheim colonists to "not mix in politics," though perhaps he meant to say "German politics," since he also noted that he was writing as a "loyal Canadian." Apparently, identifying with a North American government was fine, since North American Mennonites believed that their Anabaptist forebears anticipated democratic governance. However, identifying with a fascist government was another story, even though Germany's Mennonites were entirely at peace with the regime for their own historical and theological reasons.[70]

Interestingly, it was not Fernheim's *völkisch* contingent that the missionaries had the most difficulty understanding, since both parties shared a modern, political vocabulary. Rather, it was the Menno Colony that Snyder singled out as a bastion of "fanaticism" in his letter to Goshen College president and Mennonite Board of Missions secretary Sanford C. Yoder. Snyder observed that the Menno Colony neither shared nor desired "harmony or cooperation" with Fernheim.[71] Snyder was firmly opposed to the Fernheim Colony's Nazi contingent, but at least theirs was an extremism that could be debated on intellectual and theological grounds. That of the Menno Colony Mennonites could not. Though Snyder observed that it would be difficult to change the Fernheim colonists' minds, he intuited that it would be nearly impossible to do the same with the Menno colonists.

The missionaries' most troubling discovery, however, had less to do with theology and more to do with Paraguayan politics and the MCC's bottom line. During their conversations with sympathetic Fernheimers,

[68] "Litwiller to Bender," May 1, 1940, f. 69, b. 54, H. S. Bender papers, Hist. Mss. 1-278, AMC.

[69] Ibid., "Snyder to Yoder," May 1, 1940, f. 2/13, Elvin Snyder papers, Hist. Mss. 1-113, AMC.

[70] It may have been the case that Litwiller's declaration of being a "loyal Canadian" was included in his letter to put potential US censors at ease. "Litwiller to Bender," May 1, 1940, f. 69, b. 54, H. S. Bender papers, Hist. Mss. 1-278, AMC.

[71] "Elvin Snyder to Yoder," May 1, 1940, f. 2/13, Elvin Snyder papers, Hist. Mss. 1-113, AMC.

the missionaries learned that Kliewer was encouraging colonists to take out German citizenship papers, which threatened to forfeit the colony's privileged status in Paraguay. They also learned that Kliewer's ultimate goal was to persuade colonists to default on their MCC debts and save their money for transportation to Buenos Aires, where they would ostensibly receive free passage to Germany. With a clear majority of colonists receptive to the Nazi cause, this was a serious threat to the MCC's ability to collect the colony's debt and remain solvent.[72] Altogether, the missionaries' visit in early 1940 was a wake-up call to the MCC, because it illuminated the degree to which their vision of Mennoniteness diverged from the colony's *völkisch* drift.

Apparently, the three North American representatives emboldened the colony's preachers to hold a subsequent meeting to discuss the *völkisch* movement and its effect on the settlement. At a meeting held on April 28, 1940, most of the colony's preachers voted to not go along with the *völkisch* cause since it "creates anxiety in us and is not consistent with the Mennonite principles."[73] Yet it would take more than an injunction by the colony's preachers to break the will of the *völkisch* movement. The movement, and the possibility of repatriation that it entailed, was to many Fernheim and Friesland individuals their best and perhaps only chance of survival.

By May 1940, a line was drawn between the Fernheim colony's *wehrlos* and *völkisch* factions that largely fell along church lines. The Allianzgemeinde dominated the former, while Brüdergemeinde and Mennonitengemeinde individuals dominated the latter. Of course, a large number of colonists existed somewhere in the middle of the opposing *wehrlos* and *völkisch* poles: They sincerely wished to return to Europe if it were possible, but they remained engrossed in their immediate concerns of growing crops and meeting the next debt payment. Hence, the *völkisch* faction maintained the upper hand, not because it had to defend its ideology but because it merely had to cast doubt on the colony's viability.

Soon after this informal division, the *völkisch* contingent flexed its power by drawing up a petition to the German legation in Asunción requesting resettlement in Germany. Signatories requested German

---

[72] Ibid.; "Litwiller to Bender," May 1, 1940, f. 69, b. 54, H. S. Bender papers, Hist. Mss. 1–278, AMC.

[73] Peter Wiens, *Die K. f. K. Fernheim: ein geschichtlicher Überblick 1931–1991* (Filadelfia, Paraguay: K. f. K. Fernheim, 1992), 35.

citizenship and promised to fit themselves into the German national state, and to "do our duty unto the utmost for the German Fatherland" – which suggested their willingness to perform military service – since "the ten colonial years and the conditions in this country have persuaded us that we will never find a homeland here."[74] Kliewer enclosed a message with the petition that further explained: "The settlers here doubt that they can persevere because of economic reversals and the malaria epidemic raging in the Chaco. They are convincing themselves more and more that they can't endure it here not only from the viewpoint of economic and unhealthy conditions, but also the national-cultural viewpoint."[75] By September, the number of signatories had reached 240 families, representing a clear majority of the colony's population. Friesland made a similar request.[76] What Kliewer had intimated to Quiring the year before – that the Chaco was uninhabitable for "German" colonists – was now accepted as fact in the Fernheim Colony. The petition's popularity also indicates that colonists believed the war would be over soon and that they had a real possibility of relocating to Europe. In view of the Nazis' stunning victories, there was little chance that they would be required to perform military service and every indication that they could reap the benefits of German victory.

MCC leaders P. Hiebert, Miller, and Bender weighed in on the controversy with a strongly worded letter that was read at a colony assembly in June 1940.[77] The letter focused on a few key issues, including the repatriation scheme and Kliewer's (mis)management of the schools.[78] It also repeated a rumor that the colonists' special privileges were in danger of being revoked by the Paraguayan government due to their *völkisch* activity.[79] Echoing Siemens, the MCC exhorted the colony to remain in Paraguay by referencing Jeremiah 27:8–9 which states, "But if any nation

---

[74] "Application of Russian-German Colonists of the colony Fernheim for citizenship," May 26, 1940, in Cornelius J. Dyck, ed., *From the Files of MCC* (Scottdale, PA: Herald Press, 1980), 56.

[75] "Fritz Kliewer to German Legation, June 3, 1940," translated and enclosed in "Re: Dr. Fritz Kliewer, was. Asunción, Paraguay," June 18, 1944, Box 5563 [mislabeled 5564] (862.20210–862.20210), Entry dec. file 1940–44, RG 59, NACP, 12.

[76] Thiesen, *Mennonite and Nazi?* 143.

[77] "MCC to Oberschulzen ... in der Kolonie Fernheim," June 15, 1940, f. 69, b. 54, H. S. Bender papers, Hist. Mss. 1–278, AMC.

[78] Ibid.

[79] Thiesen argues that Paraguayan officials were likely worried about the repatriation scheme for several reasons, including the fact that the Fernheim Colony grew a major portion of the country's cotton, supplied food and materials to Paraguayan troops stationed in the Chaco, and provided a social and economic bulwark against Bolivian reprisal. See *Mennonite and Nazi?* 152.

or kingdom will not serve this Nebuchadnezzar king of Babylon, and put its neck under the yoke of the king of Babylon, I will punish that nation . . . So do not listen to your prophets, your diviners, your dreamers, your fortune-tellers, or your sorcerers, who are saying to you, 'You shall not serve the king of Babylon.'"[80] In the MCC's view, Paraguay was "Babylon" to colonists – a foreign and hostile land far removed from their imagined "Promised Land" – but the Lord willed them to embrace it and not heed the false words of Kliewer the "dreamer."

The MCC's designation of Paraguay as "Babylon" is particularly important since it highlights the eclectic application of biblical metaphors within the confession. Canada was a decadent and prideful "Babylon" to the Menno colonists in 1927, but an unrealizable "Promised Land" to the Fernheim colonists in 1929. Alternatively, the Menno Colony regarded Paraguay as one of a series of temporary "Promised Lands," while the MCC regarded it as a foreign, though benign, "Babylon." It was not as felicitous as the colonists' homeland on the Russian steppe, but serviceable enough. With the Chaco's disease, drought, and war, many Fernheim colonists experienced Paraguay neither as a "Promised Land" nor as "Babylon," but as a "Sinai Desert," that they must escape. It is therefore understandable that the Fernheim colonists had serious doubts about their Mennonite contemporaries' attempts to explain their situation in biblical language.

By the late 1930s, the vast majority of North American Mennonites had found their "Promised Land" in Canada and the United States. A few outliers, such as the aforementioned J. J. Hildebrand, used Canadian publications to advertise their *völkisch* fantasies but they were strongly criticized by most of the denomination's faithful.[81] With the United States teetering on the edge of war, MCC leaders wanted to be clear that theirs was a peaceful organization, committed to working with Allied governments, and did not conflate their Mennonite identification with a German one. In this spirit, Hiebert encouraged Legiehn to fall in line with the MCC and cut the colony's financial and organizational ties to Germany and *völkisch* organizations in Paraguay.[82] Although the colony's *wehrlos*

---

[80] ESV.

[81] Urry notes that elder Jacob H. Janzen in Canada was a key figure in the Mennonite battle against Nazism. See "A Mennostaat for the Mennovolk? Mennonite Immigrant Fantasies in Canada in the 1930s," *Journal of Mennonite Studies* 14 (1996): 73–74.

[82] "P. C. Hiebert to Julius Legiehn," March 25, 1941, f. 394 Correspondence, March 1941, b. 35, P. C. Hiebert papers, MS-37, MLA.

faction was buoyed by this stance, the *völkisch* contingent considered the MCC's entreaty as a demand to cut their lifeline.

By the fall of 1940, Kliewer had become a petty tyrant, a perfect Nazi. According to one observer, Gerhard Balzer, "Dr. Kliewer gives and takes German citizenship to and from whomever he wishes."[83] This placed Legiehn in the difficult position of trying to bind the colony together while nursing his own hope that repatriation was possible. As *Oberschulze*, he agreed with *Menno-Blatt* editor N. Siemens that politics was a disease, but he wanted to remain on friendly terms with Kliewer. In October 1940, he proposed a moratorium on the issue. The statement was titled "Recommendations for the Strengthening of Public Peace in the Fernheim Colony" and was read at a conference of the colony's preachers.[84] In general terms, the document called on both *völkisch* and *wehrlos* groups to admit that they were uncharitable toward each other and agree that they would keep all future disagreements personal and private. With the preachers' endorsement and the BDMP's assurances, both sides assented to Legiehn's tepid injunction. Pleased with the truce, Legiehn reported to the MCC that peace reigned in the Chaco. The organization remained doubtful that it would last. As the fortunes of Kliewer and Nazi Germany rose, the influence of the MCC and the wherlos declined. This was not strictly an ideological struggle between "good" and "bad," but a struggle between how colonists imagined their future and their identification as Germans and as Mennonites.

Völkisch spirits were buoyed in June 1941 when Germany's war machine leveled its sights on the Soviet Union during Operation Barbarossa. Preacher A. Harder heard the news while en route to Asunción to conduct church services for Mennonites in the capital. This event spurred him to write that Paraguay:

cannot be a permanent home [for Fernheim Colony Mennonites]! It was and is only our place of refuge ... We shall tell our children ever more of God's wonderful help in time of need, our most wonderful rescue out of Russia, the help from the German Reich and our brethren in North America ... we will stand our ground in the thorny, inhospitable Chaco until God will bring to fulfillment our burning wish, our almost insatiable longing![85]

---

[83] "Bernhard Wall to H. S. Bender," May 8, 1940, ACF.
[84] Thiesen, *Mennonite and Nazi?* 141–42.
[85] Abraham Harder, "Reisebericht," 1941, 1, f. 262 "Paraguay and Brazil 1937–1941," b. 25, General Conference Emergency Relief Board papers, I-G-I, MLA.

Although Abraham Harder was among the Mennonites that Wilhelmy had criticized for having a "Jewish name," he nevertheless longed for deliverance from the Chaco. He believed that God had plans for the Fernheim colonists and it was only a matter of time – weeks perhaps – before Germany would widen its horizons "with the hills and valleys of our old home in Russia."[86] A. Harder's statement clearly symbolizes the local and mythological way that the Fernheim colonists imagined their repatriation to Europe. It was *the* happy resolution to the struggles that had defined their time in the Chaco. As the Nazi narrative of the German nation cast the Weimar era as a sojourn through ambiguity and pain, renewed hostilities on the European continent portended a happy (comedic) finale for both Nazi and Mennonite stories.

As A. Harder was proclaiming a new destiny for the Fernheim Colony, the DAI in Germany outlined its own vision for the role of *Überseedeutschen* (oversees Germans, a term similar in meaning to *Auslandsdeutsche*) in an expanded Reich. The document was titled "Fundamental questions about a possible resettlement of the overseas *Volksdeutsche*" and was presented to the Reichskommissariat für die Festigung deutschen Volkstums (Reich Commissariat for the Strengthening of German Nationhood). Notably, the report stated that much of Paraguay's German population was interested in relocating to Germany if so allowed. According to a 1941 DAI estimate, there were about 20,000 Germans in Paraguay (likely including both Mennonite colonies), of whom it was estimated that 15,000 wished to migrate to Germany after a successful conclusion of hostilities.[87] In total, the DAI suggested there would be about 800,000 *Überseedeutschen* who wanted to return to Europe, and possibly more if host states increased their persecution of German speakers.[88]

It appeared as if the Fernheim Colony's *völkisch* stars were finally coming into alignment, for the report went on to suggest that rural *Überseedeutschen* were of high value to the Nazis' agrarian ambitions in Eastern Europe. Mentioning the Paraguayan settlers directly, the report stated, "It can be said with certainty that after the victorious conclusion of the war, a significant return migration of *Volksdeutsche* will be from overseas. The overseas Germans themselves are striving to return to the

---

[86] Ibid.
[87] Deutsche Ausland-Institut, "Grundfragen zu einer etwaigen Umsiedlung der überseeischen Volksdeutschen," GFM 33/4822, NA, 2.
[88] Ibid., 3.

realm because they are hoping to find within its boundaries an extended tree upon which they can develop their *Volk* style freely and because they want to participate in the economic prosperity of the empire."[89] Thus, as the Fernheim Mennonites looked to Germany to save them, Germany looked to South America's German speakers as a resource for the realization of its plans to Germanize Eastern Europe.

As Germany moved from victory to victory, Mennonite conscientious objectors from the United States began arriving in the Fernheim Colony to perform aid-related activities as alternative service to the US draft. North America's Mennonites had learned from the violence and confusion that was directed against conscientious objectors during the First World War, and they were now eager to provide Mennonite young men with federally sanctioned alternatives to military service. In 1940–1941, the MCC added a Civilian Public Service (CPS) component to its relief operations as an alternative to the US Selective Service and Training Act. The MCC positioned itself as the broker between the federal government, Mennonite groups, and other historic peace churches, such as the Quakers, with whom it increasingly cooperated. Within a few years, Mennonites outnumbered all other denominations in the program with 4,665 of 12,600 participants, though less than half of all Mennonite young men chose CPS over military service.[90] Thus, in the same month that A. Harder had his prophetic vision of leaving the Chaco and the DAI filed its report on repatriating overseas Germans, MCC representatives O. Miller and CPS participant John R. Schmidt arrived in the colony. O. Miller's visit was brief, but J. Schmidt remained in the Chaco for a year and a half working as a medical doctor in Fernheim's small hospital. In October 1941, a second CPS participant named Vernon H. Schmidt arrived in Paraguay and was tasked with helping build a hospital and road for the Fernheim and Friesland colonies.[91]

In early 1943, at the same time as the United States was proposing a development package to bring Paraguay back into its political orbit, the MCC was dispatching three more individuals to the colony to bring Fernheim back into its religious sphere. They were Robert W. Geigley, a lawyer from Pennsylvania; A. E. Janzen, a college

[89] Ibid., 1.
[90] Melvin Gingerich, "Civilian Public Service," *Global Anabaptist Mennonite Encyclopedia Online*, last modified April 13, 2014, http://gameo.org/index.php?title=Civilian_Publi c_Service&oldid=120961, last accessed June 7, 2018.
[91] "Orie O. Miller to Mrs. R. B. Shipley," May 17, 1944, Container 10, Entry UD 3088 (Classified General Records {Confidential File} 1936–1961), RG 84, NACP, 1–2.

professor from Kansas; and George S. Klassen, a dentist who was also from Kansas. These men were older than the CPS men and their assignment was to deal with the colony's financial problems, help draw colonists into closer fellowship with US Mennonites, and provide dental care.[92] In the United States, Mennonite men faced the condescension of their peers for not fighting in the military. Now, surrounded by Mennonites in Paraguay, they were surprised to learn that some colonists cheered the military achievements of the country that had started the war. Moreover, the volunteers held politically sophisticated and theologically justified reasons for their decisions, which did not translate well to a colony that had cut its teeth on the visceral realities of a pioneer existence that it wished to escape.

The new arrivals were accustomed to working with the US government and not against it, since the United States had made CPS service possible. To this end, they readily visited and corresponded with US diplomatic officials in the region. Soon after his arrival, G. Klassen penned a letter in which he mentioned that if he "sensed any repetition of the questionable things of the past .,, [he] would report any program activities to you [Walter E. Sewell, US military attaché] or other authorities in Asuncion."[93] On one of V. Schmidt's occasional trips to the capital in February 1943, he reported to Frost that many colonists continued to favor Germany. A few months later Schmidt encouraged Legiehn to show US propaganda films furnished by Americans. About 1,500 colonists viewed the films including, interestingly enough, many people from the Menno Colony.[94] Perhaps wishing to ameliorate US fears, on August 12, 1943, Janzen painted a sanguine picture of Fernheim colony to the US consulate in Curitiba, Brazil.[95] According to his report, the Fernheimers had been "approached by Nazi propagandists from the German legation at Asuncion" and had "readily absorbed the German indoctrination" but "at present there is no indication of pro-Nazi sympathy with the exception of two or three

[92] Ibid., Wesley Prieb, *Global Anabaptist Mennonite Encyclopedia Online*, "Janzen, Abraham Ewell (1892–1995)," last modified July 31, 2014, http://gameo.org/index.php?title=Janzen,_Abraham_Ewell_(1892–1995)&oldid=123758, last accessed June 7, 2018.

[93] "G. S. Klassen to Walter E. Sewell," March 16, 1944, Container 10, Entry UD 3088 (Classified General Records {Confidential File} 1936–1961), RG 84, NACP, 1.

[94] Thiesen, *Mennonite and Nazi?* 170–71.

[95] Janzen was visiting a small Mennonite settlement in the region.

individuals."[96] The truth lay somewhere between the Americans' competing accounts, but as the US government committed to Americanizing Paraguay's economy and domestic security, the MCC committed to Americanizing its Mennonite colonies.

In spite of US and MCC propaganda, the Fernheim Colony's repatriation scheme would not die and Kliewer's status as the intermediary between the Fernheim Colony and the DVfP remained secure. In 1943, the colony obtained news from the DVfP in Asunción that qualified *Auslandsdeutsche* who wished to "return" to Germany would be exchanged for Allied civilians in occupied Europe.[97] Consequently, on April 11, Kliewer submitted forms for his family, and ten other Fernheim families (presumably including Legiehn) who held German passports, to the DVfP and the German legation (presumably before it was closed by the Americans). He also submitted a petition on behalf of 180 families, which represented about 1,000 colonists, though he stated that "Surely one or the other is not going to return during the war, but about 130 families have expressed that they want to go if they receive passports at whatever opportunity."[98] On a national level, one US Naval Attaché intelligence report claimed that a total of 5,000 German speakers in Paraguay were considering German repatriation.[99] The transfer scheme melted away in the light of German reversals later that year, but Kliewer sustained the colony's emigration hopes, even as the MCC worked to keep the colonists settled.

---

[96] "MEMORANDUM Re: Abraham Ewell Janzen; Ukrainian Mennonites, Curitiba, Brazil" enclosed in "J. Edgar Hoover to Adolf A. Berle, Jr.," September 29, 1943 (862.20210/2599), Box 5515, Entry dec. file 1940–44, RG 59, NACP.

[97] This plan may relate to the failed 1943–44 arrangement between Nazi Germany and Western governments to exchange German nationals in the Americas for Polish and Dutch Jews holding US or Latin American papers. The Jews were held at the Bergen-Belsen "Residence Camp," in Germany until the scheme failed and they were transferred to Auschwitz. See Friedman, *Nazis and Good Neighbors*, 209–13.

[98] "Dr. Kliewer to Deutscher Volksbund," April 11, 1943; "Dr. Kliewer to the Deutscher Volksbund in Asuncion," April 11, 1943, translated and enclosed in "MENNONITE COLONIES IN PARAGUAY – DR. FRITZ KLIEWER, WITH ALIASES," September 14, 1943, Box 1, Entry UD 3090 (Paraguay U.S. Embassy, Asunción, Supplemental Confidential General Records, 1944-1947), RG 84, NACP, 5–6. For more on the colony's sentiments about returning to Europe, see "Julius Legiehn to Orie O. Miller," July 9, 1940, f. "Paraguay Fernheim Colony 1940," IX-6-3 Central Correspondence, 1931–85, MCCA.

[99] "INTELLIGENCE REPORT," November 29, 1943 (862.20234/159), Box 1, Entry UD 3090 (Paraguay U.S. Embassy, Asunción, Supplemental Confidential General Records, 1944–1947), RG 84, NACP.

A DANCE OF DEATH/A NEW BEGINNING

The stage was now set for a confrontation between the MCC representatives, their *wehrlos* compatriots, and the VRD (formerly the BDMP). Yet as it turned out, the MCC/*wehrlos* faction mostly sat on the sidelines as the colony's *völkisch* supporters eviscerated their solidarity in an attempt to control their destiny. What had begun as a personality conflict between Kliewer and one of the VRD's younger members quickly morphed into violence and vigilantism after a cantankerous shopkeeper entered the fray. Local events entwined with broader attachments as the colony became entangled in another national narrative – one of US hemispheric hegemony – which brought US legation representatives to the colony at the behest of the excitable dentist, G. Klassen.

The Roosevelt administration made a great show of its "Good Neighbor" policy during the 1930s. Yet US actions during the war signaled a return to the Monroe Doctrine, which had positioned the United States as the hemispheric watchdog against European incursion. Alarmed by events surrounding the Munich Agreement, as early as 1938 Roosevelt declared that "the United States must be prepared to resist attack on the western hemisphere from the North Pole to the South Pole, including all of North America and South America."[100] The United States subsequently stepped up its military preparedness for war as well as its diplomatic, economic, and cultural influence in Latin America. In addition to exporting pro-Allied propaganda (including the films that were shown in the colonies) and employing a range of economic "carrots" and "sticks," a prime example of the United States' new orientation was a massive internment and deportation program, which rounded up 4,058 German-speaking Latin Americans, from Mexico to Chile, and sent them to US internment camps.[101]

---

[100] Henry H. Arnold, "Report of Conference at White House" November 14, 1938, Office of the Chief of Staff, Conference Binder 1, Emergency Measures, 1939–40. Quoted in Stetson Conn and Byron Fairchild, *The Western Hemisphere: The Framework of Hemisphere Defense* (Washington, D.C.: U.S. Government Printing Office, 1960), 3.

[101] Friedman, *Nazis and Good Neighbors*, 2, 129, 164, 226. See also Stephen Fox, "The Deportation of Latin American Germans, 1941–47: Fresh Legs for Mr. Monroe's Doctrine," *Yearbook of German-American Studies* 32, 1997, 117–42; Uwe Lübken, *Bedrohliche Nähe: Die USA und die nationalsozialistische Herausforderung in Lateinamerika, 1937–1945* (Stuttgart: Fritz Steiner, 2004). The program also interned 288 Italian-speaking Latin Americans and 2,264 Japanese-speaking Latin Americans.

Paraguay never deported its suspected Nazis, but the US legation's interest and intervention in the Fernheim Colony reflects an expanding vision of US involvement in Latin America, complete with the belief that the region's governments were naive and feckless, and that their German communities were bastions of Nazi subterfuge. The Paraguayan government's flirtation with fascism made the legation especially sensitive to Nazism, and it pressured the Paraguayan military to monitor and incarcerate suspected Nazis. Yet fears of a growing Nazi presence in Paraguay did not resonate with the country's general population, even under the fascist-leaning Morínigo regime. According to one confidential memorandum written by Morrill Cody, cultural relations attaché to the US legation, in 1941 50 percent of Paraguayans were "completely indifferent to the war," 30 percent were "pro-Allied," 10 percent "favored the axis because they were winning," and 10 percent were "sincerely pro-Axis."[102] Average Paraguayans had more pressing concerns than war in Europe, but that did not stop US officials in Asunción from monitoring them, the German speakers among them, and even the subset of German-speaking Mennonites in the distant Chaco. Like German Mennonites and the Nazi government, American Mennonites and the US government shared the assumption that Paraguay and its Mennonite population would be ideologically better off if they allowed outsiders to direct their fate. And so, fifteen years after its settlement, the Fernheim Colony remained entwined in the political machinations of governments on three continents, though they lived in one of the most remote regions in the world.

The trouble started in late 1942 when Kliewer overextended his authority during a colony-wide celebration. One event required the colony's young people to jump over a fire. The practice was evocative of the deutsche Jugendbewegung (German Youth Movement) practice of jumping through a fire to rededicate oneself to Germanic values. Like a martinet, Kliewer demanded the participation of *all* the colony's young people and this presumably meant anyone younger than thirty. Yet the activity seemed quaint and silly to some of the older attendees who themselves were leaders in the VRD. Some of these young men had joined the Jugendbund nine years earlier and had grown up while Kliewer was in Germany. Now Kliewer wanted to be a dictator. His primary antagonist,

---

[102] Cody notes that the proportion of "indifferent" Paraguayans could range as high as 75 percent. Morrill Cody, "Memorandum to the Ambassador," November 9, 1943, enclosed in dispatch no. 1498 (Asuncion, 1943, 822–848), Container 8, UD 3088 (1936–1961), RG 84, NACP, 1.

Hans Neufeld, claimed; "As I repeatedly tried to defend our feeling that our age was not appropriate to these games, he became increasingly agitated and finally furious. His words still ring clearly in my ears: 'You will obey me!'"[103] Ironically, this conflict between members of the Jugendbund – the very organization that was created to subdue and unify colony youths – paved the way to the biggest disruption of the settlement's peace.

Subsequent confrontations ensued regarding Kliewer's unfair treatment of some VRD members and his injunction against dancing. Class was also an issue. H. Neufeld and his allies, even those who were over thirty, were referred to as "boys" because they did not own land. As a result, they were effectively "second-class citizens" and could not vote in colony elections.[104] Combined with Kliewer's self-styled position as the gatekeeper to Germany, the situation spiraled into a face-off between his supporters and a smaller group clustered around H. Neufeld.

The first sally came from the H. Neufeld group, whose members posted anti-Kliewer posters around the colony on November 1 (a Sunday) that called into question the credentials of Kliewer's doctorate degree. Unwilling to resolve the issue within the bounds of the VRD, on November 6, Kliewer asked *Oberschulze* Legiehn to publicly condemn H. Neufeld's group. His reasoning was that they "do not want to submit."[105] The implication of Kliewer's letter was that he represented peace, unity, and the concerns of the community and that everyone he disagreed with did not. Kliewer's supporters raised their own posters on November 8 (also a Sunday).[106] As usual, Legiehn was indecisive and issued a public statement calling for a moratorium on the issue – there would be no investigation and no attempt at reconciliation.[107] Though neither side apologized or admitted wrongdoing, Kliewer maintained the high ground since he was the leader of the VRD and the colony's intermediary with the DVfP in Asunción. The H. Neufeld group therefore asked Legiehn to give them a copy of his statement showing that the affair

---

[103] Hans (Juan) Neufeld, *Affaire Dr. Fritz Kliewer in Farnheim* [sic] *1940–1944* (Asunción: Hans Neufeld, 1988), 10.

[104] Thiesen, *Mennonite and Nazi?* 290, n. 91.

[105] Fritz Kliewer, "Darlegungen über den Zwischenfall in Philadelphia," November 6, 1942, Nachlaß Dr. F. Kliewer, ACF; P. Klassen *Die deutsch-völkish Zeit*, 94.

[106] "PROTOKOLL: einer Kol.-Versammlung," November 12, 1942, ACF; F[ritz] K[liewer], "Herr Warkentin, auf Ihre Zeilen ...," November 22, 1942, Nachlaß Dr. F. Kliewer, ACF.

[107] "PROTOKOLL: einer Kol.-Versammlung," November 12, 1942.

was finished and would not hurt their chances of returning to Germany in the event that Kliewer became vindictive (and Germany won the war).[108] Perhaps under pressure from Kliewer, Legiehn delayed and then declined to share the statement with H. Neufeld. This, in turn, prompted H. Neufeld and his compatriots to break into Legiehn's office to steal it.[109]

During their search, the H. Neufeld group uncovered something much more interesting (and damning) than the moratorium letter. Apparently, on October 8, 1942, Kliewer had written an unmailed letter addressed to the DVfP in Asunción that requested his and Legiehn's transfer out of the Fernheim colony, since even Kliewer had come to believe that the colonists' loyalty to Germany was insincere.[110] According to Kliewer, "We must make it clear that after three years our people have not advanced beyond mere lip-service in spite of all our labors of instruction and enlightenment. Most of them are so hidebound by religious scruples that they cannot accept the national-socialist idea." Further on he stated, "We are doubtful as to whether there is any object in bringing such people back to Germany ... It might be far better to leave them in peace without letting any idea of leaving this country ever enter their heads." Kliewer's disillusionment went even deeper, as shown by his suggestion that "one could almost begin to doubt the theory of race and blood," owing to its failure to seamlessly tie together such widely disparate groups of people as the Fernheim Mennonites and Nazis in Germany. He concluded by noting with dismay that American volunteers in Fernheim were working to undermine the *völkisch* cause. As a loyal Nazi, Kliewer was ready to jettison his loyalty to the colony. Despite his earlier remonstrance against Wilhelmy's assessment, Kliewer conceded that the settlement's Germanness fell short of Nazi ideals.[111]

---

[108] H. Neufeld, *Affaire Dr. Fritz Kliewer*, 13–14.

[109] Ibid., 14–15; "Protokol einer Schulzenberatung," December 16, 1942, ACF; "Protokol der ausserordentlichen Mitgliederversammlung des Verband der Russlanddeutschen," December, 20, 1942, Nachlaß Dr. F. Kliewer, ACF.

[110] It remains unclear whether a version of the letter was actually sent to Schütz since US embassy correspondences claim that V. Schmidt, or someone acting for him, had "intercepted" such a message. At some point between October 1942 and May 1943, however, V. Schmidt did come into possession of the October 8 letter, which he forwarded to the MCC. See "Frost to Secretary of State," February 18, 1943, 2. This correspondence refers to "Fritz Kliewer to Gerd von Schütz," October 8, 1942, translated in "Vernon H. Schmidt to MCC," May 22, 1943, intercepted by the US Office of Censorship, no. 945, Box C295 (862.20211–862.20211), Entry dec. file 1940–44, RG 59, NACP.

[111] "Kliewer to von Schütz," October 8, 1942, translated in "Vernon H. Schmidt to MCC," May 22, 1943, 2–3.

After the letter was made public Kliewer still held a strong hand, but he was required to account for the letter before a preachers' meeting on December 10, 1942. At the meeting, he conflated the recent break-in with the youth disturbances of ten years prior and placed the blame on the H. Neufeld group.[112] A few days later, Legiehn was called before an assembly of the colony's mayors, but they delayed a decision until a general colony meeting could be held.[113] Kliewer, for his part, tried to put out the flames with the VRD during a special meeting held on December 20. His semantics were impressive. He stated that he had written the letter in a "downcast mood" and even denied that the letter was "real," because "a letter is a conversation between two or more persons, but since the conversation did not materialize, one cannot call the stolen record a letter." The result was that Kliewer retained his standing in the group, the H. Neufeld party was criticized for the break-in, and the controversy was quieted.[114]

H. Neufeld's voluntary departure to the Friesland Colony on January 4, 1943 calmed the situation further, but it also solidified the *völkisch* movement's internal divisions. On the same day, his supporters in the VRD (numbering forty-three individuals) attempted to circumvent the VRD by appealing to Asunción for direct membership of the DVfP. The VRD subsequently declined the request, forwarded a copy of the letter to Kliewer, and maintained that all Mennonites should be united under the same banner. Tensions remained high at a DVfP meeting in Asunción on February 27 when Neufeld's representative, Heinrich Warkentin, verbally "abused" Kliewer after the evening news service.[115] Subsequent negotiations between Kliewer, the H. Neufeld group, and the DVfP, went nowhere and the matter was apparently tabled.

By early 1944, there were other individuals in the Friesland colony besides H. Neufeld who were fed up with Kliewer's leadership of the VRD. Brüdergemeinde leader Kornelius Voth was one of them. In January, he accused Kliewer of no longer following God's path, since he had abandoned his faith for politics. Voth also criticized Kliewer's followers in Friesland for placing national loyalties above religious loyalties.

---

[112] Friedrich Kliewer, "Notizen für die Aussprache mit der Predigerkommission der MBG," December 10, 1942, Nachlaß Dr. F. Kliewer, ACF.

[113] "Protokoll einer Schulzenberatung," December 16, 1942.

[114] "Protokoll der ausserordentlichen Mitgliederversammlung des Verband der Russlanddeutschen," December 20, 1942, Nachlaß Dr. F. Kliewer, ACF.

[115] "DVP to Fritz Kliewer," February 5, 1943, Nachlaß Dr. F. Kliewer, ACF; "Protokoll der Stützpunktleiter-versamlung," February 23, 1943, Nachlaß Dr. F. Kliewer, ACF.

Yet Voth was not wholly against National Socialism. Rather, he claimed that Kliewer had undermined the spirit of National Socialism by telling colony pastors that their religious attitudes hindered the possibility of immigrating to Germany. According to Voth, Hitler was a champion of Christianity and he would surely allow Mennonites to live according to their religious beliefs in peace.[116] With a war in Europe that that was going badly for the Nazis, the VRD's constituency split between the Fernheim and Friesland colonies, its leadership split between Kliewer and H. Neufeld, and its members' impressions of Nazi Germany ranging across a wide interpretative terrain, the colony was ripe for open conflict.

Strangely, it was the erratic accusations of an obscure Mennonite shop-keeper named Abram Martins that unraveled the *völkisch* movement in Fernheim and Friesland. Martens operated a small general store in the Paraguayan military outpost of Fortín Lopez De Filippis, located about 95 km from Filadelfia. He was not a regular face in the colony and those who knew him found him to be quarrelsome.[117] In 1943, he was put out of business when the Fernheim Colony's economic cooperative opened a store in the same town. In January 1944, Legiehn made a trip to purchase equipment in Buenos Aires. Accompanied by Kliewer, he stopped in Asunción to draw up a new statute concerning the colony's administration with a lawyer.[118] Yet the disgruntled Martins apparently got hold of the new statute before Legiehn could return, and denounced the *Oberschulze* in an "unchristian" and "common" public letter. Based on his reading of the statute (and some old grudges), Martins claimed that among "many dark initiatives," Legiehn and Kliewer were liars, that they were trying to create a dictatorship, that Kliewer positioned himself as the gatekeeper to Germany, and that Legiehn was a fraud.[119] There was a bit

---

[116] Kornelius Voth, "Ein Offenes Wort an die M. Bruedergemeinde in der Kolonie Friesland," January 16, 1944, J. H. Franz papers, CMBS. Cited in Thiesen, *Mennonite and Nazi?* 174.

[117] "Julius Legiehn to P. C. Hiebert and Orie O. Miller," April 14, 1944, f. 431, b. 39, P. C. Hiebert papers, MS-37, MLA; Thiesen, *Mennonite and Nazi?* 173.

[118] Information on the statute and the fallout is based on competing (and perhaps unreliable) accounts from G. Klassen and Legiehn: "G. S. Klassen to Walter E. Sewell," March 16, 1944, 1; "G. S. Klassen to Orie O. Miller," March 17, 1944, f. 430, b. 38, P. C. Hiebert papers, MS-37, MLA, 2; "Legiehn to Hiebert and Miller," April 14. See also "Protokoll einer Kolonie-Versammlung," January 8, 1944, ACF.

[119] Abram Martins, "Aufruf," March 1944, ACF (The letter was originally written in February); "Legiehn to Hiebert," April 14, 1944, 2; "John R. Schmidt to MCC," March 18, 1944, f. 431, b. 39, P. C. Hiebert papers, MS-37, MLA. See also D. Loewen, "An den Schulzen in," February 21, 1944, ACF; "Protokoll: einer Amtsberatung," February 24, 1944, ACF.

of truth to his claims, since the colony cooperative represented an economic monopoly that put Martins' business at an unfair disadvantage. Less truthful perhaps was his accusation that Legiehn pursued his schemes with "satanic energy and determination."[120]

G. Klassen claimed that a number of "responsible citizens" were concerned that the new statute gave Legiehn "even more power than Hitler has" and in G. Klassen's own estimation the proposal was "rather radical" and an "absolute dictatorship!" (emphasis in the original).[121] Martin's rumors spread quickly, so the colony was on edge when Legiehn returned on February 24. Colonists called a meeting on March 3, 1944, to discuss the issue, which at this point had practically nothing do with repatriation or *völkisch* ideology.[122] The immediate outcome was the formation of an auditing committee that would (once again) investigate the colony's confidence in its leaders.[123]

One of the auditors, a Peter Rahn, was a strong supporter of Legiehn and Kliewer and rather wished to solve the problem via alternate means.[124] On March 10, he convened a secret meeting composed of Legiehn and Kliewer's supporters and they formed a plan to take a stand against anyone who opposed them.[125] It is unclear whether this meant Martins specifically, or anyone who was against Legiehn and Kliewer generally, but the next day Legiehn voluntarily stepped down from his position as *Oberschulze*.[126] Legiehn's resignation, however, did not thwart his and Kliewer's supporters from forming a posse of vigilantes to confront *all* of their opponents in an attempt to sustain their nationalist hopes through complete local control.

---

[120] Martins, "Aufruf," March 1944.

[121] "Klassen to Miller," March 17, 1944, 3; "Klassen to Sewell," March 16, 1944, 1.

[122] Kliewer's wife, Margarete Dyck, died at some point in February 1944. A US embassy report claims that soon thereafter he began "courting a sister of MARIA BUSSE, the latter being a Nazi Party member and a leader in the Nazi women's organization." See "Re: Dr. Fritz Kliewer, was. Asunción, Paraguay," June 18, 1944, 9.

[123] "Klassen to Miller," March 17, 1944, 2; "Legiehn to Hiebert and Miller," April 14, 1944, 2. See also Thiesen, *Mennonite and Nazi?* 175.

[124] Thiesen cites the announcement, signed by Peter Rahn, from the George S. Klassen papers, AR 920 K63g, CMBS (see *Mennonite and Nazi?* 175), but a 1945 testimony from Legiehn states that his secretary, Peter Klassen, arranged the meeting. See "RE: JULIUS FRIEDRICH LEGIEHN, alias Julius Legiehn," October 30, 1945, enclosed in "John Edgar Hoover to Mr. Frederick B. Lyon," November 29, 1945, Box 6734 (862.20233/1–145 to 862.20234/12–3148, Entry dec. file 1945–49, RG 59, NACP, 3.

[125] Apparently, invitations to the secret meeting were printed in Legiehn's office. "Klassen to Miller," March 17, 2, 4.

[126] Thiesen, *Mennonite and Nazi?* 176.

By this point, the colony had witnessed three failed repatriation schemes including Schröder's two plans and Kliewer's 1943 petition. Owing to Nazi reversals in Southern and Eastern Europe, the colonists' hopes were quickly fading. By the beginning of 1944, the Fernheim Mennonites sensed, but did not completely accept, that the time for building a collective narrative based on repatriation to Germany was over. Simultaneously, the advocates of that narrative – the VDA and the Nazi government – were increasingly focused on other matters: eastward toward the destruction of the Jews and other minorities and inward, toward their own survival. They no longer had the ability to project a compelling narrative of (trans)National Socialism. The vacuum left by their failure gave rise to terrifying ambiguities for the Fernheim Colony's *völkisch* contingent. As in life, so too in death, they repurposed German national glory as local glory and German national trauma as local trauma. The colony now plunged into violence as a sort of collective catharsis for its troubled history and failed aspirations. Martins was no ideologue, and H. Neufeld's problems with Kliewer were mostly personal in nature. The events of March 1944 therefore had less to do with which "side" would "win" and more to do with colonists' pent-up anxieties as to whether Nazism was a transcendent force in the world.

So it began. The night of March 11 was bright and clear, with enough light from the waning moon to see without a lantern.[127] The details (and veracity) of the accounts provided by the H. Neufeld/Martins and the Legiehn/Kliewer sides are sketchy, but according to Neufeld, the pro-Legiehn/Kliewer vigilantes' called H. Neufeld's brother, Heinrich, out of his house, beat him until he was bloody, and threatened that he would "get it better" tomorrow.[128] By contrast, Kliewer's brother, Franz Kliewer, stated that he was unaware of the event until he was en route to Filadelfia to chat with J. Günther and listen to the radio in the latter's yard. According to Franz Kliewer's story, it was here that he learned that a group of about ten or fifteen Legiehn/Kliewer supporters planned to visit Martins and demand his silence.[129]

After threatening Martins, Legiehn and Kliewer's supporters returned to Günther's yard. Soon thereafter, about ten armed men walked slowly past the front of the house. Apparently, someone had alerted the H. Neufeld group, who now took it upon themselves to defend Martins. Franz Kliewer stated that "one stopped and loaded a revolver before our

---

[127] Ibid., 176.   [128] H. Neufeld, *Affaire Dr. Fritz Kliewer*, 20.
[129] Franz Kliewer, "Aufzeichnung von Franz Kliewer," n.d., Nachlaß Dr. F. Kliewer, ACF.

eyes."[130] In response, the Legiehn/Kliewer contingent sent out riders to muster a force of about sixty men to find the prattling Martins and intimidate any H. Neufeld supporters that they happened to encounter. The vigilantes were armed with clubs, iron rods, heavy cattle whips, bush knives, and a few guns when they confronted two of H. Neufeld's men in front of Martins' house. Sharp words led to harsh blows. A running battle ensued between the groups as the vigilantes moved from house to house searching for Martins.[131] The Legiehn/Kliewer vigilantes finally decided to confront H. Warkentin, who was H. Neufeld's closest confidant in the Fernheim Colony. When they approached the house, Warkentin's mother stormed out of the door and called the men "Mahknovtsy," a pejorative referring to the anarchist Nestor Makhno, who terrorized Ukrainian Mennonites during the Russian Civil War. The insult worked on religious and national levels, by labeling the posse as (irreligious) anarchists and conflating them with their former oppressors and Germany's current enemy, the Soviet Union. Franz Kliewer reported that least one person brandished a gun, but after the confrontation with Warkentin's mother, the vigilantes skulked away.[132]

The US volunteers, J. Schmidt and G. Klassen, were notified of the situation when one of the victims came to J. Schmidt for medical aid. He proceeded to wake the dentist G. Klassen, who lived next door. G. Klassen was an excitable man and concerned with decorum. He grabbed his tropical hat (it was past midnight) and his gun, to "lock horns" with Kliewer. Before he left, his wife admonished him to "put that gun down," an order with which he grudgingly complied. J. Schmidt and G. Klassen then dashed to Kliewer's home, stood outside his window, and called on him to account for the fracas. Apparently, Kliewer acted as though he was unaware of what had happened and J. Schmidt and G. Klassen eventually returned home.[133]

Against the instructions of J. Schmidt, the authorized MCC leader in the colony, G. Klassen called the Paraguayan military outpost at Isla Po'i the next morning to dispatch a truck in case there was further violence.[134] While J. Schmidt hoped to deal with the situation through Mennonite channels, G. Klassen was eager to flex control over the *völkisch* movement

---

[130] Ibid.   [131] Ibid., "Klassen to Miller," March 17, 1944, 2–3.

[132] Franz Kliewer, "Aufzeichnung von Franz Kliewer," 178–79.

[133] Personal communication from John R. Schmidt to John D. Thiesen, August 10, 1990. See Thiesen, *Mennonite and Nazi?* 179–80.

[134] Ibid., 180; "Klassen to Miller," March 17, 1944, 3.

immediately, and especially over Kliewer. Meanwhile, rumors spread like wildfire through the colony. People poured into Filadelfia to see what would come of the previous night's disturbance. Finally, at about four in the afternoon the CPS men, Legiehn, and colony leaders persuaded the crowd to go home. An army truck with four soldiers arrived soon thereafter but proceeded on to Lopez De Filippis without incident. Nevertheless, word soon got back to Asunción that there was trouble in the colonies, piquing the interest of the Paraguayan and US governments.[135]

On March 13, 1944, the KfK denounced the violence that had taken place two days earlier in order to distance the colony from the event and those who instigated it. Another colony-wide meeting was scheduled for the next morning. About 275 people attended. As stated by G. Klassen, it was not "only young boys in the mob" but "Sunday School teachers, choir leaders, preachers sons, etc.," which in his view was especially troubling.[136] Colonists debated a change in colony administration and the conduct of the rioters, and they resolved to give the irascible Martins two months to leave the colony.[137] Despite G. Klassen's wish to have avoided the meeting by being "lifted ... by the boot straps into the good old U.S.A.," he and J. Schmidt argued that Kliewer should be forced to leave the colony, and threatened to return to the United States if he was not.[138] G. Klassen wished to see Legiehn leave as well.[139] He stated that he made his demands for himself, the MCC, and (significantly) the US government, the last of which he apparently represented.[140] At a second meeting on March 24, the victims were allowed to decide their attackers' punishments, which resulted in fourteen participants having their voting privileges suspended for one year and six participants – all underage –

[135] United States interest in the Mennonite colonies and the country's attitudes to Nazi Germany is revealed in documents generated by its Paraguayan embassy, including Philip's 1939 report. What especially caught the embassy's attention was an intercepted letter from Kliewer that stated he was prepared to "create separate fronts." See the first page of the section "German School System" in the report "Frank G. Siscoe to Mr. Ambassador," December 22, 1942, Box 1, Entry UD 3090 (Paraguay U.S. Embassy, Asuncion, Supplemental Confidential General Records, 1944–1947), RG 84, NACP.

[136] "Klassen to Miller," March 17, 1944, 3–4.
[137] "PROTOKOLL: einer allgemeinen Siedlerversammlung," March 14, 1944, ACF.
[138] "Klassen to Miller," March 17, 1944, 4.
[139] "Klassen to Sewell," March 16, 1944, 2.
[140] "PROTOKOLL," March 14, 1944. See also "Klassen to the American Embassy," April 14, 1944, reproduced in "Re: Dr. Fritz Kliewer, was. Asunción, Paraguay," June 18, 1944, 9.

being sentenced to one month's labor. The attackers admitted their wrongdoing and the victims assured colony leaders and their assailants that they would not retaliate.[141] Nevertheless, Fernheimers remained anxious that their actions would hurt the colony if they were collectively placed on a Nazi blacklist. Their fears were not misplaced, as the US legation was already considering twenty-six German nationals living in Paraguay, including Kliewer, for deportation and internment in the US.[142]

In his summary of the March 11 incident, George D. Henderson, third secretary of the US legation, reported that Paraguayan "Minister of Interior PAMPLIEGA (who was informed of the Nazi riot by Ambassador FROST) instructed Colonel Andino, Commander of the Chaco Military Territory, to detain Kliewer and Legiehn and send them to Asunción, with the idea of sending both of them to the concentration camp which was being provided for objectionable Nazis by the Paraguayan Government at this time."[143] Thus, the US legation insinuated itself between the colony and the Paraguayan government so as to monitor the Nazi activities of the former and the anti-Nazi activities of the latter. Yet an April 22 telegram intercepted by US agents addressed from Kliewer to Oscar Ketterer – Director of Asunción's German schools – indicates that Kliewer and Legiehn had remained in Puerto Casado and had received instructions from Paraguay's Minister of the Interior, Paampliega, to report to Villa San Pedro, which was much closer to the colonies.[144] Subsequent intercepted telegrams suggest that Ketterer successfully pressured the Ministry of the Interior to allow Kliewer to return

---

[141] "Julius Legiehn to P. C. Hiebert and Orie O. Miller," April 14, 1944. See also "Akt der Vermittlungskommission der Kolonie Fernheim," n.d., ACF.

[142] "Re: Dr. Fritz Kliewer, was. Asunción, Paraguay," June 18, 1944, Box 5563 [mislabeled 5564] (862.20210–862.20210), Entry dec. file 1940–44, RG 59, NACP, 1. On April 2, 1943, Frost likewise recommended that Heinrichs and all shipments to the "Fernheim Cooperativa," which were consigned through him, should be registered on the United States' "Confidential List of Unsatisfactory Consignees." See "Frost to Secretary of State," April 2, 1943.

[143] Thiesen states that Kliewer left on March 20 to find new work but subsequently quotes Henderson's report at length, which explains that Andino dispatched Kliewer and Legiehn to Puerto Casado shortly after March 11. See, *Mennonite and Nazi?* 184 and 188; George D. Henderson, "Memorandum of Trip to Chaco re Mennonite Colony," June 17, 1944, enclosed in dispatch no. 2195, Box 5563 [mislabeled 5564] (862.20210– 862.20210), Entry dec. file 1940–44, RG 59, NACP, 2–3.

[144] "Re: Dr. Fritz Kliewer, was. Asunción, Paraguay," June 18, 1944, Box 5563 [mislabeled 5564] (862.20210–862.20210), Entry dec. file 1940–44, RG 59, NACP, 1.

to the Fernheim Colony, much to the chagrin of the US legation.[145] By May 15, Kliewer and Legiehn had briefly visited Asunción but surreptitiously returned to Fernheim.[146]

On May 31, 1944, Henderson accompanied three Paraguayan military officers – Major Careaga, Major de Filippis, and Lieutenant Colonel Meyer – to Fernheim to bring Kliewer and Legiehn to justice. The officials' first stop was G. Klassen's home. G. Klassen reported that Legiehn lived less than fifty yards away and that Kliewer lived nearby on his father's ranch. After phoning Andino (now a general) to ask how to proceed, the officials visited Legiehn and Kliewer and gave them notice that they should report to Andino the next day.[147] Once "caught," the men were sentenced to a Paraguayan military internment camp in Villa San Pedro to await their fate. Soon thereafter, officials rescinded the order and the men were sent to the village of Barranqueritas, located near Friesland, where they taught school.[148] After the war, Paraguayan authorities in Asunción questioned the men and searched their houses but by the end of 1947, they were allowed to return to the colony.[149] The colony gave Legiehn work in its economic cooperative and Kliewer remained in Asunción. In 1952, both men moved with their families to a Mennonite settlement in Brazil.[150]

Thus, US Mennonites collaborated with the Paraguayan government and an increasingly imperialist US government to (1) assert Paraguayan control over a region that Paraguayans had scant knowledge of and (2) impound a Paraguayan (but also Polish and German) Mennonite who supported the repatriation of Russian-born Mennonites under the auspices of the Nazi government in Germany. G. Klassen deemed Kliewer to be entirely un-Mennonite and helped "worldly" US and Paraguayan authorities impound him, even as Kliewer deemed G. Klassen to be an American interloper in the colony's rightful Nazi-German-Mennonite destiny. Much was lost in translation, as nationalist ends blurred with transnational means in a highly local situation. Recalling the debate between the MCC and the German government over where the Moscow refugees should settle (Brazil versus Paraguay) in 1929, Mennonitism and nationalism were again purveyed to colonists through contradictory transnational vectors.

---

[145] Ibid.   [146] Henderson, "Memorandum of Trip," June 17, 1944, 2–3.   [147] Ibid.
[148] J. Edgar Hoover, cover letter to "Re: Dr. Fritz Kliewer, was. Asunción, Paraguay," June 18, 1944, Box 5563 [mislabeled 5564] (862.20210–862.20210), Entry dec. file 1940–44, RG 59, NACP.
[149] Thiesen, *Mennonite and Nazi?* 190–91, 200.   [150] Ibid., 200–1.

After Kliewer and Legiehn had been taken into custody, colony members debated whether it was right to involve Paraguayan and US authorities in their local problems. This was a surprising concern, since they had actively sought outside influence in their affairs since the colony's inception. Perhaps they felt guilty about Kliewer and Legiehn's fate, or they had finally found their elusive group cohesion via somewhat embarrassing means. Paradoxically, the colony's *völkisch* remnant structured their argument against outside involvement around the Mennonite ideal of nonresistance. According to Leslie E. Reed, first secretary at the US legation, "The pro-Nazi elements had been criticizing some of the colonists for having complained to the legation regarding the attitude of the Nazi organizers. The criticisms were based on the ground that such complaints ... were incompatible with the Mennonite doctrine of nonresistance."[151] It is unclear upon what interpretation of nonresistance the *völkisch* supporters based their argument, but they may have understood the concept as a mandate to not involve outsiders in community politics – though they certainly did not extend this criticism to the VDA. Alternately, they may have been simply trying to use the rhetoric of their *wehrlos* foes to justify their position, a tactic that was too clever by half.

Another argument emerged a few months later in the form of an anonymously published document titled *Das Mennonitische Zentralkomitee als politisches Werkzeug* (The Mennonite Central Committee as a Political Tool). The author took for granted that the colonists' most natural and valued allegiance was to the German nation but that they had been hoodwinked by a scheming MCC, which had destroyed their *völkisch* unity through a diabolical pact with the US government. Though this argument was flawed in both logic and content, the author stated that the Fernheim Colony had accepted the organization's aid without realizing that its representatives "came to us not only as Mennonites but as Americans." The author concluded that acting under "Mennonite pretenses, [the MCC] did the dirty work of the North American government" by banning Kliewer and Legiehn from the Fernheim Colony.[152] Thus, it was Mennonites from the United States who were trouble-making nationalists, not the Fernheim Colony's

---

[151] Leslie E. Reed, "Memorandum," December 7, 1944, enclosed in dispatch no. 238 (862.20234/12–744), Box 1, Entry UD 3090 (Paraguay U.S. Embassy, Asunción, Supplemental Confidential General Records, 1944–1947), RG 84, NACP, 1.

[152] Anonymous, *Das Mennonitische Zentralkomitee als politisches Werkzeug* (1944), MLA. The document is also available on the MLA website: http://mla.bethelks.edu/arc hives/ms_139/folder_23_mcc_als_werkzeug/, last accessed June 7, 2018.

völkisch leaders. Yet by this point, the debate was over. The author did not promote the *völkisch* cause – and by extension the Nazi Party's enduring glory – but instead offered a self-conscious excuse for its failure, thereby exonerating the movement and disentangling it from a future that was no longer tenable.

The intrigue that swirled around the Fernheim fiasco eventually subsided as the colonists' attention returned to more practical matters and the MCC demonstrated that it would support the colony indefinitely. The postwar years brought a flood of MCC volunteers from North America to serve in the colony's school system and provide other services. On the international level, Bender and the MCC sidelined Unruh, who was caught up in the denazification process after the war and no longer had access to the same channels and quantities of aid as Mennonites in the United States.[153] The *völkisch* era in the Fernheim Colony was over. There would be no Nazi deliverance to a German-controlled Russia. The colonists would remain in Paraguay.

The events that transpired in early 1944 represented a violent release for the colony – a "dance of death," or a "rite of spring," – to end the colony's winter of ambiguity. It likewise augured a new and permanent life in the Chaco. Their imagined repatriation to Europe – Harder's "insatiable longing" – remained unfulfilled and so the Fernheim colonists were compelled to look for new meanings and attachments elsewhere. Some Fernheimers had already made peace with remaining in the Chaco by channeling their energies into Licht den Indianern! and aligning themselves with the MCC. It is no surprise that the individuals who could not accept the path of remaining in the Chaco – the Kliewers and the H. Neufelds of the colony – responded most intensely when the possibility of a victorious return to a "Greater Germany" began losing its influence. As Nazi Germany's defeat began to look increasingly likely by mid-1944, the Fernheim Colony was already charting a new direction, as a *Mennonite* colony in Paraguay that was not as utopian as repatriation to Eastern Europe, but serviceable enough.

Interestingly, the stress and rupture caused by the quick reversal of the Fernheim Colony's collective narrative – from an anticipated comic

---

[153] Unruh voluntarily testified at the Nuremberg trials in defense of Werner Lorenz, the head of the VoMi. See Gerhard Rempel, "Review of *Fügungen und Führungen: Benjamin Heinrich Unruh, 1881–1959: Ein Leben im Geiste christlicher Humanität und im Dienste der Nächstenliebe*, by Heinrich B. Unruh," *Mennonite Quarterly Review* 84, no. 2 (2010): 278.

outcome to a tragic one – was left largely unexamined in the postwar years. Guilty speculation on the question "What if the Nazis *had* won?" is perhaps the reason why there was no objective published account of Fernheim's Nazi movement until 1990, when colony historian Peter P. Klassen released his book *Die Deutsch-völkische Zeit in Der Kolonie Fernheim, Chaco, Paraguay, 1933–1945*. By this point, however, when the key players in Fernheim's Nazi movement were either elderly or had passed, the colony could finally afford to confront its alternative narratives and mythologies without ego or shame. Mythology sows unity, history sows ambiguity, and somewhere between the two, communities remember their pasts.

It is easy to imagine that the Nazi Party's racist hubris and martial appeals found a receptive audience in every German-speaking community the world over. In 1941, Franklin D. Roosevelt declared in a radio address, "Hitler's advance guards" are gaining "footholds, bridgeheads in the New World, to be used as soon as he has gained control of the oceans."[154] Scores of pulp history books, magazines, and comics have subsequently burnished the perception that Nazi spies were found in every German-speaking community during the war years.[155] Yet this is to unfairly privilege military intrigue and politics above other interests. As Friedman notes, the Nazi mobilization of Latin America's German speakers "generated a kind of surface response commensurate with the effort that went into it."[156]

The Fernheim colonists certainly disliked the Soviet Union, cheered a Nazi victory, and were flattered by the DAI and VDA's attentions. When the opportunity arose for a new destiny in a fondly remembered environment, they readily reinterpreted their Germanness as Nazism, if only to profit from Germany's conquest. Despite Kliewer and the BDMP/VRD's agitation, colonists were generally required to focus on the mundane realities of life: the meager household budget, the next rain, cotton prices, and so on. Meanwhile, the war's effects on the Menno Colony were practically nonexistent. Menno Colony colonists was mostly absorbed in expanding both their land holdings and cotton production.[157] Though

---

[154] Buhite and Levy, eds., *FDR's Fireside Chats*, 192.
[155] Cited in Francis MacDonnell, *Insidious Foes: The Axis Fifth Column and the American Home Front* (New York: Oxford University Press, 1995), 7.
[156] Friedman, *Nazis and Good Neighbors*, 39.
[157] Abram W. Hiebert and Jacob T. Friesen, *Eine bewegte Geschichte ... die zu uns spricht: Materialien zur Entwicklungsgeschichte der Kolonie Menno: Ein Beitrag zur 75. Gedenkfeier* (Asunción, Paraguay: Chortitzer Komitee, Colonia Menno, 2002), 139–49.

the colony suffered as a result of decreased imports and exports during to the war, the year 1944 was neither the end nor the beginning of anything, but simply a continuation of the colony's local rhythms. That year was no more a turning point for them than 1933 or 1945 – ostensibly pivotal dates in the history of any "German" community. Menno Colony Mennonites wanted to retain their Germanness without being labeled German – and certainly not Nazi – and the Nazi representatives in Paraguay surely knew it. According to a 1942 letter written by Kliewer, "Almost two years ago when the subject of the settlers of the Menno colony came up for discussion at the [German] legation, and after all they are still of German blood and speech, I was told: 'Leave these people in peace – we want nothing more from them.'"[158] Such local-level distinctions matter because they demonstrate, in miniature, the breadth of opinions on National Socialism among Latin American *Auslandsdeutsche*. Even in communities that were ostensibly homogeneous, there was a range of opinions on national identifications that baffled outside observers who clung to the notion that nationalist ideology had the irresistible power to standardize large populations.

The Fernheim colonists were refugees, and their story should be understood as such. Their most pressing concerns were the elusive goals of stability and continuity. The disintegration of the Nazi's *völkisch* narrative – a seductive though ultimately unrealizable historical path – was a "tragic" development for the Fernheim colonists. Their forced expulsion from the Soviet Union was an initial trauma that they had experienced as independent families. Now they experienced a second trauma as a group. With the first trauma, others persecuted them. With the second, they persecuted each other. During the 1930s, in the middle of these tragic bookends, the Fernheim Mennonites devised a range of "comedic" destinies – as the redeemers of the Chaco's land and people through their Mennonite or German "genius." Yet it was tragedy that had brought them together and tragedy that kept them together.

The end of the Second World War did not make the Fernheim colonists less German. It simply made them a different kind of German. After the war, the colony's schools redoubled their efforts to educate their youths in German *and* Paraguayan culture. Their example reflects larger patterns among *Auslandsdeutsche*. Hoerder states that most members of the German-language diaspora reinvented themselves after the two world wars in a "quick drawingboard-like process" of disassociating themselves

---

[158] "Kliewer to von Schütz," October 8, 1942, 2–3.

from the German nation state but not their local German culture. Eventually, he argues, even these cultural markers were eroded or modified beyond recognition. Nevertheless, the Mennonites of Paraguay are unique. Hoerder claims, "Only among the distinct group of the Mennonites did a diasporic connectedness between Russian, North American, and South American colonies last through the 1950s and beyond – but this was religiocultural, not ethnocultural."[159] In their own ways, both the Menno Colony and the MCC had won the day: the former by maintaining the same type of Mennoniteness and Germanness that it had possessed before the war, and the latter through a continually evolving theology that was comfortable in a new world order of democracy and free-market capitalism.

"Emancipation" and "final solutions" are two sides of the same coin. They are both modern preoccupations.[160] The modern world celebrates freedom from social norms, political conventions, intellectual constraints, and territorial boundaries. It celebrates freedom from history and from narratives, even as it creates its own in the process of destroying others. Emancipation is the underlying sensibility of all pronouncements that humans have finally wrested control of their destiny from the gods. Yet even if there are no gods, there are always narratives, stories that arrange the vastness of time and space, provide humans with hope and fear, and make it possible for them to understand history and mythology, and – more often than not – entwine the two.

As the Menno Colony allowed the narrative of progress and its modernist teleology to wash over them – or rather, slosh them from shore to shore – they battened down the hatches and refused to accept that humans control events or that it was possible to be emancipated from the divine order. Though they remained embroiled in their own disputations, which kept them far from the Christian ideal of fraternal love, they uniformly regarded emancipation and earthly "final solutions" as deceptions that only lead to Babylon and to death.

The Fernheim colonists, composed as they were of competing factions with competing aspirations, viewed emancipation from the Chaco as emancipation from uncertainty. It was, perhaps, the only panacea for the collective ambiguities that the world had thrust upon them. For this reason, their identification as refugees – with all of the tenuous hopes and

---

[159] Dirk Hoerder, "The German-Language Diasporas: A Survey, Critique, and Interpretation," *Diaspora* 11, no. 1 (2002): 33.

[160] Modris Eksteins, *Rites of Spring* (Boston and New York: Mariner Books, 2000), xiii.

terrifying uncertainties embodied in the term – remained perhaps their most enduring condition, from their settlement in 1930 to the chaos of 1944. They remained refugees until they could no longer imagine relocating elsewhere. They remained refugees until they could reinterpret their confinement in the Chaco as emancipation from ambiguity. They remained refugees until their only option was to reinterpret their fate as destiny and to transform their "tragic" narrative into a "comedic" one themselves.

Conclusion

Schism in the soul [and] in the body social, will not be resolved by any scheme of return to the good old days (archaism), or by programs guaranteed to render an ideal projected future (futurism), or even by the most realistic, hardheaded work to weld together again the deteriorating elements. Only birth can conquer death – the birth, not of the old thing again, but of something new.

Joseph Campbell, *The Hero with a Thousand Faces*

During the twentieth century, large groups of people, united as nation states, engaged in a fevered quest to draw imaginary lines across the globe. National populations and territorial boundaries consecrated the inexorable triumph of homogenization as a social imperative and "progress" as a moral imperative. Some Mennonites – such as those living in Germany – were receptive to this development. They united with other nationally minded individuals within a bounded territory, created nationally based confessional organizations, and established historical chronologies that legitimated their nation's triumphal place in the new order. Yet there were always alternate trajectories other than the nation-state paradigm. For example, many Weimar-era Germans looked abroad to imagine a transnational network of Germans that stood in economic solidarity with the German state. Mennonite intellectuals in North America likewise imagined a global web of brethren that would tie together Mennonites living in a variety of "safe" national frameworks. The concerns of Mennonite intellectuals in Germany and North America therefore mirror to a certain degree Germany's erratic geopolitical visions during the early twentieth century, as each group struggled to determine whether a nation or a denomination should be consolidated within a specific territory or form a transnational alliance of independent enclaves.

Both options required individuals to participate in "imagined communities," whether within a consolidated geographic area or dispersed throughout the world.[1] Yet other courses remained viable too. Some Mennonite *Gemeinden*, such as the individuals who created the Menno Colony, strategically drew on multiple identifications – as farmers, German-speakers, and Mennonites – to stay in motion and preserve their local cultures. Finally, there were others who slipped between the cracks of nations and confessions alike. The Mennonites who formed the Fernheim Colony, for example, wanted to remain Mennonites in Russia, until the Soviets forced them to live by their wits and grasp at whatever identifications seemed most beneficial in the moment.

These different avenues were not unique to Mennonites. The years between 1870 and 1945 saw a massive redistribution of all kinds of people across the globe. How did this happen? How did a nation-state paradigm that was so misunderstood and that negatively affected so many individuals appear so natural and inevitable to so many others? One could create an index of political, economic, and social factors that explain this development, but it would simply ground nation states in their own cosmologies, which are predicated on humans' mastery of time and space. Nationalist writers articulated a curated chronology of the world that legitimated a specific groups' dominance over a particular space. Using primordial national mythologies that relied on political events as well as Marxist scholarship that relied on economic ones, governments legitimated their chronologies through theories of dialectical materialism and the "awakening" of national consciousness. In short, they created new mythologies – new rationalities – that glorified progress and homogenization. Like other Western mythologies, "it was not their belief that their God was the true God but their belief that all other Gods were false that proved decisive" in singling out and then persecuting those who did not join in.[2] This was a process of consent and coercion, but it was not merely a social, political, or economic one. It was a narrative one as well.

Russia's German-speaking Mennonites – with their strange customs and multiple identifications – were square pegs in the round holes of idealized national profiles. They did not fit. Or perhaps the analogy works the other way around: German-speaking Mennonites were round

---

[1] Benedict Anderson, *Imagined Communities: Reflections on the Origins and Spread of Nationalism* (London: Verso, 1983).

[2] Northrop Frye, *The Great Code: The Bible and Literature*, ed. Alvin A. Lee. (Toronto: University of Toronto Press, Scholarly Publishing Division, 2006), 134.

pegs in the square holes of nationality, since they fit various profiles, albeit awkwardly. This was a blessing and a curse, as it allowed them to move out of harm's way but provoked their relocation in the first place. In various national contexts – Russia, Canada, Germany, and Paraguay – German-speaking Mennonites were labeled as Germans and consequently fit into a larger historical debate about the variegated nature of the German-language diaspora. The kaleidoscope of significations swirling around the colonies, and by extension other German-speaking communities, was highly disturbing to German governments and host governments that had little patience for hyphenated identifications as they set about crafting their own national narratives.

During the early twentieth century, the German state and the thousands of German-speaking communities outside its borders seldom shared a sense of unity or a similar trajectory, though this did not keep the state from trying to cultivate one – from the cultural and economic connections of the Kaiserreich, to the racial and economic connections of the Third Reich. Appeals were often grounded in heavy-handed injunctions or high-minded pleas that lent a sense of immediacy, peril, or glamor to the project. Unsurprisingly, host countries and their presses often paid more attention to Reich propaganda (and feared it) than they paid to the articulations and actions of their own German-speaking populations. After all, the intrigues of a fifth column infiltrating a given country through the nefarious actions of its "foreign" minority are better narrative fodder for building a shared, national story than focusing on "foreign" citizens' workaday lives. The former portends a dramatic reversal for the host nation's fate unless immediate, collective action is taken. The latter is aimless and boring. Nationalist stories spun from the pens of journalists and politicians have to be riveting. They have to be "good" if they are to unite a constituency.

In the midst of hardening nationalist molds and national narratives that sanctified this development, separatist Mennonites adhered to a mythology that transcended time and space. They anachronistically interpreted modern events in Russia, Canada, and Paraguay through an assemblage of stories chosen from the Old and New Testaments – a timespan of roughly 4,000 years that meanders across the Mediterranean world, heaven, and hell – to legitimate their actions and their cosmology. These Mennonites found ready answers to questions about Russian military conscription in first-century Jerusalem, and answers to questions about Canadian public schooling in ancient Babylon. It was all the same. There was nothing new under the sun.

Carving a middle path between nationalists and separatist Mennonites were associative Mennonites – such as Bender and D. Toews – who used history and theology to weave a story that legitimated a clear set of religious principles that were amenable to modern, democratic governments. An important by-product of this development entailed locating spaces where Mennonites could retain a specific set of confessional peculiarities, in exchange for their political and economic loyalty. Initially, this proposition was confusing to governments and separatist Mennonites alike. Governments were confused by Mennonite intellectuals' confessional peculiarities while separatists Mennonites were confused by Mennonite intellectuals' political dealings. It took decades of conference- and institution-building, money, and publicity, to make this vision a reality – developments that were altogether unimaginable before the turn of the century. Above all, it took the dissemination and acceptance of the notion that this particular Mennonite trajectory was historically and theologically ordained and that modern, democratic governments represented a good thing for the confession.

Governments and religious groups strove to clarify their collective narratives to each other, but ended up rearticulating their own mythologies to themselves and their constituencies. Humans cannot accept new information that does not, in some way, reflect their own reality; so the German government parlayed conventional wisdom about *Auslandsdeutsche* to recast Mennonites as long-lost Germans, the MCC recast the colonists as North American-style Mennonites, and host countries labeled them as "German farmers." Separatist Mennonites could not convey their religious cosmology to government authorities, so they settled in places where they did not need to be understood. This was a moving target – Russia, Canada, Paraguay – so they relied on concepts that governments did understand, such as their ethnicity and economic productivity, to make their case. Their movement inevitability brought them to the margins (or battlegrounds) of state sovereignty, where they remained, for a time. Governments likewise tried to convey their national cosmologies to separatist Mennonites, but the only narrative tools at their disposal were the ones that they had created themselves, and so officials eventually ejected separatist Mennonites from their territories. Sometimes – as was the case with the Nazis who visited the Fernheim Colony – government representatives were heartened that Mennonites were receptive to specific aspects of their nationalist mythologies, but were dismayed to learn that they were interested mostly for local purposes. Such encounters testify to the fact that foreign concepts – articulated through ideology and theology – cannot be bestowed on a population but can only be interpreted into (or contaminated by?) local vernaculars.

Communities and nations cannot exist without consensus. Dissenting narratives – large or small – within the body politic are existential threats because they cast doubt on the naturalness of the dominant narrative. Speaking in theatrical terms, incongruent actors on the national stage compromise the audience's suspension of disbelief. Thus, the Menno colonists fell out of favor with each country that tried to force their communities into a nationalist mold, because they refused to play the part. They performed their own drama, for the benefit of a closed audience, that took them across several national stages. At the risk of overextending the analogy, the Fernheim colonists sampled different roles on different stages – flitting from one to the other over the course of fifteen years. Yet they often wore the wrong costume for the wrong performance, thereby confusing an impatient audience. They were not "German enough" during Wilhelmy's visit in 1937, nor "Mennonite enough" during the North American missionaries' visit in 1940.

Group narratives do not exist in a vacuum, they must be acknowledged – internally and externally and either positively or negatively – in order to be real. For the Menno colonists, outside validation was a negative process. They defined themselves in opposition to outside interests; in fact, they defined themselves against every entity that was not a part of their group. Negative validation gives rise to a very specific theology about nearly every aspect of life: clothing, conduct, occupation, and so on. As outsiders evaluated and attempted to influence the loyalties of separatist Mennonites these groups cultivated a sense of continuity and internal coherence that rendered the barrage of influences, recommendations, and demands uncompelling. Alternately, the Fernheim colonists hoped to define themselves in positive cooperation with outside interests at the local, national, and transnational levels. Positive external validations entail a process whereby one group – in this case, the Fernheim Colony – wishes to align with another group – in this case, German Nazis or North American Mennonites. Continuity is replaced by contingency: a new revelation or the rediscovery of an old one draws a group into closer orbit with others. Yet the Fernheim Colony's path was fraught with ambiguity because their sundry identifications were at loggerheads: their Paraguayan citizenship versus their German nationality and their German nationality versus their Mennonite religion. A group that seeks positive external validation consequently embraces a fluid interpretation of nearly everything – culture, customs, and politics – as time progresses. This process is mostly future-directed. In the words of artist Paul Klee, "One deserts the realm of the here and now to transfer one's activity into a realm of the yonder where total affirmation is possible. Abstraction."[3]

Ultimately, we must reimagine the way we understand how populations construct their cosmologies, merge their mythologies, and project collective narratives on to sacred and secular eschatologies. The ever-present now is always a handmaiden to memories and expectations, plans and happenstances ("twists") that gel, however abstrusely, into a story. These narrative umbilical cords give life to individuals and societies. They are as gossamer as they are resilient – cobwebs that we spin and become entangled in. In short, humans live inside stories, large and small, and analyzing these stories is key to understanding human activity.

The effects of government persecution on ethno-religious diasporas are illuminated and explained by analyzing the national and religious narratives that provoked their persecution and sustained their migration. On a broader level, collective narratives play a critical role in how we understand group affinities and "imagined communities." Narratives are not static, they are not predictable, and seldom do they fuse to other narratives without a great deal of contortion. Even when they do, they quickly separate out again. In the words of poet William Butler Yeats – who saw Europe's narrative of progress incinerate in the flames of the First World War – "things fall apart, the center cannot hold."[4]

There is another poem, written after another world war, a war whose violence revealed with ghastly precision the modern revulsion toward multiple, hybrid, or transient identities, personal narratives that are not easily summarized in what is perhaps the most terrifyingly intimate yet colorless book of all: the passport. It is poet Robert Frost's "Directive" and its opening lines are as follows:

> Back out of all this now too much for us,
> Back in a time made simple by the loss
> Of detail, burned, dissolved, and broken off...

Frost's narrative takes the form of a journey, a personal exodus from a world that is no longer coherent to him. He takes the reader down a neglected path, through a forest, to a house near a forgotten stream.

[3] Paul Klee, *The Diaries of Paul Klee, 1898–1918*, ed. Felix Klee (Berkeley and Los Angeles: University of California Press, 1964), 313.
[4] William Butler Yeats, "The Second Coming," *The Collected Poems of W. B. Yeats*, ed. Richard J. Finneran (New York: Scribner, 1996), 187.

His withdrawal is complete since he "only has at heart [our] getting lost" and the goal is redemption, for at the stream we will find our "watering place" where we will "drink and be whole again beyond confusion."[5] Yet Frost is not taking us back to a place. He is taking us back in time. Or rather, he is removing us from time and space altogether. By escaping the world, Frost wished to escape both history and progress – the interminable and incoherent crashing of events described by philosopher Walter Benjamin in his interpretation of Paul Klee's *Angelus Novus*. H. A. L. Fischer likewise apprehended the demise of a narrative of progress in his 1935 *History of Europe*,

Men wiser and more learned than I have discerned in history a plot, a rhythm, a predetermined pattern. These harmonies are concealed from me. I can see only one emergency following upon another as wave follows upon wave.[6]

Benjamin and Fisher shared the notion that nothing in the past makes historical sense. This is a distinctly postmodern intuition, since its bearers are painfully aware of their lost faith in progress. Yet there are still stories to be made out of these "crashings" and "waves" of modern life that have nothing to do with progress. They are narratives of death and rebirth. No beginning. No end. Perfect continuity through perfect rupture, the oscillations of an eternal plot.

Along with Frost, the Menno Colony wished to escape progress by journeying to a lonely wilderness where they could reassert their "eternal privileges" and their opposition to nationalism. Likewise, the Fernheim Colony wished to escape history through a flight to the future and their messianic deliverance to a Nazi-controlled Europe. Yet the past could not be reassembled in the present, nor could the present give rise to a future of the colonies' choosing. Neither group found exactly what they were looking for in the Chaco. They found themselves, they found each other, and in doing so, they created something new.

---

[5] Robert Frost, "Directive," *Robert Frost's Poems* (New York: St. Martins, 2002).
[6] H. A. L. Fisher, *A History of Europe* (London: Edward Arnold, 1936), v.

Bibliography

ARCHIVAL SOURCES

Canada

Mennonite Heritage Centre, Winnipeg (MHC)

Germany

Auswärtiges Amt, Berlin (PA AA)
Bundesarchiv, Berlin-Lichterfelde (BA)
Stadtarchiv, Mölln (SAM)

Paraguay

Archivo Colonia Fernheim, Filadelfia (ACF)
Archivo Colonia Menno, Loma Plata (ACM)

United Kingdom

National Archives, Kew (NA)

United States

Archives of the Mennonite Church, Goshen (AMC)
Mennonite Central Committee Archives, Akron (MCCA)
Mennonite Library and Archives, North Newton (MLA)
National Archives, College Park (NACP)

PUBLISHED PRIMARY SOURCES

Auhagen, Otto. *Die Schicksalswende des Russlanddeutschen Bauerntum in den Jahren 1927–1930.* Leipzig: Hirzel, 1942.

Balzer, Frieda. "Brush with Terror." In *The Schoenbrunn Chronicles,* compiled by Agnes Balzer and Liselotte Dueck. Translated by Henry and Esther Regehr, 65–66. Waterloo: Sweetwater Books, 2009.

Bender, Harold S. *The Anabaptist Vision.* Scottdale, PA: Herald Press, 1944.

"Die Einwanderung nach Paraguay." In *Bericht über die Mennonitische Welt-Hilfs-Konferenz vom 31. August bis 3. September 1930.* Edited by Christian Neff, 117–25. Karlsruhe: Heinrich Schneider, 1930.

"With the Mennonite Refugee Colonies in Brazil and Paraguay: A Personal Narrative." *Mennonite Quarterly Review* 13, no. 1 (1939): 59–70.

Braght, Thieleman J. van. *The bloody theater or Martyrs mirror of the defenseless Christians who baptized only upon confession of faith, and who suffered and died for the testimony of Jesus, their Savior, from the time of Christ to the year A.D. 1660.* Scottdale, PA: Mennonite Publishing House, 1950.

Buhite, Russell D., and David W. Levy, eds. *FDR's Fireside Chats.* Norman, OK: University of Oklahoma Press, 1992.

Cámara de Senadores, Paraguay. "Franquicias a los Menonitas." In *Diario de Sesiones Del Congreso – Cámara de Senadores, 32 Sesion Ordinaria, July 12, 1921.* Asunción: Imprenta Nacional, 1921.

Canada (Province). Dept. of Public Instruction for Upper Canada and Egerton Ryerson. *Special Report on the Separate School Provisions of the School Law.* Toronto: J. Lovell, 1858.

Carroll, Henry King. "Statistics of Churches," *Census Bulletin,* no. 131. Washington, D.C.: United States Census Office, October 25, 1891.

Delgado Llano, Humberto. *Complementos de la Legislacion Integral del Ramo de Colonizacion 1928–1935.* La Paz: Intendencia General de Guerra, 1938.

Doerksen, J. H. *Geschichte und Wichtige Dokumente der Mennoniten von Russland, Canada [sic], Paraguay und Mexico.* n.p., 1923.

Dyck, Cornelius J., ed. *From the Files of MCC.* Scottdale, PA: Herald Press, 1980.

Ehrt, Adolf. *Das Mennonitentum in Russland von seiner Einwanderung bis zur Gegenwart.* Berlin: Verlag von Julius Beltz, 1932.

Epp, D. H. *Kurze Erklärungen und Erläuterungen zum Katechismus der christlichen, taufgesinnten Gemeinden, so Mennoniten genannt warden.* Translated by Al Reimer. Odessa: A. Schultze, 1897; 2nd ed., Klaterinoslav: D. H. Epp, 1899; Canadian reprint of 1899 ed., Rosthern: Dietrich Epp Verlag, 1941).

Flierl, Friedrich. "Die Ausbreitung des deutschen Volkes." In *Deutsche im Ausland – im Auftrage des Reichswanderungsamtes und in Verbindung mit dem Verein für das Deutschtum im Ausland.* Edited by Friedrich Wilhelm Mohr and Walter von Hauff, 1–17. Breslau, Germany: F. Hirt, 1923.

Foght, Harold J. *A Survey of Education in the Province of Saskatchewan.* Regina: King's Printer, 1918.

Freeden, Hermann von. "Kolonisatorische Erfahrungen aus der Nachkriegszeit." *Archiv für Wanderungswesen und Auslandskunde: Studien und Mitteilungen zur Wanderungsbewegung der Kulturvölker* 4, no. 4 (1933/1934): 1–12.

"Über die Möglichkeiten der Kolonisation für die Weisse Rasse in der Tropischen Zone." In *Comptes rendus du Congrès International de Geographie Amsterdam*, 111–21. Leiden, Netherlands: E. J. Brill, 1938.

"German Imperial and State Citizenship Law. July, 22 1913." *The American Journal of International Law* 8, no. 3, Supplement: Official Documents (1914), 217–27.

Goodman, Glen. "The Enduring Politics of German-Brazilian Ethnicity," *German History* 33, no. 3 (2015): 423–38.

Gross Brown, Sigfrido (Sigifredo). *Las Colonias Menonitas en el Chaco.* Asunción: Imprenta Nacional, 1934.

Hamilton-Temple-Blackwood, Hariot Georgina, Marchioness of Dufferin and Ava. *My Canadian Journal 1872–8: Extracts from My Letters Home Written While Lord Dufferin Was Governor-General.* London: John Murray, 1891.

Harder, Abraham, Gerhard Isaak, Johann Teichgräf, Jakob Siemens, and Nikolai Wiebe. "An die Mennonitische Weltkonferenz in Holland." In *Der Allgemeine Kongress der Mennoniten gehalten in Amsterdam, Elspeet, Witmarsum (Holland) 29. Juni bis 3. Juli 1936.* Edited by D. Christian Neff, 83. Karlsruhe, Germany: Heinrich Schneider, 1936.

Hiebert, Peter C. *Mitteilungen von der Reise nach Süd-Amerika.* Hillsboro, KS: Mennonite Brethren Publishing House, n.d.

Hildebrand, Peter. *Odyssee wider Willen: Das Schicksal eines Auslandsdeutschen.* Oldenburg, Germany: Heinz Holzberg Verlag, 1984.

Hildebrandt, Gerhard. *Die Mennoniten in der Ukraine und im Gebiet Orenburg: Dokumente aus Archiven in Kiev und Orenburg.* Göttingen, Germany: Der Göttinger Arbeitskreis, 2006.

Hopkins, J. Castell. *The Canadian Annual Review of Public Affairs.* Toronto: Canadian Annual Review, ltd., 1920.

Jubiläumskomitee der Harbiner Gruppe. *Die Flucht über den Amur: ein Zeugnis von Gottvertrauen und Mut.* Filadelfia, Paraguay: Jubiläumskomitee der Harbiner Gruppe, 2007.

Kasdorf, Hans. *Design of My Journey: An Autobiography.* Fresno, CA: Center for Mennonite Brethren Studies; Nürnberg. Germany: VTR Publications, 2004.

Klassen, Wilhelm. "Painful Paths." In *The Schoenbrunn Chronicles.* Compiled by Agnes Balzer and Liselotte Dueck. Translated by Henry and Esther Regehr, 34–38. Waterloo: Sweetwater Books, 2009.

Kliewer, Friedrich (Fritz). *Deutsche Volksgruppe in Paraguay: Eine siedlungsgeschichtliche, volkskundliche, und volkspolitische Untersuchung.* Hamburg: Hans Christians, 1941.

"Die Mennoniten-Kolonie Friesland in Ostparaguay." *Mennonitische Geschichtsblätter* (Emden, Germany) 3 (1938): 58.

"The Mennonites of Paraguay." *Mennonite Quarterly Review* 11, no. 1 (1937): 92–97.

"Mennonite Young People's Work in the Paraguayan Chaco." *Mennonite Quarterly Review* 11, no. 2 (1937): 119–30.

"Vortrag von Fritz Kliewer über Paraguay." In *Der Allgemeine Kongress der Mennoniten gehalten in Amsterdam, Elspeet, Witmarsum (Holland) 29. Juni bis 3. Juli 1936.* Edited by D.Christian Neff, 75–78. Karlsruhe, Germany: Heinrich Schneider, 1936.

Kraemer, Gustav. *Wir und unsere Volksgemeinschaft 1938.* Crefeld, Germany: Crefeld Mennonitengemeinde, 1938.

Kraft, Siegfried. *Die rußlanddeutschen Flüchtlinge des Jahres 1929/1930 und ihre Aufnahme im Deutschen Reich: Eine Untersuchung über die Gründe der Massenflucht der deutschen Bauern und ein Beitrag zur Kenntnis der Behandlung volksdeutscher Fragen im Weimarer Zwischenreich.* Inaugural Dissertation zur Erlangung der Doktorwürde einer Hohen Philosophischen Fakultät der Martin Luther-Universität Halle-Wittenberg. Halle, Germany: Eduard Klinz Buchdruck-Werkstätte, 1939.

League of Nations. "Arrangement with Respect to the Issue of Certificates of Identity to Russian Refugees." July 5, 1922. *League of Nations Treaty Series* 13, no. 355. www.refworld.org/docid/3dd8b4864.html. Last accessed June 7, 2018.

"Conference on Russian and Armenian Refugee Questions, Report by the High Commissioner, June 5, 1926," 3. http://biblio-archive.unog.ch/Dateien/Cou ncilDocs/C-327-1926_EN.pdf. Last accessed August 8, 2019.

"Dispute between Bolivia and Paraguay-Annex 1099 and 1099(a)." *League of Nations Official Journal* 10, no. 1 (1929): 253–56

"Documentation Concerning the Dispute Between Bolivia and Paraguay." *League of Nations Official Journal* 10, no. 2 (1929): 264–74.

"Refugees in China. Communication from the Delegates of Paraguay to the League of Nations-Annex 1972." *League of Nations Official Journal* 13, no. 7 (1932): 1338–40.

Lebow, Richard Ned. "The Future of Memory," *Annals of the American Academy of Political and Social Science* 617 (2008): 25–41.

Neufeld, Hans (Juan). *Affaire Dr. Fritz Kliewer in Farnheim [sic] 1940–1944.* Asunción: Hans Neufeld, 1988.

Neufeld, Kornelius K. *Flucht aus dem Paradies: Damals vor Moskau.* Weisenheim am Berg, Germany: Agape, 2005.

Quiring, Walter. "The Canadian Mennonite Immigration into the Paraguayan Chaco." *Mennonite Quarterly Review* 8, no. 1 (1934): 32–45.

"The Colonization of the German Mennonites from Russia in the Paraguayan Chaco." *Mennonite Quarterly Review* 8, no. 2 (1934): 62–72.

Deutsche erschliessen den Chaco. Karlsruhe, Germany: Heinrich Schneider, 1936.

Regehr, Johann. "Death in Schoenbrunn." In *The Schoenbrunn Chronicles.* Compiled by Agnes Balzer and Liselotte Dueck. Translated by Henry Regehr and Esther Regehr, 39–46. Waterloo: Sweetwater Books, 2009.

Republica del Paraguay. "Ley N. 514." *Republica del Paraguay Registro Oficial Correspondiente al año 1921, Primer Semestr.* Asunción: Imprenta Nacional, 1921.

Rüdiger, Hermann. "Zahl und Verbreitung des deutschen Volkes." In Paul Gauß, *Das Buch vom deutschen Volkstum: Wesen, Lebensraum, Schicksal.* Leipzig: F. A. Brockhaus, 1935.

School Attendance Act. *The Revised Statutes of Saskatchewan, 1920,* Chapter 111 (Assented to November 10, 1920). www.publications.gov.sk.ca/redirect.cfm ?p=66948&i=74287. Last accessed June 7, 2018.

Simpson, John Hope. *The Refugee Problem: Report of a Survey.* London: Oxford University Press, 1939.

Toews, Bernhard. *Reise-Tagebuch des Bernhard Töws 1921: Chacoexpedition mit Fred Engen.* Kolonie Menno, Paraguay: Abteilung Geschichtsarchiv, Schulverwaltung der Kolonie Menno, 1997.

Verhandlungen des Reichstags: IV Wahlperiode 1928, vol. 426. Berlin: Reichsdruckerei, 1930.

Wiebe, Gerhard. *Causes and History of the Emigration of the Mennonites from Russia to America.* Translated by Helen Janzen. Winnipeg: Manitoba Mennonite Historical Society, 1981.

Wilhelmy, Herbert, and Oskar Schmieder. *Deutsche Akerbausiedlungen im südamerikanischen Grasland, Pampa und Gran Chaco.* Wissenschaftliche Veröffentlichungen, Neue Folge 6. Leipzig: Deutsches Museum für Ländkunde, 1938.

Willms, H. J. *At the Gates of Moscow: God's Gracious Aid Through a Most Difficult and Trying Period.* Translated by George G. Thielman. Yarrow, BC: Columbia Press, 1964.

NEWSPAPERS AND MAGAZINES

Canadian Magazine (Toronto)
Chicago Daily Tribune
Deutsche Post aus dem Osten (Berlin)
Deutsche Warte (Asunción)
Deutsche Zeitung für Paraguay (Asunción)
El Diario (Asunción)
Evening Ledger (Philadelphia)
Gospel Herald
Kalender des Auslanddeutschtums (Stuttgart)
Kämpfende Jugend (Fernheim, Paraguay)
El Liberal (Asunción)
Literary Digest (New York)
Menno-Blatt (Fernheim, Paraguay)
Mennonite
Mennonitische Geschichtsblätter (Emden, Germany)
Mennonitische Jugendwarte (Elbing, Germany)
New Outlook (New York)
New York Times

Philadelphia Enquirer
Rote Fahne (Berlin)
Saskatoon Star Phoenix
Steinbach Post (Canada)[1]
Times of India
La Tribuna (Asunción)
Völkischer Beobachter (Munich)
Völkischer Kurier (Munich)
Winnipeg Free Press
Das Wochenblatt (Asunción)

REFERENCE SOURCES

Global Anabaptist Mennonite Encyclopedia Online. http://gameo.org/index.php? title= Welcome_to_GAMEO. Last accessed August 8, 2019.

Ratzlaff, Gerhard, Jakob Warkentin, Uwe S. Friesen, Gundolf Niebuhr, Hans Theodor Regier, Beate Penner, and Lily August. *Lexikon der Mennoniten in Paraguay.* Asunción: Verein für Geschichte und Kultur der Mennoniten in Paraguay, 2009.

SECONDARY SOURCES

Alexopoulos, Golfo. *Stalin's Outcasts: Aliens, Citizens, and the Soviet State, 1926–1936.* Ithaca, NY: Cornell University Press, 2003.

Anderson, Benedict. *Imagined Communities: Reflections on the Origins and Spread of Nationalism.* London: Verso, 1983.

Applegate, Celia. *A Nation of Provincials: The German Idea of Heimat.* Berkeley, CA: University of California Press, 1990.

Arendt, Hannah. *The Origins of Totalitarianism.* New ed. New York: Harcourt, Brace, Jovanovich, 1973.

Avery, Donald. "Ethnic and Class Relations in Western Canada During the First World War: A Case Study of European Immigrants and Anglo-Canadian Nativism." In *Canada and the First World War: Essays in Honour of Robert Craig Brown.* Edited by David MacKenzie, 272–99. Toronto: University of Toronto Press, 2005.

Balibar, Etienne. "The Nation Form: History and Ideology." In *Race, Nation, Class: Ambiguous Identities.* Edited by Etienne Balibar and Immanuel Wallerstein, 86–106. London: Verso, 1991.

Barbian, Nikolaus. *Auswärtige Kulturpolitik und "Auslandsdeutsche" in Lateinamerika 1949–1973.* Wiesbaden: Springer, 2013.

Barkun, Michael. *Disaster and the Millennium.* Syracuse, NY: Syracuse University, 1986.

[1] From a collection of newspaper clippings compiled by Andrea Dyck and Royden Loewen.

Barzun, Jacques. *From Dawn to Decadence: 500 Years of Western Cultural Life: 1500 to the Present*. New York: HarperCollins, 2000.

Basch, Linda, Cristina Blanc-Szanton, and Nina Glick Schiller. *Towards a Transnational Perspective on Migration: Race, Class, Ethnicity, and Nationalism Reconsidered*. New York: New York Academy of Sciences, 1992.

Bassler, Gerhard P. "German-Canadian Identity in Historical Perspective." In *A Chorus of Different Voices: German-Canadian Identities*. Edited by Angelika E. Sauer and Matthias Zimmer, 72–89. New York: Peter Lang, 1998.

Beaujot, Roderic P., and Don Kerr, eds. *The Changing Face of Canada: Essential Readings in Population*. Toronto: Canadian Scholars Press, 2007.

Bell, Duncan S. A. "Mythscapes: Memory, Mythology, and National Identity." *British Journal of Sociology* 54, no. 1 (2003): 63–81.

Bernecker, Walther L. and Thomas Fischer. "Deutsche in Lateinamerika." In *Deutsche im Ausland, Fremde in Deutschland: Migration in Geschichte und Gegenwart*. Edited by Klaus Bade, 197–214. Munich: C. H. Beck, 1992.

Bickelmann, Hartmut. *Deutsche Überseeauswanderung in der Weimarer Zeit*. Wiesbaden: Steiner, 1980.

Bjork, James. *Neither German Nor Pole: Catholicism and National Indifference in a Central European Borderland*. Ann Arbor, MI: University of Michigan Press, 2008.

Blamires, Cyprian P., ed. *World Fascism: A Historical Encyclopedia*, vol. 1. Santa Barbara, Denver, Oxford: ABC CLIO, 2006.

Blickle, Peter. *Heimat: A Critical Theory of the German Idea of Homeland*. New York: Camden House, 2004.

Block, Ulrike. "Deutsche Lateinamerikaforschung im Nationalsozialismus – Ansätze zu einer wissenschaftshistorischen Perspektive." In *Der Nationalsozialismus und Lateinamerika: Institutionen – Repräsentationen – Wissenskonstrukte I*. Edited by Sandra Carreras, 7–22. Berlin: Ibero-Amerikanisches Institut Preußischer Kulturbesitz, 2005.

Bönisch-Brednich, Brigitte. "Migration, Gender, and Storytelling: How Gender Shapes the Experiences and the Narrative Patterns in Biographical interviews." In *German Diasporic Experiences*. Edited by Mathias Schulze, James M. Skidmore, David G. John, Grit Liebscher, and Sebastian Siebel-Achenbach, 331–44. Waterloo: Wilfrid Laurier University Press, 2008.

Boyd, Monica, and Michael Vickers. "100 Years of Immigration in Canada." In *The Changing Face of Canada: Essential Readings in Population*. Edited by Roderic P. Beaujot and Don Kerr. Toronto: Canadian Scholars Press, 2007.

Braun, Jacob A. *Im Gedenken an jene Zeit: Mitteilungen zur Entstehungsgeschichte der Kolonie Menno*. Loma Plata, Paraguay: Jacob A. Braun, 2001[?].

Breunig, Bernd. *Die Deutsche Rolandwanderung (1932–1938): Soziologische Analyse in historischer, wirtschaftlicher und politischer Sicht, mit einem Geleitwort von Johannes Schauff*. Munich: Nymphenburger, 1983.

Bridenthal, Renate. "Germans from Russia: The Political Network of a Double Diaspora." In *The Heimat Abroad: The Boundaries of Germanness*. Edited by Krista O'Donnell, Renate Bridenthal, and Nancy Reagin, 187–218. Ann Arbor, MI: University of Michigan Press, 2005.

Brinkmann, Tobias. "'German Jews'? Reassessing the History of Nineteenth-Century Jewish Immigrants." In *Transnational Traditions: New Perspectives on American Jewish History*. Edited by Ava F. Kahn and Adam Mendelsohn, 144–164. Detroit, MI: Wayne State University Press, 2014.

Brodbeck, David. *Defining Deutschtum: Political Ideology, German Identity, and Music-Critical Discourse in Liberal Vienna*. New York: Oxford University Press, 2014.

Brown, Kate. *A Biography of No Place: From Ethnic Borderland to Soviet Heartland*. Cambridge, MA: Harvard University Press, 2004.

Brubaker, Rogers. *Ethnicity Without Groups*. Cambridge, MA: Harvard University Press, 2004.

"The 'Diaspora' Diaspora." *Ethnic and Racial Studies* 28, no. 1 (2005): 1–19.

Nationalism Reframed: Nationhood and the National Question in the New Europe. Cambridge, UK: Cambridge University Press, 1996.

Brubaker, Rogers, Margit Feischmidt, Jon Fox, and Liana Grancea. *Nationalist Politics and Everyday Ethnicity in a Transylvanian Town*. Princeton, NJ: Princeton University Press, 2006.

Bruno-Jofre, Rose. "Citizenship and Schooling in Manitoba, 1918–1945." *Manitoba History* 36 (Autumn/Winter 1998–1999). Last updated October 23, 2011. www.mhs.mb.ca/docs/mb_history/36/citizenship.shtml. Last accessed June 7, 2018.

Bryce, Benjamin. "Linguistic Ideology and State Power: German and English Education in Ontario, 1880–1912." *The Canadian Historical Review* 94, no. 2 (2013): 207–33.

Buchenau, Jürgen. *Tools of Progress: A German Merchant Family in Mexico City, 1865–Present*. Albuquerque, NM: University of New Mexico Press, 2004.

Burbank, Jane, and Frederick Cooper. *Empires in World History: Power and the Politics of Difference*. Princeton, NJ: Princeton University Press, 2010.

Bush, Perry. "'United Progressive Mennonites': Bluffton College and Anabaptist Higher Education, 1913–1945." *Mennonite Quarterly Review* 74, no. 3 (2000): 357–80.

Carr, David. "Narrative and the Real World: An Argument for Continuity." *History and Theory*, 25, no. 2 (1986), 117–31.

Casteel, James E. "The Politics of Diaspora: Russian German Émigré Activists in Interwar Germany." In *German Diasporic Experiences: Identity, Migration, and Loss*. Edited by Mathias Schulze, James M. Skidmore, David G. John, Grit Liebscher, and Sebastian Siebel-Achenbach, 117–29. Waterloo: Wilfrid Laurier University Press, 2008.

"The Russian Germans in the Interwar German National Imaginary." *Central European History*, 40, no. 3 (2007): 429–466.

Chesterton, Bridget María. *Grandchildren of Solano López: Frontier and Nation in Paraguay, 1904–1936*. Albuquerque, NM: University of New Mexico Press, 2013.

Clifford, James. "Diasporas." *Cultural Anthropology* 9, no. 3 (1994): 302–38.

Confino, Alon. *The Nation as a Local Metaphor: Wurttemberg, Imperial Germany, and National Memory, 1871–1918*. Chapel Hill, NC: University of North Carolina Press, 1997.

Conn, Stetson, and Byron Fairchild. *The Western Hemisphere: The Framework of Hemisphere Defense*. Washington, D.C.: U.S. Government Printing Office, 1960.

Conrad, Sebastian. *Globalisation and the Nation in Imperial Germany*. Cambridge, UK: Cambridge University Press, 2010.

Conrad, Sebastian, and Dominic Sachsenmaier. "Introduction: Competing Visions of World Order: Global Moments and Movements, 1880s–1930s," in *Competing Visions of World Order: Global Moments and Movements, 1880s–1930s*. Edited by Sebastian Conrad and Dominic Sachsenmaier, 1–27. New York: Palgrave Macmillan, 2007.

Correll, Ernst. "The Mennonite Loan in the Canadian Parliament, 1875." *Mennonite Quarterly Review* 20, no. 4 (1946): 255–75.

Crerar, Adam. "Ontario and the Great War." In *Canada and the First World War: Essays in Honour of Robert Craig Brown*. Edited by David MacKenzie, 230–72. Toronto: University of Toronto Press, 2005.

Cronon, William. "A Place for Stories: Nature, History, and Narrative." *Journal of American History* 78, no. 4 (1992): 1347–76.

Cupitt, Don. *What Is a Story?* London: SCM Press, 1991.

Curtis, Bruce. *Building the Educational State: Canada, West, 1836–1871*. London, ON: Falmer, 1988.

Dirks, Gerald E. *Canada's Refugee Policy: Indifference or Opportunism?* Montreal: McGill-Queen's University Press, 1977.

Drekonja-Kornat, Gerhard. "Nationalsozialismus und Lateinamerika. Neue Kontroversen," *Wiener Zeitschrift zur Geschichte der Neuzeit* 6, no. 2 (2006): 109–18.

Dueck, Abe J. "Mennonite Churches and Religious Developments in Russia 1850–1914." In *Mennonites in Russia 1788–1988: Essays in honour of Gerhard Lohrenz*. Edited by John Friesen. 149–81. Winnipeg: CMBC Publications, 1989.

Dyck, Harvey. *Weimar Germany and Soviet Russia 1926–1933: A Study in Diplomatic Instability*. London: Chatto and Windus, 1966.

Eklof, Ben, John Bushnell, and Larissa Zakharova, eds. *Russia's Great Reforms, 1855–1881*. Bloomington, IN: Indiana University Press, 1994.

Eksteins, Modris. *Rites of Spring*. Boston and New York: Mariner Books, 2000.

Eley, Geoff, and Ronald Grigor Suny. "Introduction: From the Moment of Social History to the Work of Cultural Representation." In *Becoming National: A Reader*. Edited by Geoff Eley and Ronald Grigor Suny, 3–37. New York: Oxford University Press, 1996.

Ens, Adolf. "Becoming British Citizens in Pre-WW I Canada." In *Canadian Mennonites and the Challenge of Nationalism*. Edited by Abe J. Dueck, 69–88. Winnipeg: Manitoba Mennonite Historical Society, 1994.

— *Subjects or Citizens? The Mennonite Experience in Canada, 1870–1925*. Ottawa: University of Ottawa Press, 1994.

Epp, Frank H. *Mennonite Exodus: The Rescue and Resettlement of the Russian Mennonites Since the Communist Revolution*. Altona, MB: Canadian Mennonite Relief and Immigration Council, 1962.

— *Mennonites in Canada, 1786–1920: The History of a Separate People*. Toronto: Macmillan of Canada, 1974.

— *Mennonites in Canada, 1920–1940: A People's Struggle for Survival*. Toronto: Macmillan of Canada, 1982.

— *Mennonite Peoplehood: A Plea for New Initiatives*. Waterloo: Conrad Press, 1977.

Epp, Marlene. *Mennonite Women in Canada: A History*. Winnipeg: University of Manitoba Press, 2008.

Eyford, Ryan. *White Settler Reserve: New Iceland and the Colonization of the Canadian West*. Vancouver: UBC Press, 2006.

Farcau, Bruce W. *The Chaco War: Bolivia and Paraguay, 1932–1935*. London: Praeger, 1996.

Finger, Thomas. "Confessions of Faith in the Anabaptist/Mennonite Tradition." *Mennonite Quarterly Review* 76, no. 3 (2002): 277–97.

Fisher, H. A. L. *A History of Europe*. London: Edward Arnold, 1936.

Fitzpatrick, Sheila. *Everyday Stalinism: Ordinary Life in Extraordinary Times*. New York: Oxford University Press, 1999.

Fox, Stephen. "The Deportation of Latin American Germans, 1941–47: Fresh Legs for Mr. Monroe's Doctrine," *Yearbook of German-American Studies* 32 (1997): 117–42.

Francis, E. K. *In Search of Utopia: The Mennonites in Manitoba*. Glencoe, IL: Free Press, 1955.

— *Interethnic Relations: An Essay in Sociological Theory*. New York: Elsevier, 1976.

Fretz, Joseph Winfield. *Immigrant Group Settlement in Paraguay: A Study in the Sociology of Colonization*. North Newton, KS: Bethel College, 1962.

Freund, Alexander. "Introduction." In *Beyond the Nation? Immigrants' Local Lives in Transnational Cultures*, 3–17. Toronto: University of Toronto Press, 2012.

Friedman, Max Paul. *Nazis and Good Neighbors: The United States Campaign Against the Germans of Latin America in World War II*. Cambridge, UK: Cambridge University Press, 2003.

Friesen, Abraham. *In Defense of Privilege: Russian Mennonites and the State Before and During World War I*. Winnipeg: Kindred Productions, 2006.

Friesen, Martin W. *Canadian Mennonites Conquer a Wilderness: The Beginning and Development of the Menno Colony First Mennonite Settlement in South America*. Translated by Christel Wiebe. Loma Plata, Paraguay: Historical Committee of the Menno Colony, 2009.

— *New Homeland in the Chaco Wilderness*. 2nd ed. Translated by Jake Balzer. Loma Plata, Paraguay: Cooperativa Chortitzer Limited, 1997.

Friesen, Peter M. *The Mennonite Brotherhood in Russia (1879–1910)*. Translated by J. B. Toews. Fresno, CA: Mennonite Brethren Board of Christian Literature, 1978.

Friesen, Richard J. "Saskatchewan Mennonite Settlements: The Modification of an Old World Settlement Pattern." *Canadian Ethnic Studies* 9, no. 2 (1977): 72–90.

Friesen, Uwe S. "Der Erschließungsprozess des Gran Chaco seit dem Späten 19. Jahrhundert." *Jahrbuch für Geschichte und Kultur der Mennoniten in Paraguay* 14 (2013): 23–76.

"Martin W. Friesen: Ein Leben im Dienste der Gemeinschaft." *Jahrbuch für Geschichte und Kultur der Mennoniten in Paraguay* 5 (2005): 53–90.

Fröschle, Hartmut. *Die Deutschen in Lateinamerika: Schicksal und Leistung.* Basel: Horst Erdmann, 1979.

Frost, Robert. "Directive." In *Robert Frost's Poems.* New York: St. Martins, 2002.

Frye, Northrop. *Anatomy of Criticism: Four Essays.* Edited by Robert D. Denham. Toronto: University of Toronto Press, 2006.

The Double Vision: Language and Meaning in Religion. Toronto: University of Toronto Press, 1991.

The Great Code: The Bible and Literature. Edited by Alvin A. Lee. Toronto: University of Toronto Press, Scholarly Publishing Division, 2006.

Fulda, Bernhard. *Press and Politics in the Weimar Republic.* Oxford: Oxford University Press, 2009.

Gatrell, Peter. *The Making of the Modern Refugee.* Oxford: Oxford University Press, 2013.

Gaudig, Olaf and Peter Veit. *Der Widerschein des Nazismus: Das Bild des Nationalsozialismus in der deutschsprachigen Presse Argentiniens, Brasiliens und Chiles 1932–1945.* Berlin: Wissenschaftlicher, 1997.

Gellner, Ernest. *Nations and Nationalism.* Ithaca, NY: Cornell University Press, 1983.

Gerlach, Horst. *Die Russlandmennoniten: Ein Volk unterwegs.* Kirchheimbolanden, Germany: Horst Gerlach, 1992, 49.

Giesbrecht, Donovan. "Metis, Mennonites and the 'Unsettled Prairie,' 1874–1896." *Journal of Mennonite Studies* 19 (2001): 103–11.

Glassie, Henry. *Material Culture.* Bloomington, IN: Indiana University Press, 1999.

Gleich, Albrecht von. *Germany and Latin America, Memorandum RM-5523-RC.* Santa Monica, CA: RAND Corporation, 1968.

Goossen, Benjamin W. *Chosen Nation: Mennonites and Germany in a Global Era.* Princeton, NJ: Princeton University Press, 2017.

"Into a Great Nation: Mennonites and Nationalism in Imperial Germany, 1871–1900." Honors history thesis, Swarthmore College, 2013.

Götz, Norbert. "German-Speaking People and German Heritage: Nazi Germany and the Problem of Volksgemeinschaft." In *The Heimat Abroad: The Boundaries of Germanness.* Edited by Krista O'Donnell, Renate Bridenthal, and Nancy Reagin, 58–82. Ann Arbor, MI: University of Michigan Press, 2005.

Grams, Grant. *German Emigration to Canada and the Support of Its Deutschtum During the Weimar Republic.* New York: Peter Lang, 2001.

Granatstein, J. L. "Conscription in the Great War." In *Canada and the First World War: Essays in Honour of Robert Craig Brown.* Edited by David MacKenzie, 62–75. Toronto: University of Toronto Press, 2005.

Green, Nancy L., and Francois Weil, eds. *Citizenship and Those Who Leave: The Politics of Emigration and Expatriation*, Urbana and Chicago: University of Illinois, 2007.

Gregory, Brad S. *Salvation at Stake: Christian Martyrdom in Early Modern Europe*. Cambridge, MA: Harvard University Press, 1999.

Grow, Michael. *The Good Neighbor Policy and Authoritarianism in Paraguay: United States Economic Expansion and Great Power Rivalry in Latin America During World War II*. Lawrence, KS: Regents Press of Kansas, 1998.

Guenther, Alan M. "'Barred from Heaven and Cursed Forever': Old Colony Mennonites and the 1908 Commission of Inquiry Regarding Public Education." *Historical Papers 2007, Canadian Society of Church History: Annual Conference, University of Saskatchewan, 27–29 May 2007* (2008): 129–48.

Guenther, Titus F. "*Ältester* Martin C. Friesen (1889–1968): A Man of Vision for Paraguay's *Mennogemeinde.*" *Journal of Mennonite Studies* 23 (2005): 185–211.

"Theology of Migration: The *Ältesten* Reflect." *Journal of Mennonite Studies* 18 (2000): 164–76.

Harder, Helmut. *David Toews Was Here, 1870–1947*. Winnipeg: Canadian Mennonite University Press, 2006.

Harder Horst, René D. *The Stroessner Regime and Indigenous Resistance in Paraguay*. Tallahassee, FL: University Press of Florida, 2007.

Harms-Baltzer, Käte. *Die Nationalisierung der deutschen Einwanderer und ihrer Nachkommen in Brasilien als Problem der deutsch-brasilianischen Beziehungen, 1930–1938*. Berlin: Colloquium, 1970.

Harvey, Elizabeth. "Emissaries of Nazism: German Student Travelers in Romania and Yugoslavia in the 1930s." *Österreichische Zeitschrift für Geschichtswissenschaften* 22, no. 1 (2011), 135–60.

Heinzen, James W. *Inventing a Soviet Countryside: State Power and the Transformation of Rural Russia, 1917–1929*. Pittsburgh, PA: University of Pittsburgh Press, 2004.

Hiebert, Abram W., and Jacob T. Friesen. *Eine bewegte Geschichte ... die zu uns spricht: Materialien zur Entwicklungsgeschichte der Kolonie Menno: Ein Beitrag zur 75. Gedenkfeier*. Asunción, Paraguay: Chortitzer Komitee, Colonia Menno, 2002.

Hilton, Stanley. *Hitler's Secret War in South America 1939–1945*. Baton Rouge, LA: Louisiana State University Press, 1981.

Hobsbawm, Eric J. *Nations and Nationalism Since 1780: Programme, Myth, Reality*. Cambridge, UK: Cambridge University Press, 1990.

Hobsbawm, Eric J., and Terence Ranger. *The Invention of Tradition*. Cambridge: Cambridge University Press, 1983.

Hoerder, Dirk. "The German-Language Diasporas: A Survey, Critique, and Interpretation." *Diaspora* 11, no. 1 (2002): 7–44.

Huebert, Helmut T. *Events and People: Events in Russian Mennonite History and the People That Made Them Happen*. Winnipeg: Springfield Publishers, 1999.

Hughes, James. *Stalinism in a Russian Province: Collectivization and Dekulakization in Siberia*. Basingstoke, UK: Macmillan, 1996.

Hughes, Matthew. "Logistics and the Chaco War: Bolivia Versus Paraguay, 1932–1935." *Journal of Military History* 69, no. 2 (2005): 411–37.

Humphries, Mark Osborne. *The Last Plague: Spanish Influenza and the Politics of Public Health in Canada.* Toronto: University of Toronto Press, 2013.

Hutton, Christopher. *Race and the Third Reich: Linguistics, Racial Anthropology and Genetics in the Dialectic of Volk.* Cambridge: Polity, 2005.

Huxman, Susan Schultz, and Gerald Biesecker-Mast. "In the World but Not of It: Mennonite Traditions as Resources for Rhetorical Invention." *Rhetoric & Public Affairs* 7, no. 4 (2004): 539–54.

Hyman, Paula E. *The Jews of Modern France.* Berkeley and Los Angeles, CA: University of California Press, 1998.

Isaak, Helmuth. *Your Faith Will Sustain You, and You Will Prevail.* Translated by Jack Thiessen. Norderstedt, Germany: Books on Demand, 2014.

Jantzen, Mark. *Mennonite German Soldiers: Nation, Religion, and Family in the Prussian East, 1772–1880.* South Bend, IN: University of Notre Dame Press, 2010.

"'Whoever Will Not Defend His Homeland Should Leave It!' German Conscription and Prussian Mennonite Emigration to the Great Plains, 1860–1890." *Mennonite Life* 58, no. 3 (2003). https://ml.bethelks.edu/issu e/vol-58-no-3/article/whoever-will-not-defend-his-homeland-should-leave/. Last accessed June 7, 2018.

Janzen, William. *Limits on Liberty: The Experience of Mennonite, Hutterite, and Doukhobor Communities in Canada.* Toronto: University of Toronto Press, 1990.

Judson, Pieter M. *Guardians of the Nation: Activists on the Language Frontiers of Imperial Austria.* Cambridge, MA: Harvard University Press, 2006.

"When Is a Diaspora Not a Diaspora? Rethinking Nation-Centered Narratives About Germans in Habsburg East Central Europe." In *The Heimat Abroad: The Boundaries of Germanness.* Edited by Krista O'Donnell, Renate Bridenthal, and Nancy Reagin, 219–47. Ann Arbor, MI: University of Michigan Press, 2005.

Juhnke, James. *A People of Two Kingdoms.* Newton, KS: Faith and Life Press, 1975.

Vision, Doctrine, War. Scottdale, PA: Herald Press, 1989.

Kaethler, Frieda Siemens, and Alfred Neufeld, eds. *Nikolai Siemens der Chacooptimist.* Weisenheim am Berg, Germany: Agape, 2005.

Kalin, Rudolf, and J. M. Berry. "Ethnic, National and Provincial Self-Identity in Canada: Analyses of 1974 and 1991." *Canadian Ethnic Studies* 27, no. 2 (1995): 1–15.

Keim, Albert N. *Harold S. Bender, 1897–1962.* Scottdale, PA: Herald Press, 1997.

Kenley, David. *New Culture in a New World: The May Fourth Movement and the Chinese Diaspora in Singapore, 1919–1932.* New York: Routledge, 2003.

Kershaw, Ian. *The Hitler Myth: Image and Reality in the Third Reich.* Oxford, UK: Oxford University Press, 1987.

King, Jeremy. *Budweisers into Czechs and Germans: A Local History of Bohemian Politics, 1848–1948.* Princeton, NJ: Princeton University Press, 2002.

Klassen, Burt. "Puerto Casado – 16 Monate Wartzeit an der Tür zum Chacoinneren." *Jahrbuch für Geschichte und Kultur der Mennoniten in Paraguay* 13 (2012): 7–30.

Klassen, Peter P. *Die deutsch-völkish Zeit in der Kolonie Fernheim, Chaco, Paraguay, 1943–1945: Ein Beitrag zur Geschichte der auslandsdeutschen Mennoniten während des Dritten Reiches.* Bolanden-Weierhof, Germany: Mennonitischer Geschichtsverein e.V., 1990.

The Mennonites in Paraguay Volume 1: Kingdom of God and Kingdom of This World. Translated by Gunther H. Schmitt. Filadelfia, Paraguay: Peter P. Klassen, 2003.

The Mennonites in Paraguay Volume 2: Encounter with Indians and Paraguayans. Translated by Gunther H. Schmitt. Filadelfia, Paraguay: Peter P. Klassen, 2002.

"Die Namen der Dörfer wanderten mit." *Jahrbuch für Geschichte und Kultur der Mennoniten in Paraguay* 13 (2012): 7–30.

"Die Rolle des Mennonitischen Zentralkomitees (MCC) in den Konflikten der Mennonitenkolonien in Paraguay." *Jahrbuch für Geschichte und Kultur der Mennoniten in Paraguay* 2 (2001): 35–58.

Klautke, Egbert. *The Mind of the Nation: Völkerpsychologie in Germany, 1851–1955.* New York: Berghahn 2013.

Klee, Paul. *The Diaries of Paul Klee, 1898–1918.* Edited by Felix Klee. Berkeley and Los Angeles, CA: University of California Press, 1964.

Kleinpenning, Jan M. *Integration and Colonisation of the Paraguayan Chaco.* Nijmegen: Katholieke Universiteit Nijmegen, 1986.

Klippenstein, Lawrence. "FUNK, JOHANN." *Dictionary of Canadian Biography* 14, www.biographi.ca/en/bio/funk_johann_14E.html. Last accessed June 7, 2018.

"Western Local Mennonite Teachers' Conference – An Early Minute Book." *Manitoba Pageant* 22, no. 2 (1977), www.mhs.mb.ca/docs/pageant/22/men noniteteachers.shtml. Last accessed June 7, 2018.

Kordan, Bohdan S. *No Free Man: Canada, the Great War, and the Enemy Alien Experience.* Montreal and Kingston: McGill-Queen's University Press, 2016.

Kotsonis, Yanni. "'Face-to-Face': The State, the Individual, and the Citizen in Russian Taxation, 1863–1917," *Slavic Review* 63, no. 2 (Summer, 2004): 221–46.

Kroetsch, Robert. "Closing Panel." In *Acts of Concealment: Mennonite/s Writing in Canada.* Edited by Hildi Froese Tiessen and Peter Hinchcliffe. Waterloo: University of Waterloo, 1992.

Kwan, Jonathan. "Transylvanian Saxon Politics, Hungarian State Building and the Case of the Allgemeiner Deutscher Schulverein (1881–82)." *English Historical Review* 127, no. 526 (2012): 592–624.

Lapp, John A., and Ed van Straten. "Mennonite World Conference 1925–2000: From Euro-American Conference to Worldwide Communion." *Mennonite Quarterly Review* 76, no. 1 (2003): 7–45.

Lebow, Richard Ned. "The Future of Memory." *Annals of the American Academy of Political and Social Science* 617 (2008): 30.

Lehmann, Heinz. *The German Canadians: Immigration, Settlement, and Culture.* Edited and translated by Gerhard P. Bassler. St. John's, NL: Jesperson Press, 1986.

Lehr, John C., John Everitt, and Simon Evans. "The Making of the Prairie Landscape." In *Immigration and Settlement, 1870–1939.* Edited by Gregory P. Marchildon, 13–56. Regina: Canadian Plains Research Center, 2009.

Lekan, Thomas. "German Landscape: Local Promotion of the *Heimat* Abroad." In *The Heimat Abroad: The Boundaries of Germanness.* Edited by Krista O'Donnell, Renate Bridenthal, and Nancy Reagin, 141–66. Ann Arbor, MI: University of Michigan Press, 2005.

Letkemann, Peter. "Mennonite Refugee Camps in Germany, 1921–1951: Part I – Lager Lechfeld." *Mennonite Historian* 38, no. 3 (2012): 1–2.

"Mennonite Refugee Camps in Germany, 1921–1951: Part II – Lager Mölln." *Mennonite Historian* 38, no. 4 (2012): 1–2 and 10.

Lichti, James Irvin. *Houses on the Sand? Pacifist Denominations in Nazi Germany.* New York: Peter Lang, 2008.

Loewen, Harry. "Anti-Menno: Introduction to Early Soviet-Mennonite Literature (1920–1940)." *Journal of Mennonite Studies* 11 (1993): 23–42.

"A House Divided: Russian Mennonite Nonresistance and Emigration in the 1870s." In *Mennonites in Russia 1788–1988: Essays in Honour of Gerhard Lohrenz.* Edited by John Friesen. 127–43. Winnipeg: CMBC Publications, 1989.

"Intellectual Developments Among the Mennonites 1880–1917," *Journal of Mennonite Studies* 8 (1990): 89–107.

Loewen, Royden. "'As I Experienced Them Myself': The Autobiographical German-Language Immigrant Woman in Prairie Canada, 1874–1910." In *A Chorus of Different Voices: German-Canadian Identities.* Edited by Angelika E. Sauer and Matthias Zimmer, 119–42. New York: Peter Lang, 1998.

"'The Children, the Cows, My Dear Man and My Sister': The Transplanted Lives of Mennonite Farm Women, 1874–1900." *Canadian Historical Review* 73, no. 3 (1992): 344–73.

Family, Church, and Market: A Mennonite Community in the Old and the New Worlds, 1850–1930. Toronto: University of Toronto Press, 1993.

Hidden Worlds: Revisiting the Mennonite Migrants of the 1870s. Winnipeg: University of Manitoba Press, 2001.

Village Among Nations: "Canadian" Mennonites in a Transnational World, 1916–2006. Toronto: University of Toronto Press, 2013.

Lübken, Uwe. *Bedrohliche Nähe: Die USA und die nationalsozialistische Herausforderung in Lateinamerika, 1937–1945.* Stuttgart, Germany: Fritz Steiner, 2004.

Luebke, Frederick C. *Germans in the New World: Essays in the History of Immigration.* Urbana-Champaign: University of Illinois Press, 1990.

Lumans, Valdis O. *Himmler's Auxiliaries: The Volksdeutsche Mittelstelle and the German National Minorities of Europe 1933–1935.* Chapel Hill, NC: University of North Carolina Press, 1993.

MacDonnell, Francis. *Insidious Foes: The Axis Fifth Column and the American Home Front.* New York: Oxford University Press, 1995.

Mainka, Peter Johann. *Roland und Rolândia Gründungs – und Frühgeschichte einer Deutschen Kolonie in Brasilien (1932–1944/45).* São Paulo: Cultura Acadêmica/Instituto Maritus-Staden, 2008.

Malkki, Liisa. *Purity and Exile: Violence, Memory, and National Cosmology Among Hutu Refugees in Tanzania.* Chicago: University of Chicago Press, 1995.

Manz, Stefan. *Constructing a German Diaspora: The "Greater German Empire," 1871–1914.* New York: Routledge, 2014.

Marrus, Michael. *The Unwanted: European Refugees from the First World War Through the Cold War.* Philadelphia, PA: Temple University Press, 1985.

Martin, Terry. *The Affirmative Action Empire: Nations and Nationalism in the Soviet Union, 1923 1939.* Ithaca, NY: Cornell University Press, 2001.

"The Russian Mennonite Encounter with the Soviet State, 1917–1955." *The Conrad Grebel Review* 20, no. 1 (Winter 2002): 5–59.

McCormick, P. L. "Transportation and Settlement: Problems in the Expansion of the Frontier of Saskatchewan and Assiniboia in 1904." In *Immigration and Settlement, 1870–1939,* ed. Gregory P. Marchildon, 81–102. Regina: Canadian Plains Research Center, 2009.

McCreedy, David. *Rural Guatemala, 1760–1940.* Stanford, CA: Stanford University Press, 1994.

McKeown, Adam. "Global Migration, 1846–1940." *Journal of World History* 15, no. 2 (2004): 155–89.

McLaren, John. "Creating 'Slaves of Satan' or 'New Canadians'? The Law, Education, and the Socialization of Doukhobor Children, 1911–1935." In *Essays in the History of Canadian Law: British Columbia and the Yukon.* Edited by Hamar Foster and John McLaren. Toronto: University of Toronto Press, 1995.

Mick, Christoph. *Sowjetische Propaganda, Fünfjahrplan, und deutsche Rußlandpolitik 1928–1932.* Stuttgart: Franz Steiner, 1995.

Mitcham, Samuel W., *The Rise of the Wehrmacht: The German Armed Forces and World War II,* vol. 1. Westport, CT: Praeger, 2008.

Mitchell, Tom. "The Manufacture of Souls of Good Quality: Winnipeg's 1919 National Conference on Canadian Citizenship, English-Canadian Nationalism, and the New Order After the Great War." *Journal of Canadian Studies* 31, no. 4 (Winter 1996–1997): 5–28.

Mora, Frank and Jerry Cooney. *Paraguay and the United States: Distant Allies.* Athens, GA: University of Georgia Press, 2007.

Moreira, Pedro. "Juden aus dem deutschsprachigen Kulturraum in Brasilien: Ein Überblick." In *Das Kulturerbe deutschsprachiger Juden: Eine Spurensuche in den Ursprungs.* Edited by Elke-Vera Kotowaski. Berlin: Walter De Gruyter, 2015.

Mowry, David P. *German Clandestine Activities in South America in World War II.* Ft. Meade, MD: Office of Archives and History of the National Security Agency and Central Security Service, 1989.

Mühlen, Patrik von zur. *Fluchtziel Lateinamerika: Die deutsche Emigration 1933–1945: politische Aktivitäten und soziokulturelle Integration.* Bonn: Neue Gesellschaft, 1988.

Müller, Jürgen. "The Mennonite Experience in Paraguay: The Congregational and Theological Experience." *Conrad Grebel Review* 27, no. 1 (Winter, 2009): 20–35.

Nationalsozialismus in Lateinamerika. Die Auslandsorganisation der NSDAP in Argentinien, Brasilien, Chile und Mexico, 1931–1945. Stuttgart, Germany: Verlag Hans-Dieter Heinz, 1997.

Naranch, Bradley. "Inventing the Auslandsdeutsche: Emigration, Colonial Fantasy, and German National Identity, 1848–71." In *Germany's Colonial Pasts.* Edited by Eric Ames, Marcia Klotz, and Lora Wildenthal. Lincoln, NE: University of Nebraska Press, 2005.

Neufeld, Alfred. "The Mennonite Experience in Paraguay: The Congregational and Theological Experience," *Conrad Grebel Review* 27, no. 1 (2009).

"Nikolai Siemens: Ein Wanderer zwischen Welten." *Jahrbuch für Geschichte und Kultur der Mennoniten in Paraguay* 6 (2005): 91–113.

Neufeldt, Colin. "The Flight to Moscow, 1929." *Preservings* 19 (2001): 35–47.

"'Liquidating' Mennonite Kulaks (1929–1930)." *Mennonite Quarterly Review* 83, no. 2 (2009): 221–91.

"Re-forging Mennonite *Spetspereselentsy*: The Experience of Mennonite Exiles at Siberian Special Settlements in the Omsk, Tomsk, Novosibirsk and Narym Regions, 1930–1933." *Journal of Mennonite Studies* 30 (2012): 269–14.

Newton, Ronald C. *The "Nazi Menace" in Argentina, 1931–1947.* Stanford, CA: Stanford University Press, 1992.

Päßler, Jan. "Kuriositäten und Wissenswertes aus Paraguays Vergangenheit." *Das Wochenblatt* (Paraguay). Last modified January 22, 2012. http://wochenblatt.cc/nachrichten/kuriositaten-und-wissenswertes-aus-paraguays-vergangenheit-teil-8/. Last accessed June 7, 2018.

Penny, H. Glenn. "Latin American Connections: Recent Work on German Interactions with Latin America." *Central European History* 46, no. 2 (2013): 362–94.

Plett, Delbert F. "'Poor and Simple?' The Economic Background of the Mennonite Immigrants to Manitoba, 1874–1879." *Journal of Mennonite Studies* 18 (2000): 114–28.

Pommerin, Reiner. *Das Dritte Reich und Lateinamerika: Die deutsche Politik gegenüber Süd- und Mittelamerika 1939–1942.* Dusseldorf: Droste, 1977.

Prentice, Alison. *The School Promoters: Education and Social Class in Mid-Nineteenth Century Upper Canada.* Toronto: McClelland and Stewart, 1977.

Prokop, Manfred. *The German Language in Alberta: Maintenance and Teaching.* Edmonton: University of Alberta Press, 1990.

Quesada, Alejandro. *The Chaco War 1932–95: South America's Greatest War.* Oxford: Osprey Publishing, 2011.

Ratzlaff, Gerhard. *Cristianos Evangélicos en la Guerra del Chaco 1932–1935.* Asunción: Gerhard Ratzlaff, 2008.

Ein Leib, viele Glieder: die mennonitischen Gemeinden in Paraguay: vielfältige Gemeinde, kämpfende Gemeinde, begnadete Gemeinde. Asunción: Gemeindekomittee-Asociación Evangélica Mennonita del Paraguay, 2001.

"Die paraguayischen Mennoniten in der nationalen Politik." *Jahrbuch für Geschichte und Kultur der Mennoniten in Paraguay* 5 (2004): 59–91.

Zwischen den Fronten: Mennoniten und andere evangelische Christen im Chacokrieg 1932–1935. Asunción: Gerhard Ratzlaff, 2009.

Ratzlaff, Heinrich. *Ältester Martin C. Friesen: Ein Mann, den Gott brauchen konnte.* Loma Plata, Paraguay: Geschichtskomitee der Kolonie Menno, 2006.

Reagin, Nancy R. "German Brigadoon? Domesticity and Metropolitan Perceptions of *Auslandsdeutschen* in Southwest Africa and Eastern Europe." In *The Heimat Abroad: The Boundaries of Germanness.* Edited by Krista O'Donnell, Renate Bridenthal, and Nancy Reagin, 248–88. Ann Arbor, MI: University of Michigan Press, 2005.

Redekop, Calvin. *Strangers Become Neighbors: Mennonite and Indigenous Relations in the Paraguayan Chaco.* Scottdale, PA: Herald Press, 1980.

Reimer, Gerhard. "The 'Green Hell' Becomes Home: Mennonites in Paraguay as Described in the Writings of Peter P. Klassen, A Review Essay." *Mennonite Quarterly Review* 76, no. 4 (2002): 460–80.

Rempel, Gerhard. "Review of *Fügungen und Führungen: Benjamin Heinrich Unruh, 1881–1959: Ein Leben im Geiste christlicher Humanität und im Dienste der Nächstenliebe,* by Heinrich B. Unruh." *Mennonite Quarterly Review* 84, no. 2 (2010): 275–78.

Renan, Ernest. "What Is a Nation?" In *Becoming National: A Reader.* Edited by Geoff Eley and Ronald Grigor Suny, 42–55. New York: Oxford University Press, 1996.

Richtik, James M. "The Policy Framework for Settling the Canadian West 1870–1880." *Agricultural History* 49, no. 4 (1975): 613–28.

Ricœur, Paul. *Memory, History, Forgetting.* Chicago: University of Chicago Press, 2004.

Time and Narrative. 2 vols. Translated by Kathleen Blamey and David Pellauer. Chicago: University of Chicago Press, 1988.

Rinke, Stefan. "German Migration to Latin America." In *Germany and the Americas: Culture, Politics, and History, a Multidisciplinary Encyclopedia,* vol. 1. Edited by Thomas Adam, 27–31. Santa Barbara, Denver, Oxford: ABC CLIO, 2005.

"Der letzte freie Kontinent." Deutsche Lateinamerikapolitik im Zeichen transnationaler Beziehungen, 1918–1933. 2 vols. Stuttgart, Germany: Hans-Dieter Heinz Akademischer Verlag, 1996.

Roth, John D. "The Complex Legacy of the Martyrs Mirror Among the Mennonites in North America." *Mennonite Quarterly Review* 87, no. 3 (2013): 277–16.

Rout Jr., Leslie B., and John F. Bratzel. *The Shadow War: German Espionage and United States Counterespionage in Latin America During World War II.* Frederick, MD: University Publications of America, 1986.

Rowney, Don K. "Imperial Russian Officialdom During Modernization." In *Russian Bureaucracy and the State: Officialdom from Alexander III to Putin*. Edited by Don K. Rowney and Eugene Huskey, 26–45. Basingstoke: Palgrave Macmillan, 2009.

Rutherdale, Robert. *Hometown Horizons: Local Responses to Canada's Great War*. Vancouver: University of British Columbia Press, 2004.

Said, Edward. "Beginnings." In *Narrative Dynamics: Essay on Time, Plot, Closure, and Frames*. Edited by Brian Richardson, 256–66. Columbus, OH: Ohio State University Press, 2002.

Sammartino, Annemarie. "Culture, Belonging and the Law: Naturalization in the Weimar Republic." In *Citizenship and National Identity in Twentieth-Century Germany*. Edited by Geoff Eley and Jan Palmowski, 57–72. Stanford, CA: Stanford University Press, 2008.

The Impossible Border: Germany and the East 1914–1922. Ithaca, NY: Cornell University Press, 2010.

Sargent, Howard. "Diasporic Citizens: Germans Abroad in the Framing of German Citizenship Law." In *The Heimat Abroad: The Boundaries of Germanness*. Edited by Krista O'Donnell, Renate Bridenthal, and Nancy Reagin, 17–39. Ann Arbor, MI: University of Michigan Press, 2005.

Savin, Andrey I. "The 1929 Emigration of Mennonites from the USSR: An Examination of Documents from the Archive of Foreign Policy of the Russian Federation." *Journal of Mennonite Studies* 30 (2012): 45–55.

Sawatsky, Rodney J. "Canadian Mennonite Nationalism? The 49th Parallel in the Structuring of Mennonite Life." In *Canadian Mennonites and the Challenge of Nationalism*. Edited by Abe J. Dueck, 89–110. Winnipeg: Manitoba Mennonite Historical Society, 1994.

History and Ideology: American Mennonite Identity Definition Through History. Kitchener, ON: Pandora Press, 2005.

Sawatzky, Peter G. "The Paraguayan Corporation: The Agency Which Facilitated the Mennonite Settlement in the Chaco." History Senior Seminar paper. Goshen College, 1965.

Schiffauer, Werner. "Migration and Religiousness." In *The New Islamic Presence in Western Europe*. Edited by Thomas Gerholm and Yngve Georg Lithman, 146–58. London: Mansell, 1988.

Schroeder, William, and Helmut T. Huebert. *Mennonite Historical Atlas*. 2nd ed. Winnipeg: Springfield Publishers, 1996.

Scott, James. *Seeing Like a State: How Certain Schemes to Improve the Human Condition Have Failed*. New Haven, CT: Yale University Press, 1998.

Sissons, C. B. *Bi-lingual Schools in Canada*. London: J. M. Dent, 1917.

Sivan, Emmanuel, and Jay Winter, eds. *War and Remembrance in the Twentieth Century*. Cambridge: Cambridge University Press, 1999.

Skran, Claudena M. *Refugees in Inter-War Europe: The Emergence of a Regime*. New York: Oxford University Press, 1995.

Smith, Anthony D. *The Ethnic Origins of Nationalism*. Oxford: Basil Blackwell, 1986.

Nationalism. London: Verso, 2006.

Smith, Daniel L. *The Religion of the Landless: The Social Context of the Babylonian Exile.* Bloomington, IN: Meyer-Stone Books, 1989.

Snyder, Timothy. *Reconstruction of Nations: Poland, Ukraine, Lithuania, Belarus, 1569–1999.* New Haven, CT: Yale University Press, 2003.

Stahl, Kurt Daniel. "Zwischen Volkstumspflege, Nationalsozialismus und Mennonitentum, unveröffentlichte wissenschaftliche." Jena: Wissenschaftliche Hausarbeit zur Ersten Staatsprüfung für das Lehramt an Gymnasien im Fach Geschichte, 2007.

Stahl, Sandra K. D. *Literary Folkloristics and the Personal Narrative.* Bloomington, IN: Indiana University Press, 1987.

Staples, John. "Religion, Politics, and the Mennonite Privilegium in Early Nineteenth Century Russia: Reconsidering the Warkentin Affair."*Journal of Mennonite Studies* 21 (2003): 71–88.

Stayer, James M., Werner O. Packull, and Klaus Deppermann. "From Monogenesis to Polygenesis: The Historical Discussion of Anabaptist Origins." *Mennonite Quarterly Review* 49, no. 2 (1975): 83–121.

Sutherland, Neil. *Children in English-Canadian Society.* Toronto: University of Toronto Press, 1976.

Swyripa, Frances. *Storied Landscapes: Ethno-Religious Identity and the Canadian Prairies.* Winnipeg: University of Manitoba Press, 2010.

Sylvester, Kenneth Michael. *The Limits of Rural Capitalism: Family, Culture, and Markets in Montcalm, Manitoba 1870–1940.* Toronto: University of Toronto Press, 2001.

Thiesen, John D. *Mennonite and Nazi? Attitudes Among Mennonite Colonists in Latin America, 1933–1945.* Kitchener, ON: Pandora Press, 1999.

"The Mennonite Encounter with National Socialism in Latin America, 1933–1944." *Journal of Mennonite Studies* 12 (1994): 104–17.

Thompson, John Herd. *The Harvests of War: The Prairie West, 1914–1918.* Toronto: McClelland and Stewart Limited, 1978.

Toews, John B. "Brethren and Old Church Relations in Pre-World War I Russia: Setting the Stage for Canada." *Journal of Mennonite Studies* 2 (1984): 42–59.

"The Origins and Activities of the Mennonite *Selbstschutz* in the Ukraine (1918–1919)." *Mennonite Quarterly Review* 46, no. 1 (1972): 5–39.

"The Russian Mennonites: Some Introductory Comments." *Mennonite Quarterly Review* 48, no. 3 (1974): 403–8.

Tulchinsky, Gerald. *Canada's Jews: A People's History.* Toronto: University of Toronto Press, 2008.

Unruh, Heinrich B. *Fügungen und Führungen: Benjamin Heinrich Unruh, 1881–1959: Ein Leben im Geiste christlicher Humanität und im Dienste der Nächstenliebe.* Detmold, Germany: Verein zur Erforschung und Pflege des Russlanddeutschen Mennonitentums, 2009.

Unruh, John D. *In the Name of Christ: A History of the Mennonite Central Committee and Its Service 1920–1951.* Scottdale, PA: Herald Press, 1952.

Urry, James. "After the Rooster Crowed: Some Issues Concerning the Interpretation of Mennonite/Bolshevik Relations During the Early Soviet Period." *Journal of Mennonite Studies* 13 (1995): 26–50.

"The Mennonite Commonwealth in Imperial Russia Revisited." *Mennonite Quarterly Review* 84, no. 2 (2010): 229–47.

"Mennonites, Nationalism and the State in Imperial Russia." *Journal of Mennonite Studies* 12 (1994): 65–88.

Mennonites, Politics, and Peoplehood: Europe-Russia-Canada 1525–1980. Winnipeg: University of Manitoba Press, 2006.

"A *Mennostaat* for the *Mennovolk*? Mennonite Immigrant Fantasies in Canada in the 1930s." *Journal of Mennonite Studies* 14 (1996): 65–80.

None but Saints: The Transformation of Mennonite Life in Russia 1789–1889. Winnipeg: Hyperion Press, 1989.

"Of Borders and Boundaries: Reflections on Mennonite Unity and Separation in the Modern World." *Mennonite Quarterly Review* 73 (1999): 503–24.

"The Russian Mennonites, Nationalism and the State 1789–1917." In *Canadian Mennonites and the Challenge of Nationalism.* Edited by Abe J. Dueck, 21–68. Winnipeg: Manitoba Mennonite Historical Society, 1994.

"The Russian State, the Mennonite World and the Migration from Russia to North America in the 1870s." *Mennonite Life* 46, no. 1 (1991): 11–16.

Vertovec, Steven. "Religion and Diaspora." In *New Approaches to the Study of Religion 2: Textual, Comparative, Sociological, and Cognitive Approaches.* Edited by Peter Antes, Armin W. Geertz, and Randi R. Warne, 275–304. Berlin: Walter de Gruyter, 2008.

Wagner, Jonathan. *A History of Migration from Germany to Canada, 1850–1939.* Vancouver: University of British Columbia Press, 2006.

Warkentin, Erwin. "Germany's Diplomatic Efforts During the 1929 Mennonite Immigration Crisis." *Mennonite Historian* 31, no. 3 (2005): 4–5.

"The Mennonites Before Moscow: The Notes of Dr. Otto Auhagen." *Journal of Mennonite Studies* 26 (2008): 201–20.

Weaver, J. Denny. *Keeping Salvation Ethical: Mennonite and Amish Atonement Theology in the Late Nineteenth Century.* Scottdale, PA: Herald Press, 1997.

Wells, Allen. "American-Resident Migration to Western Canada at the Turn of the 20th Century." In *Immigration and Settlement, 1870–1939.* Edited by Gregory P. Marchildon. Regina: Canadian Plains Research Center, 2009.

Tropical Zion: General Trujillo, FDR, and the Jews of Sosua. Durham, NC: Duke University Press, 2009.

Wiebe, Petr P. "The Mennonite Colonies of Siberia: From the Late Nineteenth to the Early Twentieth Century." *Journal of Mennonite Studies* 30 (2012): 23–35.

Wiens, Peter. *Die K. f. K. Fernheim: ein geschichtlicher Überblick 1931–1991.* Filadelfia, Paraguay: K. f. K. Fernheim, 1992.

Yeats, William Butler. "The Second Coming." *The Collected Poems of W. B. Yeats.* Edited by Richard J. Finneran. New York: Scribner, 1996.

Yoder, John Howard. "Exodus and Exile: The Two Faces of Liberation." *Cross Currents* 23 (Fall 1973): 297–309.

Zacharias, Robert. *Rewriting the Break Event: Memories and Migration in Canadian Literature.* Winnipeg: University of Manitoba Press, 2013.

Zahra, Tara. "Imagined Noncommunities: National Indifference as a Category of Analysis." *Slavic Review* 69, no. 1 (2010): 93–119.

Zahra, Tara. *Kidnapped Souls: National Indifference and the Battle for Children in the Bohemian Lands, 1900–1948*. Ithaca, NY: Cornell University Press, 2008.

Zhuk, Sergei I. *Russia's Lost Reformation: Peasants, Millennialism, and Radical Sects in Southern Russia and Ukraine, 1830–1917*. Baltimore, MD: Johns Hopkins University Press, 2004.

Index

CPSIA information can be obtained
at www.ICGtesting.com
Printed in the USA
BVHW041719280921
617699BV00005B/29